PROPERTY LAW IN CHINA

Unlock the intricacies of Chinese property law with this groundbreaking book, perfect for legal practitioners, scholars and international investors. This comprehensive guide delves into the complexities of Chinese property law, offering detailed analysis, practical case studies and insightful global comparisons. Understand the evolution and current landscape of property law in China and see how theoretical principles are applied in real-world scenarios. Whether you're navigating cross-border property issues, developing legal strategies or seeking an academic resource, this book is an invaluable tool. Authored by a recognised expert, it combines scholarly rigour with practical expertise, making it an essential addition to your legal library.

PROFESSOR LEI CHEN, PhD, is Chair in International Arbitration and Chinese Law at Durham University, UK. His research areas are property law, contract law and international arbitration. He is a member of the European Academy of Sciences and Arts and a titular member of the International Academy of Comparative Law. Lei Chen is an Adjunct Chair Professor at Shandong University.

This book offers far more than a presentation of 'transition and trend' of Chinese property law. It gives a thorough overview of modern Chinese property law and is an incredible source for both academics and practitioners written by an expert in the field.

Sjef van Erp,
Emeritus Professor of Law, University of Amsterdam

Professor Chen's book provides a precise interpretation of the Civil Code and judicial positions, enriched by case law and scholarly commentaries. Its insightful analysis of topics such as the real security system, condominium ownership, and civil customs, along with its status as the most updated resource, makes it indispensable for scholars, practitioners, and anyone seeking a deep understanding of Chinese property law.

Liming Wang,
Professor of Law, Renmin University of China, Beijing

Socialist but also Romanist, Chinese property law presents an intriguing mixture of legal traditions. To this important and complex body of law Professor Lei Chen offers a lucid and authoritative guide which will be of value to comparative lawyers or to anyone with an interest in Chinese law.

Kenneth Reid,
Emeritus Professor of Scots Law, University of Edinburgh

Professor Lei Chen has written the authoritative guide to property law in China. This masterful work goes well beyond a comprehensive account of current doctrine and property institutions to portray how the fundamental concept of property has changed in contemporary China to reflect economic reforms and rapid urbanization. This book is a must-read for scholars, students, practitioners, and policymakers.

Amnon Lehavi,
Provost and Professor of Law, Reichman University, Israel

PROPERTY LAW IN CHINA

Transition and Trend

LEI CHEN
University of Durham

CAMBRIDGE
UNIVERSITY PRESS

CAMBRIDGE
UNIVERSITY PRESS

Shaftesbury Road, Cambridge CB2 8EA, United Kingdom

One Liberty Plaza, 20th Floor, New York, NY 10006, USA

477 Williamstown Road, Port Melbourne, VIC 3207, Australia

314–321, 3rd Floor, Plot 3, Splendor Forum, Jasola District Centre, New Delhi – 110025, India

103 Penang Road, #05-06/07, Visioncrest Commercial, Singapore 238467

Cambridge University Press is part of Cambridge University Press & Assessment, a department of the University of Cambridge.

We share the University's mission to contribute to society through the pursuit of education, learning and research at the highest international levels of excellence.

www.cambridge.org
Information on this title: www.cambridge.org/9781009194129

DOI: 10.1017/9781009194112

When citing this work, please include a reference to the DOI 10.1017/9781009194112

First published 2025

A catalogue record for this publication is available from the British Library

Library of Congress Cataloging-in-Publication Data
Names: Chen, Lei (Lawyer), author.
Title: Property law in China : transition and trend / Lei Chen, University of Durham.
Description: Cambridge, United Kingdom ; New York, NY : Cambridge University Press, 2025. | Includes bibliographical references and index.
Identifiers: LCCN 2024057758 (print) | LCCN 2024057759 (ebook) | ISBN 9781009194129 (hardback) | ISBN 9781009194105 (paperback) | ISBN 9781009194112 (epub)
Subjects: LCSH: Property–China. | Acquisition of property–China. | Adjoining landowners–China. | Condominiums–Law and legislation–China. | Homestead law–China. | Land use–Law and legislation–China. | Servitudes–China. | Right of property–China. | Possession (Law)–China.
Classification: LCC KNQ640 .C446 2025 (print) | LCC KNQ640 (ebook) | DDC 346.5104–dc23/eng/20241203
LC record available at https://lccn.loc.gov/2024057758
LC ebook record available at https://lccn.loc.gov/2024057759

ISBN 978-1-009-19412-9 Hardback

CONTENTS

1

The Institution of Property in China

1.1 The Reach of Property Law

This book contains an account of the basic elements of Chinese property law. The book aims to use these elements of property law to identify fundamental features of the evolutionary concept of property in a socialist-transitioning China. China's unique political and economic system meshes socialism and a market economy. From a legal perspective, property is more than just something tangible: property is not a thing. Still, it embodies a human being's relationship with the outer world. Property is not just about individual entitlement and exclusion, but a system.[1] Individuals do not live alone, and diverse institutional arrangements have been developed to affect the allocation and exercise of property rights.[2] In essence, it is recognised that property extends beyond a concrete object to a power relationship – a relationship of social and legal legitimacy between a user and a thing.[3] This conceptual understanding of property rights seems common sense in many ways. The Civil Code (CC)[4] provides explicitly that "the Property Book [of the Code] governs the civil relationships arising from the entitlement and use of

[1] Joseph. W. Singer and Jack. M. Beermann, 'The Social Origins of Property' (1993) 6 *Canadian Journal of Law & Jurisprudence* 217.

[2] Elinor Ostrom, *Governing the Commons: The Evolution of Institutions for Collective Action* (Cambridge University Press 1990).

[3] Kevin Gray and Susan Gray, *Elements of Land Law* (5th edn, Oxford University Press 2009).

[4] The Civil Code was enacted on 28 May 2020 by the plenary session of the Thirteenth National People's Congress (NPC). The Third Session of the Thirteenth NPC adopted the CC. The CC has seven parts and 1,260 articles. The seven parts, in turn, are General Provisions, Property Rights, Contracts, Personality Rights, Marriage and Family, Right of Inheritance, and Tort Liability and Supplemental Provision. The CC came into force on 1 January 2021, and the then current General Principles of the Civil Law, the Contract Law, the Property Law, the Tort Law, the Guarantee Law, the Marriage Law, the Law of Succession and the Adoption Law were repealed simultaneously.

things."[5] Therefore, property law governs the allocation of rights and obligations in relation to immovable and movable property. Without any exaggeration, property law has resided in people's day-to-day lives because it defines our relationship or status to a tangible or intangible thing at any time, whether as landlords, tenants, mortgagees, lien holders, easement holders, copyright owners, security interest assignees or just as a licensee or a member of the general public.

Notwithstanding its pivotal importance, it appears that embracing property rights in China is more cherished yet less critically scrutinised. Property rights are regularly portrayed as essential to the rule of law, individual liberty, good governance and the efficient use of all land resources. Consequently, this book traces the changing perceptions of property rights from socialist public ownership and collective land use to contemporary private property rights influenced by economic reforms and rapid urbanisation. It also discusses how China's political system, cultural heritage and social policies have shaped its property law framework.

1.2 Historical Developments of Property Law in China

In a vast and historically rich country like China, the perspective that considers land as intrinsically tied to both the State's fiscal capacity and the well-being of commoners implies that complex property law systems existed even in ancient times. However, the property systems from the Qin Dynasty to the Tang Dynasty (221 BC to AD 618) have been relatively underexplored, largely due to the limitations of surviving archives. Recent studies on the property systems during the Tang and Song Dynasties have shed light on this historical period. In Southern China, investigations into the property systems of the Song Dynasty reveal that, under the Southern Song regime, a significant number of peasant households possessed private land.[6] Notably, the research delves into the roles of three distinct categories of land workers: the land guest,

[5] Article 205 CC. For an English translation of the Chinese CC, see Lei Chen et al., *The CC of the People's Republic of China: English Translation* (Brill 2021).

[6] The "Collected Regulations of the Southern Song Dynasty" (Nansong Lüling / 南宋律令). This compilation of legal regulations and statutes provides insights into the legal framework governing various aspects of society, including land rights, during the Southern Song Dynasty (1127–1279).

the field servant and the tenant guest.[7] These detailed examinations yield several key findings.

Firstly, evidence suggests widespread private land ownership during the Song Dynasty. Secondly, contrary to common assumptions, the ownership pattern appears rather fragmented. Many small landholders participated in the market, contributing to a less severe issue of land concentration. Thirdly, the legal relationships among various stakeholders in landholding have been delineated, providing insights into the intricate legal framework governing land ownership during this historical period. These research findings collectively contribute to a deeper understanding of the complexity and dynamics of property ownership and relationships in ancient China, particularly during the Tang and Song Dynasties.

More tellingly, most academic literature has focused on the landholding systems during the Ming and Qing dynasties. It has been argued that the land administration system was largely self-regulated during this period. The State's central coercive power was limited and fragile throughout the nineteenth century.[8] Case law through archive studies in the nineteenth century suggests that local courts at some localities rarely attempted to award adjudicative decisions in non-criminal cases.[9] The primary reason is that kinship-oriented mediation was a popular practice to settle socio-economic disputes outside of court.[10]

Nonetheless, it is beyond doubt that in ancient China there was no specific land law governing the entitlement and enforcement of property rights. Rather, customary land law, which was not a hard-and-fast rule, primarily guided the market practices on land transfers and alienation.[11] At different times, the State was willingly or unwillingly idle when it

[7] Joseph P. McDermott, 'Charting Blank Spaces and Disputed Regions: The Problem of Sung Land Tenure' (1984) 44 *The Journal of Asian Studies* 13.

[8] Loren Brandt, Debin Ma and Thomas. G. Rawski, 'From Divergence to Convergence: Re-evaluating the History behind China's Economic Boom' (2014) 52 *Journal of Economic Literature* 45.

[9] Philip C. C. Huang, *Civil Justice in China: Representation and Practice in the Qing* (Stanford University Press 1996).

[10] Joseph P. McDermott. 'Village Institutions in the Early and Mid-Ming', in *The Making of a New Rural Order in South China* (Cambridge University Press 2013).

[11] For example, see the significance of customary land law in Hong Kong's New Territories before it was subjected to British rule in Patrick H. Hase, *Custom, Land, and Livelihood in Rural South China: The Traditional Land Law of Hong Kong's New Territories, 1750–1950* (Hong Kong University Press 2013), pp. 3–5.

came to exercising coercive power to issue and enforce property rights.[12] Instead, there was a "societal enforcement" of property rights in many ways. The State gave tacit consent to private property rights while specifying the obligations, such as paying land taxes. Some scholars suggest that ancient Chinese land institutions should be understood less from the perspective of formal entitlements and more through economic reality and market-based land transfers by means of sales, lease, sublease and subdivision between topsoil rights and subsoil rights[13] or *dian quan*.[14] Significantly, Chinese property customs, largely influenced by hierarchical Confucian kinship networks,[15] granted greater powers of redemption to landowners who had pledged their land.[16] This approach was advantageous for debtors, as it enabled them to maintain redemption rights over the pledged property indefinitely. This practice was deeply rooted in Confucian-influenced kinship structures, emphasising familial ties and relationships, shaping the dynamics of property rights and debt redemption in Chinese society.[17]

In a nutshell, ancient China has witnessed the interplay between the two models in the land administration system subject to the changes in sociopolitical and economic conditions: a quintessential state law model which takes land rules as only a part of the state penal code; and a civil customs-oriented practice direction model which regards civil customs as an integral part of legal pluralism.

China began its first legal system reform during the late Qing Dynasty by drafting a modern CC patterned after the German model adopted by Japan.[18] Although this draft was never in use, it established the civil law tradition in the Chinese legal system. The blossoming of civil law

[12] Melissa Macauley, *Social Power and Legal Culture: Litigation Masters in Late Imperial China* (Stanford University Press 1998).

[13] Michael J. E. Palmer, 'The Surface–Subsoil Form of Divided Ownership in Late Imperial China: Some Examples from the New Territories of Hong Kong' (1987) 21 *Modern Asian Studies* 1.

[14] Mio Kishimoto, 'Ming Qing Shidai de Zhaojia Huishu Wenti' ['The Issue of "Zhaojia" and "Dian" Redemption in the Ming and Qing'], in T. Hiroaki (ed), *Empirical Studies on Chinese Legal History* [《中国法制史考证》] (China Social Sciences Press 2003).

[15] Mio Kishimoto, 'Property Rights, Land, and Law in Imperial China', in Debin Ma and Jan Luiten van Zanden (eds), *Law and Long-Term Economic Change: A Eurasian Perspective* (Stanford University Press 2011).

[16] Taisu Zhang, 'Social Hierarchies and the Formation of Customary Property Law in Pre-industrial China and England' (2014) 62 *The American Journal of Comparative Law* 171.

[17] *Ibid.*

[18] Philip C. C. Huang, *Code, Custom, and Legal Practice in China: The Qing Dynasty and the Republic Compared* (Stanford University Press 2002), pp. 15–18; Youjiong Yang, *Chinese*

occurred under the Kuomintang government. In 1930, the first Chinese CC was promulgated. After revising and re-examining the Qing Dynasty's Draft CC,[19] the Republican CC Drafting Committee drew on the experience of civil law countries, including Germany, Japan and Switzerland, to develop its civil law legislation.[20] Not surprisingly, the CC of the Republic of China (ROC CC) (1929–1931), enacted before the Chinese Communist Party came into power in 1949, had already enshrined several general principles with respect to social function. When the ROC CC was drafted, the prevailing view was that social harmony precedes absolutist individual rights. This closely reflects the traditional Chinese natural law philosophy that conciliation, mediation and compromise are the preferred approaches to settling civil disputes. One can readily observe this concept within several provisions of the ROC CC: "Liberty may not be restricted unless it is contrary to public order or good morals"[21] or "a juristic act which is contrary to public order and good morals is void."[22] However, perhaps the most telling are these two articles: "A right cannot be exercised for the main purpose of causing injury to another,"[23] and "no retention over a movable property can be made if the retention is contrary to public order or good morals."[24] Such provisions decree that property entails certain obligations, and its use should serve the public interest.

Prior to the formation of the People's Republic of China (PRC) in 1949, most of the rural land belonged to feudal landlords and rich farmers, while peasants were only tenant farmers and did not own any land.[25] Shortly after its foundation, the PRC instituted a land collectivisation programme that replaced private farming under the 'land-to-the-tiller' policy from 1947. This land tenure system formed in Mao's era was

Contemporary Legal History [《中国近代法制史》] (Zhonghua Wenhua Shiye Chubanshe 1958), p. 24.

19 Jianfu Chen, *From Administrative Authorisation to Private Law: A Comparative Perspective of the Developing Civil Law in the People's Republic of China* (Springer 1995), p. 14.

20 Lei Chen, 'The Historical Development of the Civil Law Tradition in China: A Private Law Perspective' (2010) 78 *The Legal History Review* 159.

21 Article 17(2) CC.

22 Article 72 ROC CC.

23 Article 148 ROC CC.

24 Article 930 ROC CC.

25 Wenjia Wang, *The History of Chinese Land Systems* [《中国土地制度史》] (Cheng Chung Book 1988).

modelled on the former Soviet Union system.[26] This was apparent from the PRC Constitution enacted in 1954, which shared a high degree of similarity with the 1936 Soviet Union Constitution concerning the content and contour of the land tenure system. Liu Shaoqi, the then PRC president, told the National People's Congress (NPC) at their first plenary session, during which the 1954 Constitution was passed:

> When the Constitution Drafting Committee worked on the draft, it used as reference materials the earlier and later constitutions of the Soviet Union and the constitutions of other people's democracies. The experience of the advanced socialist countries headed by the Soviet Union has greatly assisted us. Our draft constitution combines Chinese experience and international experience. Our draft constitution is not only the product of the people's revolutionary movement in our nation, but it is also a product of the international socialist movement.[27]

Distinct from the Eastern European countries that retained most of their original legal frameworks after their communist revolutions,[28] all the pre-existing legislation enacted during the republic was obliterated as soon as the PRC was founded.[29] Consequently, the former regime, in which affluent bourgeois landlords consolidated land and resources, was entirely abolished. Agricultural land and housing were distributed to farmers and the working-class masses to unleash the productive forces constrained by the restrictive conditions of the Kuomintang era.[30] They were also guaranteed a wide range of property rights, for instance, the right to farm and reside on the land and to buy, sell or transfer the land to another party.[31] The Chinese Agrarian [Land] Reform Law (Land Reform Law)[32] was one of the new regime's first pieces of legislation

[26] Lei Chen, 'Legal and Institutional Analysis of Land Expropriation in China', in Hualing Fu and John Gillespie (eds), *Resolving Land Disputes in East Asia: Exploring the Limits of Law* (Cambridge University Press 2003)

[27] Ahy Chen, 'Socialist Law, Civil Law, Common Law, and the Classification of Contemporary Chinese Law', in Jan Michiel Otto, Maurice V. Polak, Jianfu Chen and Yuwen Li (eds), *Law-Making in the People's Republic of China* (Kluwer Law International 2000), p. 57.

[28] John Quigley, 'Socialist Law and the Civil Law Tradition' (1989) 37 *American Journal of Comparative Law* 781, 802.

[29] Chen (n. 20), at 168–70.

[30] Philip C. C. Huang, 'Rural Class Struggle in the Chinese Revolution: Representational and Objective Realities from the Land Reform to the Cultural Revolution' (1995) 21 *Modern China* 105.

[31] Jialin Zhang, 'China's Slow Motion Land Reform' (2010) 159 *Policy Review* 59, 60.

[32] Albert P. Blaustein, *Fundamental Legal Documents of Communist China* (Fred B. Rothman & Co, 1962), p. 276.

promulgated. Article 1 of the Land Reform Law provides that "the land ownership system of exploitation by the landlord class shall be abolished and the system of peasant land ownership shall be introduced to liberate and develop the rural production, and thus embark on New China's industrialisation."[33] In particular, Article 30 recognises the notion that the land in the hands of farmers is considered their private property: "Once the agrarian reform is done, the People's Government shall issue title deeds and recognise the right of all land owners to manage freely, buy, sell or rent out their land."[34]

Subsequently, the 1954 Constitution codified the peasants' right to own land, departing from the earlier concept of socialising land, which was the crux of the Bolshevik land policy.[35] Nevertheless, since private land ownership was incompatible with the basic Marxist creed of public ownership, the communists established collective farms.[36] As a result, private ownership underwent a transformation through the cooperative movement, transitioning to collective ownership, except for some very small private plots situated around the farmers' residences.[37] In the 1950s, China experienced a notable era often termed the "Golden Age" of developing its legal system within the PRC. During this period, China actively sought to adopt a range of ideologies, institutions and practices from the Soviet Union, particularly in the realms of politics, economics and social structures.

Moreover, during the Soviet Union era, legislative texts from the Soviet system were commonly considered reference materials in the drafting of laws. A significant aspect of this era was the doctrine of socialist ownership, encompassing ownership by cooperatives, mass enterprises and state ownership.[38] Following the socialist legality, all land and natural resources in the PRC became the subject of socialist public ownership. This came in two forms: land in rural areas held by labouring masses through collective ownership or land in urban areas held through state ownership.[39] Such transformation in land ownership was attained in two ways: either by confiscating the land that remained during the period of

[33] *Ibid*, p. 279.

[34] Article 30 Land Reform Law.

[35] Article 8 PRC Constitution 1954.

[36] James T. H. Tsao, *China's Development Strategies and Foreign Trade* (Lexington Books, 1987), p. 14.

[37] *Ibid.*

[38] William. E. Butler, *Soviet Law* (2nd edn, Butterworths 1988), pp. 180–81.

[39] Articles 9 and 10 PRC Constitution 2004.

Nationalist rule[40] or through the policy of socialist transformation that started in 1953.[41] By the latter strategy, private enterprises that owned much of the remaining land in urban areas were first forced to be joined as state–private enterprises. By 1956, the central government had finished nationalising those joint enterprises.[42] The two procedures simultaneously complemented the State's consolidation of land in urban areas.

The process of collectivising land carried on during the era of Mao Zedong's Great Leap Forward. As part of the overall scheme to strengthen communism, the agricultural cooperatives were integrated and amalgamated into the larger People's Communes.[43] On top of abolishing private ownership of land, the communes took over livestock and tools for private economic activities.[44] Unlike the Soviet Union, where the State had an exclusive title to all land and assigned its perpetual use to different land users,[45] the Chinese State only retains the title to urban and industrial land, leaving rural land to the collectives. It is contended that the Chinese system resembles the Romanian land framework in which the State merely claimed the title to urban and industrial land and conferred ownership of rural land to the tillers.[46] The 1982 PRC Constitution has embraced the notion of public ownership of land in China: "The state owns land in the cities and land in the rural and suburban areas is owned by the collectives ... No organisation or individual may appropriate, buy, sell or otherwise engage in the transfer of land by unlawful means."[47]

However, under the collective People's Commune system, economic incentives were lacking to encourage farming productivity. Considering the outright failure of the People's Commune system, the decentralisation of collective ownership to the production team was carried out in the early 1960s. As a result, the production team became the de facto

[40] Victor Lippit, *The Economic Development of China* (M. E. Sharpe 1987), p. 109.

[41] *Ibid*, p. 110.

[42] William C. Kirby, 'China Unincorporated: Company Law and Business Enterprise in Twentieth-Century China' (1995) 54 *The Journal of Asian Studies* 43.

[43] Marsh Marshall, *Organizations and Growth in Rural China* (Palgrave Macmillan 1985), pp. 46–47.

[44] *Ibid*, p. 47.

[45] Liz Alden Wily, 'Collective Land Ownership in the 21st Century: Overview of Global Trends' (2018) 7 *Land* 68.

[46] John Newbold Hazard, *Communists and Their Law: A Search for the Common Core of the Legal System of the Marxian Socialist States* (The University of Chicago Press 1969), p. 157.

[47] Article 10 PRC Constitution 2004.

manager of the land in most villages, and this system was retained up to the mid-1980s.[48] China embarked on a new path marked by significant economic and social transformations when the Cultural Revolution ended. As an integral part of Deng's reforms, the Household Responsibility System (HRS) was introduced to replace the People Commune system as a family-oriented farming system in villages.[49] Under the HRS, the land is contracted to individual households for fifteen to thirty years. The decentralisation of land usage from the collective to the household level incentivised the peasants to improve farming productivity. As a result, agricultural production boomed, and rural incomes soared.[50] The HRS was initially conducted as an experiment in several designated areas. Due to its success, it was soon introduced and implemented nationwide.

From the mid-1980s to the end of the 1990s, the Chinese Central Government encouraged village collectives to employ agricultural land for building up Township and Village Enterprises (TVEs).[51] Rural peasants were encouraged to "leave the land but not the countryside" to work in the newly initiated TVEs. This essentially allows the use of agricultural land for non-agricultural (mainly manufacturing) purposes. The Rural Land Contracting Law (RLCL), implemented in 2002, secures the households' rights of use and possession by allowing the enforcement of thirty-year land use contracts to prevent large-scale arbitrary reallocations of land and allow transfers of land between the households.[52] Generally, under the current land system, farmers have two land use rights over rural land: the right to contract the land for agricultural production and the right to construct a residential homestead on the land.

[48] Chris Bramall, 'Chinese Land Reform in Long-Run Perspective and in the Wider East Asian Context' (2004) 4 *Journal of Agrarian Change* 107.

[49] James K. S. Kung, 'Choice of Land Tenure in China: The Case of a County with Quasi-private Property Rights' (2002) 50 *Economic Development and Cultural Change* 793.

[50] This was so despite the fact that its success was short lived, for various reasons. Some attributed this to the tenure insecurity. See Roy L. Prosterman, Tim Hanstad and Ping Li, 'Can China Feed Itself?' (1996) 5 *Scientific American* 90. Others thought that the reason was the low farm-gate price instead of property rights. See James K. S. Kung, 'Equal Entitlement versus Tenure Security under a Regime of Collective Property Rights: Peasants' Preference for Institutions in Post-reform Chinese Agriculture' (1995) 21 *Journal of Comparative Economics* 82.

[51] This policy eventually became a piece of legislation to the same effect. See Articles 12 and 28 Town and Village Enterprise Law 1996.

[52] Ping Li and Roy L. Prosterman, 'From Collective to Household Tenure: China and Elsewhere', in Roy L. Prosterman, Robert Mitchell and Tim Hanstad (eds), *One Billion Rising: Law, Land and the Alleviation of Global Poverty* (Leiden University Press 2009).

Around the same period in the mid-1990s, urban China struggled to provide sufficient housing given rapid urbanisation and exploding population.[53] China has toned down public power by distributing more private interests, wealth and status to people.[54] Thus, creating functioning property institutions has been put on the legislature's agenda.[55] China introduced a new policy to create wealth by marketising housing to ease the housing burden.[56] It also amended its Constitution to recognise privately owned and transferable land use rights.[57] However, because early land rights were in their infancy, the free market economy was officially characterised as a form of socialist well-being.[58]

In 1994, the State Council executed a comprehensive national housing reform policy on housing privatisation and commercialisation[59] to serve two purposes better: (1) relieving the government's obligation to maintain and manage buildings which were constructed to accommodate state employees; and (2) ensuring private property ownership (after further constitutional reform). The policy stated, "private and non-public sectors of the economy are major components of the socialist market."[60] More significantly, the constitutional reform legally equated private property

[53] Mark T. Kremzner, 'Managing Urban Land in China: The Emerging Legal Framework and Its Role in Development' (1998) 7 *Pacific Rim Law & Policy Association Journal* 611, 611–22.

[54] David Kennedy, 'Laws and Developments', in John Hatchard and Amanda Perry-Kessaris (eds), *Law and Development: Facing Complexity in the 21st Century: Essays in Honour of Peter Slinn* (Cavendish Publishing 2003), pp. 17–19.

[55] 'China to Issue Real Estate Registration Rules by June 2014' (Beijing: Xinhua, 17 May 2013) <www.chinadaily.com.cn/business/2013-05/17/content_16506420.htm> accessed on 28 May 2022.

[56] In 1988, the State Council embarked on a staged housing reform by instituting national housing reform in urban areas. The housing reform provided a ten-year blueprint that would expedite the commercialisation of residential property and reduce state subsidies of housing. See James Lee, 'From Welfare Housing to Home Ownership: The Dilemma of China's Housing Reform' (2000) 15 *Housing Studies* 61, 66.

[57] On 9 September 1987, the first trial concerning the commercialisation of land use rights took place in Shenzhen. This trial led to an amendment to Article 10 of the Constitution enacted on 12 April 1988 to permit the assignment of the right to use land. The amended Constitution (1988) stated: "[t]he right to use land may be transferred according to law." Soon thereafter, Article 2 of the Land Administration Law was revised stipulating that "the right to use State owned or collectively owned land may be assigned pursuant to the law."

[58] Peter Ho, 'Who Owns China's Land? Policies, Property Rights and Deliberate Institutional Ambiguity' (2001) 166 *The China Quarterly* 394.

[59] The Decision of the State Council on Furthering Housing Reform in Urban Areas (1994).

[60] Article 11 PRC Constitution (amended on 15 March 1999).

with state-owned property,[61] so citizens' private property rights were legally protected. It also promised corresponding compensation for government expropriations and recognised private property ownership as a fundamental freedom.

Despite these reform efforts, China lacked a sufficiently comprehensive land law, resulting in contradictory property law statutes,[62] inconsistent administrative regulations,[63] overloaded Supreme People's Court (SPC) judicial interpretations[64] and conflicting local practices.[65] Consequently, the early Chinese land law suffered from a wide range of issues such as fragmentation, structural weaknesses, inconsistent application, corruption and incompatibility with sustainable development. Thus, China's land laws call for further reform to keep pace with social evolution.[66]

In response to these issues, the NPC promulgated the Property Law in 2007.[67] This legislative move was designed to protect property rights by identifying different property types, safeguarding title security and providing greater economic stability in the real property marketplace.[68] Particularly noteworthy is that Article 4 of the Property Law protects

[61] Article 13 PRC Constitution (amended on 15 March 1999).

[62] For example, the Land Administration Law (promulgated by the Standing Committee of the NPC on 29 August 1998, effective since 1 January 1999).

[63] Examples include the Provisions Concerning the Administration of Private Houses Owned by Foreigners (1984) and the Interim Regulations on the Assignment and Transfer of Rights to Use State-Owned Land in Urban Areas (1990).

[64] For instance, the SPC Interpretation on the Application of Some Provisions of the Law of Security by the SPC.

[65] Examples include the Guiding Rules on the Management Corporation and Its Executive Council (promulgated by the municipal government of Shenzhen City on 17 January 2005).

[66] The legislative implementation of the property law has been controversial, disjointed and time consuming. As early as 1994, the Chinese legislature devised a plan to enact the code, but it was not until 1998 that a drafting panel was even tasked with the drafting. In October 1999, the drafting panel completed a model draft consisting of twelve chapters containing 435 articles. In 2000, a model property law draft was also completed. Thereafter, in consultation with these two model drafts, the Standing Committee of the NPC deliberated and pruned its legislative draft seven times. Ultimately, eight parliamentary deliberations were held from December 2002 to March 2007.

[67] The enactment of the Chinese property law immediately attracted international media's attention. See, for example, 'China's Clause Four: The Recognition of Property Rights Is an Ideological Landmark' (*The Times*, 17 March 2007) <www.martinfrost.ws/htmlfiles/mar2007/china_clause4.html> accessed 2 February 2023; see also, 'Chinas Volkskongress billigt Eigentumsgesetz', *Frankfurter Allgemeine Zeitung*, 16 March 2007.

[68] Lei Chen, 'The New Chinese Property Code: A Giant Step Forward?' (2007) 11 *Electronic Journal of Comparative Law* 1.

individual property rights from any entities, including the public sector and private developers.[69]

The implementation of the Property Law has significantly aligned Chinese legal practice with the principles of Article 17 of the Universal Declaration of Human Rights, which affirms the right to property ownership both individually and in association with others and protects against arbitrary deprivation of property.[70] This legislation, primarily concerned with land ownership rights, extends its influence beyond mere property claims, impacting broader sociopolitical and economic rights. The introduction of private property rights in real estate has facilitated the development of property associations, which are pivotal in managing shared residential and commercial spaces. These associations often function as mini-governments, making decisions that affect local communities directly. The active participation of property owners in these associations not only enhances community management but also fosters local democratic governance.[71] This shift is particularly significant in a context like China, where such grassroots democratic practices can encourage greater civic engagement and political participation. The promulgation of the Property Law also mirrors the state's response to the growing demands of China's burgeoning middle class, which has increasingly asserted its need for clear and secure private property rights. By clarifying and demarcating these rights, the law responds to socioeconomic shifts and the aspirations of a significant segment of society. The establishment of a robust legal and institutional framework under the Property Law serves multiple social functions. It not only recognises and delineates existing property rights but also ensures that these rights can be enforced at a low cost and with relative ease. This facilitates the exercise of property rights, which can have widespread social benefits, including enhancing economic stability, promoting investments and encouraging responsible property management and development.[72]

[69] Article 4 PRC Property Law 2007. The new property law should contain the fundamental principle that any legally acquired property, whether public, private, owned by the state or by collectives, should be given fair and equal protection.

[70] Article 17 of the Universal Declaration of Human Rights, UN Doc A/810 (12 December 1948).

[71] Mark D. Kielsgard and Lei Chen, 'The Emergence of Private Property Law in China and Its Impact on Human Rights' (2014) 15 *Asian-Pacific Law & Policy Journal* 94.

[72] Thomas W. Merill and Henry E. Smith argue that property rights are good against the whole world, thus requiring rules that reduces the costs of information for a broad-ranging yet unspecified group of potential violators. See Thomas W. Merill and Henry

In 2008, the third full meeting of the Seventeenth Chinese Communist Party (CCP) Central Committee suggested "progressively harmonising the real estate markets in urban and rural areas and that legally obtained collectively-owned construction land in rural areas should possess rights equivalent to state-owned land."[73] In November 2016, the government issued a guideline to promote and standardise "the transfer of the right to use land from rural residents to commercial entities,"[74] emphasising annual payments. The guideline also recommended the separation of land ownership rights, contractual management rights and management rights. Nevertheless, the Chinese government remained hesitant to alter the rural collective ownership system, asserting that regardless of any adjustments to the land system, the fundamental structure of rural collective ownership should not be dismantled.[75]

The General Provisions of Civil Law of 2017, the first part of the Civil Code, explicitly states that civil subjects shall conduct any civil activity in a resource-saving and environment-friendly manner.[76] Given the phraseology and scope of the provisions, one might argue that the social function of the property has taken root in contemporary Chinese legislation.

1.3 The Constitutional Property Clause

Balancing the competing rights and interests over property is one of the most important social functions of property law in China. Land as an institution embodies a bundle of interwoven public and private rights. Initially, there was no provision for private property in the 1982 PRC Constitution. Due to the dramatic economic and social changes, the PRC Constitution was amended several times to entrench private property

E. Smith, 'Making Coasean Property More Coasean' (2011) 54 *Journal of Law and Economics* 77.

73 Shitong Qiao and Frank Upham, 'Evolution of Relational Property Rights: A Case of Chinese Rural Land Reform' (2015) 100 *Iowa Law Review* 2479.

74 'China Promotes Transfer of Farmland Use Right' (English.gov.cn, 31 October 2016) <https://english.www.gov.cn/policies/latest_releases/2016/10/31/content_281475479420893.htm> accessed on 28 May 2022.

75 Lei Chen, 'The Evolution of the Property System in China: Between the Socialist Heritage and Liberal Market', in Hualing Fu, John Gillespie, Pip Nicolson and William Edmund Partlett (eds), *Socialist Law in Socialist East Asia* (Cambridge University Press 2018).

76 Article 9 General Provisions of Civil Law 2017, now the first Book of the Chinese CC.

Table 1.1 *Current legal framework concerning property rights in China*

Year	Title	Type of Statutory Instruments	Implications
1986 (amended in 1988, 1998, 2004, 2019)	Land Administration Law	National legislation by the standing committee of the National People's Congress (NPC)	Specific legislation governs the land title system and land use rights in urban and rural areas.
1988	Constitutional Amendment	Constitution (Amendment)	The amendment recognised privately owned and transferable land use rights in urban China.
1994	The decision to deepen the reform of the urban housing system	Administrative Regulation by the State Council	The non-market/welfare housing era in China is ended with housing privatisation.
1994	The Urban Real Estate Management Law	National Legislation by NPC	The statute governs the steps to develop real estate in urban land.
2001	Demolition Regulation	Administrative Regulation	The first-generation regulation on expropriation.
2003	The Property Management Regulation	Administrative Regulation issued by the State Council	The first general property management rules on condominium governance.
2004	Constitutional Amendment	Constitution (Amendment)	China amended its 1982 constitution to guarantee private property ownership and human rights.

2007	The Property Law	National Legislation by NPC	The first comprehensive property law is a cornerstone in the Property Law Book of the Chinese CC.
2010	The Law on the Mediation and Arbitration of Rural Land Contract Disputes	National Legislation by NPC	A special law deals with disputes arising from the contracting management of rural land.
2011	The Regulations for Expropriation and Compensation for Houses on State-owned land	The State Council	The second-generation rules governing urban land expropriations.
2014	Interim Regulation on Real Estate Registration	Administrative Regulation	An administrative regulation addresses the land registration system, aiming to introduce a unified property registration system nationwide.
2020	The CC	National Legislation by NPC	A comprehensive CC has seven parts and 1,260 articles. The seven parts are General Provisions, Property Rights, Contracts, Personality Rights, Marriage and Family, Right of Inheritance, and Tort Liability and Supplemental Provision.

constitutionally.[77] In 1988, the first step was taken through a PRC constitutional amendment to recognise privately owned and transferable land use rights in urban China.[78] The 1999 constitutional amendment states, "The individual economy, private economy, and other non-publicly owned economies within the scope defined by the law are important components of the socialist market economy."[79]

In contrast, the 2004 constitutional amendment guarantees the right to hold private property.[80] This recent amendment caused legislative changes, improving the country's legal framework for trading in real estate, stocks, bonds and other forms of property. Although private property is protected by various means under Chinese law, the constitutional amendments are conspicuous because they acknowledge the right to private property as a fundamental freedom. This is a symbolic milestone that pre-empts the enactment of further laws relating to property. Consequently, the CC provides equal protection to privately owned, state-owned and collectively owned property.[81]

The Chinese land tenure system is still socialist. The dichotomy between land ownership and land use rights shows this. All urban land is state owned, and all rural land is collectively owned. In brief, there is no private land ownership in China. However, under the Chinese Constitution, the highly commercialised land use right is created to separate itself from land ownership.[82] As a result, while the land is still publicly owned, the land use right granted to individuals or private entities can be freely transferable for value. The current legal framework governing land expropriation for rural land requires that all non-agricultural use be held over state-owned land.[83] Where the land is collectively owned in rural areas, it must first be taken by the state and converted into state-owned land.[84] Because land is publicly owned in China, expropriation only involves the summary withdrawal of land use rights.

[77] Hanri Mostert and Lei Chen, 'The Dynamics of Constitutional Property Clauses in the Developing World: China and South Africa' (2010) 17 *Maastricht Journal of European and Comparative Law* 377.

[78] See Table 1.1.

[79] Article 11 Constitution (1999 Amendment).

[80] Article 13 PRC Constitution (amended on 14 March 2004 at the 2nd session of the 10th NPC).

[81] Article 207 CC.

[82] Article 10 PRC Constitution.

[83] Article 43 Land Administration Law.

[84] Article 44 Land Administration Law.

Before the housing privatisation occurred in 1994, the expropriation of urban housing was mainly aimed at serving the needs of urban revitalisation. Expropriations were largely government oriented and benefitted the public by improving living conditions.

However, the Urban Real Estate Management Law (the UREML)[85] changed the nature of expropriations with regard to urban housing. The law created a number of de facto monopolies that rendered the implementation of fair compensation almost impossible. The UREML and the Land Administration Law require that large new construction projects be completed on state-owned land. Since the local government is the only authority that may assign a piece of state-owned land to developers or take collectively owned land and convert it to state-owned land, the local government effectively monopolises the supply of land available for construction.[86] Hence, the entrepreneurial interest of local governments is unavoidably intermingled with public interest.[87] However, the UREML only allows developers with licences and the necessary qualifications to construct in urban areas; individuals, organisations and enterprises are, therefore, unable to build their housing.[88] For the investors to maximise profit in redevelopment, a private developer removes the residents from a piece of land at a low price, redevelops the area and sells the real estate at a markedly higher price.

Property rights cannot exist as social and economic institutions without laws defining their structure and obligations. As mentioned earlier, the Chinese Constitutional Property Clause prohibits the government from taking private property for public interest without fair compensation. However, the public interest requirement in the past three decades was a veritable black hole open to wide and potentially self-serving interpretations. This renders such a clause a relatively toothless provision that cannot hold local governments accountable for their actions.[89] Moreover, the compensation mechanism does not require local governments to consider relevant factors, such as the logistical costs of moving, the value inherent to the property's location, the value stemming from

[85] The Urban Real Estate Management Law of 1994 by the Standing Committee of the NPC.

[86] Peter Ho, *Developmental Dilemmas: Land Reform and Institutional Change in China* (Routledge 2009), pp. 44–48.

[87] Sally Sargeson, 'Full Circle? Rural Land Reforms in Globalizing China' (2004) 36 *Critical Asian Studies* 637, 640.

[88] Article 30 UREML.

[89] Article 45 Land Administration Law 2019 amendment provides a list of situations which constitute public interest.

the short supply of or high demand on the land, and the farmers' employment and social security issues. To tackle these matters, the State Council issued the expropriation regulations listing the situations where land-taking fulfils the public interest requirement.[90] The expropriation regulations are more transparent and thus increase government accountability.[91] The key formalised procedures are to notify property owners and solicit opinions.[92] Local governments must comply with a mandatory review process before they expropriate. Therefore, its enactment is a significant step towards protecting individual property rights. However, the 2011 expropriation regulations do not apply to rural land expropriations. Many forced evictions and land disputes are still taking place in rural areas. Until 2019, when the Land Administration Law was amended, the rural land expropriation was addressed in the same manner as on the urban land.

1.4 Rural Land Reform

Moving from urban land to a rural tenure system, the picture is even more concerning. While the belief that property rights promote prosperity and safeguard against arbitrary intrusion has long been the norm in economic theory,[93] in China, property rights are weak and vulnerable to the varying dictates of government policies. Unfortunately, many Chinese farmers learned this lesson the hard way. As noted earlier, China employs a bifurcated system of land use rights, differentiating between urban and rural lands. In the past, while urban land use rights have been commercially transferable, rural land has been collectively owned and was effectively non-transferable. Though a village collective could transfer rural construction land use rights to individuals, such a transfer would be subject to consent from two-thirds of the villagers' representatives and the township authority.[94] Furthermore, households

[90] The Regulaiton for Expropriation and Compensation for Houses on State-owned Land in 2011.

[91] Siyi Tu [涂四益], 'From Demolition to Expropriation: Problems, Solutions and Difficulties in China' [《从拆迁到征收–当下中国拆迁面临的问题、出路及难点》] (2010) 3 *Wuhan University Law Review* [《法学评论》] 49.

[92] Lei Chen, 'The Legal and Institutional Analysis of Land Expropriation in China', in John Gillespie and Hualing Fu (eds), *Resolving Land Disputes in East Asia* (Cambridge University Press 2015), pp. 76–83.

[93] Yoram Barzel, *Economic Analysis of Property Rights* (Cambridge University Press 1997).

[94] Article 63 Land Administration Law.

that wish to transfer their contracting management rights must give preference to potential transferees in the same collective.[95] However, several low-key machinations have seen this arrangement evolve.

In 2007, the State Council allowed Chengdu and Chongqing as pilot localities to register and transfer collective agricultural land.[96] This new pilot scheme on rural land transfer could be to individuals outside the collective. Politically, these moves were significant, as they indicated that the top leadership signalled the will to terminate the bifurcated urban and rural land tenure systems.[97] Since then, Chengdu has been implementing and fine-tuning many concrete policies to establish a legal and institutional framework for markets in rural property rights.[98] Specifically, village authorities can register a person-based land use right at the village level for the homestead right (residential construction right), and there is now a household-based registration for the farmland use right. At the central level, while there are concerns over the potential for rural landlessness,[99] there are also political constituencies for liberalising rural land markets to reduce social instability caused by potential land conflict. These constituencies are supported by technocratic arguments that a rural property market is essential to allow farmers access to credit.[100] At the provincial level, there have been some attempts to "cross the river by feeling the stones" through experiments with transfers of rural land rights. The past decade, in particular, has seen pilot projects on transfers of rural land rights in almost every province in China.[101]

95 Article 33 Rural Land Contract Management Law.

96 National Development and Reform Commission (NDRC), The Circular approving Chongqing and Chengdu as the Special Experimental Zones for Coordinated Rural and Urban Development areas (Fā gǎi jīng tǐ [2007] No 1248). This notice was dated 7 June 2007.

97 Guangdong has actually been made a provisional laboratory even earlier than Chengdu and Chongqing.

98 Xiaoming Guo [郭晓鸣], *'Coordinating Urban and Rural Development and Rural Land Transfer Reform: An Empirical Study Based on Chengdu "Experimental Zone"'* [《统筹城乡发展与农村土地流转制度变革：基于成都"试验区"的实证研究》] (Science Press China 2012), pp. 23–27.

99 Qinguo Meng, *A Study on China's Rural Land Reform* (Law Press China 2009), pp. 80–81.

100 Qirena Zhou, *Property Rights and Institutional Transformation: Empirical Study of China* (Peking University Press 2004), pp. 15–18.

101 There are many other places in China carrying out the experiments on rural land transfer. The notable examples include Wenzhou in Zhejiang Province, Suzhou in Jiangsu Province, Shuangliu, Chengdu in Sichuan Province and Nanhai, Foshan in Guangdong Province.

Permitting transactions in rural land use rights would be a major milestone in the economic liberalisation of China.[102] Currently, demand for land in rural China is satisfied by state-based models of expropriation and by converting the legal status of rural land rather than through interpersonal exchanges of property rights. Not surprisingly, the current model is a cause for widespread land conflicts in China as state officials appropriate the benefits of transitions to higher-value uses of land – an arrangement I have dubbed "government gains, farmer pains."[103] Rural land transactions would appear to offer a more equitable alternative to state-based mechanisms of property rights exchange. This, in turn, would likely increase the efficient use of rural land in much of China.

However, allowing the contractual transfer of rural land use rights is a sensitive sociopolitical topic in China, not only due to the potential unrest arising from the aggrieved farmers but also because it raises issues stemming from citizens' potential engagement with the state. Therefore, although the Chengdu and Chongqing pilot reforms started as early as 2007, when turning these policies into legal provisions by assessing the effectiveness of these rural land reform pilot studies, the legislative process has been very scrupulous and cautious. The CC is still nebulous about the legal nature of the land management right carved out of the right of contractual land management. This is to say, whether the land management right the outsider investors may hold is a property right or contractual right remains unsettled. The CC only provides that the holder of land management rights can possess the land within the time limit stipulated in the contract,[104] and land management right with a term of more than five years is created when the underlying contract of grant becomes effective.[105] There is no strict need to register it to be effective. These are only two provisions specifically pertaining to land management right. Therefore, it would be audacious to conclude that the

[102] To allow legally recognised transactions of rural land does not amount to total privatisation of rural land, as zoning (land planning) ordinances will still apply for the sake of food security and nature preservation as well as preservation of indigenous people's "family land." I thank Professor Frank Upham for making this point.

[103] Chen (n. 92), p. 80.

[104] Article 340 CC.

[105] Article 341 CC: "A land management right with a term more than five years is created at the moment when the underlying contract of grant becomes effective. The parties may apply to the registration office for the registration of the right to land management; such right cannot be alleged against a bona fide third party without registration."

land management right is a property right given the above wordings, even though the two articles are included in the usufructuary rights in the CC.[106] Hence, market signals are introduced in fine-tuning state planning and offer benchmarks for improving economic efficiency. The combination of free-market dynamics and state planning represents a distinctive experiment, and Chinese lawmakers seem to produce an intentional ambiguity through this compromised expression.[107]

1.5 Protection of Property Rights

1.5.1 Exercising Property Rights

One of the guiding philosophies of property rights in China is a form of community-driven responsibility.[108] It emphasises that the rights enjoyed by property owners are no longer absolute and unrestricted. As with many other jurisdictions, the acquisition, content and exercise of property rights are subject to limitations imposed by public and private law. The obligational aspect of property rights dictates that the enjoyment of property rights is inherently subject to socially conditioned constraints and state-directed control of land use and transfer. Hence, exercising property rights is not an absolute freedom and must adhere to specific principles. Firstly, the exercise of property rights must conform to the requirements of national law and observe public order and good customs.[109] The exercise of property rights must not violate prohibitive provisions of the law, such as creating a mortgage or lien on property prohibited by the state.[110]

Secondly, while the law encourages individuals to exercise their rights legitimately, exercising rights must have reasonable limits to avoid harming national interests, social public interests, or the legitimate rights and interests of others.[111] The principle of prohibiting the abuse of rights demands that property owners should not use their rights in an improper way that harms the interests of others.

[106] See more discussions at Chapter 6.

[107] Ho (n. 86).

[108] Ting Xu and Wei Gong, 'Community-based Individual Property Rights: Developing the "Bundle of Rights" Perspective in the Chinese Context' (2020) 28 *Asia Pacific Law Review* 138.

[109] Article 8 CC.

[110] Article 399 CC.

[111] Article 132 CC.

Thirdly, exercising property rights should adhere to the good-faith principle. The principle of good faith and credit, as a fundamental provision in civil law, not only constrains general civil legal actions but also imposes constraints on acquiring and exercising property rights. The lawful exercise of property rights contributes to establishing a harmonious economic order, ensuring the smooth flow of property transactions.[112] For example, neighbouring property owners must handle relationships based on beneficial production, convenient living, mutual assistance and fairness principles.[113]

Fourthly, property owners must contribute to resource conservation and environmental protection.[114] For example, condominium owners' behaviour should reasonably align with resource conservation and environmental protection principles.[115] The exercise of usufructuary rights should comply with the principles of reasonable resource utilisation and ecological environment protection.[116]

1.5.2 Remedies

1.5.2.1 Proprietary Remedies

Where a dispute arises over the title to or content of a property right, an interested party may claim to confirm the right.[117] Where the property right is infringed, the owner can bring a claim seeking proprietary remedies. The owner need not be the direct possessor of the property. Under Chinese law, there are four types of proprietary remedies: return of the property[118]; repair, redo, replacement or restoration[119]; removal of disturbances[120]; and a prohibitory injunction.[121]

The former two suggest that the owner may require the possessor to return the property. It simply represents an action *in rem* that reflects the idea of property sovereignty – I find my property and give it back to me. This is also known as *rei vindicatio*, which empowers an owner to claim

112 Article 7 CC.
113 Article 288 CC.
114 Article 9 CC.
115 Article 286 CC.
116 Article 326 CC.
117 Article 234 CC.
118 Article 235 CC.
119 Article 237 CC.
120 Article 236 CC.
121 *Ibid.*

his property from whoever possesses it. When possession has been wrongly deprived by others who refuse to return the property upon demand, the property right holder has a claim to demand the return of the property.[122]

An owner instituting the *rei vindicatio* bears the burden of proof and must prove that (1) she is the owner or a co-owner of the property; (2) the defendant has possession or detention of the thing at the moment the action is brought; (3) the defendant is in an unauthorised possession of the property.[123]

Since *rei vindicatio* is a claim *in rem* tied to ownership, it cannot be assigned. Once the *rei vindincatio* claim is successful, the possessor must surrender the property to its owner in its present state and at its present place. If the possessed property is damaged, a claim can be made for repair, redoing or replacement of the damaged item or restoration to its original status.[124]

The *rei vindicatio* aims to restore the thing along with its fruits.[125] Whether the consumed fruits are recoverable remains unanswered in Chinese law. It is proposed that the bona fide possessor only restore unconsumed fruits while the mala fide possessor must also make good consumed fruits. Nonetheless, the bona fide possessor should compensate for the expenses incurred for maintaining the property.[126] It implies that the mala fide possessor must bear the costs for getting the property ready for return.

The *actio negatoria* aims to prevent any physical infringement of the thing by a third party. Where a property right has been or is likely to be obstructed, the right holder may claim for removal of the obstacle or elimination of the danger.[127] These claims do not depend on fault but merely require the unlawfulness of the interference. An interference is any state which contradicts the contents of the property right.

The situation that calls for this remedy must pose an actual or potential threat to the owner's possession. It is not based on the owner's understanding of the circumstance but must be objectively inferred from the facts. A common situation is when a development plan reveals that it

122 Article 235 CC.
123 Liming Wang [王利明], *Property Law* [《物权法》] (China Renmin University Press 2015), pp. 41–42
124 Article 237.
125 Article 460 CC.
126 *Ibid.*
127 Article 236 CC.

will encroach on the boundary of neighbouring land. This can be understood as a prohibitory interdict claim. A person may resort to this when the property is wrongly interfered with without taking possession away from the person.

1.5.2.2 Concurrence with Tortious Remedies

If the infringer has caused damage to the property, he is liable to compensate the property right owner or request to bear other civil liabilities.[128] There is a link between proprietary and tortious remedies. Under Chinese law, they share the same requirements between spoliation claims and prohibitory interdicts. This means the person must be in possession immediately before the damage to the property occurred and that the property must still exist when the claim is made. Notably, many return-of-property clauses/remedies in Chinese law exist.[129] In addition to proprietary and tortious remedies, Article 985 of the CC in the section on unjust enrichment provides that a property right holder can claim for the return of profits if (1) the infringer is without lawful excuse and has made a profit due to the infringement and (2) the infringement has caused the possessor a loss.[130] However, it should be noted that any wrongful possessor is responsible for returning profits to the property holders.[131] As such, there is a great deal of inconsistencies in the case law due to confusion caused.[132]

To be considered an infringement, an illegitimate action must take place that causes interference with the possessor's ability to control the property. Malicious intent is not required. Even innocent interference is considered an infringement that allows the possessor to seek legal protection. There are scant provisions addressing property protection in the CC. This is because some influential scholars advocate that "employing the tortious claim for infringement replacing the proprietary claim is the best solution to fulfil the task of protecting property rights."[133] The key

[128] Article 238 CC.

[129] For example, Articles 53 (1), 157, 179 (4), 227, 245, 312, 314, 432, 462 and 985 CC.

[130] Article 985 CC.

[131] Article 460 CC.

[132] Yuxiang Ding [丁宇翔], 'Constructing the System of Restitution of Things in the CC' [《民法典中返还原物制度的构建》] (2019) *Financial and Economic Law Review* [《财经法学》] 67.

[133] Yi Wang [王轶], 'How Does the CC Protect Property Rights' [《民法典如何保护物权》] [2019] *Chinese Law Review* [《中国法律评论》] 71, pp. 71–73.

difference is that a tortious claim requires fault as a constituting element, while a proprietary claim does not.

In summary, the property owner has recourse to a few remedies if his property entitlement is infringed upon or if the property is damaged. Technically, proprietary, tortious and enrichment remedies are available under Chinese law. Four proprietary remedies exist. The *rei vindicatio* aims to restore physical control over the property if the owner is deprived of possession. Tortious remedies differ from proprietary ones because they are actions against a person to claim compensation for damage or injury to the owner. However, such a conceptual difference has been largely blurred in the rule design of the Chinese CC.

2

Sources and Basic Principles of Property Law

2.1 Subject Matter of Property Law

This chapter examines the conceptual understanding of Chinese property law, such as its basic principles, sources and classification of property. In China's socialist system, property ownership is categorised into three types: state, collective and private. The Chinese Constitution guarantees the right to hold private property. The 2004 constitutional amendment will lead to legal changes that will improve the country's legal framework for trading in housing, stocks, bonds and other kinds of property.

The law of property is a system of legal rules that regulate legal relationships between legal subjects regarding a specific legal object, namely a thing. Article 205 of the CC stipulates that the Property Book governs the civil relationships arising from the entitlements to and use of things. This relation can be factual, such as possession and lien, or legal, such as ownership and limited real rights.

Since property law concerns the relationship between private individuals regarding a thing, it falls within private law. This does not mean that the various legal rights recognised by property law, especially ownership, are not subject to restrictions under public law or environmental law rules.[1]

Property law distinguishes itself from other branches of private law, including the law of persons, family law, the law of succession and the law of obligations. The law of persons concerns only legal subjects and deals with the incidence of natural and juristic personality; family law regulates legal relations flowing from blood relationship or marriage; the law of succession deals with the devolution of property upon death; and

[1] For example, Article 9 CC provides that civil subjects shall carry out civil activities in a way that is good for the conservation of resources, as well as ecological and environmental protection. Article 326 CC provides that the usufructuary right holder shall comply with provisions of law on the protection, rational exploitation of resources and ecological and environmental protection when exercising its rights.

the law of obligations concerns relations in terms of which a person, called a creditor, is entitled to demand performance from another person, a debtor.

Like many other jurisdictions, Chinese law distinguishes a contractual right from a property right. Contractual rights are created by agreements between parties, which bind the contracting parties and no one else.[2] In contrast to a contractual right, which only binds certain persons in legal connection, a property right required by the excludability in particular binds the whole world. In this sense, property rights are often described as rights *in rem* or real. This denotes that it is universally binding on all who encounter the object. It is not required for a real right holder to agree with any other individual to exercise his right. The property right carries the power to bind any person to not deal with the property in a manner that is against the wishes of the property right holder.

Finally, the property law belongs to substantive and not procedural law. Naturally, the rules of civil procedure play a role where ownership, possession or limited real rights in respect of a thing are enforced.

2.2 Definition and Features of Property Rights

Being a system highly influenced by German law, the modern Chinese legal system traditionally adopts a distinction between property rights (物权) and personal rights (also referred to as obligatory rights [债权]). This separation significantly alters the interpretation and application of the laws regarding whether the title has passed in any given situation, especially in cases where multiple purchasers exist.[3] The doctrine of property transfer has never been universally accepted by the legal academia, which will be explained in detail in Chapter 3.

In light of the significant economic development and technological advancement, the use of a property is diversified and is no longer limited

[2] Obligations to third parties can arise under third-party beneficiary rules, but these rules are widely regarded as uncharacteristic exception in Chinese law. For more details, see Lei Chen, 'Relaxations of Contractual Privity and the Need for Third Party Rights in Chinese Contract Law', in Mindy Chen-Wishart, Alexander Loke and Stefan Vogenauer (eds), *Studies in the Contract Laws of Asia II: Formation and Third Party Beneficiaries* (Oxford University Press 2018).

[3] This refers to the situation where a seller of a property enters into sale and purchase agreement with more than one purchaser [一物多卖]. While this topic is seldom discussed in other jurisdictions, it is a hot topic in China.

to its physical utilisation of the property. Similarly, using, profiting from and trading on one's obligatory right as if it is a property are also not uncommon anymore. However, it is argued that such is only a merge of the effects of the rights but not of the rights themselves. It remains true that an obligatory right is a tool to obtain a property right, which is the goal.

Article 114 of the CC provides a statutory definition of property rights: A property right is the right holder's exclusive right to dominate a particular thing in accordance with the law directly. Property rights include ownership, usufructuary rights and security interests.[4] While the statutory definition is abridged, it can still be deduced that a property right in and of itself gives the holder direct control of a particular property to the exclusion of others.

As a civil law system influenced by Roman law, ownership dominates the whole of property law under Chinese law. All other property interests are designed and benchmarked by their relationship with ownership, thereby establishing a conceptual and institutional hierarchy of property interests.[5] Dominance provides a person full control of the property, and excludability makes such control exclusive to that person.[6] Any other person interfering with the property against the right holder's wishes is considered an infringement of the right holder's right. Dominance describes not only physical control but also legal control. Therefore, it is possible for an owner to physically depart from his or her property and still be able to dispose of it. This legal control is the basis of an owner's power to recover their property in cases where the property is lost or stolen.

The combination of dominance and excludability makes a property right not only a type of property relationship between a person and the property but also an impersonal relationship.[7] The first type is obvious, as a 'property right' gives a person direct and immediate control over a property. A property right is also an interpersonal relationship because it

[4] Article 114 CC.

[5] Andre J. van der Walt, *Property in the Margins* (Bloomsbury Publishing 2009), p. 26.

[6] William Blackstone, *Commentaries on the Laws of England (volume 1)* (J. B. Lippincott Co., 1893), p. 2: ". . . that sole and despotic dominion which one man claims and exercises over the external things of the world, in total exclusion of the right of any other individual . . ."

[7] Liming Wang [王利明], *Research on Real Property Rights* [《物权法研究》] (3rd edn, Renmin University of China Press 2013), vol. I, p. 6.

gives a right to the real right holder and an obligation to all others not to cause any harm to the real right holder's property.[8]

2.3 Sources of Property Law

Property law is one of the branches of law in which the principles of German law have been influential to a large extent (emphasis on the distinction between movables and immovables[9]; the system of land registration)[10] and in which the principles of common law play a subordinate role (in respects of construction land use right,[11] condominium management[12] and floating mortgage).[13] Most importantly, property law has been developed further by national legislation, administrative regulations, departmental rules and cases.

Because of its civil law tradition, Roman law still forms the dogmatic basis of modern property law in China. Roman law influence is manifested in the clear distinction between ownership and possession and that between ownership and limited real rights; the perception of ownership as an indivisible right which confers on an individual the widest possible powers in relation to a thing; the emphasis on delivery as a prerequisite for transfer of ownership in a movable[14]; right of habitation (personal servitude)[15]; and the doctrinal basis of accessoriness in real security.[16]

In a nutshell, Chinese property law primarily finds its sources in the Constitution, laws, administrative regulations, local regulations, autonomous and specific regulations, departmental rules of the Ministries, judicial interpretations, civil customs[17] and international treaties.[18]

Initially, there was no specific provision governing private property in the 1982 Constitution. With rapid economic and social conditions

[8] Kevin Gray, 'Equitable Property' (1994) 47 *Current Legal Problems* 157, 160: "Property is what we have in things, not the things that we think we have . . . property is not a thing at all, but a socially approved power-relationship in respect of socially valued assets."
[9] Article 115 CC.
[10] Article 208 CC.
[11] Article 344 CC. Inspired by the law of government lease (formerly crown lease) in Hong Kong.
[12] Article 271 CC.
[13] Article 396 CC.
[14] Article 224 CC.
[15] Articles 366 and 377 CC.
[16] Article 407 CC.
[17] Article 10 CC.
[18] Lei Chen, 'Continuity and Change: Some Reflections on the Chinese CC' (2021) 29 *Asia Pacific Law Review* 287.

changes, the Constitution was amended a few times to embrace the idea of private property.[19] The 1999 constitutional amendment provides that "individual private and other non-public economies that exist within limits prescribed by law are major components of the socialist market economy."[20] Further, the 2004 constitutional amendment guarantees the right to hold private property and gives equal protection to private, state-owned and collectively owned property.[21]

Despite the lack of constitutional review in Western democracies, the constitutional amendments are significant, as they recognise the right to private property as a fundamental freedom. This is a symbolic milestone that pre-empts the enactment of further laws relating to the property.[22] They introduced a notion of private property right into the Chinese legal system that underpins a free and sustainable market economy. Nevertheless, the principles for constitutional property protection in China have yet to be translated into more concrete implications.[23] The significant role of the Chinese Constitution in property law is often overlooked, primarily due to the absence of a substantial constitutional review.

As with many other jurisdictions around the globe, the Property Right Book of the CC cannot provide an exhaustive list of property rights provisions alone. Inevitably, many statutory instruments, including special national legislation, administrative regulation and departmental rules, have contributed to developing property law rules. Hence, the notion of "in accordance with the law" mentioned in the CC needs to be construed broadly, including the provisions of the CC per se and other provisions of national legislation.

Take special national legislation, for example. There are three pieces of legislation concerning land administration in the Chinese legal framework: (1) the Land Administration Law, which stipulates the fundamentals of China's legal framework on land administration and how to convert collective-owned land into state-owned land; (2) the Urban

[19] Hanri Mostert and Lei Chen, 'The Dynamics of Constitutional Property Clauses in the Developing World: China and South Africa' (2010) 17 *Maastricht Journal of European and Comparative Law* 377.

[20] Article 11 of the PRC Constitution (amended on 15 March 1999 at the 2nd session of the 9th NPC).

[21] Article 13 of the PRC Constitution (amended on 14 March 2004 at the 2nd session of the 10th NPC).

[22] Mostert and Chen (n. 19).

[23] *Ibid.*

Real Estate Administration Law (UREAL), which mainly prescribes how a party obtains land use rights relating to the state-owned land; and (3) the Rural Land Contracting Law (RLCL), which deals with how the rural households obtain the right to land contractual management in the collectively owned land in the rural areas.

In addition, there are relevant pieces of legislation concerning certain types of property rights from private law and administrative law perspectives, such as Forest Law,[24] Mineral Resources Law,[25] Maritime Law,[26] Civil Aviation Law,[27] the Prevention and Control of Desertification Law,[28] Grassland Law,[29] the Law on the Mediation and Arbitration of Rural Land Contract Disputes,[30] the Intangible Cultural Heritage Law,[31] Fisheries Law,[32] Water Law,[33] the Law on the Administration of the Use of Sea Areas,[34] Wetlands Protection Law,[35] Soil and Water Conservation Law,[36] Urban and Rural Planning Law,[37] Construction Law,[38] the Trust Law,[39] the Assets Appraisal Law, the Law on the State-Owned Assets of Enterprises[40] and the Foreign Investment Law.[41]

Furthermore, the State Council (the central government) issued some administrative regulations governing certain types of property rights,

[24] The Forest Law (Adopted on 20 September 1984; Amended on 29 April 1998, 27 August 2009 and 28 December 2019).

[25] The Mineral Resources Law (Adopted on 19 March 1986).

[26] The Maritime Law (Adopted on 7 November 1992).

[27] The Civil Aviation Law (Adopted on 30 October 1995).

[28] The Desertification Prevention and Control Law (Adopted on 31 August 2001; Amended on 26 October 2018).

[29] The Grassland Law (Adopted on 18 June 1985; Revised on 28 December 2002; Amended on 27 August 2009, 29 June 2013 and 29 April 2021).

[30] The Law on the Mediation and Arbitration of Rural Land Contract Disputes (Adopted on 27 June 2009).

[31] The Intangible Cultural Heritage Law (Adopted on 25 February 2011).

[32] The Fisheries Law (Adopted on 20 January 1986).

[33] The Water Law (adopted on 21 January 1988; Amended on 27 August 2009 and 2 July 2016).

[34] The Law on the Administration of Sea Areas (Adopted on 27 October 2001).

[35] The Wetlands Conservation Law of the People's Republic of China (Adopted on 24 December 2021).

[36] The Water and Soil Conservation Law (Adopted on 29 June 1991; Amended on 25 December 2010).

[37] The Urban and Rural Planning Law (Adopted on 28 October 2007).

[38] The Construction Law (Adopted on 1 November 1997).

[39] The Trust Law (Adopted on 28 April 2001).

[40] The Law on the State-Owned Assets of Enterprises (Adopted on 28 October 2008).

[41] The Foreign Investment Law (Adopted on 15 March 2019).

such as the Realty Management Regulation,[42] the Interim Regulation of Immovable Property Registration,[43] the regulation on the Expropriation of Urban Buildings on State-owned Land and Compensation[44] and the Regulations on Nature Reserves.[45]

The courts have already been instrumental in developing property law. On the one hand, the courts have issued judicial interpretations and other judicial documents to flesh out the general rules in the CC, such as the 2020 SPC Interpretations on the Application of the Property Book of the CC (I).[46] On the other hand, the courts have provided detailed legal tests to determine a certain type of popular dispute. For instance, with the advent of regulatory restrictions on the house purchaser in China, the courts have developed a set of rules governing the effectiveness of "purchasing an apartment under another's name" to settle disputes without equitable rules found in the common law of trust.[47]

While China is not a case law jurisdiction like the United States and England,[48] Chinese judges tend to pay regard to prior court decisions with the advent of the guiding cases system introduced by the SPC.[49] The Chinese judiciary has started mass publicity of its decisions or rulings since 2012.[50] This facilitates the transparency and the wide use of prior

[42] The Property Management Regulations (Issued by Order No. 379 of the State Council on 8 June 2003; Amended for the first time on 26 August 2007; Amended for the second time on 6 February 2016; Amended for the third time on 19 March 2018).

[43] The Interim Regulation on Real Estate Registration (Issued by Order No. 656 of the State Council on 24 November 2014; Amended according to the Decision of the State Council on Amending Some Administrative Regulations on 24 March 2019).

[44] The Regulation on the Expropriation of Buildings on State-owned Land and Compensation (Adopted at the 141st executive meeting of the State Council on 19 January 2011).

[45] The Regulations on Nature Reserves (Adopted at the 24th executive meeting of the State Council on 2 September 1994).

[46] The SPC Interpretation (I) on the Application of the Property Book of the CC.

[47] Article 2 of the SPC Interpretation (I) on the Application of the Property Book of the CC; 辽宁中集哈深冷气体液化设备有限公司诉徐沛欣，(2020) 最高法民再328号 [*Liaoning CIMC Haisheng Cryogenic Gas Liquefaction Equipment Co., Ltd., Xu Peixin*, (2020) SPC Min Zai No. 328].

[48] Unlike precedents under the common law system, China's guiding cases do not have the status of legal source. Thus, they do not have the mandatory binding force on judicial decisions.

[49] The Organic Law of the People's Courts was amended to allow the SPC to issue guiding cases which are discussed and approved by expert committees of the Judicial Committee. See Articles 18 and 37 of the Organic Law of the People's Courts.

[50] Lei Chen, Zhuang Liu and Yingmao Tang, 'Judicial Transparency as Judicial Centralization: Mass Publicity of Court Decisions in China' (2021) 31 *Journal of Contemporary China* 726.

decisions by the parties, lawyers and judges. One empirical study suggests that the "Chinese judiciary operates much more similar to its homologues in the United States and elsewhere than their written opinions."[51] Suppose a judge finds that a guiding case may share some similarity to a pending case during the trial or encounters a situation where a party, lawyer or prosecutor proposes that a guiding case be referred to and applied. In that case, the judge should prepare a similar-case search report and record the scope, targets, analysis process and findings of the reference search, regardless of whether the case is eventually referred to or applied. Particularly, for cases where the final decision is not to refer to the guiding cases, "more sufficient grounds of argument" should be given during deliberations of the collegial panel or discussions at the specialised judges' meeting during the judicial process.[52]

The relevant ministries and commissions issue numerous departmental rules, providing technical implementation rules. Examples are the Administrative Measures for the Circulation of Rural Land Management Rights,[53] the Administration of Preliminary Examination of Land Use for Construction Projects[54] and the Measures for Disposal of Idle Land.[55]

Finally, the CC replaced national policies with civil custom as a source of civil law.[56] While this change is commendable, a question exists about identifying and defining civil custom. What is meant by civil custom in this connection? In Europe, the French CC addresses the *droit coutumier*, while the German CC and Swiss CC refer to the *usus modernus* and the Germanic customary law, which survived the reception of Roman law in certain respects.[57] In the Chinese CC, there is a lack of guidance. Does it mean trade usages, customary industry practices or ethical traditions in

[51] Zhuang Liu, Lars Klöhn and Holger Spamann, 'Precedents and Chinese Judges: An Experiment' (2021) 69 *The American Journal of Comparative Law* 93.

[52] In 2020, the SPC issued Guiding Opinions on Unifying the Application of Laws to Strengthen the Retrieval of Similar Cases (for Trial Implementation), which introduced the concept of "similar cases."

[53] The Measures for the Administration of Circulation of Rural Land Contracted Management Right (Adopted at the 2nd executive meeting of the Ministry of Agriculture on 7 January 2005).

[54] The Measures of the Ministry of Land and Resources on the Administration of Preliminary Examination of the Land Used for Construction Projects (Adopted at the 5th executive meeting of the Ministry of Land and Resources on 28 June 2001).

[55] The Measures for Disposal of Idle Land were issued by the Ministry of Land and Resources (currently the Ministry of Natural Resources).

[56] Article 10 CC.

[57] Roscoe Pound, 'Chinese CC in Action' (1954) 29 *Tulane Law Review* 277, 288.

certain communities? Many ethnic minority groups have developed their local customs through historical evolution. As some customs still function today, it has been argued that these local customs have been disregarded and overlooked, as they were external to China's unitary national statutory system.[58] However, the crux of the issue is that they are unsystematic, bulky and scattered. The legislator has sidestepped the legal definition of civil customs. Consequently, the Chinese courts have significant discretion to characterise and ascertain the widely recognised civil custom.[59]

In short, among all the aforementioned sources of property law, the two most crucial ones are (1) the national legislation enacted and amended by the NPC, whose Standing Committee also holds the power of enacting and amending laws other than those that the NPC should enact; and (2) the judicial interpretations by the SPC, which are interpretations made by the highest judicial organ on the specific application of law in the judicial work.

2.4 Basic Principles of Law of Property

The foundational principles serve as the guiding regulations for developing Chinese property laws and act as instructive guidelines for applying and interpreting these laws. On the one hand, these principles signify the objectives legislators strive to accomplish when creating or amending legislation, making them a product of legislative intent. On the other hand, they mirror societal perspectives on property governance, encompassing associated rights and obligations. Nevertheless, these fundamental principles encapsulate the values that underlie the entire property law system. The ensuing paragraphs will delve into the distinct explanations of each basic principle of property law, namely (1) the *numerus clausus* principle, (2) the equal protection principle and (3) the publicity principle.

2.4.1 Principle of Numerus Clausus

China adopts the principle of *numerus clausus* with some relaxation.[60] Article 116 of the CC states, "Laws provide for the types and contents of a

[58] Chen (n. 18).
[59] *Ibid.*
[60] Yun-chien Chang and Henry E. Smith, 'The Numerus Clausus Principle, Property Customs, and the Emergence of New Property Forms', 100 *Iowa Law Review* 2275

property right."[61] A literal interpretation of this article provides two consequences. First, a right can be recognised as a property right only if it belongs to one legally recognised category. The contents of each recognised property right fit into the legal stipulations. Second, it refers to 'laws' only, meaning that administrative or local regulations would not qualify. In short, the principle of *numerus clausus* dictates that there is a closed catalogue of property rights.

As a natural consequence of the strict differentiation between property rights and personal rights, the principle of *numerus clausus* means any right that arises out of any situation – for example, through agreements between the parties – can only be recognised as a property right if the said right is designated as such in the laws. This means that only real rights, modes of delivery and acquisition, which fall into one of the recognised categories, will be countenanced by the law. This principle has been recognised by civil law and common law jurisdictions. At the heart of the *numerus clausus* principle lies a protective stance over the schematic order of property law.[62] Lord Brougham reasoned in *Keppell v. Bailey* 1834 that "it must not be supposed that incidents of a novel kind can be devised and attached to property at the fancy and caprice of any owner. It is inconvenient both to the science of the law and the public weal that such a latitude should be given."[63] Otherwise, it was articulated further that "great detriment would arise and much confusion of rights if parties were allowed to invent new modes of holding and enjoying the real property."[64]

Moreover, the economic theory and the law and development ground have further justified this principle. Specifically, the standardisation of the property system by employing the principle helps to reduce information costs[65] and pinpoint the economic potential of resources to enhance what we can do with them.[66] Merrill and Smith argued that

(arguing that leading Chinese property scholars all seem to agree that the number of forms is not airtight).

61 Article 116 CC.

62 Kevin Gray and Susan Gray, *Elements of Land Law* (5th edn, Oxford University Press 2009), p. 138.

63 *Keppell v. Bailey* [1834] EWHC Ch J77, [1834] 2 My & K 517.

64 *Ibid.*

65 Thomas. W. Merrill and Henry. E. Smith, 'Optimal Standardization in the Law of Property: The Numerus Clausus Principle' (2000) 110 *The Yale Law Journal* 1.

66 Hernando De Soto, *The Mystery of Capital: Why Capitalism Triumphs in the West and Fails Everywhere Else* (Basic Books 2000), p. 200.

property law could only acknowledge a limited number of relatively simple categories for property's alienability – transactional ease fending off the otherwise overwhelming search cost.[67] The information cost–centred standardisation theory explains and justifies the rationale of the *numerus clausus* principle across legal families. Nonetheless, the information cost theory has been criticised for being disconnected from the individuality-enhancing personhood interests[68] or overemphasising institutional choice while downplaying individual preference.[69]

It is worth noting that how the *numerus clausus* principle is framed under the Chinese CC differs from other civil law jurisdictions. For example, in Europe, Article 3.3 of the Belgian CC categorises the recognised property rights: (1) ownership or co-ownership; (2) property rights to use, which are sub-categorised as usufruct, long lease and building rights; and (3) property security rights, which are sub-categorised in specific statutory rights of priority, pledge, hypothec and liens (Droit de retention).[70] In Asia, for example, Article 175 of the Japanese CC provides that no property right may be created other than those prescribed by laws, including the CC.[71]

In brief, the *numerus clausus* rule is framed either inclusively by specifying what property rights are recognised (Belgian CC) or exclusively by excluding any rights not statutorily recognised (Japanese CC). What is common is that the rule limits party autonomy, as it takes away the freedom for parties to contract for rights intended to bear the characteristics of a property right. This is in stark contrast with the freedom enjoyed under contract law, where contracting parties may agree on whatever they desire. The transaction cost theory[72] is good in the pre-digital era but stifles legal development and encourages adaptation to modern conditions. This is particularly true when comprehensive land registration in a public and transparent manner with digital technology

67 Merrill and Smith (n. 65).

68 Hanoch Dagan, *Property: Values and Institutions* (Oxford University Press 2011); Margaret Jane Radin, 'Personhood and Property' (1982) 34 *Stanford Law Review* 957.

69 Taisu Zhang, 'Beyond Information Costs: Preference Formation and the Architecture of Property Law' (2020) 12 *Journal of Legal Analysis* 1.

70 Vincent Sagaert, 'The Background and General Principles of the New Belgian Property Law' (2021) 10 *European Property Law Journal* 3, 11.

71 Japanese Law Translation: CC (Act No. 89 of 1896) <www.japaneselawtranslation.go.jp/en/laws/view/3494/en> accessed on 1 December 2023.

72 Henry Hansmann and Reinier Kraakman, 'Property, Contract, and Verification: The Numerus Clausus Problem and the Divisibility of Rights' (2002) 31 *The Journal of Legal Studies* 373, 407.

reduces the need to constrict the closed list of property rights.[73] The Chinese approach seems to restrict more public powers (statutory authorities) than private initiatives (party autonomy). This is to say, only the laws enacted by the NPC or NPCSC can recognise property rights. The State Council's Administrative Regulations, the local rules or the court decisions cannot create a new form of property right. In Japan, the court may recognise customary property rights because it has been argued that the laws include customary law.[74] The Chinese rule appears to be more rigid than other jurisdictions, but with scrutiny, the appearances do not match the reality.

The principle of *numerus clausus* has been relaxed or declined in modern times by recognising new types of real rights and a new mode of constructive delivery. Three major routes exist to relax the *numerus clausus* principle under Chinese law. First, civil custom is introduced as a source of civil law where the law remains silent, provided that it is not contrary to public order and good morals.[75] In other words, certain property rights can be created by civil custom where necessary.[76]

Second, the law could effectively prompt or nudge a contractual right into a property-like right. For example, Article 388 of the CC provides that to "create a real security interest, a collateral contract shall be entered into following this CC and other law provisions. A collateral contract refers to a mortgage contract, a pledge contract or other kinds of contracts with security functions." Here, the notion of "other kinds of contacts with security functions" is remarkable, as it allows the deviation from the rigidity of the *numerus clausus* principle. It is worth noting that Article 388 is contained in the Basic Rules of the Security Interests Part of the CC. In contrast with the *numerus clausus* principle, which promotes legal certainty and standardisation of property rights, the principle of party autonomy entails the ability of a person to act according to his or her wishes with the benefits of legal recognition of such acts, thus appearing to be the antithesis to the *numerus clausus* principle. Parties are free under contract law to decide and regulate certain rights and obligations between the parties, knowing that if the counterparty defaults, recourse to a legally backed remedy is available. A legal system

73 Gray and Gray (n. 62), p. 139.

74 Rokuya Suzuki, *Real Estate Law Lecture (Bukkenhō Kōgi)* (5th edn, Sobunsha 2007), p. 436.

75 Article 10 CC.

76 Chang and Smith (n. 60).

that embodies such a principle will provide a legal framework that endorses the acts of a person as he or she intended.

On the contrary, if the acts are not done according to the person's wishes – for example, in cases of duress or lacking mental capacity – the acts will not have legal effects. It becomes clear that the CC balances legal certainty under the *numerus clausus* principle and party autonomy under contractual freedom and market practice. However, the boundary of such contracts with security functions remains unclear. More to the point is whether this kind of security contract creates a real security interest – that is, a property right. The CC is silent because the Security Interest Part of the CC only provides a specified list of mortgages, pledges and liens.

Third, the judicial interpretations issued by the SPC may formalise a new property right when the SPC is satisfied that the maturity of the market practice warrants the rule change. This is a typical result of judicial law-making. Strictly, the *numerus clausus* principle dictates that no new property right can be created unless it is permitted by law. Law in this context refers to the national legislation enacted by the NPC or its Standing Committee. The SPC judicial documents are not qualified to create a new property right. However, the Chinese judges can refer to the SPC interpretations as a legal basis to deliver the final decision. Therefore, Chinese courts can codify judicial policies in a manner similar to legislation and can function as occasional de facto legislators. For example, Articles 68 and 69 of *the SPC Interpretation on the Application of the CC Concerning the Security System* (henceforth the "SPC Interpretation on the Security System") formalise the transfer of ownership as security on a debt (*Sicherungsübereignung* or the Roman *fiducia cum creditore*). As illustrated, the CC per se does not create this type of property right and only makes such a type of security contract permissible. The speculated reason for not creating such a property right could be publicity, as the existence of real security is not discoverable by other parties and, therefore, raises a concern.

Transferring ownership as security is a common business practice. For example, a motor dealer needing to finance car purchases from suppliers might employ one of two transaction structures.[77] In the first, the supplier sells cars to a financier, who then sells them to the motor dealer. Here, the financier retains title until full payment is made by the motor

[77] Cornelius van der Merwe, *Law of Things* (Butterworths 1987), 15–19.

dealer, often facilitated through a hire-purchase agreement.[78] The second structure involves the motor dealer purchasing cars directly and securing a loan from the financier by transferring ownership without physical delivery, relying on the legal concept of *constitutum possessorium*.[79] This allows the motor dealer to retain the cars for sale while providing security on the debt. Although not explicitly mentioned in the CC, the SPC recognises such security rights, stipulating that in default situations, the creditor must obtain the property through auction or judicial sale rather than direct acquisition.[80]

The outcome of the creative tension between the *numerus clausus* principle and party autonomy has been a popular subject of elaboration among legal comparativists.[81] There are strong arguments for discarding the *numerus clausus* principle by embracing the new types of property rights in the digital and data economy era.[82] Van Erp forcefully argued that "legislation is slow, courts hesitate, and legal scholars ponder, but technology does not wait for lawyers, who find it difficult to understand this new virtual world in which they live and seem more inclined to look backwards than forward."[83] On the other hand, there are opposing arguments in favour of retaining the principle of *numerus clausus*.[84] When the Chinese Property Law and later CC were drafted, the drafters needed to decide on the content and contour of property rights. As explained earlier, the Property Law and the CC adopt the *numerus clausus* principle, thereby restricting the types and contents of a property right to those already defined in the laws. However, certain elements of party autonomy have been incorporated to ease the rigidity of the *numerus clausus* principle, given the ever-changing society we face today.

78 Article 641 CC on a right of retention of title.

79 Cornelius van der Merwe, 'Modern Application of the Roman Institution of fiducia cum creditore contracta', in Letitia Vacca (ed), *La Garanzia nella prospettiva storico-comparatisca* (G. Giappichelli Editore 2003).

80 Article 68 of the SPC Interpretation on the Application of the Civil Code Concerning Security System.

81 Vincent Sagaert, 'Property Law: Beyond Dogmas?' (2017) 6 *European Property Law Journal* 119; Michael A. Heller, 'The Boundaries of Private Property' (1999) 108 *The Yale Law Journal* 1163; Bram Akkermans, *The Principle of Numerus Clausus in European Property Law* (Intersentia 2008), p. 657.

82 Sjef van Erp, 'Ownership of Data: The Numerus Clausus of Legal Objects' (2017) 6 *Brigham-Kanner Property Rights Conference Journal* 235.

83 *Ibid.*

84 Kenneth. J. Vandevelde, 'The New Property of the Nineteenth Century: The Development of the Modern Concept of Property' (1980) 29 *Buffalo Law Review* 325.

The legislative balance is well pronounced, but the practical implications might be hard to understand. How do we understand this balance between Chinese law's *numerus clausus* principle and party autonomy? First, the *numerus clausus* principle is strictly upheld regarding *Typenzwang*, the number or enumeration of property rights.[85] Second, the content of property rights, *Typenfixieuring*, is rather relaxed and flexible. For example, the condominium right has been specifically provided on the list of property rights, but there are instances where the rules of the Property Law act as "default rules." For instance, content-wise, the rights and obligations between homeowners, such as the right to manage the property, the right to deal with the common property and the responsibility for management fees,[86] can all be freely decided.

Another example can be seen in security rights. While the CC specifically addresses mortgage, pledge and lien, it allows the parties to contractually derogate from the statutory list to create a collateral contract. The second sentence of Article 388 of the CC provides, "A collateral contract refers to a contract of charge, a pledge contract, or other kinds of contracts with security functions." It becomes clear that the CC employs open categories determined by contract freedom and market practice and avoids a rigid closed list. This practical application of "fancies are for contract, not for property, to meet the market expectations."[87]

Worldwide, legislators and academics ponder how to strike a delicate balance on the *numerus clausus* principle.[88] Under the Chinese CC, creating innominate property rights by party autonomy is impossible. Nonetheless, there is room and space for contractual freedom to determine the scope and nature of the content of nominated property rights within the closed list.

[85] This is a common practice in almost all legal systems, including civil law and common law systems. Even in common law jurisdictions, a standardisation of property rights is applied. See Brendan Edgeworth, 'The *numerus clausus* Principle in Contemporary Australian Property Law' (2006) 32 *Monash University Law Review* 387.

[86] Articles 96, 97 and 98 of the Property Law.

[87] Bernard Rudden, 'Economic Theory v Property Law: The Numerus Clausus Problem', in John Eekelaar and John Bell (eds), *Oxford Essays in Jurisprudence* (3rd edn, Clarendon Press 1987), p. 243.

[88] For example, in the Property Book of the Belgian CC entered into force in November 2020, a similar approach on balance to Chinese law was adopted. See V. Sagaert (n. 70), pp. 10–12.

2.4.2 Principle of Equal Protection

The Chinese Constitution upholds private property rights as a fundamental liberty, ensuring that legally acquired private property cannot be infringed upon.[89] Chinese Property Law delineates ownership into three categories: state, collective, and private ownership, as per the Property Law. This aligns with Article 3 of the 1986 GPCL, which guarantees that property rights belonging to the state, collectives and individuals are protected against any unauthorised interference.[90] The CC further reinforces that property rights of all civil subjects are equally safeguarded.[91] While recent laws specifically address land ownership rights, their broader implications extend to various other property rights, marking significant impacts beyond land ownership alone.

It is important to note that the principle of equal protection under Chinese Property Law does not imply homogeneity in the characteristics or management of state-owned, collective and private property. For instance, the transferability of construction land use rights (CLURs) for commercial purposes is limited to state-owned land in urban areas and does not extend to collective land in rural settings, thus highlighting a disparity in rights between state- and collective-owned lands. Nevertheless, the law's provision for equal protection to all holders of property rights is crucial. This is not only to reinforce a fundamental principle in property law but also to dispel any notion that property rights are tiered according to the status of the owner. This approach ensures that the protection of property rights is uniform across different ownership types, emphasising equity over equality in legal treatment.[92]

Despite gradual progress in acknowledging and safeguarding private property interests, the 2007 Property Law reiterates that all land is owned by the state or a collective, with the latter managed under governmental oversight, thus affirming the state's ultimate authority over land use and planning. This underscores a system of property law in China characterised by significant governmental intervention and strict regulation of property rights and responsibilities. As discussed in Chapter 1, discussions around the property are inherently value laden. Property law not only embodies numerous value judgements that reflect cultural norms

[89] Article 13 PRC Constitution.
[90] Article 4 Property Law.
[91] Article 113 CC.
[92] Article 207 CC.

and the political economy but also acts as a conduit for ideological expression. Article 206 of the CC articulates the fundamental objective of the Property Law to support and enhance the nation's socialist economic system, wherein public ownership remains central. This aims to stabilise the public economic sector while also fostering and guiding the growth of the non-public sectors.[93] Such provisions clearly indicate the legislation's strong socialist orientation.

In line with the overarching direction of the Property Law, numerous provisions are primarily focused on safeguarding state rights or facilitating state intervention in the public interest. Prior to the enactment of the CC, Article 42 of the Property Law permitted the expropriation of land owned by collectives and the expropriation of houses and other immovable properties owned by individuals, provided there was a demonstrated public need.[94] Research frequently highlights that even collective property rights are susceptible to the influences of local government policies in rural China, reflecting their relatively weaker and more vulnerable status.[95] Additionally, Article 43 of the Property Law enforces stringent restrictions on the conversion of farmland to construction land, supporting the state's policy of farmland preservation. The underlying justification for such regulations is that land demands in rural China are primarily addressed through state-driven models of expropriation and legal status alterations of the land rather than through market-based transactions of property rights. Consequently, the facilitation of rural land transactions would represent a significant step in the economic liberalisation of China, signalling a move towards a more market-oriented approach in rural land management.

Other instances of the Property Law demonstrating a public nature are the provisions specifying the ownership of certain resources. As an extension of state ownership over urban land and certain rural land,[96] natural resources such as forests, mountains, grasslands, wastelands, tidal flats,[97] mineral resources, waters, sea areas,[98] inhabited

[93] Article 206 CC.

[94] Article 42 Property Law.

[95] Ethan Michelson, 'Climbing the Dispute Pagoda: Grievances and Appeals to the Official Justice System in Rural China' (2007) 72 *American Sociological Review* 459; Eva Pils, 'Land Disputes, Rights Assertion and Social Unrest: A Case from Sichuan' (2005) 19 *Columbia Journal of Asian Law* 235.

[96] Article 249 CC.

[97] Article 250 CC.

[98] Article 247 CC.

islands[99] and wildlife resources, including wild animals and vegetation,[100] are considered state property. Further, radio spectrum resources,[101] cultural relics[102] and public infrastructure facilities[103] belong to the state.[104] The purpose of specifying the state ownership over these resources is to prevent any loss of state property in situations where the belongingness of a resource is in doubt. The predominant state ownership is partly because the Chinese property law is still ideologically heavily slanted in favour of socialism. Another reason could be what Carol Rose articulated: the "inherently public property" theory in certain kinds of property.[105] When turning property rights underpinned by the "publicness" from the "unorganised public" into a governmentally organised public, the government might be the most useful manager where many persons desire access to or control a given property.[106] To echo this, Benkler argued that in the age of the knowledge economy, public legal directives are preferred over exclusion-orientated private property for the use of, for example, the radio spectrum.[107] Nonetheless, it must be noted that while rejecting private property in these circumstances, neither Rose nor Benkler favours misguided or intrusive government interventions.

The dominant state ownership is so ubiquitous under Chinese law that in the case of lost property, if no one claims the ownership within a year from the date of the finding announcement made by the relevant government agency, the property belongs to the state.[108]

Therefore, while the equal protection principle is commendable, individual property rights are weaker than state and collective ownership. One way to argue this is by surveying chapter V of the Property Book of the CC, which deals with state, collective and private ownership. It has twenty-five articles in total. Mathematically, it is interesting to note that

[99] Article 248 CC.
[100] Article 251 CC.
[101] Article 252 CC.
[102] Article 253 CC.
[103] Article 254 CC.
[104] Article 255 CC.
[105] Carol Rose, 'The Comedy of the Commons: Custom, Commerce, and Inherently Public Property' (1986) 53 *The University of Chicago Law Review* 711.
[106] Richard Stroup and John Baden, 'Externality, Property Rights, and the Management of Our National Forests' (1973) 16 *The Journal Law and Economics* 303, 306–309.
[107] Yochai Benkler, 'From Consumers to Users: Shifting the Deeper Structures of Regulation toward Sustainable Commons and User Access' (2000) 52 *Federal Communications Law Journal* 561.
[108] Article 318 CC.

out of the twenty-five articles, fourteen govern state ownership (Articles 246–259), six (Articles 260–265) govern collective ownership and only two (Articles 266–267) specifically deal with private ownership. The final three articles address property belonging to corporate bodies (Articles 268–270). In addition, without specifying a remedy or punishment, this chapter is more appropriate to be taken as a guiding principle.

2.4.3 *The Publicity Principle*

The publicity principle is a guiding principle of Chinese property law. Closely linked with the principle of *numerus clausus*, property rights have a third-party effect and should, therefore, be public. The transfer of movables is affected only by delivery, since delivery publicises to the outside world a change of ownership.[109] In the case of immovables, the publicity principle demands that the transfer of a real right in immovables is effected by registration of the transfer in the land registration office.[110] A public member can ascertain the owner of a specific apartment or shop and by which limited real rights the land is burdened.

For the creation and transfer of a real right to be effective, registration is required in most instances of immovable properties. Therefore, how land registration operates is crucial to the property transfer system. It is worth noting that this rule is not invariable, and as a result, not all immovable property rights are created or transferred upon registration. Instead of a uniform approach, the Chinese legislators adopted a fragmented approach to whether registration is a condition precedent for creating an immovable property right. For instance, while the right of habitation must be created through registration,[111] the real servitude right does not need to be created through registration. A contract is sufficient to create a valid real servitude right.[112] While the right to use construction land is created upon registration,[113] a right to land contractual management is created when such a contract becomes effective.[114]

Registration is not required to acquire a real right in the case of movables. Otherwise, it would have been too burdensome, generating a

[109] Article 208 CC.
[110] *Ibid.*
[111] Article 368 CC.
[112] Article 374 CC.
[113] Article 349 CC.
[114] Article 333 CC.

high search cost. Instead, delivery is the rule governing the transfer of movable properties. However, as various constructive modes of delivery are applied to manifest possession, the publicity principle is less strictly adhered to in movables than immovables. This is also prevalent in real security, where the movable property is mortgaged; the mortgagee cannot allege against the purchaser who has paid a reasonable consideration.[115]

2.5 Classification of Property

Things as the subject matter of property rights include immovables and movables. If a legal provision recognises a particular right as the subject matter of a property right, such provision prevails.[116] The CC's definition of property is fairly sketchy. However, academic commentaries classify things according to their relation to a person and their nature.

2.5.1 *Classification according to Their Relation to a Person*

Where things are classified according to their relation to a person, there are *res extra commercium*, things out of commerce, including state-owned property, collective property and property belonging to corporate bodies;[117] and *res in commercio*, or things in commerce, including privately owned property and unowned property (*res nullius*).

2.5.1.1 State-owned Property

In the Chinese context, property owned by the state, as stipulated by law, is considered the property of the state, meaning it belongs to the entire populace.[118] Therefore, no organisation or individual may acquire ownership of immovable or movable property exclusively owned by the state.[119] The State Council exercises the ownership of state-owned property on behalf of the state.[120] Additionally, state organs, including the statutory bodies set by the state, possess the right to possess and use both

115 Article 404 CC. Read with Article 396 CC and Article 181 of the 2007 Property Law concerning floating charge.

116 Article 115 CC.

117 Different from some other jurisdictions, there is no such thing as religious property in the CC, although this type of property has been provided in academic drafts of the Property Law as early as in 2007.

118 Article 246 (1) CC.

119 Article 242 CC.

120 Article 246 (2) CC.

immovable and movable property under their direct control.[121] They also have the right to dispose of such property following the law and relevant regulations set forth by the State Council.

Moreover, enterprises funded by the state shall have their investment responsibilities represented by the State Council or local people's governments that enjoy the rights of the investing entity.[122] To emphasise, the CC expressly affirms that state-owned property is afforded legal protection, and it explicitly prohibits any organisation or individual from engaging in activities such as embezzling, looting, privately dividing, detaining or destroying state-owned property.[123] As a result, state ownership is predominant in China compared to collective and private ownership despite the equal protection principle.

Beyond the socialist ideology explanation, there are additional reasons why a significant portion of resources remains state-owned in China. Technically, delineating and enforcing rights in land and tangible private property are straightforward processes. However, regarding rights in wildlife, including animals[124] and underground waters,[125] the challenges in ascertaining and enforcing these rights are more complex. For example, owning a bottle of river water might be feasible, but owning the entire river is practically impossible.

The emergence of private property rights is often contingent on a cost–benefit analysis. Private property rights are more likely to emerge when the internalisation benefits associated with these rights outweigh the costs of establishing and enforcing them. Regarding resources such as wildlife and natural elements, the complexity and cost associated with defining and protecting individual property rights may contribute to the preference for state ownership, where the state acts as the custodian of these resources on behalf of the entire populace.[126] Resources will remain unowned or open access if the cost exceeds the benefits.[127] Indeed, it is unsurprising that these less straightforward properties, such as wildlife and certain natural resources,[128] are treated as state owned in China.

[121] Article 255 CC.
[122] Article 257 CC.
[123] Article 258 CC.
[124] Article 251 CC.
[125] Article 247 CC.
[126] Harold Demsetz, 'Toward a Theory of Property Rights' (1967) 57 *American Economic Review* 347, offering an economic theory of the evolution of property rights.
[127] *Ibid.*
[128] Article 250 CC.

Carol Rose's theory of network effects provides another perspective. According to this theory, certain resources should be inherently considered public properties because their value increases as more people use them. In such cases, the collective ownership by the state aligns with the idea that these resources are better managed and optimised for the benefit of the entire population.[129]

The radio spectrum resource is a prime example illustrating the network effects theory.[130] Essentially, this theory aligns with a cost–benefit analysis. For instance, leaving rivers as open-access resources would imply zero access costs, encouraging more people to use them. In Chinese law, the government heavily regulates the permissible uses of state properties, imposing specific restrictions on their use. While the access cost is lower than what it might be if these properties were privately owned, it is not necessarily zero.

This economic analysis resonates with China's socialist heritage, where the prevailing belief is that the cost of establishing private property rights over natural resources is higher than the benefits derived from such private property rights. Consequently, Chinese legislators seem convinced that maintaining state ownership over natural resources is a more viable and beneficial approach.

However, two standing issues concerning state-owned property exist in the Chinese legal framework. First, considering the widespread state ownership, introducing the public trust or state guardianship doctrine could be beneficial to address the state's responsibility and ensure the sustainability of natural resources. As a trustee or guardian, the state must protect natural resources by preventing unreasonable exploitation and seeking compensation for losses.[131] This obligation stems from the unique relationship established by the state's ownership of its sovereign capacity and the public's expectation that the state holds common resources for the benefit of the entire population. While the institutions and their managing staff are held legally responsible if they abuse their

[129] Rose (n. 105).

[130] Article 252 CC.

[131] It is worth noting that in June 2017, the NPC Standing Committee amended the Civil Procedure Law and the Administrative Procedure Law formally establishing the procuratorial public interest litigation system. Under this system, the procuracy offices are in a position to lodge a public interest litigation on behalf of the state in environmental damage disputes. But the CC, which was enacted later, does not formally introduce the public trust or state guardianship principle.

powers, neglect their duties and cause losses to state-owned assets,[132] there is no mechanism to hold the state as a guardian accountable for the property owned by the entire populace. Secondly, connected to the above-mentioned point, such state-owned property should not be susceptible to accession or any other form of original acquisition.[133]

2.5.1.2 Collective Property

Article 260 of the CC establishes a legal definition for collectively owned immovable and movable property, encompassing various categories such as land, forests, mountains, grasslands, wastelands, tidal flats, buildings, production facilities, farmland irrigation facilities and facilities for education, science, culture, sanitation, sports and other properties owned by collectives.[134] All collective members are considered owners of these collectively owned immovable and movable properties.[135] While the statutory provision outlines the scope and content of collective-owned property, it does not explicitly define its characteristics. Notably, a distinction exists in China's land tenure system, where urban land is state-owned and commercially transferable while rural land is primarily collectively owned.

In the Chinese context, "collective" typically refers to a collective entity at the local level, often associated with rural communities. Specifically, it may refer to a village collective, a group of villages or a township collective.

Regarding the right to dispose of collective-owned property, the CC provides clarity. When village farmers collectively own land, forests, mountains, grasslands, wastelands or tidal flats, the property rights are exercised on behalf of the collective by either the village committee or the collective economic organisation.[136] In cases where more than two collective groups own such property within a village, the property rights are exercised by the collective groups or the group economic organisation. If township farmers collectively own such property, the ownership is

[132] Article 259 CC.

[133] State-owned property is typically subject to the condition that it cannot be acquired through acquisitive prescription. More to the point, Chinese property law does not recognise the acquisitive prescription despite its being provided in various academic drafts and advocated by scholars.

[134] Article 260 CC.

[135] Article 261 CC.

[136] Article 263 CC.

exercised by a collective economic organisation of the township.[137] This legal framework ensures that the rights to collectively owned property are managed and exercised by specific entities, such as village committees, collective economic organisations or group economic organisations, depending on the nature and extent of collective ownership. Where a decision made by a village committee or the person in charge infringes the lawful rights of any collective member, such member may commence a legal proceeding to cancel it.[138]

However, certain collective decision-making procedures are warranted for some important matters. The collective members decide the following matters: (1) land contractual management plan and land contracting to external organisations or individuals; (2) adjustment of the contracted lands among the holders of the right to land contractual management; (3) methods for the use and distribution of land compensation fees and other expenses; (4) the change in ownership of collectively funded enterprises and other related matters; and (5) other matters prescribed by law.[139] Specifically, a village committee or a village group shall publicise the collective property status following the laws, the administrative regulations, the articles of association and village by-laws. Members have the right to inquire and duplicate relevant documents.[140]

2.5.1.3 Property Owned by Corporate Bodies

There are properties which belong to a corporate body but not to individuals. For example, things can be owned by a statutory body (事业单位) or a military unit. Notably, all these properties owned by corporate bodies are sub-species of state-owned property in the Chinese context. Legally speaking, the statutory body or the military unit acts as a representative or the agent to exercise the property rights on behalf of the state or the entire people. However, it should be noted that there is a distinction between legal persons recognised as such by public law, such as government functionaries and the registered social group legal persons, and private law legal persons, such as limited companies, listed companies and not-for-profit organisations.[141] There seems to be no reason why private law legal persons cannot be regarded as private

137 Article 262 CC.
138 Article 265 CC.
139 Article 261 (2) CC.
140 Article 264 CC.
141 Article 268 CC.

property holders. The CC provides specific provisions for these two types: Article 269 deals with private law legal persons, including for-profit and not-for-profit legal persons,[142] while Article 270 addresses the property protection of the social group legal persons and charity legal persons (donor-funded legal persons).[143]

Interestingly, the property belonging to unincorporated organisations is missing in chapter V of the Property Rights Book. Unincorporated organisations include but are not limited to sole proprietorships, partnership enterprises and professional service organisations without a legal personality.[144] Assuming that this is not an oversight, one could only speculate that such properties owned by unincorporated organisations are protected by analogy to private properties.

The private property right has gradually taken root in the Chinese legal landscape in the last three decades through constitutional amendments and special legislation. After the Chinese Communist Party came to power in 1949, it repealed the legal system of the Republican era and transplanted a portion of the 1950s Soviet legal system into it.[145] According to the classical proletarian theory, laws became instrumental in political class struggle rather than restricting government power and protecting individual rights. Hence, private property rights were severely reduced during the planned economy period.[146] Under the CC, a private individual is entitled to own their lawful income, houses, daily necessities, means of production, raw materials and other immovable and movable property.[147]

Moreover, lawful private properties shall be protected by law from being embezzled, looted or destroyed by any organisation or individual.[148] These provisions are not just rhetoric. Shortly after introducing private property in China, property owners found that they had increased bargaining power. These stakeholders' attitudes changed from supplication to rights-based demands as they enjoyed wider success.[149]

142 Article 269 CC.
143 Article 270 CC.
144 Article 102 CC.
145 Lei Chen, 'The Historical Development of the Civil Law Tradition in China: A Private Law Perspective' (2010) 78 *The Legal History Review* 159.
146 Lei Chen, 'The New Chinese Property Code: A Giant Step Forward?' (2007) 11 *Electronic Journal of Comparative Law* 1.
147 Article 266 CC.
148 Article 267 CC.
149 Yongshun Cai, 'China's Moderate Middle Class: The Case of Homeowners' Resistance' (2005) 25 *Asian Survey* 777; Jiangang Zhu and Chao Wang, 'Seniors Defending Their Rights – Strategies and Culture in Collective Action: The Homeowners Rights

Homeowners possess the willingness and justification to challenge arbitrary decisions and request involvement in the formulation of rules.[150] Thus, they enjoyed a greater sense of entitlement and a more effective voice in matters affecting their interests.[151] For example, homeowner protests are typically collective actions by self-governing community associations. Expressions of dissent frequently take the shape of public protests, direct appeals to the government, signature and letter campaigns, litigation, negotiation, appeals to the courts or NPC,[152] antagonistic action or even appeals to the media.[153]

2.5.2 Classification according to Their Nature

2.5.2.1 Corporeal and Incorporeal Property

The distinction between corporeal things (*res corporales*) and incorporeal things (*res incorporales*) dates back to Roman law. Material objects that could be felt or touched, such as land, clothes and furniture, are corporeal. Abstract conceptions, namely objects having no physical existence but having a monetary value, like rights of various kinds (including inheritance rights, personal rights and copyrights), are classified as incorporeal. Various rights are classified as things because they are considered capable of being the objects of real rights, such as shares in a company and bills of lading. The CC expressly provides for the pledge of rights.[154]

Classifying a thing as corporeal or incorporeal remains crucial in practical applications. This distinction holds significance in various contexts, especially in dividing things into movables and immovables. Possession applies solely to corporeal things, whether movable or

Movement in Lijing Garden, Guangzhou' (2007) 40 *Chinese Sociology & Anthropology* 5; Benjamin L. Read, 'Assessing Variation in Civil Society Organizations: China's Homeowner Associations in Comparative Perspective' (2008) 41 *Comparative Political Studies* 1240.

150 David Kelly, 'Citizen Movements in China's Public Intellectuals in the Hu-Wen Era' (2006) 79 *Pacific Affairs* 183.

151 Mark D. Kielsgard and Lei Chen, 'The Emergence of Private Property Law in China and Its Impact on Human Rights' (2013) 15 *Asian-Pacific Law and Policy Journal* 94.

152 Lei Chen and Mark D. Kielsgard, 'Evolving Property Rights in China: Patterns and Dynamics of Condominium Governance' (2014) 2 *The Chinese Journal of Comparative Law* 21.

153 Ying Wu and Nm Yip, 'The Homeowners' Protest in Beijing and Guangzhou: Rightful Resistance and Beyond' (2010) 5 *The International Journal of Interdisciplinary Social Sciences: Annual Review* 513, pp. 519–20.

154 Article 440 CC.

immovable. Consequently, modes of acquiring ownership based on possession apply exclusively to corporeal things.

Similar to numerous jurisdictions, the concept of incorporeal property is undergoing continuous evolution in the digital age. A prime example of this complexity is determining whether a cryptocurrency, such as Bitcoin, qualifies as property. If it does, the question arises whether it should be categorised as incorporeal or *sui generis* property. Notably, although cryptocurrencies, despite being a frequent subject of legal disputes in Chinese courts, are not explicitly addressed in the CC, the Code does, for the first time, offer legal protection to virtual network property.[155] Secondly, Chinese courts have consistently recognised cryptocurrency as virtual property, marking a shift from initial resistance in the preceding years.[156] The challenging doctrinal issue arises from the fact that while the CC asserts legal protection for virtual property, it does not provide a clear definition or specification of its nature.

Furthermore, virtual property is not explicitly listed in the closed catalogue of property rights governed by the *numerus clausus* principle. Consequently, the courts have avoided directly addressing whether cryptocurrency is unequivocally considered property.[157] Instead, Chinese courts base their decisions on Article 127 of the CC, recognising the economic value of cryptocurrency and subsequently offering legal remedies through tort law or contract law.[158]

Continuing with the inquiry, classifying cryptocurrency as a virtual property within the realm of incorporeal property remains an unanswered conceptual question in legislation. In a significant development in February 2021, the Shanghai Baoan People's Court addressed a

155 Article 127 CC.

156 吴某与上海耀志网络科技有限公司、浙江淘宝网络有限公司案（2019）浙0192民初1626号 [*Wu v. Shanghai Yaozhi Internet Technology Co., Ltd., Zhejiang Taobao Network Co., Ltd.* (2019) Zhejiang 0192 Min Chu No. 1626]; 李某、布兰登·斯密特诉闫某案（2019）沪01民终13689号 [*Li, Brandon Smit v. Yan, etc.* (2019) Hu 01 Min Zhong No. 13689]; 陈某诉张某案（2020）苏1183民初3825号 [*Chen v. Zhang* (2020) Su 1183 Min Chu No. 3825].

157 Comparatively, in Japan, a civilian jurisdiction, cryptocurrency has been held by the Tokyo District Court not to be a property: Kelvin Low and Ying-Chieh Wu, 'The Characterization of Cryptocurrencies in East Asia', in David Fox and Sarah Green (eds), *Cryptocurrencies in Public and Private Law* (Oxford University Press 2019), p. 199; nonetheless, in English law, following a series of partially reasoned or ambiguous decisions, Bitcoin was held to be property for the purposes of an interim proprietary injunction; see *AA v. Persons Unknown & Ors, Re Bitcoin* [2019] EWHC 3556 (Comm).

158 See n. 156.

Bitcoin case.[159] The Court reasoned that Bitcoin possesses characteristics such as value, scarcity and disposability. Thus, it has the features of an object of rights and meets the requirements to be considered virtual property. Therefore, Bitcoin has the attributes of virtual property and virtual commodities and should be protected by law.[160] This suggests that there appears to be a notable relaxation of the *numerus clausus* principle in Chinese jurisprudence regarding cryptocurrencies.

In summary, in the absence of explicit legislative guidance, there is an evolving interpretation regarding the nature of cryptocurrency as property within the Chinese judiciary. Although constrained by the *numerus clausus* principle, which categorises property in a fixed and exhaustive list, Chinese courts have a growing consensus that cryptocurrencies can be considered virtual property, implying ownership rights. Chinese courts increasingly apply property law principles to protect cryptocurrencies, recognising them as subject to established property norms.

2.5.2.2 Movable and Immovable Property

In Chinese law, one of the most fundamental classifications is the distinction between movables and immovables.[161] This categorisation, with roots in Roman law and widespread acceptance in civil law jurisdictions, has been adopted in Chinese legal frameworks and further affirmed through case law.

The CC per se does not provide a legal definition of immovable and movable properties. Under the Immovable Property Registration Interim Regulation, immovable property refers to land, housing and woods attached to the land and sea waters.[162] Immovable things cannot be moved from one place to another without damage or change of form. A thing is considered movable if it is not immovable. Specifically, it is movable if it can be moved from one place to another without being damaged or losing its identity. Things that can move independently, such as animals, are also movables. The distinction between movables and immovables is not time honoured due to technological advancement. What is immovable today may be movable tomorrow.

[159] 程红与施玉莲案（2020）沪0113民初23704号[*Cheng Hong v. Shi Yulian* (2020) Hu 0113 Min Chu No. 23704]

[160] *Ibid.*

[161] Article 115 CC.

[162] Article 2 CC.

The importance of distinguishing between movables and immovables becomes evident when considering the following aspects: (1) concerning the method of acquisition, contracts for the sale of immovables typically require written documentation, while contracts for the sale of movables can be oral or conducted through actions; (2) for movables, a valid transfer of ownership can occur through delivery, whereas immovables necessitate mandatory registration in a property registration office; (3) the creation of security rights in immovables involves registering a mortgage contract or deed, while movables can be pledged through delivery; (4) while legal restrictions on the transfer of movables are minimal, Chinese law imposes numerous limitations on the use and possession of immovables; and (5) according to Chinese private international law, the applicable law for immovables is determined by the location of the property, whereas there is no equivalent exclusive jurisdiction rule for movables.[163] Understanding these distinctions is crucial for legal and practical reasons, influencing the requirements, processes and legal consequences of transactions involving movables and immovables in the Chinese legal context.

[163] Article 36 of the Law of the People's Republic of China on Choice of Law for Foreign-related Civil Relationships.

3

Property Acquisition

3.1 Introduction

In property law, the distinction between original and derivative methods of acquiring property rights centres on the mechanism of acquisition – whether it involves a unilateral act or a bilateral transaction. Original acquisition occurs without the cooperation of a prior owner and can be through natural processes or by law, such as harvesting natural fruits, creating a new object (*specificatio*) or combining or mixing materials (*commixtio et confusio*). In contrast, derivative acquisition involves a transfer of property rights from an existing owner, typically executed through a contractual arrangement, such as a sale or exchange.

It is crucial to distinguish between the contractual agreement, which initiates the intent to transfer property rights, and the actual transfer or conveyance of those rights. For movables, the transfer typically involves physical delivery, while for immovables it necessitates registration. Although Chinese property law borrows heavily from the German legal system,[1] the rules governing the derivative acquisition of property showcase significant deviations, illustrating a tailored approach that accommodates specific legal and cultural contexts within China.

3.2. Original Acquisition

Under Chinese law, the scope for the original acquisition of property is relatively limited, reflecting the predominance of state ownership. Several examples illustrate how state control pervades even the most fundamental aspects of property rights. For example, wild animals belong to the state; therefore, there is no such thing as appropriation (*occupatio*) of the wild animals in China, thus eliminating the possibility for individuals to

[1] Lei Chen, 'Continuity and Change: Some Reflections on the Chinese CC' (2021) 29 *Asia Pacific Law Review* 287.

claim ownership through capture.[2] Another example, commonly found in other legal systems, is that acquisition by prescription (acquiring rights through long-term use or possession) is notably absent in Chinese law, as neither the Civil Code (CC) nor other legal statutes provide for such a method of property acquisition. This absence further underscores the restrictive nature of property rights under Chinese law. More to the point, the rules for acquiring lost property are stipulated in the "Special Provisions on Acquisition of Ownership" chapter of the CC. If lost property is not claimed within a designated period, it defaults to state ownership.[3] This provision effectively turns the state into the default recipient of unclaimed property, further entrenching state control over property rights. The final example is where an estate is neither inherited nor subject to a legacy; such an estate will belong to the state for public use.[4] Where the deceased is a member of a collective organisation, the estate will pass to the organisation.[5] These examples highlight that in China, the principle of unclaimed or unowned property defaulting to state ownership is a fundamental rule, reflecting the overarching framework of state control over property. This approach underscores the state's omnipotent role in property rights.

Original acquisition of property under Chinese law includes several distinct methods such as collecting fruits, accession, manufacture (*specificatio*) and bona fide acquisition. Notably, in the Chinese legal context, the lost property also falls under original acquisition. If a lost item is not claimed within the specified announcement period, it legally transitions to state ownership. This transition is classified as an original acquisition because it occurs via a statutory mandate outlined in the CC, independent of the original owner's intent.

This section will, therefore, concentrate on exploring the nuances of lost property, along with the acquisition of fruits, accession, manufacture and bona fide acquisition. Each of these methods represents a legal mechanism through which property rights are established not through transfer from a previous owner but directly as a result of legal or natural processes. This analysis will provide a clearer understanding of how property rights are initiated and recognised under Chinese law, highlighting the specific conditions and legal foundations associated with each method.

[2] Article 251 CC.
[3] Article 318 CC.
[4] Article 1160 CC.
[5] *Ibid.*

3.2.1 *Lost Property*

The 1986 GPCL unambiguously provided that if a buried or concealed object's owner is unknown, the object shall belong to the state.[6] There is no special provision in the CC governing unowned property. However, the CC provides relatively detailed rules governing lost property. The owner or any other right holder has the entitlement to claim the recovery of lost property.[7] If the lost property is in possession of a transferee due to a transfer, the right holder can claim against the person without the power of disposition for damages or against the transferee for the return of the property.[8] The right holder has a two-year window from the date of knowledge of the transferee's identity to make such claims.[9] If the transferee purchased the lost property through auction or from a qualified seller, the right holder, when claiming the return, must reimburse the expenses paid by the transferee.[10]

Finders of lost property must notify the right holder promptly or hand over the property to relevant authorities.[11] The competent department receiving the property must inform the right holder or publish an announcement if the identity is unknown.[12] Both finders and competent departments must keep the lost property in good custody.[13] Otherwise, they are liable for damages or loss caused by intention or negligence.[14] When reclaiming lost property, the right holder must reimburse finders or competent departments for necessary expenses.[15] If a reward is offered for finding lost property, the right holder must fulfil promised obligations when reclaiming it.[16] A finder who converts lost property for personal use has no right to reimbursement or to demand the fulfilment of promised obligations.[17] Lastly, lost property unclaimed within a year from the announcement date becomes state owned.[18]

[6] Article 79 of the General Principles of the Civil Law of the People's Republic of China 1986, which has been repealed on 31 December 2020.
[7] Article 312 CC.
[8] *Ibid.*
[9] *Ibid.*
[10] *Ibid.*
[11] Article 314 CC.
[12] Article 315 CC.
[13] Article 316 CC
[14] *Ibid.*
[15] Para. 1 of Article 317 CC.
[16] Para. 2 of Article 317 CC.
[17] Para. 3 of Article 317 CC.
[18] Article 318 CC.

In the highly controversial ebony wood case,[19] the local government agency confiscated the ebony wood from the finders on the grounds of the unlicensed salvage operation and transportation. The plaintiff made two claims. The first claim is to set aside the administrative penalty decision, and the second is to return the confiscated ebony wood, as the plaintiff claims to be the owner.[20] In the first instance, the court has sidestepped the second claim regarding who is entitled to the lost and hidden ebony wood. Instead, it focused its analysis on the legality of the administrative penalty decision giving rise to confiscation. The court ruled that the administrative penalty decision must be struck down, as it was issued without sufficient evidence and proper procedures.[21] However, the court did not order the return of the ebony wood.[22] On appeal, the court of the second instance upheld such a decision and reasoned that the ebony wood belonged to the state.[23]

The court reasoned that the wood, categorised as either a buried object, cultural relic, wildlife or natural resource, should belong to the state according to the Chinese legal framework. This decision is grounded in the principle that such items, when discovered, automatically become state property under existing laws that prioritise state ownership over natural resources and cultural heritage. However, this ruling faced criticism from some legal scholars who contested the application of such broad state ownership.[24] They argued that in this particular instance, the state did not inherently own the ebony wood and proposed that a "finder keeper" rule, based on possessory title, should be applied by analogy to favour the plaintiff.[25] This suggestion aims to liberalise the interpretation of the law to allow individuals who find unowned objects to claim ownership, thereby encouraging more personal initiative and potentially rewarding discovery.

[19] 屈保龙诉南昌市林业局 [*Qu Baolong v Nanchang City Forestry Bureau*] (2015) 洪行终字第 5 号 [(2015) Hong Xing Zhong No. 5].

[20] 屈保龙诉南昌市林业局 [*Qu Baolong v Nanchang City Forestry Bureau*] (2014) 东行初字第 14号行政判决书 [(2014) Dong Xing Chu Zi No. 14].

[21] *Ibid.*

[22] *Ibid.*

[23] 屈保龙诉南昌市林业局 [*Qu Baolong v Nanchang City Forestry Bureau*] (2014) 东行初字第 14号行政判决书 [(2014) Dong Xing Chu Zi No. 14].

[24] Keke Jin [金可可], 'On the Ownership of Ebony Wood – Also on the Types and Limits of State Ownership' [《论乌木之所有权归属—兼论国家所有权之种类及其限度》] (2015) 3 *Oriental Law* [《东方法学》] 82.

[25] *Ibid.*

Despite the appeal of this argument for a more liberal and individual-centric approach to property rights, the challenge remains that Chinese law does not formally recognise a "finder keeper" rule as found in some other legal systems.[26] The debate thus highlights a tension between maintaining state control over certain resources and adapting legal frameworks to enhance individual rights and incentives potentially.

More to the point, even in a jurisdiction where the finder keeper rule is allowed, such as England, a primary distinction is drawn between hidden or buried things under the land surface and things found merely resting on the land surface.[27] In the former situation, under English law, the landowner or usufructuary right holder has a stronger claim, as they are regarded as enjoying possession of things embedded or concealed within the ground.[28] Under Belgian law, the ownership of the hidden property will be equally divided between the finder and the owner of the land on which the object is found.[29] In the latter, in the absence of clear possessory intent on the landowner's part, the finder's claim appears more compelling. Applying these rules in the present case, as the river belongs to the state, the ebony wood found in the riverbed is more likely than not owned or at least half-owned by the state unless there is strong evidence to suggest that the state does not manifest any intention to control the river. However, it is nearly impossible to succeed because the CC clarifies that the river belongs to the state. So, the key issue at stake is not about what the technical rule should be applied to determine the owner. The root cause of the decision is the predominance and ubiquitousness of state ownership under the Chinese property law.

Nonetheless, the CC provides that where drifting objects are picked up or buried or hidden objects are discovered, the relevant provisions on finding lost property shall be referred to and applied.[30] At least, under the CC, lost property belongs to the state only after no one reclaims it one year after the lost-and-found announcement.[31] However, such a rule still grants the state a privileged position in owning unowned property. This

[26] Chang, Yun-chien. 'Property Law with Chinese Characteristics: An Economic and Comparative Analysis'. (2012) 1 *Brigham-Kanner Property Rights Conference Journal* 345.

[27] Kevin Gray and Susan Gray, *Elements of Land Law* (5th edn, Oxford University Press 2009), p. 41.

[28] *Ibid.*

[29] Article 3.59 §3 of the Belgian CC.

[30] Article 319 CC.

[31] Article 318 CC.

is because Chinese law does not formalise the property occupation rule (*occupatio*) as a way of the original acquisition of ownership.[32] As a result, no one can claim the title of the unowned property (*res nullius*), unlike the lost property.

3.2.2 Fruits

In legal terms, certain assets, known as the principal thing, can naturally produce outputs or income referred to as fruits. These fruits are defined as the regular yields from the principal thing that accrue without diminishing or altering its essential substance. This definition is pivotal, as it highlights that for any product to be classified as a fruit, it must emerge from the principal thing without degrading its inherent properties.

An important distinction to make in this context is that minerals, which require extraction and consequently lead to significant alteration or degradation of the land, are not considered fruits. This is because their extraction inherently compromises the physical integrity of the principal thing – land. Thus, unlike agricultural produce or dividends from investments, which qualify as fruits due to their non-destructive generation from the principal thing, minerals do not meet this criterion due to the irreversible change they impose on their source.

Fruits are differentiated into natural fruits (*fructus naturales*) and civil fruits (*fructus civiles*). Natural fruits are fruits that are brought forth by nature from fruit-bearing things. Examples are apples, oranges and crops such as wheat, wool, eggs and milk. Natural fruits are thus the products of natural forces or industry. Because fruits are accessories of a special kind separated from the principal thing, usually the owner of the principal thing acquires separation of the ownership of the fruits as individual things. A dispossessed owner can claim the principal thing and its fruits with his *rei vindicatio*. Under the CC, natural fruits are obtained by the owner of a fruit-bearing thing as a default rule unless the parties agree otherwise.[33]

Under specific conditions, fruits may deviate from following the ownership of the principal thing. In certain circumstances, a bona fide possessor, a usufructuary or a lessee has the potential to acquire the

[32] Shiyang Wen [温世扬], '<The CC> The Conservation, Progress and Defects of Property Ownership' [《<民法典>物权编的守成、进步与缺憾》] (2021) 2 *Law Science Magazine* [《法学杂志》] 56.

[33] Article 321 (1) CC.

fruits. Ownership of natural fruits, upon separation, is automatically acquired by owners and bona fide possessors without requiring additional action. In contrast, a usufructuary and a lessee acquire the fruits through an explicit act of gathering or collection, not by merely separating the fruits but by taking possession of them as if they were their own. The unresolved question pertains to resolving a dispute between the owner and the usufructuary, asserting their entitlement to the fruits. According to the CC, the usufructuary is entitled to the natural fruits in such a scenario unless there is an agreement between the parties specifying otherwise.[34]

In contrast, civil fruits are non-organic returns generated from an item either by operation of law or due to a legal act.[35] These proceeds arise from the ownership or business dealings involving the item, such as loan interest, lease rents and mineral rights royalties. Given that civil fruits result from a legal relationship, acquiring these returns is typically guided by agreements between the involved parties.[36] In cases where there is no agreement or the agreement is unclear, the acquisition of civil fruits follows established trade practices.[37] Gathering civil fruits entails considering the relevant expenses incurred in obtaining these fruits.[38]

For instance, if A entered into an agency agreement to manage B's investment funds in the stock market, the contract was later deemed invalid due to its violation of mandatory legal provisions. The question arises about the legal ramifications of the contract's invalidity, specifically the scope of recovery from A to B. When a contract is declared invalid or revoked, all property acquired due to that contract must be returned.[39] Therefore, the term "all property obtained because of the contract" clearly includes the principal sum and interests, with the latter being the civil fruits of the principal sum of the investment money.[40]

34 *Ibid.*

35 Liming Wang [王利明], *Research on Real Property Rights* [《物权法研究》] (3rd edn, China Renmin University Press 2013), vol. I, p. 21.

36 Article 321 (2) CC.

37 *Ibid.*

38 Article 430 CC.

39 Article 157 CC.

40 This approach has been widely taken in Chinese case law. For example, see a SPC case, 上海民生投资有限公司与吉林省东力投资集团公司（2006）民二终字第145号 [*Shanghai Minsheng Investment Co., Ltd. v Jilin Dongji Comprehensive Investment (Group) Co., Ltd.* (2006) SPC Min Er Zhong No. 145.]

In summary, under the CC, the default rule is that the owner of the principal thing also owns the natural fruits produced. This default can be altered if there is an agreement to the contrary between the parties involved. The Chinese approach to the allocation of fruits emphasises adherence to mutual agreements between parties. This provision ensures clarity and predictability in property relations, affirming the rights of owners while allowing for flexibility through contractual agreements.

*3.2.3 Accession (*acceeessio*)*

A composite thing may consist of the principal thing, accessories and auxiliaries. A house, for example, consists of the basic framework (principal thing), the roof, doors and windows (accessories), and the keys to the doors of the house (auxiliaries). Things that previously enjoyed a separate existence become associated with a principal thing because of a physical or functional connection (accessories) or a mere economic connection (auxiliaries) with the principal thing. However, not all things associated with a principal thing are necessarily accessories or auxiliaries. For example, furniture in a house or oil paintings hung on a living room wall can remain independent.

A principal thing is an independent entity capable of being the subject of legal rights. In contrast, an accessory assumes the role of a component or an integral part of the principal thing by becoming integrated into it. Once an accessory is affixed to a principal thing, it relinquishes its independent identity and becomes an inseparable part. Examples of accessories include items firmly affixed to land, such as buildings, constructions, trees, plants and seeds sown in the ground. This principle also extends to objects incorporated into movable assets, such as a wheel attached to a motor vehicle. Determining the categorisation of components as principal or accessory can be challenging. In cases where something is affixed to the land, the land is invariably regarded as the principal thing, and the fixture is deemed the accessory. Conversely, with movables, an accessory is generally identified as an item that serves a purpose, complements or adds decorative elements to the principal thing.[41]

An accessory, physically or functionally attached to a principal thing, becomes an integral part of the composite entity. In such cases, the owner of the principal thing is automatically recognised as the owner of the

[41] Wang (n. 35), p. 19.

accessory by operation of law. However, when the accessory is detached, it can exist independently as a separate object. Even though an accessory maintains its own identity, it may function in a subordinate capacity to a principal thing. For instance, items like keys to a house or a spare car wheel are considered accessories to the principal things (the house or the motor vehicle) without losing their distinct characteristics.

An auxiliary is an object that, while maintaining its distinct identity, serves the economic purpose of the principal thing permanently rather than temporarily. An auxiliary is presumed to follow the principal unless there is a clear contrary intention or unless surrounding circumstances, customs and community usages indicate otherwise. Therefore, when a principal thing is sold, encumbered with a mortgage, pledged or made the subject of a usufruct, the auxiliaries of the principal thing are generally included by default.[42] However, this inclusion can be modified by an agreement between the parties.[43] Notably, the CC delineates principal and accessory things without distinguishing between accessories and auxiliaries.[44]

3.2.4 *Manufacture* (specificatio)*, Mixing and Fusing* (commixtio et confusio)

Manufacture involves an individual acquiring ownership of a newly created item by using someone else's materials to create a completely new object without the original owner's consent. Mixing refers to the combination of solid materials owned by different individuals, while fusing relates to the blending of liquids from multiple owners, also done without consent. Neither mixing nor fusing involves the attachment of an accessory to a principal thing or the creation of an entirely new product. In cases of mixed or fused materials, co-ownership is determined based on the proportion of each party's contribution to the final mixed product.

The CC provides a guideline of entitlement to property resulting from specification, mixing or fusing.[45] If the parties agree on this matter, the agreement takes precedence.[46] The law applies without an agreement or in cases of ambiguity. If there is no specific legal provision, the

[42] Article 320 CC.
[43] *Ibid.*
[44] *Ibid.*
[45] Article 322 CC.
[46] *Ibid.*

determination is based on principles prioritising making the utmost use of the property and protecting the party without fault.[47] Where the party at fault or determining property entitlement damages the other party, compensation must be provided in full or partially.[48] The requirement for compensation serves as a mechanism to address any losses or damages suffered by the non-at-fault party due to the actions or decisions regarding property entitlement.

This legal framework aims to establish fair outcomes when disputes arise over property entitlement from processes like specification, mixing or fusing, ensuring accountability for any harm caused to the non-at-fault party. However, while the CC seeks to balance the autonomy of parties to define their property rights through agreements, it does not provide any detailed rule per se other than the determining factor of making the most use of the property to determine the property entitlement.

3.2.5 Bona Fide Acquisition

When a property is transferred by someone without the legal authority to do so, the original owner typically has the right to recover that property. However, under certain conditions, the recipient (transferee) may legally acquire ownership rights, even if the transferor lacks the necessary authority. This is governed by the bona fide acquisition rule, a legal principle designed to balance the interests of all parties involved in the transfer. The rule takes into account the practical aspects of the transaction and aligns with broader principles of good faith and fairness.

The transferee acquires ownership of such property if the following conditions are met: (1) the transferee acted in good faith during the transfer; (2) the transfer is executed at a reasonable price; and (3) the transferred immovable or movable property has been properly registered, as required by law, or delivered to the transferee when no registration is necessary.[49] In such a circumstance, the original owner cannot take back the property but can seek damages from the person lacking the power of disposition.[50]

The transferee must have acted in good faith during the property transfer. This implies that they were unaware of any wrongdoing or lack

[47] *Ibid.*
[48] *Ibid.*
[49] Para. 1 of Article 311 CC.
[50] Para. 2 of Article 311 CC.

of authority on the part of the transferor. The emphasis on good faith in the transferee's actions promotes fairness. If the transferee genuinely believed they were acquiring the property legally, they are protected. However, as an abstract legal concept, the term *good faith* in this context emphasises the innocent, a subjective mental state of the transferee during a transaction. Therefore, the concept of good faith is subjective and challenging to determine objectively. It may lead to disputes over the transferee's state of mind during the transaction. It is for this reason that the SPC pronounced a criterion of good faith, which stipulates:

> When a transferee acquires real or personal property without knowing that the transferor lacks the disposal right, and without significant negligence, the transferee should be considered in good faith. If the true owner claims that the transferee does not act in good faith, the burden of proof shall be borne by the claimant.[51]

In light of this, the definition of good faith hinges on the requirement that the party involved does not have gross negligence. How to define gross negligence? It generally involves a failure to exercise reasonable care or a marked departure from the level of care that a reasonable person would exercise in a similar situation. It implies a more severe degree of negligence compared to ordinary negligence. In legal terms, gross negligence is often characterised by reckless or wilful disregard for the rights or safety of others. Specifically, the SPC provides a list of gross negligence in the context of bona fide acquisition of immovable property,

> 1) there is a valid objection registration on the registration book; 2) within the effective period of pre-registration, the consent of the unregistered property rights holder has not been obtained; 3) the registration book records relevant matters where judicial or administrative authorities have legally ordered, decided to seal, or restricted real property rights in other ways; 4) The transferee knows that the registered subject of rights on the registration book is incorrect; 5) The transferee is aware that someone else has legally acquired real property rights.[52]

When the transferee acquires personal property, if the transaction's object, place or timing does not conform to customary trading practices, it shall be deemed that the transferee has significant negligence.[53]

[51] Article 14 of the SPC Interpretation on the Application of the Property Rights Book of CC (I) (the SPC Interpretation of Property Book"), effective on January 1, 2021.

[52] Article 15 SPC Interpretation of Property Book (I).

[53] Article 16 SPC Interpretation of Property Book (I).

It is important to note that while the above SPC rules provide useful guidance, the specific criteria for gross negligence can vary depending on the context. Courts may consider factors such as the level of awareness, the degree of care exercised, the relationship between the transferor and the transferee, and the seriousness of the consequences of the negligence. In practice, the following situations have been regarded as constituting gross negligence for bona fide acquisition, such as where the transferee purchased real estate without actually inspecting the property[54]; where the transferee failed to fulfil the substantive examination duty when there existed a special relationship between the transferee, the true property rights holder and the transferor (e.g. parents and child, siblings)[55]; where the transferor is married, the transferee failed to examine the spouse's opinion during the transaction[56]; and where a professional financial institution failed to conduct a formal review during the transaction.[57]

When assessing the bona fides of a transaction, a Chinese court considers several critical factors to determine its legitimacy. These factors include (1) the timing, location and condition of the property involved; (2) the age, educational background, professional experience and prior transaction history of the parties; (3) the nature of the relationship between the parties; (4) whether there was a physical inspection of the property or verification of registration certificates in cases involving special movable property; (5) the marital status of the person transferring the property and the status of the property within the marital assets; and (6) whether the recipient of the property is a professional institution. These criteria help to ensure that the transaction adheres to principles of fairness and good faith.

The fairness of a property transfer is heavily contingent on it being conducted at a reasonable price, a key factor in assessing whether the transaction was free from duress and not undervalued. This criterion is essential for evaluating the good faith of the transferee. The concept of a

[54] 昊壮公司诉百桂公司、达胜公司、房铁公司（2016）桂0102民初2228号民事判决 [*Nanning Haozhuang Real Estate Development Co. Ltd v Nanning Dasheng Real Estate Development Co. Ltd & Hangtie Co Ltd.* (2016) Gui 0102 Min Chu No. 2228]

[55] 徐振富诉徐文有 (2019)津01民终2401号 [*Xu Zhenfu v Xu Wenyou* (2019) Jin 01 Min Zhong No. 2401]

[56] 郑诉蒋（2015）京二中民终字第01033号 [*Zheng v Jiang* (2015) Jing Er Zhong Min Zhong No. 01033]

[57] 山东日发纺织机械有限公司诉华融金融租赁股份有限公司金华分公司 （2016）浙07民终5303号 [*Shandong Rifa Textiles Machinery Co., Ltd v Huarong Leasing Co. (Subsidiary Company)* (2016) Min Zhong No. 5303]

reasonable price, however, can vary and potentially lead to disputes regarding property valuation. In China, where sophisticated property appraisal systems and land registration offices are prevalent, an independent appraiser is typically engaged to assess the price's reasonableness when disputes arise. Despite this, questions remain about what constitutes a reasonable price. For example, if the payment is 68 per cent of the appraised value, the determination of its reasonableness may still be subjective and open to interpretation by the courts. Thus, Chinese courts often exercise considerable discretion in making these judgments, reflecting the complexities involved in defining and enforcing the concept of a reasonable price in property transactions.

Depending on the type of property and applicable legal standards, the transfer of property must be formalised either through proper registration with the relevant authorities or through the physical delivery of the property to the transferee. These requirements serve to cement the legal certainty and stability of property transactions by providing clear mechanisms to resolve disputes over unauthorised transfers. Chinese law strives to balance conflicting interests and foster equitable outcomes in property transfers. The existence of the bona fide acquisition rule plays a significant role in shaping the theoretical framework of property transfers in China, a topic that will be explored in further detail in the following section.

3.3 Property Transfer Theory

In legal systems that differentiate between property rights and obligations, there is a clear distinction between the promise to transfer property and the actual transfer of ownership. Under Chinese law, an agreement between the current owner and the prospective owner is both necessary and sufficient to initiate the transfer of property. However, it is crucial to note that ownership does not transfer merely based on the agreement itself. The transition of ownership is only formalised and recognised legally upon the fulfilment of specific formalities, such as delivery or registration, as mandated by the applicable legal framework. This ensures that ownership is clearly and effectively transferred in accordance with the law.[58]

[58] While this is the case under the Chinese law, in the German legal system, registration and delivery are not merely formalities but are juridical acts with the transferor's intent to convey embodied in the real contract.

A comparative law survey suggests two main dividing lines in the property transfer theory. The first is the intent alone system versus the intent plus system, also known as the consensual versus delivery (*traditio*) system. The second is the abstract system versus the causal system.[59]

Under the intent alone system, property rights pass on the conclusion of the contract, save for agreements to the contrary (when the parties so intend in English law).[60] In other words, a valid sale contract completes the property transfer. On the contrary, under the *traditio* system, although a contract creates obligations, property transfer requires an additional element, delivery or conveyance to transfer a property right. As the term "delivery" is limited to the context of corporeal movables rather than all tangibles,[61] it is perhaps more sensible to employ the phrase "intent plus" instead. The "intent plus" system refers to a conveyance process that involves an additional distinct stage to finalise the transfer, incorporating various methods as mandated by law. The specific nature of the "plus" element may vary, encompassing actions such as delivery, execution of a deed, or registration.

Under Chinese law, the agreement giving rise to transfer is strictly separated from the delivery or registration itself.[62] Immovable property is transferred by registration and movables by delivery. The conventional wisdom by Chinese legal academics rejects the German-style separation. At the same time, it contends that Chinese law does have a "separation" principle in property transfers: the cause of a conveyance is separate from the result of that conveyance.[63] What Chinese scholars refer to as the

[59] See, e.g. 'Transfer', in Sjef van Erp and Bram Akkermans (eds), *Cases, Materials and Text on National, Supranational and International Property Law* (Hart Publishing 2012); Vincent Sagaert, 'Consensual versus Delivery Systems in European Private Law: Consensus about Tradition?', in Wolfgang Faber and Brigitta Lurger (eds), *Rules for the Transfer of Movables* (Sellier 2008), p. 10.

[60] Gray and Gray (n. 27), pp. 1073–77.

[61] Delivery used to be a way of transferring fee simple to land in the English legal history before 1925, where there was a symbolic ceremony called 'livery of seisin' taking place on the very land where the transferor placed a clod of earth into the hands of the transferee. This was abolished as a way of conveyance by s 51(1) of the Law of Property Act 1925 which states that "delivery" is no longer suitable to represent land conveyance.

[62] Article 208 CC.

[63] See Huixing Liang [梁慧星], 'Is Juridical Act of Real Rights Recognised in Chinese Civil Law?' [《我国民法是否承认物权行为》] (1989) 6 *Chinese Journal of Law* [《法学研究》] 56; Liming Wang [王利明], 'On Several Issues Concerning Juridical Act of Real Right' [《物权行为若干问题探讨》] (1997) 3 *Chinese Legal Science* [《中国法学》] 58; Xianzhong Sun [孙宪忠], 'The Principle of Separation between the Reason and the

"separation principle" actually embodies an "intent plus" model, where the transfer of ownership for both movable and immovable property necessitates not only a contract but also either delivery or registration.[64] Thus, Chinese law demonstrates the application of the "intent plus" system, distinctly steering away from a strict separatist approach, which would distinctly isolate the contractual agreement from the transfer of ownership.[65]

The agreement creates only personal rights and obligations; an additional transaction is required to transfer ownership from one party to the other. Consequently, there are two separate legal acts, each having its requirements. This is also the position when the two transactions occur simultaneously, as is normally the case. In such a case, it is always possible to distinguish between the agreement which gives rise to the personal obligation to transfer and the actual transfer of the movable or immovable. One reason for adhering to the requirement of delivery and registration for the passing of ownership is the publicity brought by delivery and registration.

The *traditio* approach can be further divided into causal and abstract systems. The causal theory dictates that transferring a property right depends on a valid underlying contract. On the contrary, the underlying contract (obligation) and the act of transfer (consisting of the proprietary contract plus delivery or registration) are completely separate under the abstract system. As this logic goes, the abstract theory does not make the transfer of a property right dependent on the validity of the underlying contract.[66] A party could become the legal owner through an underlying contract in error, and a transfer by a legally incompetent person will pass ownership to the transferee.[67] Since the transferee can, in these circumstances, usually be forced by order of a court to restore what has been acquired, the consequences *inter partes* are not far-reaching. However, a transfer by the transferee to a bona fide third party will have far-reaching consequences because the original owner will have no remedy against the bona fide third party.

Result of the Alteration of Property Rights' [《论物权变动的原因及其结果的区分原则》] (1999) 5 *Chinese Journal of Law* [《法学研究》] 28

64 Articles 209 and 224 CC.

65 Zhicheng Wu and Lei Chen, 'Revisiting Property Transfer Theory: English Law and Chinese Law Compared' (2023) 43 *Legal Studies* 259.

66 *Ibid.*

67 *Ibid.*

Chinese law adopts a causal system rather than an abstract system.[68] There has been a long-standing debate among Chinese scholars since the 1980s over whether Chinese law should adopt abstraction[69] or causality.[70] Although valuing its doctrinal refinement as von Savigny and his disciples advocated, most Chinese legal scholars took a dim view of this theory. Among those, the strongest anti-abstractionist argument is that the "causal system plus bona fide acquisition" model strikes a perfect balance between the security of the property and the security of the transaction. Such a model protects good faith purchasers, so they are prioritised over the transferor as long as all constituent elements of bona fide acquisition are met.[71] Bad faith purchasers do not enjoy this protection. It is worth noting that Chinese law doctrinally views a bona fide acquisition as an independent acquisition by operation of law.[72]

Before determining whether a real right has been transferred, the first step is to examine whether a valid and enforceable contract exists. If the contract is invalid, there will not be a property transfer. If the underlying contract is valid and enforceable, it is necessary to investigate whether the stipulated formality rules have been followed to transfer a real right over the property.

68 *Ibid*

69 Xianzhong Sun [孙宪忠] *General Principles of Real Rights Law of China* [《中国物权法总论》] (2nd edn, Law Press China 2009), pp. 412–56; Yunsong Ge [葛云松], 'Study on the Theory of Real Juridical Act' [《物权行为理论研究》] 16 (2004) *Peking University Law Journal* [《中外法学》] 702; Diyu Xu [徐涤宇], 'A Teleological Explanation of the Abstraction Principle' [《物权行为无因性理论之目的论解释》] (2005) 2 *Chinese Legal Science* [《中国法学》] 84.

70 Yi Wang [王轶], *On the Transfer of Real Rights* [《物权变动论》] (China Renmin University Press 2001), pp. 311–32; Tian Yin [尹田], *Comments and Thoughts on Property Law Theories* [《物权法理论评析与思考》] (China Renmin University Press 2004), pp. 190–215; Jianyuan Cui [崔建远], 'A Positivist Analysis of the Concept of Juridical Act of Real Rights and Chinese Civil Law' [《从解释论看物权行为与中国民法》] [2004] *Journal of Comparative Law* [《比较法研究》] 60.

71 Huixing Liang and Huabin Chen [梁慧星、华彬], *Property Law* [《物权法（第六版）》] (6th edn, Law Press China 2016), p. 97; Liming Wang [王利明], *Property Law* [《物权法》] (China Renmin University Press 2015), p. 56.

72 Article 311 and 313 CC; Jianyuan Cui [崔建远], *Commentaries of the Chinese CC: Book on Property Rights* (Vol. I) [《中国民法典释评：物权编（上下卷）（上)》] (China Renmin University Press 2020), p. 528; Xianzhong Sun and Guangxin Zhu [孙宪忠与朱广新], *Commentaries CC: Book on Property Rights* (Vol. I) [《民法典评注: 物权编（上卷）》] (China Legal Publishing House 2020), p. 476. In contrast, English law doctrinally considers the good faith purchase as a mere exception to the *nemo dat* starting point. See William Swadling, 'Restitution and Bona Fide Purchase', in William Swadling (ed), *The Limits of Restitutionary Claims: A Comparative Analysis* (UKNCCL 1997).

Before the Property Law was enacted, the formality rules for creating a property right were contained in Article 72 of the GPCL 1986. Article 72 provided that unless the law stipulates otherwise or the parties agree otherwise, the property obtained by a contract or other lawful means shall be transferred upon the delivery of the property itself.[73] This article has to be viewed in context. When the GPCL was enacted in 1986, there was no transferable land use right, even in urban China. Therefore, there was no need to establish a land registration system. Without a land registration system, the GPCL nonetheless stressed that a property right could be created when the property was transferred in addition to an underlying contract. Whatever "the property is transferred" means, the contract alone would not convey the title. This is the genesis of the intent plus system in Chinese law.

Under the Property Law, registration was required for immovable property[74] and delivery of movables.[75] Without an underlying agreement, a property right would not be created under Chinese law. As a general rule, ownership will not pass if any of the above-mentioned requirements are not complied with.

Paragraph 1 of Article 597 of the CC provides that if the seller lacks the authority to dispose of the subject matter, preventing the transfer of ownership, the buyer has the right to terminate the contract and insist that the seller be held responsible for the breach of contract.[76] Meanwhile, Article 15 of the Property Law was reproduced word by word in Article 215 of the Chinese CC. It states that,

> A contract entered into by the parties concerning the creation, alteration, transfer or extinction of immovable property rights shall become effective upon the formation of the contract unless otherwise provided by law or agreed by the parties, and the failure to register the property right shall not affect the validity of the contract.

Thus, the above provisions clarify that the transferor's power of disposition is a determining factor of the validity of the conveyance but not necessarily of the underlying contract. While the scholarly debates are ongoing and unsettled as to whether the Chinese law should remain unitary or go towards a separatist approach, the SPC interpreted such a

[73] Article 72 General Principles of Civil Law.
[74] Article 15 Property Law.
[75] Article 23 Property Law.
[76] Para. 1 of Article 597 CC.

change in the Chinese CC in a pro-separatist way.[77] In recent years, judgments given by higher courts (i.e. the SPC and the High People's Courts [HPCs]) show a trend that there are more cases explicitly recognising the principle of separation[78] than those explicitly denying the principle of separation.[79]

Finally, the question of whether Chinese law adopts an abstract or causal system for the transfer of property rights remains theoretically unresolved, as neither the CC nor any SPC interpretations provide a definitive stance. Moreover, the SPC has not issued a landmark ruling to clarify this aspect of Chinese law. However, an analysis of judicial decisions suggests a tendency towards a causal approach.[80]

Evidence of this is seen in the rulings at the HPC level in which judgments that directly address the debate between causality and abstraction predominantly support causality.[81] Similarly, at the Intermediate People's Court (IPC) level, there is a noticeable inclination against the principle of abstraction,[82] with more judgments explicitly rejecting it than affirming it.[83] This pattern across various levels of the judiciary

[77] Enforcement of CC Group of the SPC (ed), *Understanding and Applying the Book on Contracts of the Chinese CC* (People's Court Press 2020), p. 861.

[78] 河南金石联科工程技术有限公司与中国建设银行股份有限公司周口分行案 [*Henan Jinshi Lianke Engineering Project Technology Co Ltd and China Construction Bank Co Ltd Zhoukou Branch*] (2018) 最高法民申5669 [(2018) SPC Min Shen No. 5669]; 交通银行股份有限公司陕西省分行诉王菊梅 (2018) 最高法民申4883号 [*Bank of Communications Co Ltd Shaanxi Branch v. Wang Jumei* (2018), SPC Min Shen. No. 4883].

[79] 胡喜柱邢磊民事判决书 (2018) 冀民终737号 (2018) [*Hu Xizhu v. Xing Lei* (2018) Ji Min Zhong. No. 737]; 胡建军、高有林案 (2019) 赣民终705号 [*Hu Jianjun v. Gao Youlin* [2019] Gan Min Zhong No. 705]; 韩高伟. 青海怡海房地产开发有限公司 (2020) 青民终83号 [*Han Gaowei v. Qinghai Yihai Real Estate Development Co Ltd* (2020) Qing Min Zhong. No. 83].

[80] Wu and Chen (n. 65).

[81] 孙良与吴焕堂案 (2015) 粤高法民一申字第1187号 [*Sun Liang v. Wu Huantang* [2015] Yue Gao Fa Min Yi Shen No. 1187]; 北京京华信托投资公司与王会文二审民事判决书 (2019) 京民终145号 [*Beijing Jinghua Trust and Investment Co Ltd v. Wang Huiwen* (2019) Jing Min Zhong No. 145].

[82] 北京京华信托投资公司与刘九海一审民事判决书 (2016) 京02民初217号 [*Beijing Jinghua Trust Investment Co Ltd v. Liu Jiuhai* (2016] Jing 02 Min Chu No. 217]；成敏瑜、黄清文与魏彩莲、深圳市金融联融资担保有限公司二审判决书 (2019) 粤03民终21735号 [*Cheng Minyu v. Wei Cailian* (2019), Yue03 Min Zhong. No. 21735]; 大冶市保安镇城镇化建设有限责任公司;刘继平二审民事判决书，(2021) 川16民终10号 [*Daye Baoan Urban Development Co Ltd v. Liu Jiping* (2021) Chuan16 Min Zhong No. 10].

[83] 李瀚洋诉左亮 (2017) 苏01民终1869号民事判决 [*Li Hanyang v. Zuo Liang* (2017) Su 01 Min Zhong No. 1869].

suggests a prevalent judicial preference for a causal system where the validity of property transfers is linked to the underlying legal cause or basis of the transaction.

3.4 Special Property Transfer

There are four instances in which ownership in an estate passes automatically (without delivery or registration), namely on (1) marriage in the community of property,[84] (2) judicial order by the courts or arbitral award by arbitration institutions or expropriation decision by the government,[85] (3) death,[86] and (4) factual acts such as lawful construction or demolition of houses[87] or lawful occupation.[88] The first instance is a mode of derivative acquisition, fully dealt with under the law on marriage and family. For example, it was held by a Beijing Court that marriage, as an objective fact, already has the characteristic of publicity, and there is no need for another publicity to transfer the property title.[89] In Chinese law, succession on death[90] and ownership passing on a division of common property (*adiudicatio*) are also recognised as derivative acquisition modes.[91]

Nonetheless, a property transfer caused by a judicial order, an arbitral award or an expropriation decision creates some concerns in practice. First, when the property transfer is caused by a judicial order or an arbitral award, the transfer or conveyance occurs when the judicial order or arbitral award becomes binding and effective.[92] The property transfer between the litigating parties sounds straightforward. Still, when the party to whom either court judgment or arbitral award has awarded a property right transfers such a property right to a third party, the original party must go through registration.[93] Without registration, the third

84 Article 1062 CC.
85 Article 229 CC.
86 Article 230 CC.
87 Article 231 CC.
88 Article 1 of the SPC Interpretation on Several Issues Concerning the Condominium Ownership Trials.
89 A SPC gazetted case (2014) 12: (2014) 三中民终字第09467号 [[2014] San Zhong Min Zhong Zi No. 09467].《最高人民法院公报》2014年第12期 [*SPC Gazette* (2014) 12]
90 Read Article 230 CC with paragraph 1 of Article 1121, which provides that inheritance shall commence at the death of the deceased.
91 Article 1087 CC.
92 Article 229 CC.
93 Article 232 CC.

party may not know about this change in property title due to a lack of publicity. As a result, this may undermine the transaction security and potentially generate some unnecessary litigations. To tackle this, the CC provides that any disposition of immovable property rights has no proprietary effect without being registered if the law requires registration.[94] Therefore, registration is still needed for practical purposes if the party awarded a property right under a judicial order or an arbitral award intends to sell the property or obtain a mortgage.

Second, a problem arises when a property transfer occurs as a result of an expropriation decision made by a local government. The plain language in Article 229 implies that the property title changes when the expropriation decision becomes effective. Hence, it is crucial to ascertain when the expropriation decision is deemed effective for property title transfer. Does it mean the effective date pronounced by the government when issuing an expropriation decision? If so, this is problematic, as it would be against the rule of law. How can a government decision be given the same legal status as a judicial order or an arbitral award for the purpose of property transfer? Government decisions are not and should not be final and effective. Therefore, they are open to challenges by affected parties, in this instance the expropriated. There are well-established rules and procedures under the Chinese Administrative Litigation law against government decisions, including expropriation decisions.[95] Thus, if the property transfer occurs when the government's decision is issued, that will create an unnecessary hassle when the affected parties successfully challenge the government's decision.

For this reason, the effective date of an expropriation decision should be interpreted as the date when the expropriation compensation is provided if no administrative litigation is involved. If the compensation plan is in dispute before the court, the effective date should be when a final court judgment is issued. Such an interpretation is derived from the expropriation provision contained in the CC, which provides,

> where houses or other immovable property owned by organisations or individuals are expropriated, compensation shall be provided under the law; the lawful rights and interests of the expropriated persons shall be safeguarded. Where the residences of individuals are expropriated, the residential conditions of the expropriated individuals shall also be guaranteed.[96]

[94] *Ibid.*
[95] Article 12(5), Article 12(11) and Article 61 Administrative Litigation Law of the PRC.
[96] Para. 3 of Article 243 CC.

Certain conditions must be met if some factual acts cause the property transfer, such as lawful construction and housing demolition. First, not all factual acts are taken to constitute a property transfer without registration or delivery. The CC only specifies lawful construction and housing demolition for this purpose. Second, such factual acts must be lawful. The construction must be carried out with all the legally required permits or licenses. Third, the construction or demolition must be completed. If the construction work has not been completed, then the object of the property right does not exist. As a result, there could not be a property transfer or conveyance. Still, why can such factual acts per se lead to the property transfer? China experienced construction booms in the last three decades when its economy took off. Hence, there were many situations where real rights could be established by legally constructing houses for self-occupation without registration. Although there is a lack of registration, the buildings created by such acts cannot be treated as unowned property. Therefore, property rights over such buildings are legally recognised, favouring the builder/developer with full licences. For example, when a farmer builds a house on his homestead on rural land, he acquires the ownership of the house from the day the construction is completed. However, this policy consideration will fade in the long run when the land registration system gradually gains ground in rural land in view of the rural land transfer policy. Still, at the moment, registration is needed if the builder/developer intends to dispose of the completed houses to a third party, according to Article 232 of the CC.

3.5 Land Registration System

3.5.1 Historical Development

In view of the Chinese law position on the property transfer theory, it is necessary to delve into the design and characteristics of the land registration system in the case of immovable property. Even for a tiny apartment, those with property rights will have more incentives to invest in their properties, and they can use their properties as collateral for credit. In economic terms, an effective property information system is a public good.[97] When property information is made transparent and accessible,

97 Stuart Banner, 'Transitions between Property Regimes' (2002) 31 *The Journal of Legal Studies* 359, 362.

the system allows for effective planning incorporating demographics, land use and environmental impact assessments.[98] Because the benefits are so dispersed and the costs of setting up a standardised property system are high, some form of state intervention is necessary to establish a national system for registering land information, particularly valuing rights and collecting consents.[99] With the emergence of private property interests, creating functioning property institutions has been put on the legislature's agenda. Real property titles have become hallmarks of citizenship, personhood and social justice.[100]

Before 1988, the fundamental rule pertaining to all land in China was no individual rights on the land.[101] In 1988, Chinese law allowed the transferability of urban land use rights (LURs) by amending its Constitution.[102] The recognition of the LURs generated a building construction boom and unprecedented commercial dealings in the real estate and housing industry.[103] However, housing privatisation has challenged other related institutional frameworks, particularly the land registration system.

98 Kluas Deininger, *Land Policies for Growth and Poverty Reduction* (World Bank 2003), vol. I, pp. 24–25 and 31–32.

99 Benito Arruñada, 'Property Enforcement as Organized Consent' (2003) 19 *The Journal of Law, Economics, and Organization* 401.

100 Katherine Verdery, 'Fuzzy Property: Rights, Power, and Identity in Transylvania's Collectivization', in Michael Burawoy and Katherine Verdery (eds), *Uncertain Transition: Ethnographies of Change in the Post socialist World* (Rowman and Littleffield Publishers 1999), pp. 53–82.

101 George C. S. Lin and Samuel P. S. Ho, 'The State, Land System, and Land Development Processes in Contemporary China' (2005) 95 *Annals of the Association of American Geographers* 411.

102 The amended Constitution of 1988 states that "the right to use land may be transferred according to law." Soon thereafter, Article 2 of the Land Administration Law was revised and the revised version stipulates that "the right to use State owned or collectively owned land may be assigned pursuant to the law." The commercialisation of LURs was first tried in Shenzhen on 9 September 1987 and was formally adopted when Article 10 of the Constitution was amended on 12 April 1988 to permit the assignment of the right to use land.

103 Mark Selden and Aiguo Lu, 'The Reform of Landownership and the Political Economy of Contemporary China', in Mark Selden (ed), *The Political Economy of Chinese Development* (Armonk & ME Sharpe, 1993), pp. 107–205. However, Ellickson made the counter-argument that the land use right in urban China may put economic growth into peril. See Robert C. Ellickson, 'The Costs of Complex Land Titles: Two Examples from China' (2011) 1 *Property Rights Conference Journal* 281.

While the first departmental rule concerning land registration was introduced in 1982,[104] the State Council published the Rules Concerning the Administration of Private Housing in the Urban Area in 1983.[105] This rule demands that owners of private households in urban areas apply for registration; going through the investigation and confirmation process, they can obtain the certificate of household ownership.[106] In addition, when there is a transfer of ownership, the related parties should apply to register the transfer of ownership.[107]

By implementing these rules, the household registration system was thus standardised. The next significant legislation on land registration was the UREAL in 1994.[108] Under this law, the owners will legally obtain real estate ownership only upon registration.[109] In addition, the various departmental rules have been promulgated subsequently to fine-tune the details.[110]

The promulgation of the 2007 Property Law reflected state commitments and the middle class's appeals to clarify and demarcate private property rights.[111] The Property Law aimed to set up an institutional framework that recognises property rights, enforces them at low cost and facilitates holders to exercise them easily to be socially beneficial.[112]

104 The Provisional Regulation Concerning Urban Housing Title Management of 1982.

105 The Rules Concerning the Administration of the Private Households in the Urban Area, which is an administrative regulation issued by the State Council in 1983 and has been repealed.

106 Article 6 of the Rules Concerning the Administration of the Private Households in the Urban Area.

107 *Ibid.*

108 The Urban Real Estate Administration Law of 1994.

109 Concerning the land use right, it should be noted that Article 16 of the Interim Regulations on the Assignment and Transfer of Urban State-owned Land Use Rights (issued on 19 May 1990, and revised on 29 November 2020 by the State Council) provides that the land grantee, after paying all the land use right premiums, is required to go through the registration process and obtain the land use certificate.

110 For example, the Measure Dealing with the Pre-sale of Urban Commodity Housing issued by the Ministry of Construction in 1994 and the Measure Concerning Urban Real Estate Mortgage issued by the Ministry of Construction in 1997.

111 Lei Chen, 'Private Property with Chinese Characteristics: A Critical Analysis of the Chinese Law on Property of 2007' (2010) 18 *European Review of Private Law* 983; Yun-chien Chang, 'Property Law with Chinese Characteristics: An Economic and Comparative Analysis' (2011) 1 *Brigham-Kanner Property Rights Conference Journal* 345.

112 Thomas Merill and Henry Smith argued that property rights are good against the whole world, thus requiring rules that reduce the costs of information for a broad-ranging yet unspecified group of potential violators. Thomas. W. Merrill and Henry. E. Smith, 'Making Coasean Property More Coasean' (2011) 54 *Journal of Law and Economics* 77.

A property registration system has been established to provide title security and boost transaction efficiency. In line with the Property Law, more detailed Measures of Land Registration have also been introduced by the Ministry of Land and Resources and the Measures of Housing Registration by the Ministry of Housing and Urban-Rural Development in 2007 and 2008, respectively. Some details, such as identifying the immovable property, methods of recording and indexing, and powers of review by the Registrar, are provided. Since the CC has kept the provisions concerning the land registration system in the Property Law intact, the following sections will explore salient features of the Property Law.

3.5.2 Registering Land Use Rights and Building

In China, immovable property registration is provided by registrars at the local government level as a type of public service.[113] In the past, the registrations of land and housing were separate.[114] For urban housing registration in China, the owner has to register with two different authorities to obtain two different entitlement certificates: a certificate for the LUR with the state land administration authority and a certificate for the housing on the land (housing ownership) with the housing authority.[115] To be specific, the LUR of state-owned and collectively owned land, the mortgage over LUR, easement and other property rights were registered with the land authority at the local level.[116] The housing transfer and other housing-related rights were registered at the Housing Registrar.[117] Nonetheless, a trend has recently developed; notably, in 2014, the Interim Regulation on Real Estate Registration was promulgated to issue a single certificate by merging the LUR and housing ownership deeds.[118] In essence, this marks the introduction of the uniform land registration system over immovable property, which means

113 Paragraph 1 of Article 210 CC.

114 Lei Chen, 'Land Registration, Property Rights and Institutional Performance in China: Progress Achieved and Challenges Ahead' (2014) 44 *Hong Kong Law Journal* 841.

115 Patrick Randolph and Jianbo Lou, *Chinese Real Estate Law* (Kluwer Law International 2000), pp. 167–71.

116 Article 2(1) of the Measures of Land Registration.

117 Article 2 of the Measures of Housing Registration.

118 Article 5 of the Interim Regulations on Real Estate Registration.

that one Registrar uniformly regulates the scope, authority and registration measures at the local government level.[119]

Under Chinese law, a vivid expression about the relationship between the land and the house erected on the land is "house moves with the land, and land moves with the house." This expression indicates that the house and the land are inseparable in real estate. In other words, when a property is transferred or dealt with, the house and the land are transferred together. This concept implies a close and integral relationship between the physical structure (house) and the underlying piece of land. It underpins the idea that any transaction involving one will affect the other, and the two should be registered in one certificate.

3.5.3 A Hybrid System of Mandatory and Voluntary Models

When the Property Law was drafted, there was a debate on the choice of property registration model within the civilian system to emulate. The final decision was to adopt a hybrid approach, combining the mandatory and voluntary models. The difference is that the mandatory model, mainly German-influenced, requires registration to establish a right to land or buildings. In contrast, in the voluntary model, mainly French-inspired, registration merely declares the existence of rights already created. The French model, also called the voluntary system, is characterised by parties' consent, and registration shall not affect the validity of the sales contract in transferring land. The contract is valid when parties consent to its terms and conditions. The registration only makes the transaction effective against third parties, but it does not give the creditor greater rights against third parties than against the person whose property is encumbered.[120] In contrast, the German model, sometimes called the mandatory system, is far more rigid and supervisory than the French model, since without registration there is no property right.[121] A civil law notary is often required in the German

[119] Para. 2 of Article 210 CC.

[120] Jacob H. Beekhuis et al., Structural Variations in Property Law, *International Encyclopaedia of Comparative Law* (vol. VI) (Mohr 2004), p. 53

[121] Article 873 of the *Bürgerliches Gesetzbuch* (BGB) requires both deed/contract of sale and registration for validity.

model, for a property right cannot exist without being notarised and registered.

In China, a hybrid registration system operates under the current laws. The general provisions in the CC provide that "[t]he creation, alteration, transfer or extinction of immovable property rights shall become effective upon registration following the law; it shall not become effective without registration unless otherwise provided by law. According to law, the ownership of natural resources owned by the State may not need to be registered."[122]

From the above provisions it appears *prima facie* that the Chinese land registration system adopts the German system, as the Code stipulates that a change of certain property rights will only take effect when duly registered. Failing to register means no legal effect on the establishment, modification, transfer and lapse of rights in real property. The property rights only become effective when recorded in the register of immovable property.[123] Second, where the law specifies that no registration is required, the property right becomes effective upon the conclusion of the contract, and the failure to register the property right shall not affect the contract's validity.[124] There are many exceptions in the same legislation to this "no registration, no property right" norm. Exceptions refer to the voluntary system not mandating registration to effectuate the property interest. Third, the state-owned natural resources do not need to be registered.

Specifically, under Chinese law, the LUR of the urban construction land, the real estate ownership, the right of habitation and the mortgage right of real property will come into effect after registration.[125] In contrast, the recordation of contractual management rights of rural land, the use rights of rural housing sites, the easement and the floating charge merely enable them to stand against third parties. Table 3.1 surveys the scope of application of the two different models in China.

[122] Article 209 CC.

[123] Article 214 CC.

[124] Article 215 CC.

[125] Donald Clark, 'China's Stealth Urban Land Revolution' (2014) 62 *The American Journal of Comparative Law* 323, arguing that the nature of urban LURs in China is not significantly different from those land tenure systems commonly regarded as featuring private owners.

Table 3.1 *Operation of the dual registration systems*

Type of System	For Registration of	Specification
Mandatory System	Property	Alienation and Mortgages of Flats, Buildings and Other Fixtures[126]
		Creation of Mortgage of Uncompleted Buildings[127]
	Land Use Right	Transfer and Mortgage of the Right to Use Construction Land[128]
	Sea Areas Use Right	Transfer and Mortgage of the Right to Use Sea Areas[129]
	Right of Habitation (Personal Servitude)	Creation of the Right of Habitation[130]
Voluntary System	Property	Creation, Alteration, Transfer or Extinction of the Property Rights of Vessels, Aircraft and Motor Vehicles[131]
		Mortgage of Movable Property[132]
	Land Use Right	Exchange or Transfer of the Right to Rural Land Contractual Management[133]
		Transfer, Modification and Cancelation of the Right to Homestead Use in Rural Land[134]
	Praedial Servitude	Creation of Servitude[135]

126 Article 349 CC.
127 Article 402 CC.
128 *Ibid.*
129 *Ibid.* It is notable that the CC does not explicitly require a mandatory registration of the transfer of the right to use sea areas.
130 Article 368 CC.
131 Article 225 CC.
132 Article 403 CC.
133 Article 335 CC.
134 Article 363 CC.
135 Article 374 CC.

3.5.4 *Functions of the Land Registration System*

When registration is needed to trigger the transfer of property interests,[136] the scope of the Registrar's authority to review documents deserves discussion. Generally, when applying for registration, an applicant must provide proof of ownership and other required documents, such as those defining the boundary and area of the immovable property,[137] and pay the registration fees.[138] A Registrar then verifies the proof of ownership and other required documents provided by the applicant, inquiries the applicant about the relevant matters, and finally registers relevant matters truthfully and timely. The Registrar can perform other duties as provided by laws or administrative regulations.[139] Where it is necessary to prove relevant immovable property registration matters further, the Registrar may require the applicant to submit additional documents and conduct an onsite inspection.[140]

This indicates that the Chinese Registrar is vested with extensive verification powers to check the authenticity of the contract for sale. However, comparatively, the Chinese Registrar's review powers are less than their German counterparts. In Germany, the Registrar's review powers extend to examining whether the documents reflect that the applicant has a genuine and substantive right to the property.[141] In addition, the German Registrar also has the power to verify whether the property description, such as the location, size and boundary, matches the reality.[142] If the Registrar suspects any fraud or mistake, a registration application may be suspended pending further investigation.[143]

This is not the case in China, as, firstly, Chinese Registrars are part of a governmental agency rather than part of the judiciary. Administrative officers do not enjoy the wide powers and discretion vested in and exercised by judicial officers. Unlike Germany, China does not have a mandatory registration model for all property rights, as explained earlier. The Registrar is forbidden from demanding the appraisal of

136 Exceptions do exist, such as the application of the declarative system as illustrated above.
137 Article 211 CC.
138 Article 223 CC.
139 Para. 1 of Article 212 CC.
140 Para. 2 of Article 212 CC.
141 Murray Raff, 'Characteristics of the International Model of Land Title Registration Illuminated by Comparative Study of the German and Torrens Systems' (2012) 1 *European Property Law Journal* 54.
142 *Ibid.*
143 Section 44 of the *Grundbuchordnung* [Land Registry Code].

immovable property, requiring repeated registration on grounds such as an annual inspection, or any other act beyond the scope of registration duties.[144]

Secondly, since a right entails an obligation, having a strong power to verify denotes an obligation to make the registration entries reliable and conclusive. Otherwise, the liability for compensation when making a mistake may arise. Under Chinese law, the title certificate to immovable property is the proof of ownership of such property not only for the registered owner but also for a third party relying on the deeds registry.[145] An interesting question may arise regarding a discrepancy between the title certificate held by the registered owner and the entries on the land register held by the Registrar. All entries on the land register are deemed or presumed to be correct unless there is evidence showing a mistake or defect of the Registrar.[146] In other words, the entry on the land register prevails over the title certificate in case of discrepancy unless there is a proven mistake or defect on the part of the Registrar. The SPC has long held this position, even before the enactment of the CC. In *Sichuan Jufeng Real Estate Development Co Ltd v. Dazhou Radio and Television College*, it was held by the SPC that the title holder of the real estate at issue should be determined based on the records in the land register. Although the Dazhou municipal government had announced the cancellation of the state-owned land use certificate as proof of real estate ownership of the land involved, it did not change the entry in the land register. Hence, the cancellation of the state-owned land use certificate by the Dazhou municipal government has not changed the ownership of the land use right involved.[147]

Thirdly, at the practical level, it is not viable for a municipal Registrar, with merely a few dozen staff and having to deal with tens of thousands of applications every month, to be vested with the German-like strong review power. The Registrar's staff are also not trained well enough to exercise a strong review power. Therefore, under Chinese law, the Registrar only requires additional documents and carries out an on-site

144 Article 213 CC.

145 Article 216 CC.

146 Article 217 CC.

147 四川省聚丰房地产开发有限责任公司与达州广播电视大学案（2014）民申字第56号[*Sichuan Jufeng Real Estate Development Co Ltd v. Dazhou Radio and Television College* (2014), SPC Min Shen No. 56].

property inspection when necessary.[148] Otherwise, it will register based on the examination of the documents submitted by the applicants.[149]

Nonetheless, despite the aforementioned, the effect of registration warrants a strong review power by the Registrar. This is because, under Chinese law, once registered, a bona fide acquirer of ownership can safely assume that the registered person is the owner.[150] Meanwhile, the rights of a true owner are debilitated because if the true owner does not apply for rectification of an incorrect entry on the register before the bona fide acquirer who paid the reasonable consideration completes the registration, the true owner's right will be lost.[151] For this reason, the state assumes responsibility for incorrect registration and is liable to pay for damage suffered because of such registration. Therefore, the state should normally take extensive steps to avoid incorrect registration.

Since the key function of land registration is to ensure transparency and publicity, public access to information in the registry is crucial. However, this leads to many practical questions, including the class of persons entitled to inspect the registry record and whether the Registrar can operate an open-door policy allowing all persons to examine the land registration information freely. According to Article 218 of the CC, only those who can show that they have a legitimate interest in inspecting the land registry will be allowed to apply for access.[152] However, the CC does not prescribe whether the inspecting parties must pay a fee for such a purpose. Due to the legal protection of personal information or privacy, no inspecting party can disclose or illegally use the right holder's registration documents.[153] The detailed procedures to access the land registry have been fine-tuned in the Interim Regulations on Real Estate Registration.

3.5.5 Liability for Mistakes and Fraud

The CC allows the Registrar to compensate those who suffer losses due to inaccurate registration.[154] It is not uncommon to encounter some

[148] Para. 2 of Article 212 CC.
[149] *Ibid.*
[150] Article 216 CC.
[151] Article 311 CC.
[152] Article 218 CC states, "a right holder or an interested party may apply to inquire about or duplicate the registration documents of immovable property, and the registration office shall provide them."
[153] Article 219 CC.
[154] Para. 2 of Article 222 CC.

mistakes and fraud in registration. First, the mistake can be attributable to the negligence of the Registrar's officers. Second, the discrepancy between the record and the true legal position may be due to a transferee's fraud, forgery and mistakes. Third, there may be a malicious conspiracy between the Registrar's officers and the party who provided forged documents.

In the first instance, the party who suffers a loss can rely on the principles of tort liability and the institution's vicarious liability for negligent or intentional wrongdoings of its officials. In the second situation, where the loss is caused by the person who committed fraud, the fraudulent party is liable for the loss caused under the fault-based liability regime. This is to say that when the fraudulent party submitted a forged document, and the Registrar's staff exercised proper due diligence but did not discover the forgery, the fraudulent party should bear the liability to pay compensation. Any party providing false application materials for registration and causing damages to another person shall be liable for compensation.[155] Similarly, when a Registrar causes damages to a party because of the inaccuracy, the Registrar shall undertake the liability for compensation.

Nevertheless, even though rectification is done, rectification may not compensate for some losses. For example, expenses may have been incurred to obtain legal advice, or there may be a loss of chance of a sale. Whether this amounts to damages caused by the Registrar and whether such damages should be compensated have not been made clear in the CC. However, the person who suffers losses because of an error or omission in the register should be entitled to compensation, irrespective of rectification. After making compensation, the Registrar has the right to recourse against the person liable for such a mistake.[156] As a rule of thumb, the party claiming compensation shoulders the burden of showing that a mistake or error was made or false information was provided.

Complications arise when there is a conspiracy between the Registrar's staff and the fraudulent party. In this situation, which is possible though highly improbable, will the Registrar, the fraudulent party or both be liable to pay compensation? If both, is it based on proportionate liability, or just the one whom the party that suffered a loss chooses to claim against? The CC does not address this issue, and the position is thus left to the specific registration rule to determine. The Interim Regulation on

[155] Para. 1 of Article 222 CC.
[156] *Ibid.*

Real Estate Registration only provides that the Registrar staff shall be liable for compensation or held criminally responsible when engaging in false registration, destroying or forging, or arbitrarily modifying the registry entries without authorisation, or committing other acts of abuse of power or dereliction of duty.[157] While this is commendable, it does not address the issue of proportional liability in case of conspiracy.

When inaccuracies in registration are corrected, the individual benefitting from such rectification should be compensated by the Registrar for any losses incurred due to the error. A contentious issue arises concerning the legal nature of the Registrar's liability for this compensation: Is it a governmental administrative liability or a civil liability? The distinction is significant, as it affects the extent of loss recovery. Under administrative liability, only direct losses are compensable, whereas civil liability allows for the recovery of actual losses incurred. The debate over which type of liability applies has led to divergent opinions among legal scholars and inconsistent rulings in case law. Some significant judgments have treated the Registrar's liability as an administrative issue, whereas other rulings by Chinese courts have classified it as a civil matter.[158] Many academics advocate for recognising the Registrar's liability as civil rather than administrative, arguing that this would facilitate full compensation for actual losses.[159]

However, the CC does not clearly define whether the Registrar's liability should be treated as fault-based civil liability, administrative liability or otherwise. This ambiguity leads to varied interpretations and practices among the courts, and it is likely that this inconsistency will persist. It is important to note that registrants have a duty of care towards

[157] Article 30 Interim Regulations on Real Estate Registration.

[158] 赵国权、赵国良等与李元顺、镇江市住房和城乡建设局纠纷 [2016] 苏民申 5948 号民事裁定书 [*Zhao Guoquan et al. v. Li Yuanshun and Zhenjiang Housing and Urban-Rural Development Bureau* (2016) Su Min Shen No. 5498 Civil Ruling]; 常援朝、陈霞等与夏邑县住房和城乡规划建设管理局城乡建设行政管理审判监督 [2016] 豫民申 376 号 [*Chang Yuanchao et al. v. Xiayi County Housing and Urban-Rural Planning and Development Bureau, Urban-Rural Development Administration Management* [2016] Yu Min Shen No. 376]; in addition, the SPC recently categorised the Registrar's compensatory liability for mistake into the group of civil disputes via property rights disputes in its Cause of Action of Civil Cases Circular The SPC's Circular Cause of Actions [2011] 法发 [Legal Development] No. 41.

[159] Rongzhen Wang [王荣珍], 'Judicial Dilemma and Legislative Reflection on the Compensatory Liability of Real Estate Registration Organizations in Our Country' [《我国不动产登记机构赔偿责任的司法困境与立法反思》] (2019) 37 *Tribune of Political Science and Law* [《政法论坛》] 106.

the Registrar. This obligation includes the responsibility to inform the Registrar of any known or reasonably foreseeable issues, as the Registrar holds the right to seek restitution from any party whose negligence contributed to the registration inaccuracies.[160] This implies that the Registrar's liability may be mitigated if the loss can be attributed to the applicant's breach of their duty of care, limiting the Registrar's exposure to compensation claims. Thus, applicants must ensure full and accurate disclosure to avoid complications and potential liability.

When the Registrar is held accountable for compensation due to its errors, it is imperative that there are sufficient financial resources available to cover all potential claims for recovery of losses. It is practical to ensure that public funds are not excessively drained by errors, whether clerical or fraudulent. The CC and the Interim Regulation of Real Estate Registration do not specify the mechanisms for creating and managing indemnity funds to address this issue. It appears that such details are expected to be covered by a specific statute. To address this, two key recommendations are proposed:

First, the insurance fund set up to cover such liabilities should not provide overly broad coverage. It ought to exclude compensation for errors, omissions and misdescriptions that occur because an applicant or their agent failed to inform the Registrar about the creation, amendment or termination of registrable rights. Liability on the part of the Registrar should be limited to the extent that losses are not due to any breach of duty of care by the applicant. In instances where the applicant fails in their duty to provide accurate and complete information, the liability should fall on the applicant rather than the Registrar.

Second, while establishing an internal insurance fund is essential, it is equally important to enforce strict disciplinary rules for Registrar staff to prevent malpractice and enhance the quality of land registration services. This would help to minimise the occurrence of errors and the subsequent financial burden on the insurance fund.

In conclusion, individuals who suffer loss of property interest due to flaws in the land registration process should be entitled to compensation. This entitlement should be dual-natured: firstly, they should have the right to seek redress from the person responsible for the loss;

[160] Para. 2 of Article 222 CC.

and secondly, they should be able to claim compensation from the registration insurance fund. This approach ensures a balanced remedy system that protects public funds while providing fair compensation for affected parties.

3.5.6 *Objections and Advance Notice*

Two remedies are available when an inaccuracy shown on the register arises from a mistake or fraud. One is rectification, and the other is monetary compensation. A party who believes an error has been made in the register may apply for rectification.[161] If the party whose interests are affected consents in writing to such rectification or there is evidence to prove the error in the registration, the Registrar shall rectify it accordingly.[162] Under Chinese law, there is strong protection for the bona fide acquirer at the expense of the original owner regarding property transfer.[163] A rectification will not be done if the person in whose favour the property was registered was in good faith unless that person consents to the rectification. Consequently, without the consent of a bona fide acquirer, the registered title of the bona fide acquirer should remain unchanged even if there is a transactional error arising from the invalidity of the conveyance in the acquirer's favour.

If the affected party does not agree to the rectification, it may apply for an objection.[164] When the Registrar accepts and records such an objection, the recorded objection ceases to be effective if the affected party fails to file a lawsuit within fifteen days from the recorded date of the objection.[165] Chinese law does not allow a Registrar to determine whether the objection is groundless. Supposedly, when the Registrar receives an objection, it will first consider whether or not the objection has any chance of success. However, the Registrar has no active role to play in this regard under Chinese law. When the Registrar does not rectify the record on its own or the registered party does not agree to change the register, the Registrar has no choice but to register the objection. The objection will lapse if the party that files an objection does not lodge a lawsuit within fifteen days.

[161] Para. 1 of Article 220 CC.
[162] *Ibid.*
[163] Article 311 CC.
[164] Para. 2 of Article 220 CC.
[165] *Ibid.*

When the objection is recorded improperly and causes damage to the registered party, they may claim against the applicant for damages.[166] This provision appears sensible, as it maintains a delicate balance between the stakeholders. With a closer look, if there is a genuine inaccuracy on the register, the party whose interest has been infringed upon must file a lawsuit if neither the Registrar nor the registered party agrees to rectify it promptly. This approach requires a party filing the objection to commence a court proceeding. Otherwise, the objection will soon lapse.

On the other hand, if there is no genuine mistake and the request for rectification is groundless, thus causing a loss to the registered party, the registered party may claim damages against the party who applies for the objection. However, Chinese law does not specify the liability base, duty standard and recoverable loss extent in the legislation or administrative order. Therefore, the Chinese courts have significant discretion to characterise and ascertain the legal test for the objecting party's liability.

There is an inevitable "registration gap" between the conclusion of the sale and purchase contract, the purchase price payment and the time when the buyer's title is registered. Some legal risks arise from this registration gap period. For example, in the case of a double sale, the seller may enter into a sale contract with a second buyer at a higher price when the contract with the first buyer has already concluded. This can be called a competing deed risk, specifically the risk that the second buyer's application reaches the Land Register first. Another risk is the insolvency risk – that is, the seller is insolvent, and the sold property may be subject to liquidation. To tackle this, Chinese law introduces an advance notice system, a functional equivalent of "official search with priority" in England and Wales[167] and "*Vormerkung*" ("caution") in Germany.[168]

Advance notice may be registered when the parties enter into a sale and purchase agreement for immovable property to ensure the realisation of the property right in the future.[169] After the advance notice registration, any disposition of the immovable property without the consent of the right holder of the advance notice registration shall have no proprietary effect.[170] To illustrate, a notice is placed on the register

166 *Ibid.*
167 Schedule 3, Part 3 of the Land Registration Fee Order 2009 (SI 2009/845).
168 Article 883–8 of the BGB.
169 Para. 1 of Article 221 CC.
170 *Ibid.*

that the seller intends to transfer the title to the buyer. This notice does not confer on a buyer a real right, as the "no registration, no real right" rule is strictly applied to the urban land use rights, buildings and other fixtures. However, until the buyer is duly registered and dealing with a third party, for example, the second buyer, in case of a double sale, may not cause a property transfer without the consent of the person who lodges the notice/caution because the third party can search the register and thus know the existence of such a notice/caution. It is worth noting that using advance notice is optional under Chinese law.

However, after the advance notice registration, if the underlying contractual right is extinguished or no application for registration is submitted within ninety days from the date the formal registration can be carried out, the advance notice registration ceases to be effective. There are two related issues. First, in case of a conflict of interests between a mortgagee who has registered an advance notice and a sitting tenant, whose interest would gain priority? Second, who bears the burden of proof to show that the advance notice ceases to be effective if the formal registration is not done within the statutorily prescribed period? To clarify the position under Chinese law, it is apposite to summarise the facts of the following case.

In *Huangshi Dongfang Sub-branch of the Agricultural Bank of China v. Mei Hehua*,[171] the appellants signed a commercial lease contract for a shop on 4 November 2009 for a five-year lease from 1 January 2010 to 31 December 2014. When the lease contract was concluded, the respondent bank had already registered the mortgage for the premises, including the area of the shop. However, such mortgage registration was subsequently cancelled on the register in October 2012.

During the same period, the respondent bank secured an advance notice of mortgage on the premises based on a mortgage agreement. Subsequently, on 18 January 2014, the appellants entered into a lease agreement extending until 31 January 2025. Following a default on the mortgage, the respondent initiated legal proceedings to enforce the security right against the mortgagor. In May 2014, through civil mediation, the Court of First Instance reached a mediated settlement agreement that recognised the respondent's priority right to enforce the security right. On 10 September 2015, the Court of First Instance issued

[171] 梅荷花诉中国农业银行股份有限公司黄石东方支行案 [2017] 鄂02民终1078号 [*Huangshi Dongfang Sub-branch of the Agricultural Bank of China Co Ltd v. Mei Hehua* (2017) E 02 Min Zhong No. 1078].

an enforcement order permitting the respondent to acquire the property at a previously agreed price.[172] Later, on 29 September 2015, the respondent formally registered the mortgage over the secured property. Consequently, the respondent filed a lawsuit at the Court of First Instance to terminate the extended lease contract.

The Court of First Instance ruled in favour of the respondent, finding that the advance notice of the mortgage, registered in October 2012, was sufficiently publicised, and thus, the appellants were or should have been aware that the property was encumbered by a mortgage. Despite this knowledge, the appellants proceeded to sign the extended lease agreement. Therefore, the Court held that the lease agreement could not take precedence over the registered mortgage, effectively ruling against the appellants' interest in the property.[173]

The lessees appealed, alleging that the advance notice differed from the formal registration. In the appellant's submission, the Court of First Instance mistakenly took the respondent as a registered mortgagee, granting it a right to break the lease. Also, the appellants are not the parties to the mediated settlement agreement issued by the Court of First Instance. Such a court document is based on an agreement between the parties, and under Chinese law, the agreement cannot create a real property right, such as a mortgage, unless registered.

The appellate court upheld the decision against the appellants, diverging slightly in its reasoning from the Court of First Instance. While the lower court had acknowledged the existence of a mortgage right based on the advance notice, the appellate court referred to it as a "quasi-mortgage right" following the registration of the advance notice. The appellate court determined that the appellants failed to demonstrate that the respondent had intentionally delayed formal registration of the mortgage, which should have been completed within three months following the advance notice in October 2012 but was not done until after the lease extension was signed in January 2014. Consequently, the appellate court found that the advance notice registration remained effective at the time the lease was extended.

172 中国农业银行股份有限公司黄石东方支行诉梅荷花等 [*Agriculture Bank of China Co., Ltd Huangshi Dongfang branch v Mei Hehua* [2014] 鄂黄石中执字第00211-4号 [(2014) E Huangshi Zhong Zhi Zi No. 00211-4].

173 中国农业银行股份有限公司黄石东方支行与被告梅荷花、任超案 (2016) 鄂0202民初1291号 [*Agriculture Bank of China Co., Ltd Huangshi Dongfang branch v Mei Hehua, Ren* Chaoyi, (2016) E 0202 Min Chu No. 1291].

Furthermore, the appellate court emphasised that allowing any disposition of the property under an advance notice without the consent of the party who filed the notice would undermine the legislative intent behind the advance notice system. Therefore, the appellate court concluded that the extended lease agreement could not override the advance notice, effectively negating the lease in favour of the quasi-mortgage right held by the respondent. This interpretation ensures the protection of the rights of parties who register an advance notice against subsequent transactions that could potentially conflict with their registered interest.

At first glance, this case focuses on the rule of *emptio non tollit locatum* (the sale does not break the lease).[174] A lessee's rights limit a landlord's proprietary rights, and the rule prevents the landlord from selling (in this case, a forced sale due to the mortgage default) the property as free from all obligatory rights. However, with a closer look into the reasoning provided by the appellate court, three points on the effectiveness of advance notice registration are worth discussing. First, the court seems to suggest that the right obtained through the advance notice registration is not a real right but a quasi-real right between contractual and real rights. Whether the SPC and other Chinese courts endorse and share this perception remains to be seen because, under the *numerus clausus* principle, there is no such notion in the CC. An SPC ruling held that the advance notice registration is used to preserve a proprietary claim, and the registration content is the claim of the real right, which can be excluded from subsequent changes in the real right.[175] In other words, the SPC has sidestepped the legal nature of advance registration in the ruling. It is expected to have another similar case reaching the SPC for a definite answer to this question.

Second, the court placed the burden of proof on the tenant to show that the party who lodged an advance notice deliberately failed to conduct a proper and formal registration within the statutorily prescribed period when it could. The CC does not specify who bears the burden of proof, but in practice, should the Registrar be in the best position to advise the Court when a formal registration can be done, given that the

[174] Article 725 CC provides that any change in ownership of the leased item during the period in which the lessee possesses the item in accordance with the lease contract shall not affect the validity of the lease contract.

[175] 邵仁忠诉威海广信房地产开发有限责任公司案 (2020)最高法民申3576号民事裁定书 [*Shao Renzhong v. Weihai Guangxin Real Estate Development Co Ltd* (2020) SPC Min Shen No. 3576 Civil Ruling].

Registrar has all the necessary documents on the register? It seems unfair and unbalanced for the lessee to prove that the Respondent deliberately failed to register, given that the formal registration is only to be lodged by the Respondent to the Registrar. The lessee is not involved in the formal registration process.

Third, the standard of proof is also questionable. The CC provides that if there is no formal registration submitted within ninety days from the date when the registration can be carried out after the advance notice registration, the advance notice registration shall cease to be effective.[176] The court should take an objective approach by relying on Article 20 of the Property Law.[177] The state of mind of the relevant parties who do not register is not explicitly addressed. It is stated that the advance notice lapses when there is a failure to lodge a formal registration within three months after the advance notice when the Respondent can do so. Whether the concerned party deliberately or negligently fails to follow up with a formal registration is irrelevant. Notably, the Appellants are sitting tenants before the advance notice has been registered in this case. They did not sign a lease contract after the advance notice was registered. To what extent does the law expect the sitting tenants to check the register during the lease? Furthermore, in this case, the Respondent only lodged the formal registration after the Court of First Instance issued an enforcement order. Hence, what is at stake is when the concerned party can lodge a formal registration. When the CC is silent on the issues mentioned above, it is expected to see predictable judicial opinions from the SPC to clarify the Chinese law position in this regard.

3.6 Delivery

As explained, the *traditio* system dictates that although a contract creates obligations, transferring a property right requires an additional element, delivery or conveyance. There are two essentials of *traditio*: delivery and the requisite intent. Under Chinese law, the creation or transfer of movable property rights becomes effective upon delivery unless otherwise provided by law.[178] Movable property is delivered by the transfer of

[176] Para. 2 of Article 221 CC.

[177] It should be noted that the applicable law in this case was the Property Law because the CC was enacted later. But Article 20 of the Property Law has almost identical provisions as Article 221 CC.

[178] Article 224 CC.

possession. Therefore, delivery is a statutory publicity method for transferring movable property. Without delivery, the contract cannot pass on the title to the transferee unless the law provides otherwise. Here, the exceptions under Chinese law mainly refer to two instances. First, in respect of a charge over movable property, the charge is created when the underlying contract of charge becomes effective.[179] Therefore, delivery is not required to create a charge over the moveable property. Second, in case of retention of title, the parties may, in a sales contract, agree that the ownership of the goods vests in the seller where the buyer fails to pay the price or perform other obligations.[180] In such a situation, even if the delivery has taken place, and the possession has been transferred from the seller to the buyer, the ownership of the good may not pass to the buyer subject to the contractual agreement between the parties.

Initially, delivery occurs if the movable property is handed over to the transferee. Upon handing over the property, the transferee takes physical possession of it. Handing over the property shows the transferor's and transferee's state of mind. This is called actual delivery (*traditio vera*). Later, the law appreciates that it is sufficient to constitute delivery if the transferee is in such a position to exercise physical control over the property whenever the transferee intends. Because there is less publicity than actual delivery when the movable property is not physically handed over, it is termed "constructive delivery" (*traditio ficta*) to be distinguished from actual delivery.[181]

In most cases, delivery takes the form of physically handing the portable thing to the transferee. Gradually, even the property rights to vessels, aircraft and motor vehicles can be created, transferred and extinguished by delivery.[182] However, given their high values, such a transfer by delivery cannot be alleged against a bona fide third party without registration.[183] Nonetheless, constructive delivery usually occurs when objects that cannot be handled easily are delivered or when it is impractical or unsuitable to deliver them physically. Inspired by Roman law with its civil law tradition, Chinese law has adopted the constructive delivery system comprising three different forms.

179 Article 403 CC. It is notable that such a right of charge cannot be alleged against a bona fide third party without a prior registration.

180 Article 641 CC.

181 Cornelius van der Merwe, *The Law of Things* (Butterworths 1987), pp. 34–38.

182 Article 225 CC.

183 *Ibid.*

First, *traditio brevi manu*, or delivery with the shorthand, occurs when the transferee is already in possession of the property but on a basis other than ownership, for example, as a lessee, a borrower, or on a mandatory basis. The pre-existing possession by the transferee satisfies the requirement of physical control, and only the intention element must be satisfied for ownership to pass. In this situation, the CC provides that the disposition shall become effective when the civil juridical act takes effect.[184] That means that the ownership of the property passes as soon as the parties have the requisite intention to transfer. In essence, such a delivery entails the words of authorisation as evidence of the requisite intention.[185] No further physical handing over is required when a sale contract incorporating the requisite intention to transfer becomes effective.

Second, attornment, or delivery by instruction, is a method of delivery developed in English law and received in Chinese law.[186] This refers to situations when the moveable property to be transferred is in the physical control of a third party who holds it on behalf of the transferor. For example, A wants to transfer her car, which she has left with a car repair garage, to B. Attornment occurs by A instructing the garage to hold the car on B's behalf and the garage and B agree that the former will hold the car on the latter's behalf. In such a situation, delivery is effectuated by attornment because the transferor instructs the third party to hold the movable property no longer on their own behalf but on behalf of the transferee. In practice, delivery by instruction is often used in warehousing contracts. For example, a delivery note is a certificate for collecting the warehoused item. A bearer of the delivery note may assign the right to collect the warehoused item by endorsing and having the depositor sign or stamp the delivery note.[187] The conditions for this form of delivery are: (1) the third party has already held the movable property lawfully before the transfer of ownership; (2) the transferor has a right of vindication against the third party; and (3) there must be a tripartite agreement or meeting of minds of the three interested parties that the holder will subsequently hold the thing on behalf of the transferee and not on behalf

[184] Article 226 CC.

[185] Paul du Pleissis, *Borkowski's Textbook on Roman Law* (6th edn, Oxford University Press 2020), p. 185.

[186] Article 227 CC.

[187] Article 910 CC.

of the transferor. When these conditions are met, ownership passes by attornment instead of handing over the movable property.

Third, *constitutum possessorium*, is recognised explicitly in the CC.[188] *Constitutum possessorium* was used to facilitate leaseback arrangements whereby the vendor became the tenant of the sold property.[189] This form of delivery is, in a certain sense, the reverse of *traditio brevi manu*. The transferor retains physical control of the property to be transferred but acknowledges that the transferee is the owner. *Constitutum possessorium* thus results in the transfer of ownership, although the transferor continues to hold the property. Thus, a transfer is effected primarily based on intention.[190] The party must prove that the following requirements have been fulfilled: (1) the transferor must be the owner and the possessor of the thing at the moment of the transfer; (2) there must be a common intention that the transferor retains possession; and (3) there must be a proven contractual relationship under which the transferor becomes the possessor.

A question arises whether any other constructive delivery method is recognised in Chinese law apart from the three mentioned above. Roman law and comparative law show that other forms of constructive delivery are recognised in other jurisdictions, such as symbolical delivery (*traditio symbolica*) when a document is drawn up recording a property transfer or when keys to a building are handed over.[191] Delivery with the long hand (*traditio longa manu*) is when the moveable property's size, weight or nature makes its physical removal difficult or inconvenient. Examples are bulky things, such as a large quantity of wood, sand or heavy farming machinery. However, one Chinese HPC answered this question negatively, holding that Chinese law does not recognise any constructive delivery form other than the three contained in the legislation.[192] Moving forward, it is not surprising that the SPC or another Chinese court may develop a new form of constructive delivery in view of technological developments.

188 Article 228 CC.
189 Pleissis (n. 184), p. 186.
190 van der Merwe (n. 181).
191 *ibid.*
192 青岛源宏祥纺织有限公司诉港润（聊城）印染有限公司案 [*Qingdao Yuanhongxiang Textile Co Ltd v. Gangrun (Liaocheng) Printing and Dyeing Co Ltd*] a SPC gazetted case accessible at < http://gongbao.court.gov.cn/Details/3cd383841a8014afb01979f91ddb35.html> accessed 10 September 2023.

3.7 Summary

Chinese law distinguishes between the formalities required for transferring ownership of immovables and movables. For immovables, such as real estate in urban areas, land registration is typically mandatory to convey title. However, not all rights concerning immovable property require registration; for example, servitude rights or rural land homestead rights can be created or transferred without formal registration.

Despite significant progress in developing efficient property registries for urban real estate over the past two decades, China still faces challenges in fully documenting and defining individual legal rights to land. The need for a uniform registration system across the nation is critical to facilitate land transactions, use land as collateral for credit, and improve land administration. One of the most pressing issues is the liability arising from errors or negligence by Registrars in performing their duties, underscoring the necessity for ongoing monitoring and enhancement of the registry system.

In the case of movables, title transfer requires delivery, which can be either actual or constructive. Constructive delivery encompasses three forms, all of which emphasise the intention to transfer possession more significantly than the physical act of transfer itself. Disputes in such transfers often involve third parties, and courts must assess the bona fides of all parties involved to determine whose interests take precedence. This approach ensures that the rightful ownership is recognised and upheld in cases of conflicting claims.

4

Co-ownership and Neighbour Relations

4.1 Co-ownership

4.1.1 Categories of Co-ownership and Undivided Share

Co-ownership occurs when two or more individuals or organisations hold concurrent interests in the same property, which can be either movable or immovable.[1] This arrangement typically arises out of the desire for multiple uses of the property and the distribution of risk among the owners. In co-ownership, the property is not physically divided among the co-owners. Rather, each co-owner possesses an undivided share of the entire property. For example, if A and B are co-owners of an apartment, they do not each have a claim to distinct parts of the apartment. Instead, they each hold an undivided interest in the whole property. Similarly, if A and B are co-owners of two bottles of Moutai, a premium Chinese distilled liquor, their ownership does not extend to one specific bottle each; they are jointly entitled to both bottles in undivided shares.

Co-ownership of undivided shares allows multiple parties to own the same asset simultaneously without segregating it into distinct portions.[2] Such ownership can be established through various mechanisms including contracts, partnerships, bequests and marital arrangements, providing flexibility in the management and utilisation of shared property.

Chinese law recognises two distinctive types of co-ownership, namely co-ownership by shares and common ownership.[3] These terminologies are translated from Chinese into English and may cause confusion to some extent for a comparativist audience. For example, English law has a dichotomy between joint tenancy and tenancy in common, and a striking feature of joint tenancy under English law is the right of survivorship,

[1] Article 297 CC.
[2] Liming Wang, *Property Law* (2015), 184.
[3] Article 297 CC.

meaning that upon death, a co-owner's interest falls to the remaining joint owners. Under Chinese law, neither co-ownership by shares nor common ownership operates a right of survivorship. The CC does not deal with the right of survivorship, since it does not contain provisions for the situation when one co-owner dies.

Furthermore, the division between legal and equitable joint tenancy, as found in English law, is absent in Chinese law. Thus, joint tenancy in English law differs dramatically from common ownership in Chinese law. Despite the absence of a right of survivorship, common ownership under Chinese law could arise from certain relatively long-term relationships between the co-owners, such as marriage, family or partnership. Common ownership is regarded as a legal consequence of the relationship. Additionally, common ownership can be terminated where there is a compelling reason to do so or where the basis of the co-ownership ceases to exist. Severance, which is required under English law to convert joint tenancy into tenancy in common, is not necessary to terminate common ownership.

Also, in Scottish law, there are common property and joint property.[4] Still, while employing a similar terminology, common property under Scottish law differs from common ownership under Chinese law because each co-owner of the Scottish common property can dispose of her share at any time. On the contrary, under Chinese law, co-owners under co-ownership by shares can dispose of their share, but not co-owners of common property.

The categorisation of co-ownership under Chinese law is more akin to German law than common law, although differences exist between Chinese and German laws. Under German law, the two types of co-ownership are co-ownership by defined shares (*Miteigentum*), where every owner can deal with her share at her discretion without the consent of other co-owners, and joint ownership (*Gesamthandseigentum*), where the owners have to operate jointly and may not dispose of their share of the property on their own.[5] Despite this conceptual similarity, this

[4] Reinhard Zimmermann, Daniel Visser and Kenneth Reid, 'Co-ownership', in Reinhard Zimmermann, Kenneth Reid and Daniel Visser (eds), *Mixed Legal Systems in Comparative Perspective: Property and Obligations in Scotland and South Africa* (Oxford University Press 2005).

[5] Gerhard Dannemann et al. (eds), *German CC: Bürgerliches Gesetzbuch (BGB): Article-by-article Commentary* (C.H. Beck 2020), p. 1757.

chapter employs direct translations from Chinese to English but with detailed explanations of the features and contents of each type.

Co-ownership by shares refers to a situation where several individuals own a property in common, and each of them, in proportion to her share, owns the property together.[6] Each co-owner may freely dispose of or alienate her share without reference to other co-owners[7] but cannot change the state of the co-owned property without the consent of other co-owners. Other co-owners also have a priority right to acquire the alienated share under the same conditions.[8] Each co-owner may not necessarily be entitled to equal shares. A, B and C can, for example, be the co-owners of an apartment in equal shares, or A can have a 40% share while B has a 35% share and C has a 25 % share. Where the agreement does not exist or is equivocal, the co-owners under co-ownership by shares are entitled to request division at any time.[9] The disposition, major repair or alteration of the nature or use of a co-owned property is determined by a two-thirds majority vote of the co-owners, whose voting rights are proportionate to their share value unless otherwise agreed by the co-owners.[10]

Common ownership is created due to a certain legal relationship, for example, a partnership or a marital or family relationship. The co-owners under common ownership jointly own the immovable or movable property.[11] While the CC is silent on the situation from which common ownership arises, the case law and academic commentaries suggest that common ownership pertains primarily to marital property, family property, property of joint-partnership enterprises[12] and property jointly owned by more than one heir by will or on intestacy.[13] Marital property

6 Article 298 CC.

7 Article 305 CC.

8 *Ibid.*

9 Article 303 CC.

10 Article 301 CC.

11 Article 299 CC.

12 Articles 21 and 22 of the Partnership Enterprise Law, adopted on 23 February 1997 and amended on 27 August 27 2006, provides that: (1) prior to the liquidation of a partnership enterprise, no partner may request for dividing the properties of the partnership enterprise, unless it is otherwise provided for in this Law; and (2) unless it is otherwise provided for in the partnership agreement, when a partner assigns its entire or partial share of the properties of a partnership enterprise, it (he) shall acquire the unanimous consent of all other partners.

13 Huixing Liang [梁慧星] and Huabin Chen [陈华彬], *Property Law* [《物权法（第7版）》], (7th edition, Law Press China 2020), p. 221; Jia'an Liu [刘家安], *Property Law* [《物权法论》] (Chinese University of Political Science and Law Press 2009), p. 143.

is held under common ownership in law, as the married couple is considered one entity.[14] However, these rules can be modified by pre-nuptial agreements and marriage agreements.[15] Therefore, marital property may be subject to customised contracts and mandatory property rules. Family property can also be regarded as common property where all family members jointly invest in and manage the property. Family property is implicitly recognised as common property in Articles 308 and 1153 of the CC.[16]

There are some striking differences between co-ownership by shares and common ownership. First, under co-ownership by shares, each co-owner acquires a separate title to a separate share of the co-owned property, and the shares are separate in a legal but not physical sense. No co-owner is entitled to appropriate for her use of a specific part of the common property. In the case of common ownership, each co-owner does not have a separate share in the legal sense of the property but only a single title to the property jointly.

Second, the CC stipulates that under common ownership, any attempt to conduct a major repair or change the use or nature of a co-owned property and any attempt to dispose of a co-owned property without the permission of all co-owners is invalid unless there is an agreement between co-owners that provides otherwise.[17] In other words, absent an agreement, the default position for such a decision-making mechanism is consensus in the case of common ownership. A unilateral act of disposal by a co-owner is not allowed, as she does not have a separate share. However, concerning co-ownership by shares, the two-thirds majority rule will apply if there is no agreement between the co-owners.[18] This is because, in respect of co-ownership by shares, each co-owner can dispose of her separate share as she pleases.

[14] Article 1062 CC.

[15] Article 1065 CC.

[16] Article 308 CC: Where the co-owners fail to agree or the agreement is equivocal on whether the co-ownership is held under co-ownership by shares or common ownership, the co-ownership is deemed to be co-ownership by shares unless the co-owners have family relations or other similar relations.

Article 1153 CC: ... in respect of an estate forming part of the family common property, in the course of partitioning the estate, property owned by others shall be separated out in advance.

[17] Article 301 CC.

[18] *Ibid.*

Third, co-owners under common ownership are less individualistic than co-ownership by shares because they can only request division where there is a compelling reason or where the basis of the co-ownership ceases to exist.[19] On the contrary, co-owners under co-ownership by shares can ask for division or sell their share at any time. Furthermore, under common ownership, other co-owners do not have a right of priority when a co-owner intends to transfer her share.

When the co-owners fail to reach an agreement, or the agreement is equivocal on whether the co-ownership is held under co-ownership by shares or common ownership, the law presumes the property to be held under co-ownership by shares unless the co-owners are related by family relationship or other similar relationships.[20] Furthermore, each co-owner's share is determined by the act creating the co-ownership. When the share ownership ratio is not specified or unclear, there is a presumption of equality of shares.[21] It is recognised that there may be ways of allocating unequal shares in the property, such as by agreement, by unequal contribution to the property's purchase price, and by an unequal allocation of management functions. All the co-ownership rules will be extended to a situation where two or more organisations or individuals jointly own a usufructuary right or security right over a property.[22]

4.1.2 Rights and Obligations of Co-owners

The maxim *communio est mater rixarum* – co-ownership is the mother of disputes – is well known for a reason. Co-ownership entails cooperation and coordination among the co-owners. Every co-owner must be consulted when a legal act is proposed. No co-owner is entitled to change or improve the co-owned property independently. If the consent of a co-owner is not obtained, he can veto any legal act regarding the co-owned property. Nonetheless, a co-owner can exercise extensive control over her undivided share. Every co-owner deals with her share as she pleases. She may demand that the co-ownership relationship be terminated and that the object of co-ownership be physically divided between them. This internal tension of co-ownership may cause some collective

[19] Article 303 CC.
[20] Article 308 CC.
[21] Article 309 CC.
[22] Article 310 CC.

decision-making deadlocks. Therefore, it is apposite to understand the respective rights and obligations of the co-owners under each type of co-ownership.

A unanimity rule is required to manage property under common ownership, except for a co-owner's agreement.[23] In contrast, the CC provides for a two-thirds majority rule for the disposition or alternations and repairs of property under co-ownership by shares.[24] Such a majority decision is binding upon all co-owners. This two-thirds majority rule may be sensible to facilitate some reasonable arrangements about the use of property without being obstructed or gridlocked by a unanimity rule. However, such a one-size-fits-all approach for all decisions on the administration and management of the property, including disposition, major repairs, alterations and use, may invite questions.

A nuanced approach should be adopted by differentiating the property's disposition from its use, alterations or major repairs. Supposedly, the exclusivity of property demands assigning every property to an identifiable owner, who has the right to manage the property to exclude others. Indeed, each co-owner has a right to manage the property and veto a management decision.[25] Thus, the unanimity rule seems reasonable for fundamental matters such as major repairs and sales. Any decision which would substantially (materially) affect the property should be approved unanimously by all co-owners.

Nonetheless, when it comes to the use of property, which is less important than disposition, alterations or repairs, a two-thirds majority rule seems reasonable to avoid a deadlock. Suppose co-owners fail to reach an agreement on matters of disposition or alterations. In that case, they may seek a judicial order or terminate the co-ownership by selling *pro indiviso* shares. It is unreasonable for the minority co-owners (up to one-third share) to bear the proportional costs of alterations, repairs or leases when they object. In the case of condominium management, the CC distinguishes very important matters requiring a three-quarters majority from less important matters that fall under the two-thirds majority rule.[26] If the same logic follows, one may wonder why such a distinction between different situations regarding co-ownership is not provided.

[23] Article 301 CC.
[24] *Ibid.*
[25] Article 300 CC.
[26] Article 278 CC.

Nonetheless, the Chinese law position is that under co-ownership by shares, the co-owned property can be disposed of if the majority of co-owners so decide. A pressing issue is whether a majority of co-owners can decide to lease the property. This is not allowed in other jurisdictions, such as Scotland and South Africa, as leasing is considered an alienation. It must be done through the unanimity rule. Under the Chinese law's one-size-fits-all approach, the answer appears affirmative, whether leasing is taken as use or disposition.

Another related issue is whether there should be a departure from the unanimity or two-thirds majority rule in exceptional circumstances. In German law, each co-owner can unilaterally take any action necessary to maintain the co-owned object (*Erhaltungsmaßnahmen*) to avoid a decrease in the value of the common asset, which would result in a devaluation of the share of the acting co-owner.[27] There is no such exception provided in the Chinese CC. Perhaps it is expected to have such a provision in a management agreement among the co-owners to ease the rigidity of the unanimity or two-thirds majority rule. However, when such an agreement is lacking, this statutory provision seems necessary to avoid any unnecessary and acrimonious confrontation between the co-owners before the Chinese courts. This is because all co-owners should compensate for the costs reasonably incurred by the co-owner, taking actions to prevent the property value depreciation.

When a co-owner of the property transfers her share, other co-owners have a priority right to purchase the alienated share, akin to the right of first refusal under common law.[28] To ensure a proper exercise of such a right of first refusal, the co-owner alienating her share should promptly notify the other co-owners of the transfer condition, and the other co-owners shall exercise the right of first refusal within a reasonable period.[29] Where two or more co-owners exercise such a right of first refusal, they need to negotiate to determine their respective purchase proportions; where no agreement is reached, they exercise such right by reference to the proportion of their respective existing shares at the time of transfer.[30] It is worth noting that such a right of first refusal only applies in co-ownership by shares.

[27] Article 744 of the German CC. See also G. Dannemann et al., BGB: Article-by-article Commentary, p. 1479.

[28] Article 305 CC.

[29] Article 306 CC.

[30] *Ibid.*

Two related questions arise. First, under Chinese law, a sitting lessee has a right of first refusal when the lessor sells property subject to a lease.[31] Thus, when a co-owned apartment under a lease is to be sold, both the sitting lessee and the co-owner may claim a right of first refusal. Who has priority? The co-owner's right of first refusal derives from co-ownership, which is a property right. The lessee's right of first refusal derives from a lease contract, that is, a contractual right or an obligatory right. Under Chinese law, different from some common law jurisdictions, the lease is not regarded as a property right. Still, a contractual right,[32] a contract with proprietary effect, or a "propertised contract" in case of a sale does not break a lease.[33] According to the principles of publicity and *numerus clausus* in the CC, a property right takes precedence over a creditor's right. Therefore, the Chinese law position is that a co-owner's first refusal is superior to a lessee's first refusal.[34]

Second, if the co-owners decide unanimously to lease the property, can a co-owner enjoy a right of first refusal to lease the property if she is prepared to pay the rent required? The CC is silent on whether such a priority right to buy can be extended to a priority right to lease. On the one hand, in the CC, the notion of the right of first refusal has been confined to a preferential right to buy. In other words, the co-owner's priority right to lease was not specified as an exercisable statutory right. On the other hand, the CC provides that upon the expiry of the lease term, the lessee has a right of first refusal to renew the lease.[35] If the sitting lessee enjoys a priority right to lease as an obligation right holder,

[31] Article 726 CC.

[32] It is noteworthy that lease is not included either in the Property Law 2007 or the Property Book CC. Article 706 CC, which is in the Contract Book, provides that the validity of a lease contract is unaffected by the parties' failure to adhere to the registration or filing formalities. In its contractual aspect, lease deals primarily with the relations between the lessor and the lessee. However, such a lease contract is subject to the rules contained Articles 405 and 525 CC, namely the lease will not be affected by the sale or mortgage of the property. This gives a lease a somewhat proprietary effect. On the contrary, under English law, leasehold estate, or the term of years absolute, has been formerly marked out as a property interest in s 1(1) (b) of the Law of Property Act 1925.

[33] Yun-chien Chang and Henry E. Smith, 'An Economic Analysis of Civil versus Common Law Property' (2012) 88 *Notre Dame Law Review* 1, arguing that the 'a sale does not break a lease' doctrine only minimally propertises the lease contract.

[34] *Ibid.* See also Chinese CC Legislation Research Group led by Huixing Liang, *The Draft CC of the People's Republic of China* (Brill 2010), p. 200; Liming Wang [王利明], *Research on Contract Law* [《合同法研究》] (2nd edn, China Renmin University Press 2012), vol. III, p. 327.

[35] Article 734 CC.

why should a co-owner, as a property right holder, not be entitled to a priority right to lease? From a comparative perspective, the House of Lords (now the Supreme Court of the United Kingdom) held in *Clydesdale Bank plc v Davidson* that co-owners are not allowed to lease the property to one co-owner because the same co-owner cannot be both the debtor and the creditor in the same obligation.[36] This may seem a fairly far-fetched logic for a lawyer from a civil law background. Even in a mixed jurisdiction such as South Africa, it is permissible for the co-owned property to be leased to one of the co-owners.[37] It is a lease that is concluded between all co-owners acting together and a party who is a co-owner lessee. Hence, under Chinese law, what is certain is that it is permissible for co-owners to lease the property to one of the co-owners. Whether a co-owner has a preferential right to be a lessee remains unsettled until the judiciary provides clear guidance.

While the CC does not address the unreasonable use of the property by one or more co-owners, it seems axiomatic that the other co-owners can prevent unreasonable use of the property by demanding some injunctive relief.[38] No co-owner can enrich herself at the cost of her fellow co-owners by exploiting the property alone. A co-owner who negligently or intentionally violates the right to use one or more of her fellow co-owners is also liable for damages.[39]

The fruits and profits of the co-owned property should be divided amongst co-owners. Each co-owner has a claim to the fruits and other benefits in proportion to her share in the property unless otherwise agreed upon. Thus, co-owners who have leased a co-owned apartment become co-owners of the rent once due. Likewise, every co-owner is obliged to contribute proportionally to the necessary expenses for property management. The co-owners can have an agreement on the management expenses or other costs. Without such an agreement or when the agreement is equivocal, the co-owners bear the expenses according to the proportion of their shares under co-ownership by shares, or all co-owners bear the expenses jointly under common ownership.[40]

[36] *Clydesdale Bank plc v Davidson* (1998) SLT 522.

[37] Cornelius van der Merwe, 'Things' (2002) 27 *The Law of South Africa*, para. 408.

[38] Article 187 CC.

[39] *Ibid.*

[40] Article 302 CC.

4.1.3 Remedies

What remedies are available to a co-owner who was not consulted for any unauthorised act by other co-owners? While the CC is silent on the remedies, Chinese courts have developed a body of case law to fill the gap. First, the co-owner who objects may revoke the contract when another co-owner assigns its share without consulting all co-owners. In *Jianggan District People's Government, Hangzhou, Zhejiang v. Ren Yueying and others,*[41] the house at issue has been decided by the Court of First Instance to be co-owned by the five family members, each of whom has been allotted a one-fifth share. In this case, one co-owner unilaterally concluded an expropriation agreement with the defendant without notifying the other co-owners and received compensation of RMB 1,890,800. Therefore, the plaintiffs and other co-owners initiated a court proceeding requesting to revoke the expropriation agreement. The Court of First Instance ruled in favour of the plaintiffs by revoking the agreement. The defendant appealed. The appellant court, the Zhejiang HPC, reasoned:

> The appellant Jianggan District Government knew the house involved in this case was co-owned. However, when its negotiation with other co-owners failed many times, the appellant signed a compensation agreement and a supplementary agreement with one co-owner only. This was malicious and, therefore, administrative malpractice. At the same time, the co-owner knew that he had no right to dispose of the co-owned house alone but still signed an agreement with the appellant, harming the rights and interests of others. Therefore, the conduct of the contracting parties constituted malicious collusion and harmed the interests of the other co-owners. The agreement should thus be revoked and held invalid.[42]

In appropriate circumstances, a claim for damages can also be instituted. Before the CC, a SPC interpretation provided that "if some co-owners dispose of the co-owned property without authorisation, the disposition is generally invalid. However, suppose a third party obtains the property in good faith for value. In that case, the legitimate rights and interests of the third party shall be protected, and the loss of other co-owners shall be compensated by the person who disposes of the co-owned property

[41] 杭州市江干区人民政府诉任月英、邹飞等 [*Jianggan District People's Government, Hangzhou, Zhejiang v. Ren Yueying and others*] (2020) 浙行终821号 [(2020) Zhe Xing Zhong No. 821].

[42] *Ibid.*

without authorisation."[43] While this SPC judicial document has been repealed with the introduction of the CC, the SPC has developed a corpus of case law under its guidance. Therefore, if the co-owned property has not been transferred to a bona fide third-party purchaser for value, the dealing will be invalid. However, after the transfer to the bona fide third party, the other co-owners can seek compensation from the co-owner who committed the unauthorised division.[44]

Apart from damages, the court has wide discretion to remove building structures erected without other co-owners' consent.[45] However, suppose the co-owners who were not consulted acquiesce to the unauthorised conduct of their fellow co-owners. In that case, the court will presumably refuse to interfere on estoppel.[46] In certain instances, therefore, each co-owner can, without the cooperation or consent of her fellow co-owners, institute a claim for the recovery of the common property (*rei vindicatio*), defend a claim by a third party in connection with the common property, incur necessary (and useful) expenses in connection with the maintenance of the common property and apply for an interdict to ward off damage to the common property.

4.1.4 The Effect of Contract on Co-ownership

As shown in the preceding sections, the institution of co-ownership under Chinese law has a strong contractual flavour – that is, party autonomy in managing and administering the co-owned property. For example, co-owners can make an agreement on how the co-owners participate in the management of the co-owned property,[47] how the voting procedure is designed to pass a resolution,[48] how the co-owners bear the management expenses, charges and costs,[49] how the property

[43] Article 89 of the Opinions of the SPC on Several Issues Concerning the Implementation of the General Principles of the Civil Law of the People's Republic of China (for Trial Implementation) issued by the SPC in January 1988. Note, this SPC judicial document has been repealed with the introduction of the CC, but a corpus of case law has been developed under its guidance.

[44] Article 303 CC.

[45] 梁安平诉梁安均等[*Liang Anping v. Liang Anjun and Another*] (2015)宜民终字第485号 [(2015) Yi Min Zhong No. 485].

[46] Article 152 CC.

[47] Article 300 CC.

[48] Article 301 CC.

[49] Article 302 CC.

is divided and partitioned,[50] how the right of first refusal is to be exercised,[51] how the respective shares of the co-owners are defined[52] and how to determine whether it is co-ownership by shares or common ownership.[53] In addition, the co-owners may agree to prohibit the division of co-ownership and disallow any co-owner to request the termination of co-ownership at any time.[54] All co-owner agreements are binding from creation to termination and can vary the statutory default position.

To a large extent, property is an autonomy-enhancing institution, and one of the major legal tools is to secure and facilitate stakeholders' fundamental right to self-determination.[55] Rawls characterised "property-owning democracy" as a social system that aims to ensure the widespread distribution of property ownership, allowing citizens to engage in cooperative relationships marked by equality and freedom.[56] Autonomy is also dependent upon both material conditions and a sufficiently heterogeneous inventory of alternatives, and self-determination provides opportunities for people to alter and redesign their plans.[57] The contractualisation of co-ownership has important normative implications. Property is best understood as a legal institution that creates and protects the value inherent in the stable ownership of assets.[58] Parties can change the rules governing co-ownership by way of agreement. For example, co-owners can agree to the exclusive use of the entire property by one or more but not all co-owners. Also, co-owners can agree not to call for division within a certain time. Despite being sketchy, it is commendable that, influenced and compromised by the socialist ideology, the Chinese CC has taken this autonomy-enhancing approach to design co-ownership rules.

Nonetheless, it is worth noting that while the Chinese law of co-ownership is, to a large extent, oriented by the principle of freedom of

[50] Article 304 CC.
[51] Article 306 CC.
[52] Article 309 CC.
[53] Article 308 CC.
[54] Article 303 CC.
[55] Hanoch Dagan, *A Liberal Theory of Property* (Cambridge University Press 2021).
[56] John Rawls, *Justice as Fairness: A Restatement* (Harvard University Press 2001), pp. 111–18.
[57] Joseph Raz, *The Morality of Freedom* (Clarendon Press 1986), p. 369.
[58] Abrham Bell and Gideon Parchomovsky, 'A Theory of Property' (2005) 90 *Cornell Law Review* 531.

contract, certain proprietary features cannot be altered by contract. A prime example is where co-owners agree not to partition the property; such an agreement may be valid but is subject to an exception where co-owners have compelling reasons for partition.[59] In addition, the co-owners cannot contract out the right of first refusal exercisable when a co-owner transfers her share.[60]

4.1.5 Legal Relationship between Co-owners and Relation to Third Parties

All co-owners will bear any debts incurred by co-owners vis-à-vis a third party during the co-ownership. In the eye of a third party, Article 307 presumes a "joint and several liabilities of the co-owners for the debt, whether under co-ownership by shares or common ownership."[61] However, exceptions may arise where the third-party creditor knew that co-owners agreed to proportional liability. The implications are: (1) where it is common ownership, all co-owners bear joint and several liabilities for the joint debts, regardless of whether the co-owner is personally liable to the relevant third party; and (2) where there is an agreement on proportional liability among the co-owners, the law still presumes the joint and several liabilities unless the relevant third party was aware of the pre-existing proportional liability agreement among the co-owners. The co-owners can enjoy the claims as joint and several creditors in the case of a creditor's right. That means that where a third party has damaged the property, any co-owner alone can claim the full compensation arising from such a tort liability.

Internally, in the absence of an agreement, co-owners under co-ownership by shares enjoy the rights and bear the liabilities according to the proportion of their shares. Co-owners under common ownership shall jointly enjoy the creditor's rights and bear the liabilities.[62] For example, when a co-owner claims damages against a tortfeasor and receives the compensation, she should distribute the compensation to other co-owners accordingly. Likewise, suppose any co-owner under co-ownership by shares has first paid the joint debts alone or above her share concerning the co-owned property. The co-owner is entitled

[59] Article 303 CC.
[60] L. Wang, *Property Law*, 2015, p. 193.
[61] Article 307 CC.
[62] *Ibid.*

to recover from her fellow co-owners unless otherwise agreed by the co-owners.[63]

Surprisingly, Chinese law does not provide rules about the co-owner's successor in title. In any event, when any of the co-owners transfers her share during co-ownership, it is necessary to provide that all successors in title, such as transferees or mortgagees, will be bound by all pre-existing agreements and management decisions concerning the use of the property before the transfer if they have such knowledge. Absent such a provision, under the principle of privity of contract, agreements concluded and management decisions on the use of the property will only bind the co-owners at the time when such agreements or management decisions were reached. Consequently, the successors in title of any co-owner will not be bound by such pre-existing agreements or management decisions to which the relevant transferor was subjected. To avoid confusion, it is suggested that such a provision be introduced as legislative or SPC interpretation.

4.1.6 *Termination and Division*

No co-owner is bound to remain as a co-owner forever against her will. In the absence of an agreement to the contrary, any co-owner may demand a division of the co-owned property at any time to terminate the co-ownership and realise her share.[64] Before any co-owner claims division, the co-owners must first attempt to agree on the terms of the division. Once such an agreement is reached either expressly or tacitly, the agreement is binding on the parties and on third parties who have notice of it. If any co-owner(s) refuse to consent to a division, it is open to the demanding owner to apply for an order to resolve the matter as the court thinks fit. This can be done by division in kind (physical division) or, where it is impossible, by sale, to divide the proceeds (division by sale).

Nonetheless, culture has bearings on how the Chinese courts restrict the right to request division of co-ownership by a co-owner. Culture influences the perceptions of fairness, reasonableness and justice.[65]

[63] *Ibid.*

[64] Under co-ownership by shares, any co-owner may terminate the co-ownership by division at any time. Nonetheless, under common ownership, the co-owner cannot enjoy the same degree of autonomy to request division at any time. However, it is still permissible for them to request division in certain circumstances. See Article 303 CC.

[65] Zihan Niu and Gijs Van Dijck, 'The Impact of Culture on Chinese Judges' Decision-Making in Contractual Damages Cases' (2019) 6 *Asian Journal of Law and Society* 359.

In *Liu Keyu v. Liu Maoyong and Zhou Zhongrong*,[66] the claimant is the only daughter of the defendants, the parents. It is common for Chinese parents to purchase a house for their child's marriage out of their pockets as a gift. In this case, the parents paid the entire purchase price of an apartment. There was a written agreement between the parties that the daughter has a 90 per cent share of the apartment and each parent has a 5 per cent share. However, the apartment was registered under the joint names of the parents and the daughter without specifying the respective shares in the agreement. The daughter claims to terminate the co-ownership by asking the parents to transfer the 10 per cent share to her. As such, the daughter provides a letter of undertaking that states that:

> The parents agree to transfer 10% of the property rights to the only daughter. The daughter promised that she would not sell the apartment and that the parents would live in it until they moved to Suzhou after retirement and lived with the daughter until their death.

The court faces two issues. First, is this a co-ownership by shares or common ownership held by family members? Second, will the court entertain the request made by the daughter to terminate the co-ownership? The Court of First Instance ruled that the apartment was held under co-ownership by shares. Still, the daughter cannot divide the co-ownership, as she is obliged to support her parents, and she promised so in the letter of undertaking. The appeal court, however, ascertained the co-ownership as common ownership held by family members. When the case was submitted for retrial, the retrial court issued the final ruling that restored the first instance court ruling. It is beyond doubt that the co-ownership in this particular case should be co-ownership by shares. There are two defects in the second instance court's ruling. First, it disregards the agreement between the parties that the daughter has a 90 per cent share and the parents hold a 10 per cent share. Second, even though there is a co-ownership among the family members, such as parents and their daughter, in this case the common ownership can only be found on the condition that all of them live together. In this case, the daughter lives in Suzhou, a different city from where the parents live. More to the point, the retrial court stressed in its reasoning that while the daughter, as a co-owner, enjoys a right to request division of co-ownership, the exercise of such right is limited by Article 7 of the

[66] 刘柯妤诉刘茂勇、周忠容 (2015) [*Liu Keyu v. Liu Maoyong and Zhou Zhongrong* (2015)] 渝五中法民再终字第00043号 [Yu Wu Zhong Fa Min Zai Zhong No. 00043].

Property Law 2007, which provides that in acquiring or exercising a real right, one shall abide by the law, respect social morals and may not damage the public interests or the legitimate interests of any other person.[67] As the daughter is obliged to support the ageing parents and has indeed promised so in writing, such a cultural virtue should be upheld. As such, the daughter cannot divide the apartment, and the parents can continue living there.[68] Understanding the cultural context helps to determine the nature of the whole transaction.

As co-ownership is the mother of discord, the law should facilitate the termination and division of co-ownership at the policy level. This protects the co-owner's interest and promotes the better use of the property. The division rule is self-initiative oriented. Where co-owners have contracted not to divide the co-owned property, such agreement shall prevail, except where co-owners have compelling reasons for division.[69] Chinese law does not distinguish between an agreement barring a division for a period and one barring a division in perpetuity. In other words, it is permissible for an agreement to restrict division permanently. The grounds to override such a pre-existing agreement are (1) compelling reasons for division and (2) when the basis of co-ownership ceases to exist.[70] The key issue remains: What amounts to a compelling reason, or when does the basis of the co-ownership cease to exist? The following circumstances are considered compelling reasons: (1) the co-owners go bankrupt[71]; (2) the court takes judicial enforcement measures against the co-owned property[72]; (3) a spouse conceals, transfers, sells, damages, squanders the community property or forges a community obligation, or commits any other conduct that seriously harms the interests of the

[67] It is notable that Article 7 of the Property Law 2007 was not retained in the Property Book CC. Rather, it has been retained in the first Book, the general Provisions of Civil Law, in Article 8 CC. It reads that civil subjects shall not carry out civil activities in violation of law, nor contrary to the public order and good morals.

[68] This case has been selected into the gazetted case report by the SPC.

[69] Article 303 CC.

[70] *Ibid.*

[71] 曛川公达信律师事务所、何开发等与四川皇嘉农业集团有限公司[*Xunchuan Gongdaxin Law Firm and He Kaifa v. Sichuan Huangjia Agricultural Group Co., Ltd*] (2019)川0781民初2658号 [(2019) Chuan 0781 Min Chu No. 2658].

[72] 绻传颂诉高玉珊(2022) [*Quan Chuansong v. Gao Yushan*] (2022)] 豫05民终488号 [(2022) Yu 05 Min Zhong No.488]; SPC Property Law Research Group [最高人民法院物权法研究小组], *The Interpretation and Application of the Articles of 'the Property Law of the People's Republic of China'*[《<中华人民共和国物权法>条文理解与适用》] (People's Court Press 2007), p. 310.

community property[73]; and (4) a person for whom a spouse has a legal duty to support needs to be treated for a serious illness, while the other spouse refuses to pay related medical expenses.[74] The following situations are where courts usually hold that "the basis of the co-ownership ceases to exist": (1) the dissolution of the partnership,[75] (2) divorce,[76] and (3) the court annuls the marriage.[77] Chinese law provides that compensation shall be made if such division causes damage to other co-owners.

Co-owners may determine the means of partition by agreement. Without such agreement, the property can be partitioned if the property is capable of being partitioned and the partition will not cause depreciation in property value.[78] For example, suppose there is more than one object held jointly. In that case, the joint objects can be divided into identical parts corresponding to the co-owners' shares without reducing the objects' value. Under Chinese law, partition in kind is a default means to divide a co-owned property. However, it is subject to the following conditions. First, it must be possible to physically or legally divide the co-owned property into several parts. Second, the division of the co-owned property must be possible in such a manner as to ensure that each former co-owner will receive a new object reflecting her share in co-ownership. Third, a division may not be made if it destroys values.[79]

Where it is difficult to partition the property or where the partitioning thereof will cause depreciation in property value, the payment obtained from the sale shall be divided. Under such a circumstance, partition in kind is not permissible because such division is impossible or inappropriate for legal or physical reasons. Therefore, the co-owned property will be sold, and the sale proceeds will be distributed among the co-owners in proportion to their respective shares. The sale can be done by auction. Alternatively, all the co-owners may agree to transfer and release their interest to one of the co-owners at the agreed price. In this regard, courts have a wide discretion to effect an equitable partition amongst the co-owners. The court typically strives to physically

73 Article 1066(1) CC.

74 Article 1066(2) CC.

75 Article 74 of the SPC Interpretation (I) on the Application of the Marriage and Family Book of the Civil Code.

76 上诉人涂婷婷与林添珠等人案(2020) [*Tu Tingting (the Appellant) v. Lin Tianzhu and Another*, (2020)] 闽05民终3145号 [(2020) Min 05 Min Zhong No. 3145].

77 Article 1053 CC.

78 Para. 1 of Article 304 CC.

79 L. Wang, *Property Law*, 2015, p. 205.

divide the property among the co-owners based on the property's value and each co-owner's share.[80] If such a division is impractical or economically unfeasible, the court may, for example, allocate the property to one co-owner and instruct them to compensate the other co-owners. This form of division typically occurs in the case of indivisible properties, such as an apartment. In appropriate circumstances, the property will be sold through a public auction and the proceeds distributed among the co-owners.

Where the partitioned property acquired by a co-owner is defective, the other co-owners share the losses.[81] Any costs should be first deducted from the proceeds and jointly borne by all the co-owners before the proceeds are distributed. All expenses for necessary improvements, disproportionate gathering of fruits, and losses incurred due to the fault of a co-owner are offset against each other. In practice, when one of the heirs claims to enjoy the ownership of the house directly and to pay compensation to other heirs, the Chinese court will generally require the plaintiff to pay the compensation directly to the court or provide certain guarantees, such as escrow, to balance the rights of all parties in a fair and just manner. After the respective shares are confirmed, if the parties cannot agree on the actual division of the house, a separate lawsuit may be filed for the division of the common property.

4.2. Neighbour Relations

4.2.1. Concept

Property ownership incentivises the owners' efficient use of property and creates wealth. However, a territorial model may create barriers to access for neighbours – the stronger the owner sovereignty culture, the less potential for the property to be optimally used.[82] In modern society, where the resources are finite, land has been gradually developed to build accommodation for a growing population. Consequently, given the population density in China, one should not be surprised by the relatively high risk of disputes between neighbours. The recent quarantine and

[80] Shaokun Fang [房绍坤], 'On the Method and Effectiveness of the Judgment for the Division of Co-owned Property' [《论共有物裁判分割的方法与效力》] (2015) 11 *Shandong Social Sciences* [《山东社会科学》] 58.

[81] Article 303 CC.

[82] Thomas W. Merrill and Henry E. Smith. *The Oxford Introductions to US Law: Property* (Oxford University Press 2010), p. 183.

lockdown periods due to the COVID-19 pandemic in particular have seen a remarkable rise in neighbourhood disputes.[83]

Neighbour relation is also known as neighbour right exercisable by adjacent landowners or real rights holders. The Chinese CC employs a notion of "the holder of a real right," denoting that the scope of application is not limited to owners. A neighbour includes anyone who exercises an attribute of ownership and can be a natural or legal person. Therefore, not only an owner but also an occupier of land in whom the landowner's right is vested, such as a tenant, a usufructuary, a farmer with the agricultural land contractual management right, or a holder of an urban construction right, may invoke neighbour relation rules to assert their interests. In *Xinjiang Uygur Autonomous Region Construction Timber Processing Plant v. China Democratic League Xinjiang Industrial Development Corporation*,[84] it has been held by the SPC that the right holders include not only real estate owners but also usufruct holders, including lessees. The lessor built a building near the lessee's rented house, which affects the sunlight and ventilation of the lessee's rented house. The court ruled in favour of the lessee on the ground of an infringement of neighbour rights.[85]

Right holders of neighbouring immovable properties handle their relationships according to the principles of facilitating production and convenient living, solidarity and mutual assistance, as well as fairness and reasonableness.[86] Neighbour relation rules straddle the law of tort and the law of property. If a neighbour suffers from an infringement of her rights or interests, tort law applies; if a neighbour's use and enjoyment of her land are impaired, proprietary remedies, such as *actio negatoria*, removing obstacles and eliminating danger, are applicable.[87] While the rules governing neighbour relations are principled and general, it is a statutory limitation on the interests of individual owners, which parties cannot contract out. In *Tu Fuyan v. Wang Fuyan*, there was a dispute

[83] Lei Chen 'Self-governing Organizations and Culture: Addressing Condominium Law Developments in China' (2024) 16 (1) *Journal of Property, Planning and Environmental Law* 20–35.

[84] 新疆维吾尔自治区建筑木材加工总厂与中国民主同盟新疆实业发展总公司案 (2000) [*Xinjiang Uygur Autonomous Region Construction Timber Processing Plant v. China Democratic League Xinjiang Industrial Development Corporation* (2000)] 民终字第115号 [(2000) SPC Min Zhong Zi No. 115].

[85] *Ibid.*

[86] Article 288 CC.

[87] Article 179 CC.

concerning whether the plaintiff could enjoy the right of passage from a sale contract between his late father as a buyer and the seller.[88] The defendant, who blocked the passage, now owns the seller's land. The defendant argued that due to the change in road planning, the original right of passage is of no use, as it does not link to any public way. The plaintiff could still access the public road through another available path. Therefore, the defendant is entitled to block the passage in question, which became an exclusive use area owned by the defendant. Having examined the evidence submitted by both parties, the Yuyao Court ruled in favour of the defendant. It held that the parties could not contract out the right of passage through the sale contract. Even if the two parties agree on the right of passage in the sales contract, it is not binding on a third party. The source of the right of passage the buyer enjoys is based on the neighbour relationship, not the sales contract.[89] When the situation changes, and the buyer no longer meets the requirements of the neighbour relationship, the third party may refuse the buyer's request for passage, and the buyer has no right to bind the third party with the agreement on the right of passage in the sales contract. The appellate court upheld this ruling.

Since the neighbour relation rules are extensions or limitations on the ownership of adjacent landowners, the rules pass with the land in the event of an owner change. The responsibility for infringing the neighbour relation rights shall be on the author of the nuisance when the infringement occurred. Consequently, the landowner or occupier who caused the nuisance or a person who has succeeded to the ownership of the land on which a nuisance exists is liable.[90] A landlord is not liable for nuisances created by his tenant unless he has expressly or impliedly authorised the nuisance. If the non-continuous damage was caused before the change of the owner, the previous owner is liable to compensate for the damage.[91]

While the CC does not spell out the conditions explicitly, the case law indicates that a successful claim on neighbour relations requires the

[88] 屠福炎诉王义炎案 [*Tu Fuyan v Wang Yiyan*] (2013) 3《最高人民法院公报》[The SPC Gazette] <http://gongbao.court.gov.cn/Details/9e1b67636e6957ad92d13ff880308f.html?sw=%e7%9b%b8%e9%82%bb%e9%80%9a%e8%a1%8c%e6%9d%83> accessed on 5 September 2023.

[89] Article 87 of the Property Law; now Article 291 CC.

[90] SPC Property Law Research Group (n. 72), p. 272.

[91] 辽宁英巍良种猪专业合作社诉辽宁省高等级公路建设局案 [*Liaoning Yingwei Fine Breed Pig Professional Cooperative v. Liaoning Provincial High-grade Highway Construction Bureau*] (2013)] 民一终字第83号 [(2013) SPC Min Yi Zhong No. 83].

following conditions to be met. First, a neighbour relation must be identified between the disputing parties. The land/building of the complaining neighbour does not need to be physically adjacent to the property of the alleged wrongdoing neighbour.[92] Nevertheless, certain geographical proximity is needed. Secondly, the conduct causes annoyance, discomfort or inconvenience greater than what a normal person can be expected to endure. Tolerance for an annoyance to a certain acceptable level is expected from a neighbour. Whether a particular land use can be considered normal and acceptable is determined by the prevailing view in a community. Thirdly, the annoyance must result from an omission, conduct or act attributable to the neighbour.

4.2.2 Content

As a general rule, a holder of a real right can expect the adjacent land to provide lateral support necessary to maintain its land in a condition of stability and safety as if it were in its natural state. Thus, an owner's power to excavate the soil of her land, construct a building, or lay underground cables is limited by her duty of lateral support for the adjacent land.[93] The rationale for the duty of lateral support is not a servitude between neighbours but an obligation inherent in land ownership. A landowner who uses her land to breach her duty of lateral support, such as by causing gradual soil erosion, is liable for damages arising from the activity.[94] Similarly, when a party needs to cross over or through the neighbouring property for water, drainage, ventilation, utility services and laying electricity cable,[95] Chinese law recognises and protects the right to use neighbouring land in such a manner as to avoid causing damage to the right holder of the neighbouring immovable property.[96]

Another popular source of dispute centres on solid wastes or atmospheric discharge pollutants, water pollutants, soil pollutants, noise, light

[92] The Legal Affairs Committee of the Standing Committee of the National People's Congress (ed), *The Interpretation of the Property Law of the People's Republic of China* (Law Press 2007), p. 195.

[93] Article 295 CC.

[94] 新华日报社诉南京华厦视野有限公司案 [*Xinhua News Agency v. Nanjing Huaxia Ltd*] (1996) 47《最高人民法院公报》 [(The SPC *Gazette*] <http://gongbao.court.gov.cn/Details/74005c35afb4548e624e195230aa6b.html> accessed on 22 January 2024.

[95] Article 292 CC.

[96] Article 296 CC.

and electromagnetic radiation. Thus, noises emanating from an elevator in a high-rise building,[97] engineering works for central heating systems[98] and building operations[99] have constituted an actionable nuisance. Such disputes are closely linked with environmental protection lawsuits,[100] as sustainability underpins Chinese civil law.[101] Neighbour relation rules are invoked in certain circumstances to curtail the exercise of property rights if they harm the environment.[102] These cases often involve expert opinions from professionals to determine whether the noise or the kind of pollution exceeds the limits.[103] This allows the court to make a concrete assessment based on the expert opinions and the circumstances of the case.

Similarly, keeping pigeons in unhygienic circumstances to cause substantial interference with the physical comfort of the occupant of the land or urban premises can be an actionable nuisance.[104] Building construction shall not violate the relevant national engineering standards or block neighbouring buildings' ventilation, daylight or sunshine.[105] In practice, if the construction of buildings violates the relevant national engineering construction standards, the court would regard it as exceeding the

[97] 袁科威诉广州嘉富房地产发展有限公司案 [*Yuan Kewei v. Guangzhou Jiafu Real Estate Development Co., Ltd.*] (2015) 穗中法民一终字第5108号 [(2015) Sui Zhong Fa Min Yi Zhong No. 5108].

[98] 沈海俊与机械工业第一设计研究院[*Shen Haijun v No.1 Design and Research Institute of Machinery Industry*] (2016) 皖民申840 [(2016) Wan Min Shen No. 840].

[99] 吴国金与中铁五局（集团）有限公司、中铁五局集团路桥工程有限责任公司、贵州建工监理咨询有限公司、贵州贵安新区管理委员会 [*Wu Guojin v. China Railway No.5 Bureau (Group) Co., Ltd., China Railway No.5 Bureau Group Road and Bridge Engineering Co., Ltd., Guizhou Construction Supervision Consulting Co., Ltd, Guizhou Guian New Area Management Committee*] (2015) 筑环保民终字第2 [(2015) Zhu Huan Bao Min Zhong No. 2].

[100] Article 294 CC provides that the right holder of immovable property shall not discard solid wastes or discharge atmospheric pollutants, water pollutants, soil pollutants or such harmful substances as noise, light and electromagnetic radiation in violation of relevant provisions made by the state.

[101] Article 9 CC.

[102] Articles 1232–1234 CC.

[103] 曲忠全诉山东富海实业股份有限公司案 [*Qu Zhongquan v. Shandong Fuhai Industrial Co., Ltd.*] (2014)民申字第1782号 [(2014) SPC Min Shen No. 1782]; 袁科威诉广州嘉富房地产发展有限公司案 [*Yuan Kewei v.Guangzhou Jiafu Real Estate Development Co., Ltd.*] (2015) 穗中法民一终字第5108号 [(2015) Sui Zhong Fa Min Yi Zhong No. 5108].

[104] 尚贤菊诉励国定案 [*Shang Xianju v. Li Guoding*] (2007) 甬民一终字第152号 [(2007) Yong Min Yi Zhong Zi No. 152].

[105] Article 293 CC.

tolerance limit of ordinary people in society, and the victim may claim for the exclusion of obstruction and seek compensation for damages. Conversely, suppose it meets the national construction standards. In that case, even if a certain degree of obstruction is caused to the adjacent buildings' ventilation, lighting and sunshine, it shall be deemed that the tolerance limit is not exceeded. The owner or user of the adjacent building must tolerate it.[106]

A real right holder needs to facilitate neighbours to receive water and drainage.[107] A real right holder must allow the natural flow of water from adjoining land and cannot complain about damage caused by such water. A real right holder cannot change the natural course of surface water, causing a greater volume of water or the same volume to flow to the lower-lying land at an increased rate.[108] If this happens, the higher-lying landowner would be ordered to remove the obstruction erected or be forbidden to erect obstructing structures. Damages may only be claimed where the damage had been caused.

4.2.3 Civil Customs

The Chinese CC explicitly states that local customs will apply to determine whether the conduct in question amounts to a reasonable use when the provisions in laws or regulations handling neighbour relations are absent.[109] It is often assumed that neighbour disputes could be easily settled through mediation guided by local civil customs. However, the problem was that the local customs' content was uncertain, and their applicability was not obvious. An empirical study suggests that the percentage of neighbour dispute cases resolved through mediation was far lower than in other civil cases.[110] Even in Yunnan Province, with the highest number of ethnic minority groups in China living there, between 2014 and 2019, only around 40 per cent of the

106 SPC Property Law Research Group (n. 72), p. 283.

107 Para. 1 of Article 290 CC.

108 Para. 2 of Article 290 CC: The use of natural flowing water shall be reasonably distributed among right holders of neighbouring immovable properties. The drainage of natural flowing water shall follow its natural flow direction.

109 Article 289 CC.

110 Weihong Zhong [钟卫红] and Hanguang Weng [翁汉光], "Exploring and Analysing the Mechanism of Introducing Civil Customs in Adjudication' [《民事习惯的司法导入机制探析——以相邻关系纠纷为例》] (2009) 6 *Lingnan Journal* [《岭南学刊》] 73.

neighbourhood rights disputes handled by its basic courts were resolved through mediation.[111]

Inevitably, local customs may be invoked to adjudicate neighbour disputes.[112] In *Chang, Zhao, Fan Families v. Li Family*, the plaintiffs and the defendants were neighbours in a village in Jianchuan, Dali, Yunnan Province.[113] While the plaintiffs' houses were in the east (in the front row), the defendants' houses were in the west (in the back row). In front of these houses were paths from the north to the south leading to the road in the south. The front doors of the houses of the plaintiffs and the defendants were facing east. In 1991, under the government's town planning, the plaintiffs' houses in the east were demolished to build a road, which subsequently became a road with heavy traffic. The plaintiffs, therefore, changed the front doors of their houses, which originally faced east to the road, and made the front doors of their newly built houses face west. In July 2017, to stop the plaintiffs from having their front doors facing west, the defendants built a wall facing north and south on the path on the western side of the plaintiffs' houses, which was just 50 cm away from the walls of the plaintiffs' houses, to prevent the plaintiffs from using the path on the western side of the defendants' houses. The plaintiffs argued that since the wall built by the defendants was too high, it blocked the ventilation of the plaintiffs' houses and affected their fire evacuation safety. This was particularly true during the rainy season when the drainage system failed to work properly, and the drips from the roofs would fall on the defendants' walls, which in turn would splash onto the walls of the plaintiffs' houses, thus posing serious dangers to the plaintiffs. Due to these reasons, the plaintiffs filed a lawsuit requesting the court to order the three defendants to eradicate the danger and remove the wall that the three defendants built.

The defendants also filed a counterclaim that the front doors of the plaintiffs were originally facing east, and the pathway from the north to the south between the houses of the plaintiffs and the defendants was not the only path for the plaintiffs. The defendants also argued that since the

[111] Xiaoning Tong [童晓宁], 'Three-dimensional Remodelling: Towards Mediation with Normative Meaning—Based on the Interactive Analysis of Judges, Habits and Mediation' [《三维重塑:走向规范意义的调解—基于法官、习惯与调解的互动关系分析》] (2021) 1 *Customary Law* [《民间法》] 422

[112] Ying Lin [林鹰], 'Discussion on Cases concerning Rural Neighbour Disputes' [《浅谈农村相邻纠纷案件》] (2014) *Legal System and Society* [《法制与社会》] 218.

[113] The case discussed in this article came from the Jianchuan County People's Court; names of parties involved are deleted for privacy reasons.

wall they built was 50 cm away from the walls of the plaintiffs' houses, there were sufficient spaces for the drips from the defendants' roofs to go. Moreover, the plaintiffs also built a drainage pipe on the pathway between the houses of the plaintiffs and the defendants, which caused pollution and drainage problems. Due to these reasons, the defendants requested the court to order the plaintiffs (1) to demolish the front doors on the western side of their houses; (2) to remove the rubbish they disposed off on the pathway between their houses and that of the defendants; and (3) to demolish the drainage pipe they built on the pathway between their houses and that of the defendants, to stop causing pollution and drainage problems.[114]

The plaintiffs insisted that the rest of the problems could be negotiated if their front doors remained facing west. On the contrary, the defendants insisted that the rest of the problems could be negotiated as long as the plaintiffs demolished those doors. Both sides became acrimonious in the face of their divergent views. The core issue was whether the plaintiffs could have their front doors facing west. Why can't the plaintiffs have their front doors facing west? Why would a door's direction lead to such a dispute between neighbours? This is closely related to the civil customs of the Bai ethnic minority regarding architectural style.

The Bai accounted for more than 90 per cent of the total population of the mountainous Jianchuan County – also called "the hometown of Bai ethnic minority group."[115] For the Bai people, their houses are normally built in front of mountains with the front doors facing the river and all houses facing the same direction with the front doors facing east. Another tradition of the Bai is that the walls at the back of their houses do not have windows. "Three rooms and one wall screening" and "four houses and five courtyards" are the basic architectural styles of the Bai people, who developed such specific architectural styles based on their lifestyle as developed throughout history. Under this architectural style, there is a ditch of at least three feet (about 100 cm) in width between neighbouring houses. Pathways usually are at least six feet (about 200 cm) in width, roads are at least eight feet (about 260 cm) wide, and a few families share patios and easements. Moreover, when building a new house, the house owner must ensure that it does not block the sunlight enjoyed by the owners of the existing houses.

[114] *Ibid.*

[115] <www.yn.gov.cn/yngk/lyyn/lydt/202303/t20230317_256454.html> accessed on 11 November 2023.

As the local economy developed in recent decades, the Bai people have changed their traditional architectural styles. Especially when the pathways on the eastern side of villages were developed into streets and roads under the new urban/village plans, people began to turn their front doors facing east into walls and create doors on the western side of their houses. Such alterations often lead to disputes with neighbours living to the west of the houses being thus altered. It is not only a dispute between two neighbouring families; sometimes, the whole village or town will be involved. It is hard to settle disputes within the same village or clan, so the dispute will often go to litigation for resolution.

The problem of invoking civil customs is that it is difficult to identify the community's traditional customs,[116] thus making this case particularly appealing for analysis. The Bai people's tradition of having their front doors facing east and not having windows in the back wall of their houses was first developed because of their landscape. Since the pathways between the Bai people's houses are normally quite narrow, and there is often only one pathway per one row of houses, each pathway is used only by the people living on its western side. Such an arrangement reasonably allows people living in the front and back rows to have their respective right of passage.

The case discussed above involves three local customs. First, there should be a pathway of at least six feet (about two meters) in width between houses. However, the narrowest part of the pathway between the disputants is only 50 cm wide. Due to this, the the plaintiffs argued that the defendants' act is unacceptable and constitutes an infringement upon their property rights. Second, there should be a ditch of three feet (about one meter) in width between two neighbouring houses to catch water. Third, the crux of the contention in this case was no windows and doors in the back walls of houses.

As illustrated, both the plaintiffs and the defendants cited local customs as the justification for their arguments. For example, the plaintiffs argued that the defendants failed to observe the custom of leaving a six-foot-wide pathway for easement when building walls. However, the defendants argued that this was caused by the plaintiffs' deliberate deviation from the customs and having their front doors on the western side of their houses. The defendants contended that, by leaving 50 cm

[116] Tong (n. 111).

between the wall they built and the plaintiffs' houses, they did respect the tradition and custom of leaving three feet for the water to drain.

How should this problem be resolved in litigation? First, the judge examined the facts and found that "the right of passage is collectively owned" and "it is true that in the foundation construction plan, the Plaintiffs' passage right was approved to be facing east."[117] However, he then pointed out that the plans cannot give detailed instructions regarding the direction each house has to face, so each household is free to make its arrangements as long as others' interests are not affected. Since the passage right is collectively owned by all the house owners in the same row, the plaintiffs have the right to use it. However, if the plaintiffs failed to handle the matter properly in altering the direction of the passage, the defendants' ordinary use of their house would be adversely affected.[118] Therefore, the inquiry is whether, given the particular circumstances and the community's prevailing view, a landowner's exercise of a particular power of ownership is proper and socially acceptable. As such, restrictions must be imposed on the plaintiffs' right of passage to lessen the confrontation and promote harmony.

Presumably, where the statute is silent, the courts exercise their discretion to fill the void by invoking local civil customs. The mechanical jurisprudence oriented by state law should give way to judicial creativity. Nonetheless, it is worth noting that while the judge has referenced the local customs, he did not directly address them in the judgment. Instead, he cited Article 84 of the Property Law,[119] a general principle provision. The judge finally held that: (1) the defendants demolish the wall they built within one month from the date when the judgment came into force; (2) the plaintiffs continue to use the right of passage but cannot build any fixed installations on it; and (3) the pollutants and rubbish discarded by the plaintiffs onto the defendant's house must be cleared within one month after the relevant construction work was completed. The appellate court upheld this decision.

The court attempted a sort of judicial expediency to achieve a balance between contending claims. This is commendable. While the judge has meticulously handled the dispute, a question arises: In what circumstance can local customs be identified and addressed in the judgment? If the judge, in this case, chose to resort to Article 288 of the CC, a general

[117] *Ibid.*
[118] *Ibid.*
[119] Now Article 288 CC.

principle provision, it seems that Article 289 is of little or no use. This is because Article 288, a rather broad principle-based provision, arguably covers almost all the situations where a neighbour dispute arises. However, judges can only rely on local customs when no legislation or administrative regulation provision is found.[120]

4.2.4 *Summary*

The unencumbered exercise of the powers of ownership interest is restricted to obtain harmony when conflicting ownership interests exist. However, the rules of neighbour relations are not the only rules which restrict the unencumbered exercise of the powers of ownership. Neighbour relation rules should not be confused with servitudes,[121] even though both amount to a legal limitation on the right of ownership. First, neighbour relation rules are extensions of or limitations on ownership to limit the rights of the owner in the use of the property to promote harmony of neighbours' living and, therefore, cannot be a real right on its own.[122] In contrast, servitude is a limited real right.[123] Second, servitudes under Chinese law are created by agreement.

In contrast, neighbour relation rules are statutory rights which do not need an agreement to be applicable. Law or regulations create the neighbour relation rules, and local customs may apply in certain circumstances where there are no such provisions.[124] This implies that if a party enjoys the neighbouring right over the other under the law, she does not need to pay consideration in return for the benefit. Therefore, neighbour relation is also known as "free common goods."[125]

120 SPC Property Law Research Group (n. 72), p. 275.

121 Articles 372–385 CC.

122 L. Wang, *Property Law*, 2015, p. 174.

123 Lei Chen, 'The New Chinese Property Code: A Giant Step Forward?' (2007) 11 *Electronic Journal of Comparative Law* 1.

124 Article 289 CC.

125 This is in contrast to the restricting covenants, servitude or private contracting behaviour as articulated in the Coase Theorem resolving a negative spillover problem. Ronald Coase, 'The Problem of Social Cost' (1960) 3 *The Journal of Law and Economics* 1.

5

Condominium Ownership

5.1 Introduction

This chapter illustrates that one of the most striking hallmarks of China's economic development is the vast number of residential condominiums throughout the country. In 2018, more than 90 per cent of households in China owned homes (87 per cent in urban and 96 per cent in rural China).[1] More to the point, more than 20 per cent of Chinese households own more than one condominium, higher than those in many developed nations.[2] Naturally, the high homeownership rate in China necessitates a set of fine-tuned condominium rules. Condominiums are the dominant and growing mode of residential property in urban China, with about one-third of them managed by homeowner associations (HOAs).[3] How condominium ownership is designed and regulated has increasingly become a governmental concern in China. This chapter explains the legislative framework for identifying the key factors that make HOAs work. In addition to being a study on apartment owners, the roles of developers, local governments and non-state actors (such as property rights activists, public interest lawyers and HOAs) will be explored. The central question of this chapter relates to the apartment ownership structure most suitable for an emerging Chinese private property market. China's housing market has changed dramatically over the past few decades and is the backbone of China's transitional economy.

1 William Clark, Youqin Huang and Daichun Yi, 'Can Millennials Access Homeownership in Urban China?' (2021) 36 *Journal of Housing and the Built Environment* 69.

2 Youqin Huang, Daichun Yi and William A. V. Clark, 'Multiple Home Ownership in Chinese Cities: An Institutional and Cultural Perspective' (2020) 97 *Cities* 102518.

3 One-third is the national average. Specifically, in Shanghai, more than 90% of residential communities have set up HOAs while in Shenzhen it is only about 30%. See '深圳住宅小区业委会成立比例约三成，上海超九成 ['About 30% of Shenzhen Residential Communities have set up HOAs, and more than 90% in Shanghai'] (深圳商报 [*Shenzhen Business Daily*], 24 August 2021) <www.sohu.com/a/485334915_121010226> accessed 6 June 2022.

Condominium, also known as apartment ownership, is a unique legal institution with three prongs or elements: (1) individual ownership of an apartment, (2) joint ownership of the common areas and (3) membership in an owners' association.[4] Hence, a purchaser of a condominium acquires exclusive individual ownership of a unit and obtains joint ownership in the common property and membership in the HOA, which deals with the maintenance and management of the common areas of the condominium scheme.[5] These three components of condominium ownership are inextricably bound with each other, and as such, they can only be alienated, mortgaged or otherwise dealt with in their entirety.[6] This three-dimensional characteristic of condominiums has been accepted explicitly in the CC.[7]

Condominium ownership implies three elements: homeownership, shared responsibility and participation in community life. In other words, condominium management is closely linked to the concepts of independence of control and autonomy of unit owners.[8] It raises issues of collective action, mutual dependence and democratic participation.[9] Thus, a degree of self-governance is unavoidable as a matter of practicality. Without active participation in collective action, the effects of condominium legislation are questionable.[10] The success of condominium associations does not depend on a single controlling factor but "on a complex mixture of individual agency group dynamics, and trial and error played out against a shifting backdrop of possibilities and constraints."[11] However, they could not be generalised to fit every HOA.[12]

4 Cornelius van der Merwe, *Apartment Ownership* (Mohr Siebeck 1994), pp. 2–4.

5 Lei Chen, 'The Changing Landscape of Condominium Laws and Urban Governance in China', in A. Lehavi (ed), *Private Communities and Urban Governance* (Springer 2016).

6 Article 273 CC.

7 Article 271 CC.

8 Lei Chen and Mark Kielsgard, 'Evolving Property Rights in China: Patterns and Dynamics of Condominium Governance' (2014) 2 *The Chinese Journal of Comparative Law* 21.

9 Lei Chen and Cornelius van der Merwe, 'Reflections on the Role of the Managing Agent in South African and Chinese Sectional Title (Condominium) Legislation' (2009) 1 *Journal of South African Law (TSAR)* 22.

10 Stefan Treffers and Randy Lippert, 'Condominium Self-governance? Issues, External Interests, and the Limits of Statutory Reform' (2020) 35 *Housing Studies* 1025.

11 Benjamin Read, 'Property Rights and Homeowner Activism in New Neighbourhoods', in Li Zhang and Aihwa Ong (eds), *Privatizing China: Socialism from Afar* (Cornell University Press 2008), p. 53.

12 Yushu Zhu and Qiang Fu, 'Deciphering the Civic Virtue of Communal Space: Neighbourhood Attachment, Social Capital and Neighbourhood Participation in Urban China.' (2017) 49 *Environment and Behavior* 161.

The ROC CC (1929–1931) recognised the concept of condominiums in two relevant articles. Article 799 dealt with the cost of maintenance and repairs. Article 800 drew on customary Chinese law. It stated that an apartment owner had no exclusive use right of the main gate or entrance of their multi-unit building, which belongs to all the owners, unless local customs or specific agreements provided the owner with such a right. While these provisions are unsophisticated and sketchy, they are significant in introducing the concept of modern apartment ownership by clarifying the rights and obligations of homeowners concerning the common property.

All land has been owned either by the state in urban areas or collectively in rural areas since the PRC was founded in 1949. In 1988, China amended its constitution to recognise privately owned transferable land use rights.[13] This recognition led to an unprecedented level of condominium construction boom. Urbanisation and an exploding population intensified the financial burden on the government to provide enough housing for its citizens.[14] However, while the commercialisation of state-owned land was in its infancy, resident-tenant public housing was still characterised as a form of socialist well-being. Before enacting legislation permitting private property rights, all units were government owned, and all buildings were government managed. In the middle 1990s, the policy of privatising the housing market helped to relieve the government of its responsibility for maintaining and managing buildings originally constructed to accommodate state employees.[15]

With the sale of government property to private individuals at a concessionary rate, government control of building management also ended. With the introduction of private ownership, market value considerations dominate management decisions, resulting in more sensitivity to and greater emphasis on long-term returns. Thus, management becomes the responsibility of private, profit-driven owners. The new property law encourages this phenomenon.[16]

[13] Cornelius van der Merwe, *European Condominium Law* (Cambridge University Press 2015).

[14] Mark T. Kremzner, 'Managing Urban Land in China: The Emerging Legal Framework and Its Role in Development' (1998) 7 *Pacific Rim Law & Policy Association Journal* 611, pp. 611–22.

[15] The Constitution was again amended to ensure that private economy within the scope of law is an important building block of the socialist market economy. See Article 11 of the PRC Constitution (amended on 15 March 1999).

[16] Article 70 of the Property Law; Hua Chen [陈华], *Study on Modern Condominium Ownership* [《现代建筑物区分所有权研究》] (Law Press 1995), p. 91.

In response to this societal context, democratic governance penetrates the administrative framework, particularly at the local and neighbourhood condominium association levels. These first steps are perhaps modest, but they witness the potential game-changes to urban governance. Local governments play a role in transforming residents from tenants to property owners, thereby establishing them as stakeholders.

Despite ongoing reforms, China's condominium law framework remains incomplete, characterised by a patchwork of disparate property law statutes, somewhat inconsistent administrative regulations, an overload of judicial pronouncements and conflicting local norms. This fragmentation in the legal framework has made the system vulnerable to structural weaknesses, corruption and practices that are generally at odds with the principles of sustainable development. Given these challenges, there is a clear and pressing need for further reforms to establish a more comprehensive, consistent and regulated condominium law scheme. Such reforms are crucial for enhancing the integrity, efficiency and sustainability of condominium governance in China.

In response, in 2003, the State Council (the central government) provided the Property Management Regulation, and in 2007, the Property Law came into effect.[17] The legislation was designed as a comprehensive mechanism to regulate property, providing clear definitions for various types of property, ensuring the protection of property rights and safeguarding title security, thus providing greater economic stability in the property market.[18] Although condominium ownership has been institutionalised and the unit owner's management autonomy is statutorily recognised under the Property Law,[19] it only includes a scant fourteen articles dealing with condominium property.[20] Many important

[17] In October 1999, the drafting panel completed a model draft consisting of 12 chapters and 435 articles. See Huixing Liang [梁慧星], *Commentary on Chinese Property Law Draft* [《中国物权法草案建议稿》（合著）] (Social Science Literature Press 2000), pp. 1–88. In 2000, a model property law draft was also completed. Liming Wang [王利明], *Annotated Draft of China's Law of Things* [《中国物权法草案建议稿及说明》] (Legal Press 2000), pp. 1–67. Thereafter, in consultation with these two model drafts, the Standing Committee of the NPC deliberated and pruned its legislative draft seven times. Ultimately, eight parliamentary deliberations were held from December 2002 to March 2007.

[18] Lei Chen, 'The New Chinese Property Code: A Giant Step Forward?' (2007) 11 *Electronic Journal of Comparative Law* 1, 2.

[19] Articles 70–83 of the Property Law (2007).

[20] Lei Chen, 'The Developer's Role in the Surging Chinese Condominium Housing: through the Comparative Lens of the US System' (2010) 18 *Asia Pacific Law Review* 233, pp. 233–34.

issues are left untouched, which propels some further implementation regulations or local rules to flesh out details, such as rules pertaining to the requirement of majority for HOA resolutions, two-tier management structures and the qualification and number of HOA executive council members.

The CC contains seventeen specific articles governing condominium ownership.[21] Two notable changes deserve mentioning compared with the provisions of the Property Law. First, the proceeds or profits generated from the common property should be distributed to owners according to the participation quota.[22] Second, it has tinkered with the rules concerning the collective decision-making procedures. The owners who hold more than two-thirds of the exclusive area and owners accounting for two-thirds of the total number of homeowners must participate in the voting to constitute the quorum.[23] The issue sets a preliminary threshold not previously provided for in the Property Law.[24] In addition, the voting procedures have been adjusted accordingly regarding the exclusive unit ratio and the base number of all owners.[25] For certain important matters, the quorum of voters has been modified from double two-thirds to double three-quarters.[26] The rationale for this change was that the more important the issue, the more demanding the threshold for resolution. Unreasonable external control and limitations on the free and personal enjoyment of the right could dampen the value and allure of property. Therefore, a tightened grip on the supermajority resolution rule is introduced.[27] This protects any dissenting owners who are not present at the meeting. Moreover, since most Chinese condominium complexes are multi-building projects, a heavy financial burden is shifted to the shoulders of the consenting owners, who have to buy out the units of the dissenting owners.[28]

Meanwhile, some disappointing oversights in the CC on condominium ownership exist. A prime example is that no provision governs the

[21] Articles 271–287 CC.
[22] Article 282 CC.
[23] Article 278 CC.
[24] *Ibid.*
[25] *Ibid.*
[26] *Ibid.*
[27] Lei Chen, 'Continuity and Change: Some Reflections on the Chinese CC' (2021) 29 *Asia Pacific Law Review* 287.
[28] Lei Chen, *The Making of Chinese Condominium Law: A Comparative Perspective with American and South African Condominium Laws* (Intersentia 2010), pp. 139–40.

termination of a condominium. Worse still, neither the Property Management Regulation issued by the State Council nor local regulations address this important issue. It appears a condominium scheme will perpetually exist once created in China. Indeed, a condominium owner may not be entitled to request the court to partition the land and the buildings in the scheme to secure tenure. However, many other jurisdictions recognise the need for dissolution in certain special circumstances – the condominium scheme can be terminated by agreement by owners either unanimously or by a supermajority rule or when the building is destroyed or severely damaged.[29] Given many age-old and deteriorating buildings and natural disasters in China, there is a dire need for the legislation to fill such a gap.

5.2 Individual Property and Common Property

A condominium owner owns the individual unit exclusively and has joint ownership of the common property in the building.[30] The distinction between common property and individual property is important because all owners are collectively responsible for maintaining and repairing the common property. In contrast, owners are individually responsible for their own units' upkeep and maintenance. The owner is entitled to possess, use, profit from and dispose of the exclusive unit of a building.[31] The Judicial Interpretation of Condominium Ownership 2009 defines an individual unit or the exclusive part of a building: an individual unit must (1) have an independent structure and can be identifiable; (2) be of independent use; and (3) be registered under the name of a specific owner.

Further, the Provisional Measures on Calculation of Floor Areas and Allocation of Common Property of Commercial Housing provides that a unit consists of cubic space, the floor area of unit walls, and the balcony floor area.[32] Only half of the projected floor and balcony space, whether enclosed or open, is counted as part of the floor area of a unit.[33] The boundaries are set for the unfinished surfaces of the floors and ceilings

[29] C. van der Merwe (n. 4), pp. 126–27.
[30] Article 271 CC.
[31] Article 272 CC.
[32] Article 6 of the Provisional Measures on Calculation of Floor Areas and Allocation of Common Property of Commercial Housing.
[33] Article 7 of the Provisional Measures on Calculation of Floor Areas.

and the median line between walls when a resale, insurance or tax payment of a unit is involved. In title registration, a unit encompasses half the floor space of the dividing walls, provided the walls are not bearing walls.

While the CC provides that an owner has the right to undertake the duties concerning the common property together with other owners, it does not clearly define a common property.[34] There is a legal distinction between the common property for a multi-building condominium and the common property for a single condominium building. It is common to have a condominium scheme comprising several high-rise buildings in China. There is a master management body for a multi-building condominium scheme, and it is usually operated and administered by a single managing agent. It is necessary to distinguish a common property for the whole scheme (multiple buildings) and a common property for a single building. The common property for the whole scheme is the common elements used for all the high-rise buildings, such as their boundary fences and the main gate. The common property for a single building refers to the common elements designed solely for a specific building's use, such as its elevator and roof. The distinction between the two is prone to disputes when the common expenses are to be distributed among different buildings and unit owners. However, it is necessary to distinguish the two, since owners' contributions should be confined to expenses associated with managing and maintaining the common parts in which they have an ownership share and frequent use. Some common parts are designed for a whole scheme's use, and some are only for a single building's use.

Many Chinese local condominium regulations contain provisions concerning the management of common property for multi-building condominiums, which is termed "property management area."[35] A two-tier management structure seems attractive, as it has a master or umbrella management body at the first tier and a few subsidiary management bodies at the second tier. Thus, the subdivision plan must be drafted carefully to ascertain the equitable common expenses of a multi-building condominium. Otherwise, many disputes will abound.

Since all units are structurally interdependent, an owner can only use and enjoy the condominium unit if the owner does not infringe on other

[34] Article 273 CC.

[35] Therefore, each condominium building in a block needs to be operated by a separate management body, or one association should operate all the condominiums.

unit owners' rights. When converting a residential use into business use, Chinese law restricts the powers of an owner through not only the statutory provisions and HOA by-laws or rules but also the consent of the interested homeowners.[36] In *Zhang Yi v. Zheng Zhongwei and China Unicom Wuhan branch*,[37] China Unicom Wuham Brach (the Unicom), a telecommunications company, has concluded a tenancy agreement with Zheng Zhongwei to use the unit to accommodate telecommunications equipment. This was done to execute the urban video surveillance system project Unicom obtained from the police department in Wuhan. The plaintiff, an owner living on the upper level, has filed a case against such use. It was claimed that such a change of use needs to be consented to by the other owners in the HOA, and such use infringes upon the neighbour's health through radiation.[38] In the first instance, the court ruled in favour of the defendants because it was held that the unit was still for residential, not business, use. Even if the use of the unit changed, it would have been for public utility (i.e. telecommunications).[39] On appeal, the Wuhan IPC reversed the first instance court's ruling by ordering the defendants to dismantle the installed equipment and restore the unit to its original status. For the second instance court, it was a clear change of use, given the circumstances. In addition, Property Law provides that the plaintiff has a *locus standi* as a stakeholder to file the case.[40]

Given the restrictions imposed on condominium units, one may question whether apartment ownership is genuine property ownership. This question is answered keeping in mind the characteristics of apartment ownership. That is, the units are not structurally separated but rather structurally interdependent. Crucial to condominium living is the principle that individuals should not be allowed to compromise the integrity of the entire development through unrestricted use of their own property. Imposing certain restrictions on the use and enjoyment of each unit effectively safeguards the common interests of all owners. In other words, the justifications for these restrictions stem from the long-term benefits that accrue to every unit owner by financially

[36] Article 279 CC.
[37] 最高人民法院公告案例：张一诉郑中伟、中国联合网络通信有限公司武汉分公司案 A SPC gazetted case, see the judgment in the Chinese language at the SPC official website at <http://gongbao.court.gov.cn/Details/6a9a70d224268146817a72b6a0702d.html?sw=%e5%bb%ba%e7%ad%91%e7%89%a9> accessed on 1 July 2023.
[38] *Ibid.*
[39] *Ibid.*
[40] Articles 78 and 83 of the Property Law.

increasing the condominium's market value and preserving a stable and orderly community. Therefore, condominium ownership remains genuine ownership despite several restrictions. As shown in the above case, this perception is widely held by the general public and the judiciary in China.

5.3 Parking Space

Parking space is a thorny issue for condominium developers and owners. Worldwide, the provision of parking in a condominium scheme is a controversial issue that a condominium law must deal with. In practice, it is a popular subject of dispute. Parking spaces can be designated in many ways, either as a unit component, common property, exclusive use areas or merely by license.

In principle, condominium ownership includes such joint interest areas as parking spaces. Regardless of the method, the developer makes initial decisions regarding the parking space. A separate title certificate can be issued through property registration if the developer independently constructs the parking space and is not included in the common property. This type of parking space is generally not controversial, and the developer has the right to sell or lease it. It should not be regarded as a part of the common property. Rather, the parking space is individual property. Article 275 of the Chinese CC provides that the allocation of the ownership of parking spaces within the zoning of the apartment building should be agreed upon by the parties concerned by way of a sale, donation or lease.[41] However, parking spaces on co-owned roads or located at other co-owned sites are co-owned in undivided shares by the owners.[42]

In a nutshell, there are three major kinds of parking spaces: (1) parking spaces within the zoning of the apartment building, (2) parking spaces on the co-owned roads or located at other co-owned sites, and (3) parking spaces on roads and other sites outside the condominium buildings. First, the parking spaces within the building may be disposed of by the developer by an agreement between the parties in the form of a sale, donation or lease. Essentially, this kind of parking space is regarded as individual non-residential units held by homeowners. Second, parking spaces on the co-owned roads or other co-owned sites form a part of the

[41] Para. 1 of Article 275 CC.
[42] Para. 2 of Article 275 CC.

common property jointly owned by the homeowners in the condominium scheme. Once an HOA is established, it may be given the power to designate parking spaces, as they are considered common property. Third, if the parking space is outside the condominium buildings, they are neither an individual nor a common property. It is worth noting that the Chinese CC makes it explicit that the parking spaces and garages in the building zone planned for parking vehicles shall first meet the needs of the homeowners.[43]

Ideally, the developer should designate at least one parking space for each unit. But in day-to-day practice, a particular scheme's location, use and purpose may render parking less urgent or even impossible. Alternative arrangements are made when condominiums are located in a congested city centre with excellent public transport or zoning bylaws do not permit a parking space for each unit owner.[44] Currently, the usual practice in China is buying or renting parking spaces from developers. The question remains that despite the parking space costs paid by certain homeowners, could the homeowners who bought parking spaces through sale gain more voting rights in the collective decision-making process? The parking space issue has led to many disputes in China between developers and condominium owners and between homeowners themselves.

Some unscrupulous developers sold and let parking spaces to outside persons in the past. Also, some developers sold a parking lot to a condominium owner even though the sold parking lot has been designated as a part of the common property.[45] This seriously impaired the functioning of condominium communities, since harmony within the communities was jeopardised. Such problems could have been avoided had there been legislative provisions to deal with the issue of parking.

Regulating parking is contingent upon many factors; therefore, a one-size-fits-all approach is unfit. There are ways to draft provisions that ensure fair dealing with condominium parking spaces. In the simplest case, with sufficient parking space, the developer can set up parking spaces as individual units or as common property for exclusive use by

[43] Article 276 CC.

[44] Lei Chen and Hanri Mostert, 'The Unavoidable Necessity of Formalizing Condominium Ownership in China: A Pilot Study' (2007) 2 *Asian Journal of Comparative Law* 1.

[45] 陈秀碧与厦门源昌房地产开发有限公司等案 (2014) 厦民终字第1085号 [*Chen Xiubi v. Xiamen Yuanchang Real Estate Development Co., Ltd. and Other Owners* (2014) Xia Min Zhong Zi No. 1085].

some or all owners. Otherwise, parking spaces can be in an area of the common property, meaning that the management body retains the right to specify which unit owners can park on which part of the common property. Large mixed-use condominiums without sufficient parking spaces for either each residential condominium owner or each commercial part-owner are particularly problematic. In this case, parking spaces can be structured around "parking licenses." This means that the residential unit owners use the parking spaces overnight, whereas the commercial owners can use them during the day.

5.4 Condominium Management

5.4.1 The Function and Rights of an HOA or HOA Committee

Common property gives rise to a need for a collective decision-making mechanism. An organisation responsible for administering condominium management and maintenance must be established to safeguard the common interests. Creating a management body or an HOA is essential, since a condominium community cannot function efficiently without a management association representing all owners and handling day-to-day operations. Without such an HOA, management disputes will surely arise among unit owners. Under Chinese law, there are two homeowner bodies: a general assembly of condominium owners (HOA) to make management decisions and an executive committee (HOA executive committee) to carry them out.

In China, a condominium community is managed by the homeowners or an HOA consisting of all the unit owners. According to the CC, unit owners may decide to organise a management body.[46] The Chinese law provides that if a condominium development has only a few owners, with their unanimous consent, all owners can be jointly involved in management, so there is no need to create a separate management body.[47] However, this provision is vague, since it does not define the size of a small condominium development.

Under Chinese law, the functions of an HOA are assigned under provisions of the CC, the State Council's Regulations, the local

[46] Article 277 CC.

[47] Article 10 of Property Management Regulations (promulgated by the State Council of the PRC on 8 June 2003; revised for the first time on 26 August 2007; revised for the second time on 6 February 2016; revised for the third time on 19 March 2018).

regulations, the by-laws and the rules. Generally, there are three major functions of a management body. First, an HOA acts as a vehicle for enforcing restrictions and rules as regulated in the management rules and by-laws. Second, an HOA is a rulemaking organ to administers the condominium community's day-to-day running. Third, the management body can amend, discard, supplement or add new rules to the applicable rules or by-laws subject to the statutory provisions.

It is unusual for rules governing the functioning of the general meeting,[48] the executive committee[49] and the rules governing common property and facilities[50] to be decided by a simple majority vote. Failure to provide for the smooth transition of management will often hamper the association's ability to self-govern by unnecessarily binding the future organisation to contractors (including developer-owned commercial management companies) that limits the owners' available decision-making options and thus circumvents the democratic value of the owners' association.[51] The CC has amended the rules on collective decision-making procedures to tackle this. The preliminary threshold for less important matters is twofold: the owners must hold two-thirds of the exclusive areas, and two-thirds of the number of owners must participate in the voting.[52] This is often called the double two-thirds rule. However, the requirement has been modified from double two-thirds to double three-quarters for specifically defined matters.[53] These specifically

[48] These include, *inter alia*, the notice required for convening the general meeting, the kinds of general meetings, minimum agenda of general meetings, voting at general meetings, the quorum required for a general meeting, the representation of owners by proxies and the keeping of minutes.

[49] These include amongst others the powers and functions of the executive board, whether it must consist only of owners, whether owners may attend its meetings, whether the members are entitled to remuneration, their fiduciary obligations and their period of office.

[50] This is normally done in the so-called conduct rules of the scheme and needs more than a simple majority for amendment.

[51] The risk to the property owner is particularly heightened because of the lack of conventional constitutive documents and the developers' role in the "participation quota" that allows the developers to determine their own status early in the construction process and to ultimately dictate the terms to the fledgling scheme. See Randy Lippert and Stefan Treffers, 'Turnover or Roll Over? Property Developer Legal Avoidance and Influence on Condominium Governance in New York City and Toronto', in Randy Lippert and Stefan Treffers (eds), *Condominium Governance and Law in Global Urban Context* (Routledge 2021).

[52] Para. 2 of Article 278 CC.

[53] *Ibid.*

defined matters are: (1) raising the maintenance funds of the building and ancillary facilities; (2) renovating or reconstructing the building or ancillary facilities; and (3) changing the use of the common property or using the common property for business purposes.[54]

Take the provision for changes to the purpose/use of the common property (or its use for business operations), for example. The disposal or change of use of parts of the common property radically impacts the value of every owner's abstract share in the common property. It is usually allowed only by a unanimous resolution or the written consent of all the owners in the scheme.[55] This perhaps reflects the immaturity of the Property Law, but it is noteworthy that the CC addressed this defect by imposing a supermajority rule (i.e. three-quarters). A peculiarity of the Chinese way of determining whether a motion has been carried is that a majority, both in number and value, is required for all decisions. Given the number of homeowners in Chinese condominiums, it is nearly impossible to make any resolution to change the use of common property in practice. Homebuyers crave surety that the property they pay for will retain its essential character.

5.4.2 *Maintenance Funds*

Chinese law stipulates that a maintenance fund needs to be created,[56] with the main aim being to save for a "rainy day." A maintenance fund is needed for contingencies, because repair and maintenance costs usually exceed a management body's operating budget. A maintenance fund is a form of self-insurance that increases *pro rata* over the years to cover the repair costs. It covers many common property expenses such as the administrative cost of convening meetings, the remunerations of the administrator and executive committee members, painting the exterior wall of buildings, replacing, repairing or making good the common property, and purchasing facilities or tools for the common property.[57] Information about the raising and use of the fund shall be publicised regularly to the homeowners. The owner's right to know refers to the

[54] Para. 1 of Article 278 CC.

[55] See, e.g. s 17(1) of the South African Sectional Titles Act 95 of 1986 which requires a unanimous resolution and s 34(1) of the Singapore Building Maintenance and Strata Management Act 47 of 2004 which requires a 90% resolution.

[56] Article 53 of the 2003 Property Management Regulations.

[57] Para. 1 of Article 281 CC.

owner's right to understand the matters related to the common property, which has been specified in the SPC Interpretation Concerning Condominium Disputes.[58] In case of urgency, the HOA or the HOA executive committee may apply to use the maintenance fund according to law.[59] The maintenance account and annual budget requirements promote a condominium association's financial health in the long run. Mortgage lenders and insurers are also comfortable with an HOA that has a maintenance fund. Hence, the CC provides that the homeowners shall jointly own the maintenance funds of a building and ancillary facilities.[60]

The Chinese homeowners have a statutory obligation to pay into the maintenance fund. However, is it possible for the HOA to demand the shortfall owed by certain owners for years? A specific question is whether the request for the shortfall payment is time-barred, as the standard rule of time limitation is three years. In *Owners' Association of the Jiule Building Community (the JB HOA), Hongkou District, Shanghai v. Shanghai Huanya Industrial Corporation (the HI company)*,[61] the defendant, HI Company, did not pay the maintenance fees for the residential units of the Jiule Building it purchased in 2004. In September 2010, the plaintiff, the JB HOA, sued the defendant on behalf of all owners to recover the funds. Before the Hongkou District People's Court, the plaintiff demanded that the defendant pay the plaintiff RMB 57,566.90, the shortfall in the maintenance funds. The defendant's position was that the plaintiff had never asked for maintenance funds in the last six years since becoming a property owner in the condominium scheme. Therefore, the plaintiff's claim should be time-barred under the Chinese law. The court ruled in favour of the plaintiff. It reasoned that the right of an HOA to demand the shortfall payments of maintenance funds is a management right on behalf of all homeowners.

[58] Article 13 of the Interpretation of the SPC on Several Issues Concerning the Specific Application of Law in the Trial of Disputes over Partitioned Ownership of Building Areas (2009). See the SPC gazetted case (2011) 10: 夏浩鹏等人诉上海市闸北区精文城市家园小区业主委员会2010 [*Xia Haopeng et al and Homeowners Association of Jingwen City Community in Zhabei District*, Shanghai 2010].

[59] Para. 2 of Article 281 CC.

[60] Para. 1 of Article 281 CC.

[61] No. 65 of the Guiding Cases issued by the SPC, 上海市虹口区久乐大厦小区业主大会诉上海环亚实业总公司案 [*Owners' Association of the Jiule Building Community (the JB HOA), Hongkou District, Shanghai v. Shanghai Huanya Industrial Corporation (the HI company*] (2011) 沪二中民二（民）终字第1908号 [(2011) Hu Er Zhong Min Er (Min) Zhong No. 1908].

It will contradict the principle of fairness if certain owners are allowed not to pay into the maintenance fund while enjoying the benefits. Other owners may have paid amounts above their shares to preserve the jointly owned parts. In the second instance, the court dismissed the defendant's appeal. This ruling suggests that under Chinese law, the demand to pay the shortfall amount in maintenance funds is analogous to a claim made by a property right holder for the return of the property, to which time limits do not apply.[62]

5.4.3 *Management Structure*

The Chinese law entrusts the responsibility for efficient management to a management body consisting of all unit owners designated as an HOA. However, establishing an HOA is not mandatory for all condominium schemes in China. Suppose a condominium development has only a few owners. With their unanimous consent, all owners can be jointly involved in management; thus, creating a separate management body is unnecessary. Whether to set up an HOA is left to the owners themselves. Article 277 of the CC allows only owners to establish an HOA and its executive council.[63]

The CC contains provisions on an HOA's powers to manage and control the common property. Specifically, Article 278 provides an extensive list of powers the HOA may exercise. This article allows the association to adopt and amend rules and by-laws,[64] elect and remove executive council members of the HOA[65] and hire and discharge property management agents, other employees and independent contractors.[66] An association can also institute, defend or intervene in litigation or administrative proceedings in its name or on behalf of the owners on matters affecting the common interest, such as reckless garbage disposal, discharge of pollutants or noises, unauthorised pet breeding, illegal building works, obstruction of passages and refusal to pay property management fees.[67] Equally, if not more importantly, an association can collect and use maintenance funds for the common property.[68] The

[62] Article 196(2) CC.
[63] Article 277 CC.
[64] Article 278(1) and (2) CC.
[65] Article 278(3) CC.
[66] Article 278(4) CC.
[67] Para. 2 of Article 286 CC.
[68] Article 278(5) and (6) CC.

HOA can make contracts and incur liabilities; regulate the use, maintenance, repair, replacement and modification of common elements; and make additional improvements to the common property.[69] It remains unclear whether the notion of other important matters concerning common property[70] authorises an HOA to grant easements, leases, licenses and concessions over the common elements and to impose and receive payments, fees or charges for the use or rental of the common elements and services provided to owners.

Furthermore, Chinese law remains silent on whether an HOA can impose charges for late payment of assessments and levy reasonable fines for violations of the by-laws and rules of the association. An HOA can determine the standard of allowance or subsidy for members of the owners'executive committee and conduct an audit when the chairperson leaves office.[71] Again, whether an HOA can provide its officers and executive committee indemnification and maintain directors' and officers' liability insurance is unaddressed.

In a nutshell, any decisions or resolutions made by the HOA or its executive committee are legally binding on the owners.[72] However, an owner is entitled to initiate judicial proceedings to strike or amend a decision or resolution which allegedly infringes upon the owner's interests.[73] The condominium owners can also commence legal proceedings against the developer, the property management agent and other owners to protect their property interests.[74] In addition, some local regulations allow the HOA to amend or nullify a resolution made by the executive committee that contradicts the decision of the HOA.[75] These legal protections or remedies make HOAs a citizen-initiated and rights-based self-governing organisation, different from any other social organisation in China. The HOAs may employ legal means to make the local government listen to their concerns. Hence, in such an authoritarian system, the relationship between HOA governance and urban

[69] Article 278(7) and (8) CC.

[70] Article 278(9) CC.

[71] Article 34(8) of the Regulation of the Beijing Municipality on Property Management (2020).

[72] Para. 1 of Article 280 CC.

[73] Para. 2 of Article 280 CC.

[74] Article 287 CC.

[75] Article 34(9) of the Regulation of the Beijing Municipality on Property Management (2020).

governance led by the local government may be mutually transformative and may not necessarily be lopsided.

Nevertheless, the CC fails to provide for, as appropriate, a two-tier condominium management scheme. A two-tier scheme entails the establishment of an overarching management body overseeing an entire project at a higher level and subsidiary management bodies overseeing smaller residential units (such as single buildings in a multi-building association) and related common areas at a lower level. A two-tier management structure needs to be introduced in China because most condominiums are multi-building or mixed-use projects.[76] A two-tier approach makes owner management a less daunting enterprise, and the failure to provide for this scheme results in disproportionately high professional management involvement and reduced owner participation. Thus, the inefficiency in the national legislation creates barriers to democratic governance, as the legislation fails to anticipate and provide for a less onerous scheme.

In addition to distancing owners from management, developing multi-building or mixed-use projects in the traditional "single condominium, single association" structure creates other inefficiencies. For example, in larger condominium developments, it is financially burdensome to call meetings of all unit owners for issues related to only one building. Furthermore, unit owners in one building will often be unfamiliar with or disinterested in issues related to other buildings, making a detailed review of those issues by the umbrella organisation unduly burdensome. This also fuels owner apathy and discourages otherwise qualified volunteers from participating in management because of the required time commitment. Additionally, given that owners have limited motivation to be involved in the management issues of other buildings, a single building's management issue can usually be resolved more quickly and easily by its owners than by all the owners in the project.

5.4.4 HOA Committee Members

Problems may arise in the make-up of the HOA executive committee members. It is impractical for all owners to attend to the day-to-day management of a condominium scheme. Therefore, Chinese law

[76] Lei Chen and Mark Kielsgard, 'Evolving Property Rights in China: Patterns and Dynamics of Condominium Governance' (2014) 1 *Chinese Journal of Comparative Law* 22.

provides that the executive committee is usually elected to execute the general meeting's resolutions and administer the day-to-day affairs of the condominium complex.[77] Although the executive committee has less authority than the general meeting, its standing committee's role cannot be downplayed. Thus, the identity and qualification of executive committee members are an important issue. Under Chinese law, an executive committee member must be either a unit owner or a representative of a corporate owner.[78] This may be a potential problem. External candidates may contribute essential professional experience and skills to the executive committee, especially when there is a shortage of unit owners willing to serve as committee members, particularly in a two-tier management structure.[79] It is also noteworthy that in China, where management by unit owners is still new, finding experienced and professional executive committee members may be difficult. However, committee members will eventually acquire the necessary experience, or they may have the option to contract for the required skills. This management approach by unit owners guarantees that most executive council members have a legitimate economic stake and a personal interest in the effective management of the condominium.

Under Chinese law, the number of council members remains largely unregulated. There is no provision governing the required number of council members in either the national Property Management Regulation of 2003 or many local regulations. In practice, this may lead to problems, as the number of council members has a bearing on quorums and decision-making, even in determining a simple majority vote. However, strict regulations imposed on the number of council members represent an inflexible "one size fits all" approach that could lead to inefficiencies. In a recent local property management rule, *the Regulation of Shenzhen Special Economic Zone on Realty Management*, the condominium association specifically mandated that the executive council consist of an odd

[77] Article 15 of the Property Management Regulations, issued by Order No. 379 of the State Council on 8 June 2003; amended for the first time on 26 August 2007; for the second time on 6 February 2016; and for the third time on 19 March 2018.

[78] Article 16(2) of the Regulation on Realty Management; Article 39 of the Regulation of the Beijing Municipality on Property Management (2020). In many jurisdictions, council members do not necessarily need to be unit owners, requiring only that most executive board members must be unit owners. See § 3-103 (f) of the Uniform Common Interest Ownership Act of 1994 for the USA; see Annexure 8 Regulation 5 of the Sectional Title Act for South Africa.

[79] Cornelius van der Merwe, Sectional Titles 14-66 (2007).

number ranging from five to seventeen members.[80] However, by capping the number of members at seventeen, condominium projects will often be unable to include representatives from all subsidiary bodies or each building in many medium to large multi-building projects. This impacts the democratic character of the association and the individual owners' access to their (council) representatives. To guard against this, other local ordinances, such as the Shanghai Property Management Regulation, have stipulated that there should be an odd number of representatives, not fewer than five, with an open-ended maximum number.[81]

Thus, national legislation can be viewed as a factor that directly or indirectly impacts democratic governance. Factors directly impacting democratic governance include the simple majority requirement for most association decisions, even those constituting an organic change to common property. However, this concession is often illusory, as it must be predicated on a so-called double majority, including majorities of unit numbers and value share. The requirement of a double majority may be advisable for issues of organic change where even traditional democratic societies include greater barriers (e.g., unanimous decisions or super-majorities). However, it may be unjustified in less radical issues. The double-majority approach effectively provides veto power to those elites who collectively own more than 50 per cent of the value of the project, even though they may own fewer than 50 per cent of the units.[82] Thus, those purchasers, including corporate purchasers, who buy more expensive units are also receiving a disproportionately larger voice in the running of the condominium than other owners. Heightened drafting complexity to the national legislation could assuage these inequities while simultaneously providing for greater protection from organic changes and warranting greater market security.

5.4.5 Property Service Companies

The CC further provides that homeowners may elect to manage the scheme themselves or choose a professional management company or

[80] Article 33 of the Regulation of Shenzhen Special Economic Zone on Realty Management (2019 Revision).

[81] See Article 19 of the Shanghai Residential Property Management Regulation (2004, amended 2010).

[82] This would not allow the wealthier owners disproportionate authority to *initiate* changes, as they would still require a majority of unit owners to agree, but a minority of wealthy owners could *veto* initiatives favoured by a majority of unit owners.

another manager by a majority vote.[83] Most local statutes make it optional for owners to employ outside managers to administer the condominium scheme. Self-management usually only occurs in smaller projects where owners organise themselves into groups according to their skills to undertake the work involved in the scheme's management.[84] Many foreign condominium statutes either entrust the management of larger schemes to the owners' executive board (which usually consists of owners assisted by a managing agent) or provide for the appointment of a professional manager or managing service provider with the supervision of an HOA.[85] The CC opted for the latter alternative; a professional manager conducts its functions under the owners' supervision and should promptly respond to any enquiry the owners raise.[86] It also empowers the owners to terminate the appointment of a managing agent appointed by the developer.[87] The rationale is to frustrate the developer's effort to enter into "sweetheart" contracts with affiliated or subsidiary entities while controlling the association and binding it long term. Numerous local property management regulations either require a review of all contracts and appointments made by the developer during the initial owners' meeting or empower owners to terminate such contracts unilaterally.[88]

Under the CC, condominium owners have the power to hire or dismiss property service providers or other managing agents.[89] Local property management regulations facilitate seamless transitions from developers to condominium owners, and exempting future associations from contractual obligations enhances democratic decision-making. By binding the HOAs to long-term contracts, developer-controlled associations limit the choices available to successor owner-controlled associations. While the CC allows owners to replace the developer-appointed

[83] Article 284 CC.
[84] See generally Chen and van der Merwe (n. 9).
[85] See the provisions of the French, German and Dutch statutes referred to in van der Merwe (n. 4), p. 149.
[86] Article 285 CC.
[87] Paragraph 2 of Article 284 CC.
[88] For example, Article 24 of the Regulation of the Beijing Municipality on Property Management (effective on 1 May 2020). It grants the HOA a power to review the pre-HOA formation property service contract concluded by the developer six months before the service contract expires. Furthermore, the Beijing Regulation also caps the pre-HOA formation property service contract at two years.
[89] Article 278(4) CC.

property manager,[90] the provision for termination without penalty for other residual contracts is left to local regulation. China's legislature is naturally submissive to provincial authority on real property regulation. Still, a popular subject matter of disputes is seen when the local authority collaborates with a professional management company to undermine the democratic initiative of a HOA. The absence of drafting complexity and the failure to establish clear legal responsibility in national legislation regarding majorities and the future binding power of initial contracts are legislative deficiencies that directly and adversely affect the ongoing development of democratic governance in China.

Factors indirectly influencing democratic governance include the national legislation's failure to incorporate a provision for a two-tier management system. In this case, perhaps inadvertently, the national legislation ties the hands of owners' associations, creates costly and onerous inefficiency, and encourages owner apathy. Furthermore, while it does mandate that executive committee members have an economic interest in the condominium, the national legislation fails to guide the permissible number of executive council members. This failure allows for counterproductive local rules, such as the inadequate regulation adopted in Shenzhen referenced earlier. Enabling structural flexibility in national legislation could promote efficiency and ensure that all condominium owners have meaningful and localised democratic representation. This, in turn, would reinforce consumer confidence in their investment. However, by taking a conservative approach, the national legislation falls short of fostering market forces and tends to incentivise corruption or inefficient drafting at the local level.

Despite the changing trends and indicators, there are risks associated with the fledging democratic direction in Property Law. Among them are the risk of fiat exercised by local government overriding the condominium owner's decisions, the lack of a fully authorised judicial branch for effective enforcement of remedies, the propensity for corruption and the undue influence of developers throughout the process. This encompasses the handover to the HOA and the initial selection of management companies or other external contractors.

5.5 Local Governments' Role

The relationship between the local government and the HOA is a tricky one. On the one hand, the government needs to be submissive to the

[90] Article 76(4) Property Law (2007).

autonomy of the HOA and restrict its intervention in the HOA management, as there is a natural demand for introducing private property rights in condominiums. On the other hand, the local government also needs to step in where necessary to facilitate the creation and smooth running of the HOA. For example, the local government feels obligated to intervene when the developer did not set up an HOA within the statutorily prescribed period. The crux of the issue is where to draw the boundary under the current circumstances in China.

While both the Property Law and the CC provide for the free elections of the HOA, they also allow the local government to provide "help and instructions" for establishing the HOA and the HOA executive committee.[91] The issue of interference by local governments is tied to judicial review and especially the inefficient enforcement of judgments, as an executive mandate can circumvent judicial decisions. Some local government influence is purely ministerial, such as providing basic government services, including electricity, water and sewage. The government also assists HOAs with their initial set-up and the transfer from developers in newly constructed condominiums.

Given the relationship dynamics among developers, homeowners and local governments, local governments can substantially influence the success of condominium developments. Their job should not be limited to administering around the condominiums' edges with local zoning and subdivision ordinances. More importantly, local governments should actively facilitate the autonomy of condominium management.[92] For example, when the chairperson of the HOA executive committee fails to call a meeting requested by a committee quorum, the local government should intervene and designate one of the council members to carry out the job. This keeps the HOA functioning by avoiding a deadlock. In this sense, the local government's interference is far more effective than recourse to a local court. Another function of the local government would be to inform condominium owners of their rights and obligations in condominium life through a local government training program. Awareness raising is also needed if unit owners play a significant role in condominium governance.

Therefore, the CC has incorporated several provisions allowing the governments to play a role in condominium governance. First, the local

[91] Article 277 CC; Article 75 Property Law (2007).

[92] Shitong Qiao, 'The Authoritarian Commons: Divergent Paths of Neighborhood Democratization in Three Chinese Megacities' (2023) 71 *The American Journal of Comparative Law* 388.

governments and urban residents' committees shall guide and assist in establishing an HOA and its executive committee.[93] Second, the property-managing agent shall implement emergency management measures and other government measures and actively cooperate with the work of local governments.[94] For example, this legally justifies the local governments' enforcement of the strict COVID-19 prevention measures over condominium governance during lockdown. Third, condominium owners shall cooperate with the property-managing agent when implementing emergency management measures and other government measures.[95] Fourth, where an owner or other persons refuse to observe and perform the abovementioned duties, a party concerned may report or complain to the relevant government agency.[96] The CC has formalised the local government's role in condominium governance.

However, in some cases, there is a clash between the local government and the HOA. Originally, the local government served as the landlord for all residential property. With the emergence of private property rights, that relationship changed. Still, the local government often retained control over the common elements and charged a fee to the owners for their use.[97] While the owners eventually gained control and ownership over these elements, the local government continued to retain control over the service personnel, although the local government's role was progressively lessened.

This transition is also noticeable in newly constructed condominium projects, where developers often hesitantly release control of revenue-generating common elements and professional management companies, typically only after a dispute with the owners. In the past, it was not uncommon for the developers to align with the local government in this process or act with their support.[98]

93 Para. 2 of Article 277 CC.

94 Para. 2 of Article 285 CC.

95 Para. 1 of Article 286 CC.

96 Para. 3 of Article 286 CC.

97 For example, roads out of a building scheme are public roads. See Article 274 CC.

98 Though perhaps not strictly applicable to local government, the CC does provide for the protection of individual owners from overreaching by the HOA itself, as the CC provides that the decisions of the general meeting and the executive committee are binding on the owners unless an owner can prove that the decision adversely affects her legitimate rights and interests. See Article 280 CC. If it can be proved that prescribed procedures have been contravened, the affected owner can approach the court for invalidation of the decision within a year after he has become aware or should have become aware of the decision. See Article 12 of the SPC Interpretation on Several Issues Regarding the Application of Law

Therefore, the issue of local government interference with effective democratic governance through the HOA and the issue of judicial review and enforcement are intertwined. The continued control by a local authority outside the judiciary is at odds with democratisation and market forces. The absence of a sufficient remedy has sometimes led owners to adopt a political stance rather than a strictly legal one. Protests or speaking out have sometimes been initiated to gain higher-ranking officials' attention.[99] Because they are actual stakeholders, these protesters are more highly motivated than they would be as mere tenants. Though sometimes effective, such methods alone are perhaps unreliable in bringing about change and protecting the owners' rights, although they serve as a barometer of changing societal perceptions and expectations.[100]

Despite the permissible and ubiquitous local government interventions, greater weight seems to be placed on property rights and market forces. As owners obtain greater stakes, their rights to the property become more established and socially or culturally presumed. The trend from the public sector to the private sector is poised to ultimately transition to a free market economy and to ever greater owners' rights, and thus to more profound and reliable democratic governance, including complete control over the service personnel and management of the development.[101] In this transitional period, in one case study, the "TM complex case," a grass-roots homeowners' organisation mounted a legal challenge against the local government in Shenzhen. In this case, the TM HOA unsuccessfully relied on the judiciary to fend off illegitimate local government intervention in establishing their HOA committee.[102]

Despite local governments' interference with owners' property rights, insufficient legislation and the lack of judicial enforcement, these defects should be characterised more properly as "growing pains" that will eventually relent as market forces strengthen. One can reasonably argue that local government intervention could inhibit and restrict homeowners' control of their condominium affairs. This concern could be

in the Adjudication of Disputes over the Condominium Ownership. This provision reflects the protection of minority rights.

99 One example occurred in 1998 when the owners of the Kai Li Garden in Shenzhen staged a sit-down strike in front of the district and municipal government buildings over a dispute concerning unit ownership certificates.

100 Mark Kielsgard and Lei Chen, 'The Emergence of Private Property Law in China and Its Impact on Human Rights' (2013) 15 *Asian-Pacific Law and Policy Journal* 94.

101 *Ibid.*

102 Chen and Kielsgard (n. 76), pp. 23–25.

eased under two conditions. First, local government intervention does not mean a local government has unlimited power to intervene in the private life of the condominium community. Rather, intervention as a policy tool has a fine line drawn that lays out the circumstances under which the local government can step in. Second, not all Chinese condominium owners are familiar with properly managing their property due to their lack of experience in democratic decision-making. The local government's intervention is worthwhile at this transitional stage to lessen management problems and redress any power abuses caused by inexperienced council members. In the long run, the local government's role in condominium management should be marginal when the "my property, my destiny" mentality takes good shape.

5.6 Participation Quota

A participation quota is necessitated to demarcate an owner's common interest in the following matters: (1) the share in the common property; (2) the proportional contribution to the common expenses and the share of any common profits; and (3) the weight of a condominium owner's vote.[103] The participation quota is significant in distributing the compensation received if the property is expropriated. In short, the participation quota arises whenever the rights and responsibilities of common property are allocated.

The most relevant function of the participation quota is the allocation of the owner's contributions to the management and maintenance costs and the right to share in the common profits.[104] A prospective buyer needs to pay special attention to a development's common expenses. Financially, the entitlement to an undivided share in the common property and the voting right is less significant than contributions to common expenses and sharing in the common profits. Some unit owners may rarely attend general meetings and seldom authorise their voting rights by proxy. A default rule was set in China to allocate common expenses and distribute the income generated. If there is no otherwise stipulated agreement, these issues shall be determined based on the proportion of

[103] Cornelius van der Merwe, 'A Comparative Study of the Distribution of Ownership Rights in Property in an Apartment or Condominium Scheme in Common Law, Civil Law and Mixed Law Systems' (2002) 31 *Georgia Journal of International and Comparative Law* 101.

[104] Article 282 CC.

each owner's exclusive floor areas to the total building areas.[105] Accordingly, the "one unit, one vote" rule is the norm in China, provided that non-residential and residential projects that are very diverse in size can adopt alternative and innovative participation quotas.[106] For a mixed condominium combining commercial property with residential property, the pitfalls of the "one unit, one vote" rule are obvious, especially if the owners contributing more financially do not have more say in the management issues. Supposedly, the voting right should match the value of the property and the maintenance costs; therefore, a vote weighted by the participation quota should apply. Fortunately, in China, most condominium developments are exclusively residential ones. Moreover, the difference in size and value within one condominium building is small in many residential condominium developments.

However, alternative voting procedures may still need to be provided for condominium complexes with dramatically different sizes or mixed-use condominiums. A relative floor area formula seems fairer for allocating shares than a formula based on a simple equality rule.

Despite being mechanical, the relative floor area formula has several advantages. First, it provides certainty by being simple and easy to implement. In addition, the relative floor area formula does not need a periodic reappraisal, as is the case with the value-based quota.[107] It avoids the complications of a value-based approach, such as a periodic reappraisal. Finally, the floor area approach has been employed in residential condominium developments for years in China. More to the point, in China, the purchase price of an apartment is based on square metres, and the floor area of an apartment for sale includes the enclosed unit's floor area and its share of the floor area in the common property. Therefore, the floor area approach to determine an owner's cost for common expenses is a widely accepted default rule unless there is an alternative agreement.

Nonetheless, the CC provision leaves the door open for a developer or condominium owners themselves to determine the participation quota. Where there is an agreement on such matters, including expense sharing and income distribution of a building and the ancillary facility, such an agreement shall prevail; where the agreement does not exist or is equivocal, it shall be determined according to the proportion of the floor area of

[105] Article 283 CC.
[106] Chen and Mostert (n. 44).
[107] *Ibid.*

each unit's exclusive part.[108] If there is no stipulation in the property service contract, the relevant income is owned by the owners and cannot be included in the income of the property company. The developer's discretion is useful and necessary to distinguish between exclusive residential and non-residential or mixed-use condominiums. Unlike exclusive residential condominiums, the mixed-use condominiums vary greatly. A mixed-use project may comprise residential apartments for half of the total floor area and shops for the other half, while another scheme may allocate 35 per cent of the floor area for offices and the other 65 per cent for apartments. There are several relevant factors to determine such an allocation. Hence, it is difficult, if not impossible, to stipulate a uniform yardstick for calculating the participation quota for non-residential and mixed-use condominiums. This is apparent in the provision that the floor area formula applies only when no agreement on quotas exists.[109] This means that the agreement prevails when such an agreement on quotas exists. Moreover, as the Chinese law does not expressly mention the participation quota issue for non-residential or mixed-use condominiums, one could argue that the developer must deliberate and prepare a participation quota plan. Therefore, it is advisable to give developers the discretion to design an equitable quota plan for non-residential and mixed-use condominiums.

Secondly, the Property Law provides that the number of owners who are eligible to participate in the management of the building shall be based on the number of individual apartments or commercial units, with the qualification that all unsold units, including units sold but not yet delivered by the developer or multiple units owned by the same owner, should count as only one unit. The total number of owners shall be the sum of the outcomes obtained through the above calculation.[110] Thus, the system is determined, as far as the number of votes is concerned, via the democratic principle of "one owner, one vote" as distinct from the "one unit, one vote" rule (which would provide disproportionate voting power to developers still owning multiple units or owners who own more than one unit in the scheme).[111]

[108] Article 283 CC.

[109] *Ibid.*

[110] Article 9 §1 and §2 of the SPC Interpretation on Several Issues Regarding the Application of Law in the Adjudication of Disputes over the Condominium Ownership.

[111] On the weight attached to votes, see generally van der Merwe (n. 4), pp. 145, 154, 158 and 194.

6

Land Contractual Management Rights and Homestead Use Rights

6.1 Introduction

China has no private ownership over natural resources such as land, mining minerals and sea areas. The state or collectives own them. Therefore, any organisation or individual needs to acquire usufruct rights on natural resources owned by the state or collectives to use. Following the practice of most developed legal systems, Chinese property law regards land as having durable qualities of utility which justify its departure from other perishable forms of the resource. Therefore, some people can obtain different yet compatible rights over the same land. Usufruct is the right to possess, use and benefit from someone else's property.[1] The person who enjoys the usufruct is called the usufructuary.

The basic tenet of a usufructuary right is the right to possess, use and profit from other people's property by the parties' intentions or by operation of law. This is a separate right from the right of ownership and is an expression of the relationship between the use of property and the enjoyment of its benefits, allowing the usufructuary to use the property and derive its benefits without owning it. More significantly, it is distinguished from personal (obligatory) rights of enjoyment, such as those arising under a short tenancy or loans. While personal rights grant the creditor enjoyment of a thing through the obligation of the debtor, usufructuary rights confer a direct, real right to use and enjoy the property itself, independent of any personal obligation of another party. The contract can initiate most usufructuary rights to reflect the parties' common intentions. However, the contractual solution may not be entirely satisfactory, as the contract creates only personal rights. A risk is that when the land is alienated, the rights conferred by the contract will not be enforceable against the subsequent

[1] Article 323 CC, which provides "the holder of a usufructuary right has the right, in accordance with law, to possess, use, and profit from the immovable property and movable property owned by another person."

landowners. Another defining proprietary feature of the usufruct right is that where a usufruct right is extinguished due to expropriation or requisition, the usufructuary is entitled to receive appropriate compensation in the same manner as a property owner.[2]

The CC explicitly states that immovable and movable properties are subject to usufruct rights.[3] However, throughout usufruct, all the specified rights are created over the immovable property. It is perhaps a gap – no single usufruct over a movable property specified in the CC despite this general clause in Article 323. Under the principle of *numerus clausus*, it is anticipated to be controversial if a usufruct is recognised later over movable property.

The usufructuary shall hold the property as a responsible owner. It shall not cause damage to or diminution of the property except where it is subject to natural depletion over time. Under Chinese law, the usufruct shall comply with provisions of the law on the protection, rational exploitation of resources and ecological and environmental protection when exercising its rights.[4] The usufructuary does not own the property but does have an interest in it, which is contractually allowed by the owner or operated by law. A usufructuary right includes the land contractual management right (LCMR),[5] the right to use construction land,[6] the homestead use right,[7] the right of habitation,[8] the right of servitude,[9] the right to use sea areas,[10] the mineral exploration and mining rights,[11] the right to draw water and the right to use water areas or tidal flats for aquaculture or fishery.[12]

[2] Article 327 CC.
[3] Article 323 CC.
[4] Article 326 CC.
[5] Chapter 11 of Book 2, Property in the CC.
[6] Chapter 12 of Book 2, Property in the CC.
[7] Chapter 13 of Book 2, Property in the CC.
[8] Chapter 14 of Book 2, Property in the CC.
[9] Chapter 15 of Book 2, Property in the CC.
[10] Article 328 CC.
[11] It is worth noting that the 2007 Property Law made it explicit that mining rights and mineral exploration rights are property rights, specifically usufructuary rights. Article 123 of the 2007 Property Law provides that mineral exploration rights, mining rights, rights to draw water and the right to use water areas or tidal flats for aquaculture or fishery that are legally acquired are protected by law. This provision was kept intact in Article 329 of the Chinese CC enacted in 2020 which recognises that mineral mining rights and other exploration rights that are obtained in accordance with the law are property rights which are protected by law.
[12] Article 329 CC.

In a country without private land ownership, the usufruct is particularly significant as a manifestation of commerciality.[13] The land is not just a resource but an asset. All properties are subject to sale, lease, mortgage or other disposition to operate a functioning economy. In China, an organisation or a person has the right to possess, use and profit from natural resources owned by the state or the collective.[14] Bookchin argues that the freedom of individuals in a community to appropriate resources is merely because they are using them.[15] Given finite resources in our society, the property law is designed (1) to ensure more efficient exploitation of land and other resources; (2) to cater for the personal needs of the creator of usufruct driven by the market; and (3) to coordinate many different, and often conflicting, claims arising from the same land.

There are two ways to acquire a usufruct under the Chinese CC. First, usufruct rights such as the LCMR, the habitation right and servitude are generally created through a contract between the owner and the user, specifically that the contract is the basis for creating usufruct rights and there is no need to seek administrative approval.[16] Second, usufruct rights such as the rural homestead right, the right to use sea areas, mining exploration rights and mining rights, water rights and finishing rights need to obtain administrative permission from the competent government administrative department for their creation. In other words, usufruct rights are created through application by the owner of the right to use and approval by the competent administrative department.

Some usufruct rights must be registered to be effective while others are created upon the contract conclusion and require no registration. However, whether registration is required for creation does not correspond to how a usufruct right is set up. This is to say, for those usufruct rights created by the contract only without administrative permission, some require registration to be effective, such as habitation right.[17] However, other rights are created when the contract becomes effective,

[13] Article 325 CC states that the state implements a system of paid use of natural resources, unless otherwise provided by law.

[14] Article 324.

[15] Murray Bookchin, *The Ecology of Freedom: The Emergence and Dissolution of Hierarchy* (Cheshire Books 1982).

[16] Cui Jianyuan [崔建远], *Property Law* [《物权法》] (China Renmin University Press 2010), p. 273.

[17] Article 368.

such as the LCMR[18] and servitude.[19] Likewise, some rights needing administrative permission, such as homestead rights, do not need registration to be effective.

The duration of the usufruct rights also varies. For instance, the homestead right is perpetual, without any time limit. The allocated CLUR does not specify the time limit. However, it can be taken by the government for public use without compensation, as the user was allocated without paying a premium. The LCMR lasts between thirty and seventy years.[20] The term of a habitation right is subject to mutual negotiation between the parties.[21] More notably, a downstream usufruct might be carved out of an upstream usufruct. For example, the duration of the land management right should be no longer than the residual term of the LCMR.

This chapter selects the two designated usufructuary rights for discussion: the LCMR and the homestead use rights. In the ensuing chapter on usufruct, the right to use construction land and the right of habitation will be explored. How to create these usufructuary rights and determine questions of priority when a conflict between the usufructuary rights proves inevitable? What are the restrictions of the usufructuary rights in a heavy-handed regulatory environment? It is the law that the owner shall not interfere with exercising usufructuary rights.[22] Does it mean that under Chinese law, the usufructuary has the right to use the property to exclude the landowner? If so, is there a tragedy of anti-commons when multiple owners possess the right to exclude others from a limited resource, and none enjoy the privilege of use, with the resource being susceptible to underutilisation? Does the usufructuary have the right to transform or substantially change the property, even to enhance the property value?

6.2 Land Contractual Management Right

6.2.1 Introduction

LCMR is a legal concept related to land use rights in rural areas. The LCMR may be created over the collective-owned and state-owned land

[18] Article 333.

[19] Article 374.

[20] Article 332. The duration of contractual management on arable land is thirty years. The duration of contractual management on grassland ranges from thirty to fifty years. The duration of contractual management on forest land ranges from thirty to seventy years.

[21] Article 367.

[22] Article 326.

designated for agricultural use.[23] It is a key element of China's rural land tenure system. The LCMR is a legal product of the evolving household responsibility system implemented in China in the General Principles of Civil Law (GPCL) enacted in 1986.[24] Specifically, the LCMR can be held by individuals or over forests, mountains, grasslands, wastelands, beaches and water bodies on collectively owned or state-owned land used by collectives.[25] While the 1986 GPCL provided the notion of the LCMR, it did not specify that LCMR is a property right. However, it was located in the section with a heading on property ownership and property rights. It emerged as a way to address issues related to collective land ownership and to encourage agricultural productivity. The Land Administration Law is the first law promulgated in China on the management of land resources and regulations on land use, enacted in 1986.[26] It provides that all the land is either state owned or collective owned.[27] Table 6.1 maps

[23] Para. 2 of Article 330 CC provides that "the system of land contracting for agricultural operations is applied to arable land, forest land, grassland and other kinds of agricultural land owned by farmers collectively or owned by the State and used by farmers collectively." In addition, Article 343 explicitly states that "for state-owned agricultural land under contractual management, the relevant provisions of this Book shall be referred to and applied." Further to that, Para. 2 of Article 13 of the Land Administration Law (the 3rd amendment, effective on 1 January 2020) provides that "state-owned land designated for agricultural use can be legally contracted and operated by entities or individuals, engaging in activities such as crop cultivation, forestry, animal husbandry, and fisheries production."

[24] Para. 2 of Article 80 GPCL 1986.

[25] Article 81 GPCL 1986.

[26] The Land Administration Law has undergone four amendments since it was introduced. On 29 December 1988, the Land Administration Law was amended for the first time, adding that "the right to use state-owned land and collectively-owned land may be transferred under the law." This was a follow-up amendment in tandem with the 1988 constitutional amendment. China implements a system of paid use of state-owned land per the law, providing market access to the state-owned land. The Land Administration Law was amended for the second time on 29 August 1998. The basic state policy on farmland conservation was established in a legislative form. It was amended on 28 August 2004 for the third time, providing that the state may expropriate or requisite land and pay compensation for it when the public interest so requires. The most recent amendment of the Land Administration Law was made on 26 August 2019. It includes (1) establishing a permanent basic farmland protection system, (2) allowing collectively operating construction land to be marketised, (3) improving the legal protection of rural land expropriation, (4) streamlining the division of land use approval authority between the central and local authorities, (5) proposing the legal requirements for setting up a national land spatial planning system and (6) strengthening the protection of the homestead right on the rural land.

[27] Article 2 Land Administration Law.

Table 6.1 *Summary chart of Chinese state-owned land use rights statutory framework including SPC judicial interpretations*

Year	Title	Type of Statutory Instruments	Implications
1986 (amended in 1988, 1998, 2004, 2019)	Land Administration Law	National Legislation	Specific legislation governing LCMR in rural areas.
1986	General Principles of Civil Law (repealed on 1 January 2021)	National Legislation	Introduced a legal concept of LCMR based on the evolving household responsibility system
1998	The Implementation Regulations of the Land Administration Law (revised in 2011, 2014)	Administrative Regulation	Provides detailed procedures and guidelines for the implementation of the Land Administration Law, clarifying the administration, use and transactions of land within the legislation.
2002	Rural Land Contracting Law (amended in 2018)	National Legislation	Allows rural households to contract land for agricultural purposes, ensures long-term security of land contracts (typically thirty years) and permits transfer and sublease of land use rights under certain conditions.

2005	The SPC Interpretation on Legal Issues Concerning the Adjudication of Disputes over Rural Land Contracting (revised in 2020)	SPC Judicial Interpretation	It provides guidance on how to handle and resolve legal disputes specifically related to rural land contracting, aiming to ensure consistency and fairness in the application of laws across different cases involving rural land issues in China.
2007	The Property Law (repealed on 1 January 2021)	National Legislation	The first comprehensive legislation concerning property rights; provided a chapter on the LCMR.
2010	The Law on the Mediation and Arbitration of Rural Land Contract Disputes	National Legislation	Deals specifically with disputes arising from the contracting management of rural land.
2011	The Provisions on Several Issues Concerning the Adjudication of Administrative Cases Involving Rural Collective Land	SPC Judicial Interpretation	Contains specific guidelines and procedural rules for courts to follow when handling administrative cases related to rural collective land issues.
2015	Interim Regulations on Real Estate Registration	Administrative Regulation	Provide the framework and procedures for registering real estate in China, including LCMR in rural areas.

Table 6.1 (*cont.*)

Year	Title	Type of Statutory Instruments	Implications
2016	Opinions of the CPC Central Committee and the State Council on Steadily Advancing the Reform of the Rural Collective Property Rights System	CCP and the State Council policy document	Enhances the management, use and transfer of these rights to promote rural development and economic efficiency.
2020	The Civil Code	National Legislation by NPC	Has seven parts and 1,260 articles. The parts include General Provisions, Property Rights, Contracts, Personality Rights, Marriage and Family, Right of Inheritance, and Tort Liability and Supplemental Provision.
2020	The Opinions of the CPC Central Committee and the State Council on Establishing a Perfect System and Mechanism for Market-oriented Allocation of Factors	The CCP policy document and the State Council policy document.	Implement the reform of the rural land expropriation system and establish a fair and reasonable distribution system for the value-added benefits from the market entry of collective operational construction land.

out all the relevant statutory framework, including the SPC judicial interpretations concerning the LCMR.

Experiential rules pioneered in certain localities facilitating the decentralisation of land use from the collective to the household level incentivised the peasants to improve farming productivity. After more than a decade of practice of the household responsibility system nationwide, the RLCL, implemented in 2002, secures the households' rights of use and possession by allowing the enforcement of thirty-year land use contracts to prevent large-scale arbitrary land reallocations and allowing transfers of LCMR between the households. This system grants rural households the right to use a contracted piece of land for agricultural purposes. Specifically, the RLCL provides that the grantee under the LCMR over the collective-owned land has the right to (1) enjoy the use and income of the contracted land, (2) transfer the contracted land management rights, (3) organise production and operation and dispose of the products independently and (4) be appropriately compensated where contracted land is expropriated or occupied. Therefore, the RLCL established a stable and relatively long-term arrangement for rural land use.[28] After the initial contract period, there are provisions for renewal.[29]

When the Property Law was enacted in 2007, these rules were reinforced and fine-tuned (see discussion in Chapter 11). It has been argued that the Property Law 2007 failed to provide a genuine and systematic right-based property law regarding land use rights, and instead it is just a 2.0 version of the Land Administration Law.[30] For example, as with the Land Administration Law and the RLCL, the Property Law does not address a thorny issue of whether the LCMR can be created over the state-owned agricultural land operated by the state-owned farming or forestry estates. In other words, if a state-owned farmland or forestry land has been transferred to a private entity to manage the land for a specified

[28] The Rural Land Contract Law has been amended in 2019. Article 21 provides that "the contracting period for arable land is thirty years. The contracting period for grassland is thirty to fifty years. The contracting period for forest land is thirty to seventy years."

[29] Para. 2 of Article 21 of the RLCL states that "after the expiration of the contracting period stipulated in the preceding clause for arable land, it may be extended for an additional thirty years. For grassland and forest land, the contracting period may be correspondingly extended in accordance with the provisions of the preceding paragraph."

[30] Gu Zhang [张谷], 'Can the "Property Rights" CC be "reborn"?' [《民法典"物权编"能否"浴火重生"？》] (2016) *Speech at the International High-Level Forum on the Rule of Law and Reform* [*"法治与改革国际高端论坛"中的演讲*] <www.ghls.zju.edu.cn/ghlscn/2016/1112/c13708a1142666/page.htm> accessed on 24 January 2024.

term, does the private entity acquire a property right? The Property Law does not explicitly state that LCMR can be created under such a situation. However, it implicitly recognises that the state-owned agricultural land under contractual management can create the LCMR by referring to and applying the relevant provisions of the LCMR.[31] Often, the disputes boil down to whether contractual management, lease or franchise transfers the land use to the private entity.

Regarding land policy changes, in 2014, the No. 1 Central Document of the CCP Central Committee called for granting the right to use, occupy and generate income to farmers and allowing the lands to be subject to mortgages or liens.[32] In early 2017, the No. 1 Central Document reinforced "[t]he introduction of a rural land reform that disentangles farmland ownership rights, contract rights, and management rights, enabling farmers to increase their earnings by transferring their land use rights to individuals or entities."[33] It calls for establishing the construction land market and a land registration system and stresses the importance of collective ownership as the basis of reforms.

This accumulation of rural land reform policies eventually became the legislative changes of the Land Administration Law in 2019. Its newly added Article 45 clarifies the scope of public interest in land taking (expropriation) by specifying what amounts to the public interest to justify an expropriation.[34] This effectively restricts the scope of land expropriation, and the local government's power to expropriate rural land has been severely restrained.

In 2020, when the CC was promulgated, it not only confirmed these rules[35] but also introduced some provisions concerning the land

[31] Article 134 Property Law.

[32] The Ministry of Agriculture and Rural Affairs, <www.moa.gov.cn/gk/zcfg/qnhnzc/201401/t20140121_3743917.htm>accessed on 1 January 2023.

[33] See '中共中央国务院关于深入推进农业供给侧结构性改革加快培育农业农村发展新动能的若干意见 [Guidelines of the CCP Central Committee and State Council on Deepening Supply-Side Structural Reform of Agriculture and Accelerating the Cultivation of New Growth Drivers for Agriculture and Rural Areas]' (*Xinhua News*, 2017) < http://news.xinhuanet.com/politics/2017-02/05/c_1120413568.htm> accessed on 27 April 2020.

[34] Article 45 Land Administration Law.

[35] Under Article 330, the rural collective economic organisations implement the two-level management system that is based on household contractual management and combines centralised and decentralised operations. The system of land contracting for agricultural operations is applied to arable land, forest land, grassland and other kinds of agricultural land owned by farmers collectively or owned by the state and used by farmers collectively.

management right, which is carved out of the LCMR when the household intends to grant land use to a third party. The trajectory is clear towards a policy-orientated rule design entrenching the urban–rural divide in the Chinese land system.

The applicable laws concerning LMCR include the CC, the Land Administration Law, the RLCL, the Forestry Law, the Grassland Law and the Desertification Prevention and Control Law.[36] The LCMR straddles both the law of property and the law of contract. A contract for a certain term between the collectives and individual farm households initiates the LCMR. However, it is essentially a property right under the Chinese legal framework as the aspects of land use rights for certain terms confer to the farmers certain proprietary entitlements, not the contractual aspects. The LCMR is far-reaching, as it encompasses the most sizeable land in China concerning food productivity and safety.

6.2.2 *Content*

The right holder of LCMR takes possession of, uses and profits from the contracted arable land, forest land and grassland and carries out agricultural production such as crop cultivation, forestry, animal husbandry and so forth within the specified time limit.[37] The LCMR holder enjoys the whole property, including accessories, and receives the fruits gained from the property. The farmers may use the land by reaping natural fruits according to the usual cultivation standards in conformity with the land's intended purpose. They are also entitled to civil fruits such as the rental income from hiring out the property.

LCMR can also apply to state-owned agricultural land.[38] In China, many state-owned farms or forestry estates grant the use to individuals, households or organisations engaged in commercial farming or desertification control. In that case, the grantee over the state-owned agricultural land acquires a usufruct, a property right deserving legal protection.[39] Nonetheless, the competent government authority needs to pronounce some implementation details through administration regulations or departmental rules.

[36] For example, Articles 25 and 34 of the Desertification Prevention and Control Law address the LCMR over the collective-owned decertified land.
[37] Article 331 CC.
[38] Article 343 CC.
[39] Article 13 Land Administration Law (amended in 2019, effective on 1 January 2020).

The terms of the LCMR range from thirty to seventy years, depending on the use of the contracted land. When the contract's term expires, the farmer can renew the LCMR.[40] During its term, the grantor (usually the collectives) cannot conduct a land adjustment affecting the LCMR holder's interests unless due to special circumstances such as serious damage to the land caused by a natural disaster.[41] This confirms that the LCMR is not precarious and subject to policy change, such as land readjustment from time to time by the collectives or local townships. As a time-limited property right, the LCMR cannot be arbitrarily dispossessed during the term, meaning taken back by the collectives or the local government agencies.[42] If the contracted land is expropriated, the holder of LCMR is entitled to obtain compensation following the general rules and procedures of land expropriation.[43]

The LCMR is divided into two categories according to the two different contracting methods: family contracting and contracting through other means. Family contracting LCMR is an identity-based property right. One of the distinguishing features of family contracting is that its acquisition is inherently linked to the membership of the village collective. Only a village member, a member of the collective where the contracted land belongs, either by registered domicile or through a long period of residence, is granted the LCMR.[44]

It is difficult or nearly impossible for an outsider to acquire LCMR except where barren hills, barren ditches, barren mounds and barren beaches (known as "four barrens") and forest land[45] in rural areas are not suitable for household contracting. The four barrens may be contracted through tenders, auctions, public negotiations and other means[46] to someone outside the village if at least two-thirds of the members of the villagers' meeting or at least two-thirds of the representatives of members of this collective economic organisation consent, and the approval must

[40] Article 332 CC.

[41] Article 336 CC.

[42] Article 337 CC.

[43] Article 338 CC; Articles 60 and 65 RLCL.

[44] Article 5 RLCL stipulates: "Members of rural collective economic organizations have the right to contract land issued by their collective economic organizations in accordance with the law." Article 16 stipulates: "The contractor of family contracting is the farmer of the collective economic organization."

[45] Article 18 Forestry Law.

[46] Article 48 RLCL.

be sought from the township (town) people's government.[47] In the case of four barrens, the RLCL provides a separate category – contracting through other means.[48] When contracting rural land through other means, under equal conditions, members of the collective economic organisation have the right of first refusal to contract.[49] In short, apart from the four barrens, the transfer of the LCMR is restricted to another household within the same village.[50]

The LCMR holder is entitled to exchange or transfer the right, but it must be used for the intended purpose of the land, specifically agricultural use. No land subject to LCMR may be used for non-agricultural purposes without governmental approval.[51] The LCMR was allowed to be transferred to the household in the same collective village as early as the 2002 RLCL.[52] The transfer is based on the principle of voluntariness. The SPC pronounces that where the village collective compels the household to convey its right to a third party, the household's claim for nullifying the transfer contract should be supported by the local court that hears the dispute.[53] Therefore, granting the LCMR to outside investors, though not completely prohibited, was severely restricted. Because of ideology-driven concerns over the potential threat of corporate land acquisition to the livelihoods of farmers whose primary source of income is the land use right,[54] the law mandates that any outside investor obtain a farmer's consent before signing a contract to acquire the LCMR.[55] Moreover, members of the collective economic organisation have a right of first refusal before it is contracted to an outsider.[56]

Despite the legal protection the law and the judiciary provide, the LCMR has been weak and vulnerable to local government dictates in

47 Article 52 RLCL.

48 Chapter 3 of the RLCL.

49 Article 51 RLCL.

50 Articles 33 and 34 RLCL.

51 Article 33 RLCL.

52 Article 35 RLCL.

53 The SPC Interpretation of Applicable Laws When Reviewing Cases Concerning Rural Land Contracting Disputes of 2005.

54 Xuefeng, He [贺雪峰], 'On the Scale of Rural Land Management – Taking Anhui Fanchang City as a Subject of Discussion' [《论农地经营的规模——以安徽繁昌调研为基础的讨论》] (2011) 11 *Journal of Nanjing Agricultural University: Social Science Edition* [《南京农业大学学报: 社会科学版》] 6.

55 Article 48 RLCL (2002).

56 Articles 33 and 47 RLCL.

rural China.[57] The uneasy reality is that local governments often deviate from strictly enforcing abstract, incomplete and ambiguous national legislation and regulations. For this reason, the 2018 RLCL amendment abolished the 2002 provision that required farmers to revoke their land rights if all household members moved to cities and changed their domicile membership/Hukou to urban residents.[58] Under the previous law, the LCMR were considered inferior to property rights, as farmers would forfeit those rights when transitioning their residential status from rural to urban. Under the new law, urbanised farmers can maintain their land rights regardless of residence. They also have the option to transfer rights to an external investor while retaining the LCMR.[59] As China undergoes rapid urbanisation, this recent legislative change guarantees that the 200 million Chinese farmers presently residing in cities and those contemplating a move to an urban area in the future can do so without the risk of losing their land rights. In addition, many forced evictions and land disputes are still taking place over the LCMR held by rural villagers. It is not uncommon to have collusive alliances between the village collective, local government and commercial developers. Performance assessments of local government officials heavily emphasise factors such as GDP growth, fiscal revenues and urban infrastructure building. Although local governments enthusiastically promote local economic development, land seizures contribute to rural land tenure insecurity. Farmers are prone to forced evictions with inadequate compensation and insufficient provision of social security.[60] The root cause is the artificial differentiation of transferable urban land and non-transferable rural land. This is to say, the demand for land supply in rural China is satisfied by state-based models of expropriation through converting the legal status of rural land rather than through impersonal exchanges of property rights. To address the grievances caused by forced evictions, the RLCL and the Land Administration Law have been amended in 2018 and 2019, respectively, to allow the LCMR to be

[57] Ethan Michelson, 'Climbing the Dispute Pagoda: Grievances and Appeals to the Official Justice System in Rural China' (2007) 72 *American Sociological Review* 459; Eva Pils, 'Land Disputes, Rights Assertion and Social Unrest: A Case from Sichuan' (2006) 19 *Columbia Journal of Asian Law* 365.

[58] Para. 3 of Article 26 RLCL.

[59] Article 27 RLCL (2018 version).

[60] Lei Chen, 'The Legal and Institutional Analysis of Land Expropriation in China', in John Gillespie and Fu Hualing (eds), *Resolving Land Disputes in East Asia* (Cambridge University Press 2014), pp. 59–85.

transferred to the market. Allowing transactions in rural land use rights would be a major milestone in the economic liberalisation of China.

6.2.3 *Registration of LCMR*

The LCMR does not need to be registered; it is created when the contractual management rights agreement is concluded.[61] While registration is not essential to creating the LCMR, registration confirms the existence of the right and confers additional protections to the rights holder.[62] Those who hold LCMR are incentivised to have effective title certificates, as they need to invest and use their properties as collateral for credit. It cannot be alleged against a bona fide third party without registration.[63]

In economic terms, an effective property information system is a public good.[64] When property information is standardised and accessible, the system allows for effective planning incorporating demographics, land use and environmental-impact assessments.[65] As the benefits are so broadly dispersed and the costs of providing a standardised property system are so high, state intervention is typically necessary to establish national systems for registering land information,[66] particularly in valuing rights and collecting consents.[67] However, this economic ideal did not match the reality of land registration practice in the past.

In China, land registration has been operated as a public service by registrars at the people's government at the county level or above. The Chinese land registration system can be said to be a mixed model under a fragmented structure. To say it is a mixed model, some property rights, such as the land use right of construction land, the ownership of

[61] Para. 1 of Article 333 CC.

[62] Para. 2 of Article 333 CC.

[63] Article 335 CC.

[64] Stuart Banner, 'Transitions between Property Regimes' (2002) 31 *Journal of Legal Studies* 359, 362.

[65] Klaus Deininger, *Land Policies for Growth and Poverty Reduction* (Vol. 1) (World Bank 2003), pp. 24–25, 31–32.

[66] *Ibid.*, p. 23. ("[T]he benefits of well-defined and secure property rights and the advantages of public provision of such rights have, over history, led virtually all economically and politically advanced societies to establish state-managed systems for regulating land ownership and land transfers.")

[67] Benito Arruñada, 'Property Enforcement as Organized Consent' (2003) 19 *Journal of Law, Economics, and Organization* 401 (analysing different land administration systems in obtaining consent and enforcing *in rem* property rights).

housing,[68] habitation right[69] and the mortgage over immovable property,[70] are created only upon registration. In other words, "no registration, no property rights." In contrast, the recordation of land contractual management rights,[71] the real servitude[72] and the floating charge merely enable them to stand against third parties.[73]

The land registration system in China has a fragmented structure. To begin with, national-level registrar offices were not uniform. Before 1 March 2015, when the Provisional Regulations on Real Estate Registration came into effect to introduce the uniform registration of different types of immovable property rights, there were six main registration authorities in various departments: the state land administration, the housing authority, the mining authority, the water administration, the fishery authority and the forestry authority. Each registration authority maintained its own land registry, and there is no uniform central registry. Conflicting and inconsistent departmental interests and local governments' parochial interests hindered the systemisation of registrars. It is not uncommon to find one piece of land subject to two or multiple registered certificates by different departments.[74] This situation may be explained by the sheer expanse of Chinese rural land. Take forest land as an example. It may take some time to flesh out the implementation details on how to handle registration (design, procedure, liability from errors by the forest department); it may incur expenditures to set up the forest registry to carry out the registration and, therefore, will require budgetary approval by the State Council; it may also take some time to train the staff to be equipped with the requisite legal and practical knowledge. More to the point, the forest land in China, either state owned or collective owned, was allowed to be transferred subject to restrictions in 1998 when the Forest Law was amended. The transaction volume varies from one locality to another. If the volume is low, using the pre-existing registration office, namely the local government at the county level or above, makes sense. Therefore, fine-tuning the practical details of the forest land registration administered by the forest department is an incremental process.

[68] Article 349 CC.
[69] Article 368 CC.
[70] Article 402 CC.
[71] Article 333 CC.
[72] Article 274 CC.
[73] Articles 396 and 403 CC.
[74] In China it is known as "Two certificates over one land" [一地两证].

In December 2014, however, the State Council issued the Provisional Regulation on Real Estate Registration to introduce a nationwide uniform real estate registration system.[75] It consolidates the responsibility for the six types of certificates under a single department, the Ministry of Natural Resources. It also introduces the uniform real estate certificate format under the same centralised database. To standardise the registration and certification of LCMR and land management rights, the Ministry of Natural Resources has formulated a practice guide to facilitate nationwide uniform registration in November 2022.[76]

With a transition from collective to tradable property rights in rural land, the Chinese CC clarifies that no mandatory registration model exists on the LCMR.[77] This is to say, the creation of the LCMR is upon the conclusion of the land contractual management contract. It does not need to be registered to be created. This is a sensible approach, as the concept of transferable land use right over rural land is still evolving, and transaction volumes and property prices vary greatly from locality to locality.

- What is the demand among rural landholders for private transactions in rural land?
- What types of transactions take place over rural land?
- To what extent are farmers benefitting from transactions of rural land?

These questions help to test the evolutionary theory that property holders assert individual tradable rights when their benefits outweigh their costs. Therefore, a voluntary incremental model seems to be a natural choice.

6.2.4 *Inheritability*

The national legislative framework is ambiguous on inheritability of the LCMR. For example, Article 32 of the RLCL only provides that the proceeds obtained through land contracting can be inherited.[78] While

[75] The Provisional Regulation on Real Estate Registration was issued by the State Council on 22 December 2014 and came into effect on 1 March 2015.

[76] Ministry of Natural Resources on the Issuance of the Registration of Land Contract Management Rights and Land Management Rights Operational Specification (for Trial Implementation) and other documents Natural Resources Development [2022] No. 198, issued on 8 November 2022.

[77] Article 333 CC.

[78] Para. 1 of Article 32 RLCL.

the heirs of the LCMR over forest land or four barrens may continue to farm upon the right holder's death,[79] whether the heirs can continue to farm for residual terms over arable land is silent. The relevant SPC interpretation reiterated the above legislative provision without further clarifications.[80] Notably, the scope of heirs is not limited to members of the collective economic organisation.

Nonetheless, many local regulations passed before the RLCL granted the heirs the right to continue to farm under the contract upon the holder's death.[81] This seems to contradict the national legislation and SPC pronouncement, but local regulations are arguably more sensible than national legislation, as they are gleaned through the local practice.

Surprisingly, in most cases involving the LCMR disputes, Chinese courts did not refer to local regulations. Instead, they relied on national legislation and relevant provisions of judicial interpretations, which substantially restricted local legislative power. As a result, the vast majority of court decisions denied the inheritability of LCMR. Chinese courts reasoned that national legislation enacted by the NPC or NPCSC has priority over local rules stipulated in the Legislation Law. Therefore, Chinese courts can only interpret the laws but cannot ignore their hierarchy.

Specifically, Chinese courts first examine what category of LCMR is at issue. If it involves a family contracting the LCMR, inheritance generally does not occur. This is because the LCMR is not a property right held by

[79] Para. 2 of Article 32 and Article 54 RLCL.

[80] Article 23 of the Interpretation of the SPC on the Application of Law to the Hearing of Disputes Relating to Rural Land Contracts (2020 Amendment).

[81] For example, Article 23(2) of the 1993 Regulations on the Administration of Contracts in the Rural Collective Economy of Shanxi Province stipulates: "If the contractor of an agricultural contract dies during the contract period, the heirs of the contractor may continue the contract. If the successor does not want to contract, the contracting party and the contractor's successor shall clear the debts and liabilities during the contract period and then issue another contract." Article 17(6) of the Regulations on the Administration of Contracts for the Rural Collective Economy of Shandong Province of 1999 stipulates that if the contractor loses the ability to contract or dies, and the heirs renounce the succession, which makes the contract impossible to perform, the contract is allowed to be cancelled. In other words, if the heirs do not renounce their inheritance, the contract is allowed to continue. More examples can be seen at Article 8 of the Regulations on the Administration of Contracts for the Collective Economy of Villages, 1995; Article 10 of the Regulations on the Administration of Contracts for the Collective Economy of Rural Areas in Hubei Province (for Trial Implementation), 1996; Article 22 of the Regulations on the Administration of Contracts for the Collective Economy of Rural Areas in Guizhou Province.

individuals but the household or the family. When the head of the family is deceased, the household with other family members still exists, so no inheritance occurs.[82] Second, the household members are co-owners of the LCMR. Therefore, when the family head is deceased and the co-owner survives, there is no question of succession.[83] This is to say, in the household-based usufruct right, no inheritance occurs upon the death of one or some household members during the contracting period. If all family members die, the LCMR is extinguished, and the collective will take back the contracted land. If the heir is not a member of the collective economic organisation, he should not have the right to inherit it. Otherwise, the rights and interests of other collective members will be jeopardised.

The two aforementioned arguments put forward by Chinese courts are not tenable. They suggest that the right of survivorship under the common law rule of joint tenancy applies here. When one co-owner, such as the household head, is deceased, all the LCMR interests and rights will pass on to the surviving family members. However, Chinese law does not adopt the rule of survivorship. Therefore, the courts should address the issue of how to divide the share of the deceased household member upon death. Chinese courts are generally reluctant to explore this further, however. Before all family members die, the LCMR is taken as a property right, specifically as a co-ownership held by all family members. When the last family member dies, the courts ignore its proprietary nature by considering the LCMR only as a contract. Therefore, when the contracting party dies, the contract will end.

Consequently, the collectives are entitled to take the land back. The Chinese courts adopt a policy-oriented approach in denying the inheritability of the LCMR. However, there is a lack of effective redistribution mechanisms for rural collective economic organisations when non-inheritable agricultural land is taken back.[84] It is hoped that detailed rules will be provided to formalise its inheritability in the next legislation

[82] 王某诉王某 [*Wang v. Wang*] (2021) 京0119民初5100号 [(2021) Jing 0119 Min Chu No. 5100]; 王某诉王某 [*Wang v. Wang*] (2021) 云0623民初1614号 [(2021) Yun 0623 Min Chu No. 1614].

[83] 马某诉马某 [*Ma v. Ma*] (2021) 吉0112民初2518号 [(2021) Ji 0112 Min Chu 2518]; 蒋元桂诉蒋守良[*Jiang Yuan Gui v. Jia Shoulaing* (2021) 湘12民终1760号[(2021) Xiang 12 Min Zhong No. 1760].

[84] Su Chen [陈甦], 'The Mechanism of Inheritance of Land Contract Management Rights and Its Interpretive Debate' [《土地承包经营权继承机制及其阐释辨证》] (2016) 3 *Tsinghua Law Journal* [《清华法学》] 57.

reform, thus better protecting the farmer's property rights. When it involves land contracting through other means over forest land or four barrens, inheritance may occur. As a result, the heirs can continue land contracting for the remaining term.[85] This is because the heirs under this type of LCMR may likely not be the collective members.

An interesting scenario arises where the holder of the LCMR is a one-person family or the last surviving family member. When the holder is deceased without any other surviving family members, can her heirs who are not members of the collective continue to farm the land for the remaining term? Based on the preceding discussion, the test seems to hinge on whether the LCMR is a family contracting type or contracting through other means. A Chongqing court held that the heirs under the LCMR over forest land can continue to enjoy the land contracting for the rest of the term even if they are not members of the collective.[86] By contrast, heirs from outside of the collective under the family contract cannot enjoy the LCMR over the contracted land for the remaining term. The SPC held that after the death of the LCMR holder, if the legal heir is not listed as the contractor in the rural land contractual management registration materials or is not a family member in the family contracting method, they cannot acquire the LCMR as inheritance.[87] This is hardly convincing and may create a discrepancy between the two categories. Why are the heirs of the contracting family discriminated against by losing the right to farm for the remaining term? It is expected to be resolved by judicial rulings or legislative reform soon.

6.2.5 The Ambiguities of the Land Management Right

In the past, when engaging in non-construction, collective rural land had to be collected and stored by the local government and then go through a heavy-handed regulatory process to change the nature of the collective land into state-owned land. Transactions involving rural land present a potential alternative to state-based mechanisms for the exchange of property rights. Many local governments since 2007 have employed

[85] Para. 2 of Article 32 and Article 54 RLCL.

[86] 李乾胜与武隆区白马镇鱼光村何家沟村民小组,渝0156民初3035号 [*Li Qiansheng v. the Village Committee of Hejiagou, Yuguang Village, Baima Town, Wulong District* (2021) Yu 0156 Min Chu 3035].

[87] 管永恒等诉山西省长治市郊区人民政府 (2018) 最高法行申1731号 [*Guan Yongheng and others v. the People's Government of Changzhi Suburban District, Shanxi Province* (2018) SPC Xing Shen No. 1731].

practical approaches facilitating rural land transfer. Nevertheless, allowing the contractual transfer of rural land rights is a sensitive socio-political topic in China, not only because of histories of smallholder farmer landlessness but also because it raises issues of citizens' engagement with the state.

Given the political sensitivities, a compromise model has gained ground from the experiential practices in many localities for many years. The model involves the separation of the three rights: collective land ownership, LCMR and land management right. On the one hand, the existing rural land tenure norms remain intact by keeping the collective land ownership and the family-based LCMR. On the other hand, a new type of land management right is carved out of the LCMR to implement the land transfer. With the rapid urbanisation in the last three decades, many villagers chose to be migrant workers in urban areas while keeping the village membership. With the village membership, the villagers shave the LCMR over farmland but cannot personally engage in farming while away in cities. Against this background, in 2007, the State Council allowed Chengdu and Chongqing to conduct pilot agricultural land registration and transfer projects.[88] Policy-wise, the top leadership has signalled a clear message that it intends to end the dual urban and rural land systems, where urban land can be commercially transferred while rural land is locked and frozen. More specifically, the policy addresses a phenomenon of land abandonment when the LCMR holders do not farm themselves when migrating to cities. At the same time, outsiders are not qualified to engage. This may cause a holding-out problem. To tackle this, local governments have gradually implemented and fine-tuned many concrete policies to set up an institutional framework for markets in rural property rights.[89]

Policymakers are faced with a challenging dilemma requiring them to implement decisive measures that address both immediate and enduring issues. One of the government initiatives was to allow LCMR holders to rent out farmland to outsiders for farming within the residual terms. This is evidenced by the fact that the RLCL was amended in 2018 to formalise

[88] National Development and Reform Commission (NDRC), The Circular approving Chongqing and Chengdu as the Special Experimental Zones for Coordinated Rural and Urban Development areas (Fa Gai Jing Ti [2007] No. 1248).

[89] Xiaoming Guo, *Coordinating Urban and Rural Development and Rural Land Transfer Reform: An Empirical Study on Chengdu Model* (China Science Press 2012).

the land management right.[90] This has been further confirmed by the 2019 Amendment to the Land Administration Law. The law incorporates the experience of the transfer of collective business construction land. It removes the old law's requirement that if one is engaged in non-agricultural construction, one must use state-owned land or former collective land that has been expropriated as state owned, breaking down the legal barriers to entry of collective business construction land into the market.[91] The Land Administration Law allows landowners to hand over land to entities or individuals for use by granting or leasing the land for industrial, commercial and other business purposes, as determined in the overall land use plan and urban and rural planning and lawfully registered.[92] In other words, under the land use planning, collective business construction land can be directly transferred to the market and enjoy the same treatment as state-owned construction land, with the same rights and prices and the same access to the market, breaking through the inherent dual system of urban and rural land in China.[93]

The CC confirms such a right by allowing the LCMR holder to grant a third party or an outside investor the land management right by letting or sharing the purchase.[94] The land management right in rural areas is a land use right. It grants individuals or households within a rural collective the right to use and manage a specific piece of land for agricultural purposes, such as crop cultivation, and obtaining a profit.[95]

A land management right with a duration of more than five years is created at the moment when the underlying contract of grant becomes effective.[96] However, the parties may apply to register the land management right, and without registration, such right cannot be alleged against a bona fide third party.[97] It renders an impression that the land management right is just a right carved out of the LCMR, and the way of creation and the registration model are the same as the LCMR. However, what is

[90] Yang Wang [汪洋], 'Study on the Succession of Land Contract Management Rights: Explanation of the Legal Construction of the Existing Norms and Consideration of Legal Policies' [《土地承包经营权继承问题研究》] (2014) 4 *Tsinghua Law Journal* [《清华法学》] 129.

[91] Articles 59 and 60 Land Administration Law.

[92] Paras. 1 and 2 of Article 63 Land Administration Law.

[93] Para. 4 of Article 63 Land Administration Law.

[94] Article 339.

[95] Article 340.

[96] Article 341.

[97] *Ibid.*

different from LCMR is that the legal framework does not provide the land management right as a property right, as it did for the LCMR.[98]

Nonetheless, the CC has sidestepped whether the land management right is proprietary or contractual. The significance of this characterisation is relevant to answer two questions. First, whether the holder of the land management right is entitled to be compensated where the rural land is expropriated. Second, where the outside investor, the holder of the land management right, seeks financing by using the land management right as collateral to secure a loan, how readily the institutional lenders would agree to offer such loan if land management is not clearly defined as a property right.

The only statutory provision concerning compensation against expropriation of land management rights is found in Article 40 of the RLCL 2018 Amendment.[99] However, Article 40 only provides that the transfer of land management rights requires the parties involved to sign a written transfer contract, and one of the key clauses should address the attribution of compensation when land is expropriated.[100] The contractual stipulation may or may not entitle the land management right holder to claim compensation, even partially. In other words, it does not explicitly specify whether the holder of the land management right is entitled to compensation. At this juncture, the land management right seems to be a contractual right.

Nonetheless, the holder of the land management right through transfer, with the written consent of the contracting party, may use it as collateral for financing from financial institutions.[101] A real security right is established when the financing contract takes effect. Upon realisation

[98] Shengping Gao [高圣平], 'Allocation of Contracted Land Rights after the Amendment of the Rural Land Contract Law' [《农村土地承包法修改后的承包地法权配置》] (2019) 5 *Chinese Journal of Law* [《法学研究》] 44.

[99] Article 40 of the Rural Land Contract Law provides, "The transfer of land management rights should be governed by a written contract between the parties involved. A land management rights transfer contract typically includes the following clauses: (1) Names and addresses of the parties involved; (2) Details of the transferred land, including its name, location, area, and quality grade; (3) Transfer period, including the start and end dates; (4) Intended use of the transferred land; (5) Rights and obligations of both parties; (6) Transfer price and payment method; (7) Provisions regarding compensation in case of lawful requisition, expropriation, or occupation of the land; (8) Terms related to breach of contract and the associated responsibilities. If the contracting party entrusts someone else to cultivate the land for a period not exceeding one year, a written contract may not be necessary.

[100] *Ibid.*

[101] Para. 1 of Article 47 RLCL.

of the real security right, the security provider has the right to be compensated first concerning the land management right.[102] Here a notion of real security right indicates that the land management right may be regarded as a property right, as it is subject to a real security right.[103] Furthermore, where rural land is contracted through other means, such as by ways of bidding, auction and public consultation, and the title certificate has been registered, the holder has the power to grant another person the land management right by way of letting, share purchase and creating charge.[104]

Therefore, the answers to the two questions concerning the right's legal nature found in the same legislation are inconsistent. It is perhaps a pragmatic approach of intentional ambiguity aiming to provide more regulatory space for local governments. As laws and regulations evolve, it is advisable that future legislation may provide a definite answer on the land management right's legal nature.

6.2.6 *Women's Rights on Rural Land*

Women's property rights in rural China have been a vexing issue for decades, causing concerns. China's Constitution and the Land Administration Law grant equal land rights to men and women. The LCMR is assigned or redistributed in villages on a per-household basis. Nonetheless, in 2000, a survey conducted by the All-China Women's Federation revealed that since the first round of land-contracting distribution in 1983, the problems of belittling and discriminating against women and violating the land-contracting rights of married and divorced women and their children have been reflected to varying degrees in many parts of China.

> Since the first round of land distribution in 1983, the problem of slighting and discriminating against women and violating the right to land contracting of married women and divorced women and their children has been reflected to varying degrees in many areas of the country. In some areas, when calculating family size, women are allocated only 50 to 70 per cent of

[102] Paras. 2 and 3 of Article 47 RLCL.

[103] Xiaojun Chen [陈小君] and Chugang Xiao [肖楚钢], 'The Legal Nature of Rural Land Management Rights and the Distinction of Its Object – A Commentary on the Land Operation Rights Rules in the Property Law CC' [《农村土地经营权的法律性质及其客体之辨——兼评〈民法典〉物权编的土地经营权规则》] (2020) 12 *Zhongzhou Academic Journal* [《中州学刊》] 48, pp. 48–51.

[104] Article 342 CC.

> the land belonging to men. In some areas, even 40 per cent of working women do not have access to contracted land and homesteads. In some areas, 40 per cent of working women do not have access to contracted land or homesteads.[105]

Despite the 2002 Rural Land Contract Law, the situation did not subsequently improve; rather, it worsened. In 2015, the All-China Women's Federation further found that among rural women between the ages of 18 and 64, 21 per cent were landless in 2010 – an increase of 11.8 per cent over 2000, compared to only 3 per cent among men. Of these, 27.7 per cent lost their land due to changes in their marital status, compared to only 3.7 per cent of men.[106]

The major issue at stake appears to be married women's property rights. Married women in this context refer to women who marry and move to another village or region, commonly known as marrying out. Traditionally, when a woman marries, she moves into her husband's household and might lose rights to her natal family's land. The names listed on the contracts are often male heads of households. This makes women vulnerable, especially if they get divorced or widowed as a spouse or married as daughters. The following court case is offered as an example and to clarify the differing views of the affected women and their natal villages.

In *Han Mingli v. The Village Committee of Dahanzhuang Village, Yulin Township, Yanjin County*,[107] the plaintiff was a married woman from Dahanzhuang village in Yanjing County of the Henan Province. However, after her marriage, she did not change her household registration and still officially lives at her original residence. Moreover, she has not acquired contracted land at her new residence. She believes that changes in her marital status do not entitle her natal village to take back the LCMR she obtained under the original contract signed between the

105 Women's Rights and Interests Department of All China Women's Federation (全国妇联权益部), 'Land Contract and Women's Rights and Interests – A Survey on Violation of Women's Rights and Interests during the Second Round of Rural Land Contracting' [《土地承包与妇女权益 – 关于农村第二轮土地承包工作中妇女权益被侵害情况的调查》] (2000) 3 *Chinese Women's Movement* [《中国妇运》] 30.

106 All-China Women's Federation [中华全国妇女联合会], 'Safeguarding Rural Women's Rights and Interests in Land' [《维护农村妇女的土地权益》] (2015) 3 *Chinese Women's Movement* [《中国妇运》] 15.

107 韩明利与延津县榆林乡大韩庄村村民委员会 [*Han Mingli v. The Village Committee of Dahanzhuang Village, Yulin Township, Yanjin County*] (2015) 新中民五终字第401号 [2015 Xin Zhong Min Wu Zhong No. 401].

village and her father as the household head during the second round of land contracting. Her argument is based on the understanding that the LCMR remains unchanged for thirty years under the Rural Land Contracting Management Law. Therefore, during the thirty-year contracting period, if a woman gets married and does not acquire contracted land at her new residence, the village should not take back her originally contracted land.

On the opposing side, the village committee forfeited the plaintiff's land right by providing three justifications. First, the village's committee has unanimously approved the land adjustment of Dahanzhuang village, entitled to do so by the self-governance powers granted to the committee by Article 24 of the Organic Law of Village Committees[108] and Article 19 of the RLCL.[109] The voting results should be valid and binding. Second, although the plaintiff's household registration is in Dahanzhuang village, she and her husband have long worked outside the village. They have purchased property in another village. Therefore, she is not considered a member of the defendant's village and does not have the LCMR. Third, according to local customs and practice, a woman who marries out should not be entitled to contracted land.

The court of first instance held that the plaintiff should have the LCMR at the natal village, and no organisation or individual may deprive her of this right according to Article 6 of the RLCL, which stipulates that women and men have equal rights in rural land contracting. *Women's legitimate rights and interests should be protected during contracting, and no organisation or individual may deprive or infringe upon the land contracting rights women are entitled.*[110] In addition, the court of first

[108] Article 24 of the Organic Law of Village Committees provides that in making decisions, a villagers' committee shall apply the principle whereby the minority is subordinate to the majority. In its work the villagers' committee shall adhere to the mass line, give full play to democracy, carefully heed dissenting opinions and unremittingly exercise persuasion; it may not resort to coercion, commandism or retaliation.

[109] Article 19 of the Rural Land Contract Law provides that land shall be contracted out in accordance with the following procedures: (1) a contract-working team shall be elected by the villagers' assembly of the collective economic organisation concerned; (2) the contract-working team shall, in accordance with the provisions of laws and administrative rules and regulations, draw up and announce its contracting plan; (3) convening, according to law, the villagers' assembly of the collective economic organisation concerned to adopt the contracting plan through discussion; (4) making known to the public arrangements for the implementation of the contracting plan; and (5) concluding the contract.

[110] 黄某诉李某 [*Huang v. Li*] (2015)延民初字第821号 [(2015) Yan Min Chu Zi No. 821].

instance reasoned that Article 30 of the RLCL provides that *during the contracting period, if a woman gets married and does not acquire contracted land at her new residence, the issuer should not take back her originally contracted land. If a woman gets divorced or becomes widowed and continues to live at her original residence, or if she does not live at her original residence but has not acquired contracted land at her new residence, the issuer should not take back her originally contracted land.* The plaintiff married and continued living at her original residence, and she has not acquired contracted land at her new residence. Therefore, the Dahanzhuang village committee should not take back her originally contracted land. However, on appeal by the village, the court of second instance issued a final decision that the dispute does not fall within the civil jurisdiction of the People's Court and that the plaintiff should apply to the relevant administrative department for resolution. As a result, the first instance court ruling has been annulled.

As shown in the case above, judicial abstention is exercised by the court of the second instance by asking the parties to submit the disputes to the relevant administrative agencies. This is because the court believes that a government agency is more appropriate or competent to decide.[111] However, more recently, in a landmark case handed down by the Shandong HPC, a legal test on how to entitle and protect the marrying-out women's land rights has been refined. The court held that "marrying out woman" is not a strict legal term but a customary usage derived from rural marriage practices. Chinese law does not provide any special provisions different from ordinary villagers regarding whether women who marry out of their natal village can enjoy the same resettlement compensation as ordinary villagers. Against this background, a court should specifically examine (1) whether the household registration of the woman was still in the natal village; (2) whether the woman was still living in the village when the land compensation was provided in case of expropriation; (3) whether the woman still relies on the land of the natal village for basic livelihood; (4) what the villagers' representative assembly determines on this matter; (5) whether the woman has discharged the villager duties as other members in the village; and (6) whether the woman enjoys villager membership and benefits in another village.

[111] Xin He, 'Why Did They Not Take on the Disputes? Law, Power and Politics in the Decision-Making of Chinese Courts' (2007) 3 *International Journal of Law in Context* 203.

The Shandong court continues to reason that according to the Organic Law of Village Committees, village self-governance statutes, village rules and decisions of the villagers' meetings or representatives' meetings must not conflict with the constitution, laws and regulations, especially those that infringe upon personal rights and legal property rights of villagers. Therefore, decisions made by villagers' meetings that violate the constitution, laws, regulations and national policies, especially at the expense of women's rights, cannot serve as the basis to deny whether the woman the enjoyment of the same resettlement compensation as other villagers.

This legal test represents the current mainstream judicial position and is a significant step in enhancing the legal protection of rural women's land rights. Over the years, there have been efforts to protect women's land rights, such as encouraging the inclusion of women's names on land contracts. Eventually, women's names will be registered on land certificates for the first time.[112] The change will reinforce women's rights to access land, creating an avenue for social empowerment and a stronger voice in decision-making.

6.3 Homestead Use Right

6.3.1 *Concept and Features*

The homestead right is commonly used to describe a land use right granted to rural residents, allowing them to use a specific piece of land for residential purposes. Rural residents are granted the right to build and maintain a residence on the designated homestead land. The homestead right is usually acquired free of charge and used by farmers who are collective members. It is a welfare guarantee enjoyed by farmers based on their identity as collective members, and its primary function is to ensure their basic housing needs. Permitting homestead rights contributes to providing rural residents with land tenure security.

[112] 不动产登记暂行条例实施细则　国土资源部令第63号(2016年1月1日国土资源部令第63号公布；根据2019年7月16日自然资源部第2次部务会《自然资源部关于废止和修改的第一批部门规章的决定》修正) [Article 21 of The Detailed Rules for the Implementation of the Interim Regulations on Real Estate Registration, Ministry of Natural Resources Decree No. 63 (Published on January 1, 2016, Ministry of Natural Resources Decree No. 63; Amended according to the decision of the 2nd Departmental Meeting of the Ministry of Natural Resources on July 16, 2019, regarding the abolition and modification of the first batch of departmental regulations)].

Rural homesteads are essential to farmers' livelihoods. However, with the acceleration of urbanisation in the past three decades, many farmers chose to migrate to towns and seek new opportunities. Consequently, many rural homesteads are left vacant. With the ongoing urbanisation process in China, there have been discussions and policy changes regarding the conversion of rural land, including homestead land, for urban development. This has led to considerations about protecting homestead rights amid urban expansion. Specifically, the policymakers implemented the strategy of "rural revitalisation."[113] It is crucial to persistently prioritise resolving the "three rural issues" and comprehensively promote rural revitalisation and accelerate rural modernisation.

Turning these policies into national legislation, essentially the Chinese CC, the Land Administration Law (2019 amendment), the Rural Revitalization Promotion Law and the Implementation Regulations of the Land Administration Law provide legal support for homestead rights.

Traditionally, the homestead right was non-transferable and non-inheritable. This means that the right to use the land is tied to the specific rural household, and it cannot be sold or inherited independently of the household. The SPC confirms by ruling that a villager with a homestead right has no right to inherit the land use right for other homestead plots in the same village.[114] The homestead right is often granted for a specified duration, typically long term but not perpetually. The specific duration may vary depending on local policies and regulations. Local government authorities play a significant role in implementing and regulating homestead policies by overseeing the allocation and management of homestead land. It is important to note that specific regulations and policies related to homestead rights can vary across different regions in China. Local governments have some flexibility in implementing homestead policies, leading to variations across provinces and municipalities.

In summary, homestead rights are used by members of rural collective economic organisations over the collective-owned land and endowed with the legal right to construct houses and ancillary facilities on such

[113] The Several Opinions of the Central Committee of the Communist Party of China and the State Council on Advancing the Construction of the Socialist New Countryside (December 31, 2005) – Document No. 1 of 2006.

[114] 许德仁诉辽宁省沈阳市人民政府（2020）最高法行申14503号 [*Xu Deren v. Shenyang People's Government, Liaoning Province* (2020) SPC Xing Shen No. 14503].

land.[115] Each villager can only possess one homestead, and the area should not exceed the standards of the province, municipality or autonomous region.[116] It follows the system of villagers' application, approved and obtained free of charge by the township government through the village committee's endorsement and held for the long term.[117] Article 62 of the Land Administration Law also stipulates that the state allows rural villagers who meet the conditions to voluntarily and lawfully withdraw from homesteads when settling in cities.[118] It encourages rural collective economic organisations and their members to revitalise and utilise vacant homesteads. However, there is no specific legal provision for activating and utilising homesteads. Therefore, it provides a regulatory space to further refine the marketisation of homestead rights at the national and local policy levels.

On 30 September 2019, the Ministry of Agriculture and Rural Affairs (MARA) issued the Notice of the MARA on Actively and Prudently Promoting the Activation and Utilisation of Rural Vacant Homesteads.[119] In terms of specific reform and activation methods, the state encourages the development of new industries and formats in line with rural characteristics, such as leisure agriculture, rural tourism, catering and lodging, cultural experiences, creative offices and e-commerce, as well as integrated development projects of the primary, secondary and tertiary industries such as cold chain logistics, primary processing and warehousing by utilising vacant houses. In addition, on 28 November 2022, the MARA issued the *Interim Measures for the Management of Rural Homesteads (Draft for Solicitation of Comments)*, which stipulates that rural collective economic organisations and their members can activate and utilise legally acquired and clear-owned vacant rural homesteads through independent operation, cooperative operation, entrusted operation and other methods.[120]

[115] Article 362.

[116] Para. 1 of Article 62 Land Administration Law.

[117] Para. 4 of Article 62 Land Administration Law.

[118] Para. 6 of Article 62 Land Administration Law.

[119] The Notice from the Ministry of Agriculture and Rural Affairs on Actively and Prudently Carrying Out the Revitalization and Utilization of Idle Rural Residential Land and Vacant Houses issued by the MARA on 30 September 2019.

[120] Ministry of Agricultural and Rural Affairs of the People's Republic of China <www.moa.gov.cn/govpublic/NCJJTZ/202211/t20221128_6416131.htm> accessed on 11 October 2023.

6.3.2 *Transferability*

As mentioned earlier, although the Land Administration Law 2019 Amendment did not create a legal path for homesteads to enter the market, attempts to marketise the homestead rights have been made repeatedly by the legislature, central government and local governments.

Homesteads are central to farmers' livelihoods. Allowing farmers to mortgage their homesteads would result in them losing their homesteads and residential properties if they default on the mortgage, which would affect social stability. Therefore, the CC provides that, except as otherwise provided by law, the right to use collective-owned lands such as homesteads, self-retained land and self-retained mountains cannot be mortgaged.[121] However, based on the provisions in Article 365 regarding the timely handling of transfer and registration changes for registered homestead rights, the law does not prohibit the transfer of homestead rights.

Against this background, it is remarkable that the national legislature, NPCSC, in December 2015, issued the *Decision Authorising the State Council to Temporarily Adjust the Implementation of Relevant Legal Provisions in Administrative Regions, Including Daxing District, Beijing, and 232 Other Pilot Counties (Cities, Districts), as well as Jixian County, Tianjin, and 59 Other Pilot Counties (Cities, Districts)*.[122] This decision allows the selected pilot local governments to circumvent the rule that homestead rights cannot be mortgaged. Instead, it encourages local governments to conduct experiments to marketise homestead rights by mortgaging homestead rights in order to access the credit. Furthermore, according to *the Notice from the General Office of the China Banking and Insurance Regulatory Commission on the Construction of Innovative Demonstration Zones for Financial Services in Rural Revitalization* in 2021, under the framework of the homestead system reform pilot, conditional areas are encouraged to cautiously explore the business of using

[121] Article 399 CC.

[122] The NPCSC Decision on Authorising the State Council to Temporarily Adjust the Implementation of Relevant Legal Provisions in Administrative Regions, Including Daxing District, Beijing, and 232 Other Pilot Counties (Cities, Districts), as well as Jixian County, Tianjin, and 59 Other Pilot Counties (Cities, Districts), issued on 27 December 2015; see 全国人大常委会关于授权国务院在北京市大兴区等三十三个试点县（市、区）行政区域暂时调整实施有关法律规定的决定 [Decision of the Standing Committee of the National People's Congress on Authorizing the State Council to Temporarily Adjust the Implementation of Relevant Legal Provisions in the Administrative Areas of Thirty-Three Pilot Counties (Cities, Districts), Including Daxing District in Beijing].

homestead use rights as mortgage collateral.[123] Financing of land operating rights obtained through transfer by family farms is being explored.

According to the *Opinions of the Central Committee of the CCP and the State Council on Integrated Urban-Rural Development* issued in 2019, the state allows village collectives to transform idle homesteads that have been compensated for or abandoned collective public construction land into collective construction land for market entry with voluntary consent of farmers.[124] Therefore, idle homesteads are not completely restricted from entering the market: they can be transformed into collective construction land to develop new industries such as leisure agriculture, rural tourism, rural lodging, e-commerce and the promotion of integrated development of primary, secondary and tertiary industries.

In practice, for example, the land ticket system (地票制) in Chongqing and other regions refers to the conversion of idle rural construction land, including farmers' idle homesteads and associated land, town and township enterprise land, and rural public welfare and public facility land, into cultivated land to increase the amount of land available for farming. This is achieved through transactions conducted in land trading venues, transferring the land to entities with demand for construction land. The specific operational process of this kind of transaction involving collective construction land indicators includes land reclamation, target allocation, land ticket trading and use, ultimately resulting in the transformation of rural construction land, such as homesteads, into new urban construction land through reclamation, thereby promoting further transactions and utilisation of rural collective land resources.

Article 63 of the Rural Revitalization Promotion Law enacted in April 2021 states that the state will comprehensively use fiscal, financial and other policy measures to improve government financing guarantee mechanisms, enhance the rights of rural assets and improve and strengthen financial support and services for rural revitalisation.[125] This

[123] The Notice from the General Office of the China Banking and Insurance Regulatory Commission on the Construction of Innovative Demonstration Zones for Financial Services in Rural Revitalization, CBIRC Office Document [2021] No. 94 (*National Financial Regulatory Administration*, 1 September 2021), <www.cbirc.gov.cn/cn/view/pages/ItemDetail.html?docId=1008024&itemId=878&generaltype=1> accessed on 24 January 2024.

[124] Bullet point 2 (7) of the Opinions of the Central Committee of the Communist Party of China and the State Council on Establishing and Improving the Institutional Mechanisms and Policy Systems for Integrated Urban-Rural Development.

[125] Article 63 Rural Revitalization Promotion Law.

provision implicitly provides a legal basis for the mortgage of homestead rights.

Across the country, various pilot programs for activating and utilising homestead systems have been carried out in more developed provinces and cities. For example, in Kunshan City, Jiangsu Province, the Dianshanhu Town Homestead pilot program, as a typical case of homestead reform and management in 2022, vigorously promotes homestead reform through mortgage loans, market circulation and rental. In terms of mortgage loans, rural house mortgage loans are provided to obtain funds for rebuilding new houses. Given the widespread practice, the Chinese CC provides flexibility by stating that the laws on land administration and relevant rules of the state govern the acquisition, exercise and transfer of the homestead right land.[126] The relevant rules of the state are very broad, including state policies.

In summary, the current practice is that homestead right land is determined following the area specified by the provincial (or municipal) people's government for the collective members of rural households. The following conditions and procedures apply:

1. When farmers who are not members of rural collectives need to relocate due to geological disaster control or relief, new rural construction or centralised migration planning, they can obtain homestead rights through proper approval from the competent authority after the majority of the local rural collective members agree.
2. Suppose a collective member or a rural/urban resident who is not a collective member holds one homestead land by inheritance. In that case, they can register and obtain the right to use homestead land.
3. Non-agricultural household residents – for example, those who have moved their household registration (hukou) or overseas Chinese – who legally obtained homestead land and houses in rural areas, with no change in property rights over the years, can undergo land registration with a certificate from the rural collective and a public notice without objections for thirty days.
4. Homestead land without proof of ownership should be investigated for its historical use and current status. The village committee issues a certificate, and after a public notice period of thirty days with no objections, the township government reviews and submits it to the county people's government for approval and confirmation.

[126] Article 363 CC.

6.2.3 *Extinguishment*

It is important to note that the CC does not make a homestead right a time-limited right. In other words, the homestead right has an indefinite term. This is understandable because the homestead right is central to farmers' livelihood and would not contribute to the security and stability of farmer households. However, this does not mean the homestead right cannot be extinguished.

For example, the CC provides that the homestead right is extinguished if the homestead is destroyed due to natural disasters or other reasons. Villagers who have lost their homesteads can be reallocated to new homesteads.[127] Apart from the natural disaster, it is generally believed to interpret "other reasons" to include the following situations.

First, government authorities may acquire homestead land for public welfare projects or urban development, extinguishing homestead rights. Compensation is usually provided to the affected households. Second, the homestead right may be extinguished when town planning is modified to change land use. The affected villagers may be reallocated to new homesteads in such a circumstance. If the homestead right holder violates land use regulations or uses the homestead land for purposes other than residential, it was argued that the authorities might revoke the homestead right.[128] This may be too draconian. In such a circumstance, the local authority, through the village committee, may demand a correction following the due process procedure. If the villager does not correct upon request, the local authority may execute a readjustment or other means. This would ensure that all collective members are guaranteed a residence. Third, individuals or households may voluntarily surrender their homestead rights for various reasons, such as relocation to another village or moving their domicile to urban areas. When a registered homestead right is transferred or inherited, the concerned party should promptly change or cancel registration as stipulated by law.[129]

6.4 Summary: A Heavy-handed Regulatory Approach

The preceding discussion points to many restrictions over the LCMR or the homestead rights in rural land. First, the LCMR is restricted to

127 Article 365 CC.

128 Ping Jiang, *Chinese Property Law* (China Intellectual Property Press 2007), p. 361; Huixing Liang and Huabin Chen, *Property Law* (6th edition) (Law Press China 2016), p. 251.

129 Article 365 CC.

agricultural use, and contracting parties are limited to using the land for cultivation, farming or related agricultural purposes. In most cases, rural land designated for agricultural use is not easily convertible to non-agricultural purposes. In addition, transfer of the LCMR is subject to restrictions. Explicit permission or approval from relevant authorities is required.

Furthermore, the duration of land management contracts is limited. While many contracts are long term, they may not be perpetual. Periodic reviews or renewals may be required, and contracts might not automatically extend without examination. More to the point, in rural areas, usufructuary rights are often connected to collective land ownership. Issues may emerge concerning decision-making within the collective, especially if there are disputes or changes in the structure of collective land ownership. Besides, local governments often retain the right to requisition and reallocate rural land for larger development projects, public welfare or urbanisation. Contracting parties are subject to these government decisions. In cases of land requisition for public purposes, the usufructuary rights may be subject to reallocation. The potential for conflict arises if compensation or terms of reallocation are contested.

Contracting parties are generally required to comply with national and local laws and regulations governing land use, environmental protection and other relevant aspects. Different regions in China may have specific policies for and variances in implementing rural land contracting management rights. In other words, local governments have some discretion in tailoring policies to regional needs. Violations may lead to penalties or termination of the LCMR. Due to various restrictions imposed on the LCMR or homestead rights, one may wonder if the LCMR or homestead rights are incapable of being a property right or providing the full protection to the land use rights as is normally expected.

There are several reasons why China has implemented restrictions on homestead rights and LCMR. Historical, economic, social and political factors often shape these restrictions. It is important to note that land policies and regulations can evolve, and there have been further developments since 2020. China has undergone significant land reforms throughout its long and chaotic history. Historical land tenure issues, including large-scale land redistributions, have influenced the development of the current land management system. While elements of socialist ideology may still persist in China, restrictions are primarily designed to address historical inequities and promote a fair distribution of land resources. In many rural areas, land is collectively owned or managed.

Restrictions on individual rights may be intended to preserve communal ownership structures and prevent fragmentation of agricultural land.[130]

Given China's large population and the importance of agriculture to its economy, rural land must be primarily used for agriculture. Restrictions are placed to balance urbanisation and the preservation of agricultural land. Land laws and policies are often tied to broader social stability considerations. Restricting certain activities may be seen as a way to prevent social unrest, address land disputes and maintain order in rural areas. China has experienced rapid urbanisation, leading to a demand for land for urban development. Restrictions on homestead rights and LCMR are designed to control the conversion of rural land to urban use and manage the challenges associated with urban expansion. The Chinese government has always played a central role in land management and policy. Restrictions on homestead rights or LCMR may be part of a broader strategy to maintain control over land resources and implement national development goals.

Despite the heavy-handed approach to regulating LCMR and homestead rights, they are recognised as property right, specifically usufruct. Understanding that the reasons for restrictions on homestead rights and LCMR are multifaceted and interconnected is crucial. Additionally, laws and policies continue to evolve and are shaped by changing economic, social and environmental dynamics. Therefore, it is impossible, and potentially dangerous, to use the dictionary definitions to provide a guide to the meaning of the LCMR or homestead right because such meaning has not been fixed by technical, linguistically precise definitions divorced from the context in which the LCMR or homestead right operates. Furthermore, there is no such thing as unfettered property right, as found in any society in modern times. As theorised by Ostrom, the LCMR in rural China is a typical example of polycentric governance: rules governing land use are derived in part from household-level action and in part from government intervention.[131] In between, there is a role played by the villages or village economic organisations at the community level. Hence, it is imperative to move beyond the narrow conception

[130] Lei Chen, 'The Evolution of the Property System in China: Between the Socialist Heritage and Liberal Market', in Hualing Fu, John Gillespie, Pip Nicholson and William Partlett (eds), *Socialist Law in Socialist East Asia* (Cambridge University Press 2018).

[131] Elinor Ostrom, 'Beyond Markets and States: Polycentric Governance of Complex Economic Systems' (2010) 100 *American Economic Review* 641.

of legally enforced private property rights on which Demsetz or North relied.[132] We should instead embrace an understanding of ownership as an emergent, diverse and complex institution.[133]

However, this should not deter the central government from committing itself to deeper market reforms that bolster protections for farmers, private property and outside-of-collective investors. Private investors holding land management rights should be treated equally with state-owned enterprises (SOEs), not only in abstract legal principles but, more significantly, in industrial regulations, which often impose additional constraints on private companies, and in bank financing, where there tends to be a preference for SOEs in regards to both quantity and terms.

[132] Harold Demsetz, 'Toward a Theory of Property Rights' (1967) 57 *American Economic Review* 347.

[133] Simon Deakin and Gaofeng Meng, 'Resolving Douglass C. North's "Puzzle" Concerning China's Household Responsibility System' (2022) 18 *Journal of Institutional Economics* 521.

7

Construction Land Use Right

7.1 Introduction

The construction land use right (CLUR) refers to the legal rights granted to entities or individuals by the government to possess, use and profit from a designated piece of state-owned land for construction purposes.[1] The grantee can use such land to construct buildings, structures and ancillary facilities.[2] The CLUR is subject to land use planning, which is determined by overall urban and rural planning.[3] Construction activities must align with the designated purpose specified in the planning.[4] This right is a key component of China's land use system. The key legislation, administrative regulations and SPC judicial interpretations governing the CLUR are set out in Table 7.1.

It is worth noting that the CLUR can only be created over state-owned land. Where collective-owned land is used as construction land, it is governed by the Land Administration Law.[5] The collective construction land is divided into three categories. First, collective public welfare construction land refers to land designated for collective projects for public welfare purposes. This type of land serves the collective interest or public good, such as infrastructure projects, public facilities or other developments that benefit the community. The use and management of

[1] Article 344 CC.
[2] *Ibid.*
[3] Article 4 Land Administration Law.
[4] Article 44 Land Administration Law.
[5] Article 361 CC. Rural land in China is generally categorised into three main types: (1) collective agricultural land, which refers to land designated for agricultural production, particularly for ensuring food security. The LCMR applies to this type of land. (2) Collective construction land, which refers to land designated for collective development projects. It may include areas for industrial, commercial or infrastructure development. Collective construction land is discussed in this chapter. (3) Homestead land, which refers to land designated for rural residential purposes. This type of rural land was discussed in the previous chapter.

Table 7.1 *CLUR statutory framework including SPC judicial interpretations*

Year	Title	Type of Statutory Instruments	Implications
1986 (amended in 1988, 1998, 2004, 2019)	Land Administration Law	National legislation	Specific legislation governs the grant, use and transfer of CLUR.
1994	Urban Real Estate Administration Law (amended in 2007, 2009, 2019)	National Legislation	It regulates urban land use rights transfers, leases, and registration.
1998	The Implementation Regulations of the Land Administration Law (revised in 2011, 2014)	Administrative Regulation	It provides detailed procedures and guidelines for the implementation of the Land Administration Law, clarifying the administration, use and transactions of land within the legislation.
1998	The Regulations on the Management of Urban Real Estate Development and Operations (revised in 2011, 2028 and 2019)	Administrative Regulation	It governs the development, management and operation of real estate projects in urban areas, setting standards and requirements to ensure orderly development and to protect the interests of developers, investors and residents.
1999	The Interim Regulations on the Grant and Transfer of Urban State-owned Land Use Rights (revised in 2020)	Administrative Regulation	It covers the processes and conditions for the granting and transferring of use rights for state-owned land in urban areas, providing a legal framework to manage these rights effectively and transparently.

Table 7.1 (*cont.*)

Year	Title	Type of Statutory Instruments	Implications
2005	The SPC Interpretation on the Application of Laws in Hearing Cases Involving Disputes over Contracts for the Use of State-Owned Land (revised in 2020)	SPC Judicial Interpretation	It provides guidance on how to handle and resolve legal disputes specifically related to state-owned land use contracts.
2007	The Property Law (repealed on 1 January 2021)	National Legislation	The first comprehensive legislation concerning property rights provides a chapter on the LCMR.
2015	Interim Regulations on Real Estate Registration	Administrative Regulation	These regulations provide the framework and procedures for the registration of real estate in China, including LCMR in rural areas.
2020	The Civil Code	National Legislation by NPC	A comprehensive CC has seven parts and 1,260 articles. The seven parts, in turn, are General Provisions, Property Rights, Contracts, Personality Rights, Marriage and Family, Right of Inheritance, and Tort Liability and Supplemental Provision.
2020	The SPC Interpretation on the Application of the Property Rights Book of the CC (I)	SPC Judicial Interpretation	It provides detailed guidance on how courts should apply the property rights provisions found in the CC.

collective public welfare construction land are typically applied to and approved by the county government or above.[6] Second, collective enterprise construction land refers to the land designated or allocated for constructing enterprises or businesses. This land is typically acquired through a process that involves obtaining the necessary approvals and rights to use the land for specific industrial or commercial purposes.[7] Third, collective operating construction land refers to land designated for activities related to industry, commerce or other business operations.[8] This type of land is used by collective entities, such as cooperatives or joint ventures, to engage in various economic and construction activities. A distinguishing feature of the collective operational construction land is its market transferability.

A heavy-handed regulatory framework governs collective rural land's entry into the land market.[9] Prior to 1 January 2020, when the Land Administration Law was revised, collective land had to be converted into state-owned land through expropriation to enter the land markets.[10] Except for specific legal provisions allowing the approved use of collective land for special purposes, such as establishing township enterprises or building homes for villagers, if collective land was needed for non-agricultural construction, it had to go through collective land expropriation. After years of land reform and pilot initiatives, the Land Administration Law 2020 revision allows collective land to enter the land market, similar to state-owned land.

However, it is important to note that not all collective land can enter the market; it must meet requirements related to land type, planning conditions, use and acquisition procedures. Specifically, only collective operational construction land can enter the market, excluding other collective construction lands such as collective public welfare construction land. The land must be designated for operational purposes per the land use master plan and urban–rural planning for industrial, commercial and other purposes. Whether it can be used for residential purposes is not yet clear. The land intended for transfer must comply with specific

[6] Article 61 Land Administration Law.
[7] Article 60 Land Administration Law.
[8] Article 63 Land Administration Law.
[9] Article 44 Land Administration Law.
[10] According to Article 43 of the old Land Administration Law amended in 2004, any unit or individual needing to use land for construction must apply to use state-owned land according to the law.

procedural requirements, including signing a written contract with the landowner and obtaining the consent of two-thirds or more of the members of the village assembly or two-thirds or more of the village representatives in the case of collective economic organisations.[11]

The right to use collectively owned construction land must be obtained through application and approval by the county people's government. If the land involves agricultural land, the approval procedures for conversion must be followed.[12] Currently, the CLUR only applies to state-owned land in the CC. The collectively owned CLUR is expected to be included when the legislature is satisfied that the conditions are met to introduce a stable legal mechanism for its transferability.

State-owned land is categorised based on its designated use, such as residential, commercial, industrial or agricultural. CLURs are specific to the land's intended purpose, usually residential, commercial and industrial, and development must align with the designated use. The period for which CLURs are granted is defined in the CLUR contract. Residential land use rights often have a term of seventy years, while industrial and commercial land use rights may have terms of fifty and forty years, respectively.[13] Depending on the land's planned use and local regulations, the government may extend the term upon expiration.[14]

7.2 Creation

7.2.1 Obtaining a CLUR by Allocation or Paid Use

China implements a system for the paid use of state-owned land, with gratuitous allocation of land resources through allocation being an exception.[15] In other words, the land use right is granted by either paid use or allocation.[16] The allocation of land use rights refers to the act in which the people's government at or above the county level approves the transfer of state-owned land to its user after the land user pays compensation and resettlement fees, or does so without requiring compensation.[17]

[11] Article 63 Land Administration Law.
[12] Article 60 Land Administration Law.
[13] Article 12 Interim Regulation of Transfer of State-owned Land.
[14] Article 41 Interim Regulation of Transfer of State-owned Land.
[15] Article 54 Land Administration Law.
[16] Para. 1 of Article 347 CC; Para. 5 of Article 2 Land Administration Law.
[17] Article 23 UREAL.

No specified duration of allocated land use right exists unless the laws and administrative regulations provide otherwise.[18]

However, where the state allocates the right to use state-owned land, the scope, approval procedures and subsequent activities such as leasing, mortgage and disposal of land use rights obtained through allocation are strictly restricted. Regulatory authorities, including land administration authorities and securities regulators, pay close attention to enterprises involved in capital operations related to the allocation of land use rights during their scrutiny and review processes. For the allocated construction land, the government can recover the right to use the land without compensation based on urban development needs and only give appropriate compensation for the fixtures built on the land in light of the actual state of affairs.[19]

Therefore, creating a CLUR by way of allocation is strictly restricted.[20] The allocation of the CLUR is only granted for a specified scope of uses when necessary.[21] Land use rights are allocated mainly to government agencies, military organs and state-owned enterprises.

There are two methods to allocate the land. First, county-level or higher people's governments approve the allocation of state-owned land to land users. After the land users pay compensation, participate in resettlement and cover other related fees, the state-owned land is handed over to land users. It is worth noting that the CLUR may be created for the land surface or space either below or above the land surface separately.[22] Second, county-level or higher people's governments approve the grant of the right to use construction land by land users without compensation.

Allocation of land use rights is, in essence, an act of government to grant the land user the right to use the land free of charge. Unlike land use rights granted by paid use, land allocation is a non-market-oriented method for establishing CLURs. It is driven by the need to safeguard national interests and public welfare and follows strict legal procedures. Such an act does not require a contract. In what follows, the standard approach – obtaining a CLUR through bidding, auction, or other open-price bidding – will be discussed in greater detail.[23]

[18] Article 23 UREAL.
[19] Article 58 Land Administration Law.
[20] Para. 3 of Article 347.
[21] Article 24 UREAL.
[22] Article 345 CC.
[23] Para. 2 of Article 347.

7.2.2 A CLUR Contract

7.2.2.1 Key Terms and Conditions

There are two types of CLUR contracts. Where a competent government agency grants a CLUR to a private entity, it is termed a CLUR grant contract.[24] It also refers to the first land market. Where a holder of a CLUR transfers the remaining term to another private entity, it is called a CLUR transfer contract.[25] In this instance, it is known as entry into a secondary land market. In the following, when the term "CLUR contract" is used, it refers to both typese of contract unless otherwise specified.

Two steps exist to create a CLUR by paid use under Chinese law. First, the parties need to sign a CLUR contract in writing.[26] Second, the signed contract must be registered to be effective.[27] The concluded CLUR contract creates only a contractual right prior to registration. Only upon registration is a property right created.

Article 348 of the CC provides what the CLUR contract must contain. These items include (1) business names and addresses of the parties; (2) boundary and area of the land; (3) space occupied by the buildings, structures and their ancillary facilities; (4) use of the land and condition of planning; (5) CLUR duration; (6) land transaction fees and other expenses, as well as payment methods; and (7) methods of dispute resolution.[28]

First, the authority to grant CLUR contracts is limited to the people's government at the county level or higher.[29] In practice, a development zone management committee signs many land grant contracts. According to the SPC interpretation on state-owned land contracts, contracts signed by a development zone management committee should be invalid.[30] Before the implementation of this interpretation, the development zone management committee acted as transferors in grant contracts, which were later ratified by the natural resources authority of the municipal or county people's government; such contracts are valid.[31]

24 Article 8 UREAL; Article 8 Interim Regulation of Transfer of State-owned Land.

25 Article 39 of the UREAL governs the transfer of the state-owned land use right obtained by paid use while Article 40 governs the transfer of the land use right by allocation.

26 Para. 1 of Article 348 CC.

27 Article 349 CC.

28 Para. 2 of Article 348 CC.

29 Article 12 UREAL; Article 1 SPC Interpretation on the State-owned land contracts.

30 Article 2 SPC Interpretation on the State-owned land contracts.

31 *Ibid.*

Second, as the CLUR contract essentially addresses the land use right, it is necessary to ascertain the relationship between buildings and fixtures erected on the land and the land itself. The principle of "house follows land, land follows house" has been implemented in China for the past four decades. This principle refers to the interdependent and inseparable relationship between buildings and land use rights.[32] In essence, it means that the property rights of buildings and the term of land use rights are synchronised within the land use duration.[33] When the CLUR are transferred, the property rights of the buildings are also transferred, or the transfer of the CLUR affects the interests of related buildings.[34] This principle is commonly observed in real estate transactions in China, especially in the context of urban land use rights transfer and the sale of commercial properties. This principle is crucial for ensuring the stability and legality of real estate transactions, significantly influencing the operational dynamics of the real estate market. As such, the CC provides that ownership of the buildings, structures and ancillary facilities built by the CLUR holder is presumed to be such holder's unless there is evidence to the contrary.[35] As a corollary, where the CLUR is taken back for public purposes before its expiry, houses and other fixtures on the construction land shall be compensated, and the concerned land transaction fees shall be returned.[36]

Third, the grantee must observe the designated land use in the CLUR contracts.[37] If the grantee unilaterally changes the designated use in the contract and the grantor requests contract termination, the Chinese courts should entertain this request.[38] However, suppose the grantor consents to the land use change suggested by the grantee and the competent government agency approves such change. In that case, the grantor may request the land transfer fee adjustment based on the standard for land with the same use when filing the lawsuit.[39] In the SPC case of *Langfang Rongda Tong Real Estate Development Co., Ltd. v. Langfang Natural Resources and Planning Bureau Guangyang District Branch*, due to changes in government planning, the original planned use for the construction of a car

32 Articles 356, 357, 397, 398 and 417 CC.
33 Article 357 CC.
34 Article 356 CC.
35 Article 352 CC.
36 Article 358 CC.
37 Article 350 CC.
38 Article 6 SPC Interpretation on the State-owned land contracts.
39 Article 5 SPC Interpretation on the State-owned land contracts.

dealership was changed to a hotel construction project.[40] There were changes in the land use and an increase in the plot ratio in the involved land use right, but the grantee did not pay the required additional land transfer fees as stipulated. The competent government agency repeatedly requested the grantee to pay the additional land transfer fees, but the two parties could not agree on the amount. The SPC held that the grantee is liable for the additional payment of fees, and the amount of additional fees is based on the standards of land transfer fees for the same type of land as specified by the designated government agency at the time of filing the lawsuit.[41] CLUR are further subject to conditions outlined in the land use planning and zoning regulations.[42] These conditions may include requirements for infrastructure development, environmental protection and adherence to building standards.

Fourth, if the grantor fails to obtain the necessary grant approval, the grantee cannot request specific performance by forcing the grantor to deliver the land.[43] Rather, the grantee can only request contract termination.[44] On the other hand, land use in China is often viewed as serving the public interest. As such, the holder of the CLUR should comply with the requirements of resource conservation, ecological and environmental protection and statutory provisions on land use, albeit without prejudice to any pre-existing usufructuary right.[45] The government may reclaim land for public welfare projects like infrastructure development or urban planning initiatives.[46]

Fifth, the holder of the CLUR must pay land use fees and other expenses under legal provisions and contractual stipulations.[47] The amount is determined based on factors such as the location, type of land use and local policies. The price clause is void if a government-approved land grant sets a fee below the government-determined minimum price.[48] The transferee pays per the market-valued price. If the grantee

40 廊坊市荣达通房地产开发有限公司与廊坊市自然资源和规划局广阳区分局案 [*The Langfang Rongda Tong Real Estate Development Co., Ltd. v. Langfang Natural Resources and Planning Bureau Guangyang District Branch*] (2020) 最高法民终168号 [(2020) SPC Min Zhong 168].

41 *Ibid.*

42 Article 12 UREAL.

43 Article 4 SPC Interpretation on the State-owned land contracts.

44 *Ibid.*

45 Article 346 CC.

46 Article 58 Land Administration Law.

47 Article 351 CC.

48 Article 3 SPC Interpretation on the State-owned land contracts.

does not agree to make good the shortfall, it may seek contract termination, with resulting losses borne based on fault.[49] When CLUR holders transfer to another private entity, if the transfer price is significantly lower than the market price, the city or county government has the right of first refusal.[50] By exercising the right of first refusal, the government can intervene in the market to ensure the rational use of land resources, prevent unfair low-price transactions and promote fair and efficient allocation of land resources. On the other hand, when there is an unreasonable increase in the market price upon CLUR transfer, the city or county government can take necessary measures to intervene.[51] This is to prevent speculation in the land market and maintain stability of land prices to guard against potential risks.

7.2.2.2 Legal Nature: Civil Contract or Administrative Contract

There has been a long-standing dispute in the legal academia and judiciary regarding the nature of the CLUR contract: whether it is an administrative or civil contract. This is because the law has not clearly defined the nature of the contracts. Unambiguous characterisation of the CLUR contract is relevant and significant for legal procedures, costs, and, most of all, a chance of prevailing in a litigation.

The first view is that the CLUR contract is an administrative contract entered into by an administrative authority to achieve public interests or administrative management purposes.[52] In this contract, the administrative entity may take coercive measures or penalties unilaterally, provided it can exercise certain administrative power within the law. The Administrative Litigation Law (revised in 2014) specified government-franchised business agreements, land and house expropriation compensation agreements and other agreements as administrative agreements within the scope of administrative litigation.[53] Then, the SPC announced in a judicial document adding agreements on transferring state-owned

[49] *Ibid.*

[50] Article 26 Interim Regulation of Transfer of State-owned Land.

[51] *Ibid.*

[52] Wang Jingbo [王敬波] and Li Xiaoguo [李晓果], 'A New Exploration of Dispute Resolution in State-Owned Land Use Right Transfer: A Case Study of the Dispute over the Construction Land Use Right Transfer Contract of Jiangsu Ruihao Real Estate Company' [《国有土地使用权出让争议解决新探索——以江苏瑞豪置业公司建设用地使用权出让合同纠纷案为例》] (2017) 4 *Legal Application* [《法律适用》] 7.

[53] Article 12 Item 11 Administrative Litigation Law (2014 Revision).

natural resource utilisation rights, such as mining rights, to the scope of administrative litigation.[54] However, this provision does not mention that CLUR contracts are administrative agreements. Therefore, there remains ambiguity regarding the characterisation of CLUR contracts.

The SPC Administrative Division clarified that the initial registration of ownership or use rights of natural resources such as land is administrative licensing.[55] On 23 July 2018, the First Circuit Court of the SPC further clarified that "CLUR contracts are typical administrative agreements." This is the first official announcement by the SPC that state-owned land transfer contracts are considered administrative agreements.[56] Furthermore, in one of the published guiding cases, the SPC Administrative Division expressly announced that the CLUR contract is characterised as an administrative agreement.[57] In short, the SPC Administrative Division tends to classify CLUR contracts as administrative agreements.

Two additional justifications are provided to characterise it as an administrative contract. When the land transfer contract is characterised as an administrative agreement, the court can review the legality of administrative actions.[58] The precondition for continuing the performance of an administrative agreement is the legality of actions taken by the administrative authority. In civil litigation, the court can only review the contractual relationship itself and lacks the authority to scrutinise the

[54] Article 2 item 3 of the SPC Provisions on Several Issues Concerning the Trial of Administrative Agreement Cases, effective on January 1, 2020.

[55] 最高人民法院行政审判庭关于行政机关颁发自然资源所有权或者使用权证的行为是否属于确认行政行为问题的答复 [The "Reply of the Administrative Trial Division of the SPC on the Issue of Whether the Act of the Administrative Organs Issuing Certificates of Ownership or Use Rights for Natural Resources Belongs to the Confirmation of Administrative Acts", issued on February 24, 2005].

[56] 最高人民法院第一巡回法庭关于行政审判法律适用若干问题的会议纪要 [The Minutes of the Meeting of the First Circuit Court of the SPC on Several Issues Concerning the Application of Laws in Administrative Trials, issued on 23 July 2018].

[57] No. 76 of the SPC guiding cases, 萍乡市亚鹏房地产开发有限公司诉萍乡市国土资源局, (2014) 萍行终字第10号 [*Pingxiang Asia Peng Real Estate Development Co., Ltd. v. Pingxiang Land and Resources Bureau*] (2014) 萍行终字第10号 [(2014) Ping Xing Zhong No.10].

[58] Article 11 of the SPC Provisions on Administrative Agreement Cases stipulates that people's courts, when adjudicating administrative agreement cases, should conduct a legality review of the defendant's acts of concluding, performing, modifying and terminating administrative agreements, including whether the acts have statutory authority, whether there is an abuse of authority, whether the application of laws and regulations is correct, whether the statutory procedures are followed, whether it is obviously improper and whether the corresponding statutory duties are fulfilled.

legality of administrative actions. If the case arises from administrative actions taken by the administrative authority, the court, in civil litigation, may dismiss the parties' claims and require them to file an administrative lawsuit separately. Alternatively, the court may suspend the civil proceedings until the administrative litigation is concluded and then resume the civil trial. The separate examination of administrative and civil actions may lead to procedural delays, conflicting outcomes, and increased litigation costs for the parties involved. Therefore, filing an administrative action on the ground that the CLUR contract is an administrative contract can streamline judicial resources and facilitate administrative parties.

The other justification is cost considerations. From the pragmatic perspective of complaints, characterising the CLUR contract as a civil contract and pursuing civil litigation entails specific financial implications. According to the *Measures on the Payment of Litigation Costs*, in civil litigation, particularly in CLUR contract disputes, litigation fees are calculated based on the amount or value claimed in the lawsuit.[59] Given that these cases often involve substantial amounts, initiating civil proceedings means upfront payment of significant case acceptance fees and, in some instances, subsequent appellate case acceptance fees if the initial claims are dismissed. In contrast, if the dispute is treated as an administrative action, the litigation fees are assessed per case, with each case incurring a fee of 50 yuan.[60] This differentiation is crucial for reducing the litigation costs for the parties involved.

The choice between administrative and civil litigation CLUR contract disputes has significant financial ramifications for the parties. Opting for administrative proceedings could substantially lower litigation costs, presenting a practical consideration when deciding on the appropriate legal avenue.

On the contrary, some argue that equal civil subjects enter into the CLUR contract to define rights and obligations, so the CLUR contract is a civil contract.[61] The CLUR contract is a mutual agreement between the parties, and it is established through negotiation with adherence to the

[59] Article 13 (1) of the Measures on the Payment of Litigation Costs, State Council Decree (No. 481), issued by the State Council on 8 December 2006, effective as of 1 April 2007].

[60] Article 13 (5) Measures on the Payment of Litigation Costs.

[61] Huixing Liang [梁慧星], *Research on Civil Law Doctrine, Cases, and Legislation (Part II)* [《民法学理论、案例与立法研究（下）》] (National Administrative College Press 1999), p. 191; Liming Wang [王利明] *Property Law* [《物权法》] (China Remin University Press 2015), p. 263.

principles of equality, voluntariness and paid use. Legal equality ensures that both parties enter the land transfer contract willingly and negotiate the terms and conditions fairly and voluntarily. The legal basis supporting such characterisation is found as follows.

First, Article 11 of the Interim Regulation of Transfer of State-owned Land enacted by the State Council in 1990 states that the CLUR contract shall be concluded by the land management department of the people's government at the city or county level and the land user on the principle of equality, voluntariness and paid use.

Second, the Property Law explicitly classified the CLUR as a usufructuary right. The establishment and acquisition of this right should be through a written contract for the grant of CLUR. Therefore, it should be ascertained as a civil contract regulating property rights relationships.

Third, in the PC Provisions on Causes of Action of Civil Cases (the 2011 revision), disputes over CLUR contracts are explicitly listed as a subordinate cause of action under contract disputes. This confirms that the CLUR contracts are civil contracts, and disputes from such contracts are handled as civil litigation cases.

In light of the above, there are inconsistencies in the statutory instruments and judicial interpretations of the nature of CLUR contracts. In legal academia, as seen in an earlier discussion, civil law scholars argue that they are civil contracts, while administrative law scholars believe they are administrative contracts. This academic debate soon transformed into a battle between the civil and administrative divisions within the SPC absent legislative clarity. The nature of the CLUR contracts determines whether the claimant should file civil or administrative action following different procedures.

Nonetheless, even the SPC Administrative Division, which has been advocating that CLUR contracts should be regarded as administrative contracts, issued two different rulings within a month, one considering it an administrative contract and the other a civil one.

The case of *Huludao City Natural Resources Bureau v. Huludao Hongyi Real Estate Development Co.*[62] involved a CLUR contract between the parties signed in July 2011. The central issue is the classification of the agreement in dispute. Huludao City Natural Resources Bureau contends it falls under administrative contracts, subject to administrative litigation.

[62] 葫芦岛市自然资源局、葫芦岛鸿亿房地产开发有限公司 [*Huludao City Natural Resources Bureau v. Huludao Hongyi Real Estate Development Co.*] 最高人民法院 (2020) 最高法行申11749号 [(2020) SPC Xing Shen No. 11749].

Hongyi Company, on the other hand, argues that it should be regarded as a civil agreement, invoking civil litigation procedures. The SPC held that the CLUR contract falls under administrative agreements. It emphasised that the signatory of the CLUR contract is the land management bureau, acting as an administrative entity. Such agreements aim to achieve public interests or the rational and effective utilisation of limited land resources.

In another judgment which was handed down 20 days earlier, *Sino-Japanese Youth Exchange Center Qinhuangdao Office v. Qinhuangdao Municipal Bureau of Natural Resources and Planning and Qinhuangdao Municipal People's Government,*[63] the SPC Administrative Division ruled differently by holding that the CLUR contract in dispute was a civil contract. The reasoning is that the SPC Interpretation of State-owned land contracts explicitly places such disputes within the scope of civil litigation rather than administrative agreements. In contrast to mining rights and other state-owned natural resource usage rights agreements, state-owned land use rights contracts are under the purview of civil law.

The contradiction in these rulings reflects the ongoing debate regarding the nature of CLUR contracts. One would argue that a unified perspective and clear standards from the SPC are desired to prevent confusion. However, Chang argued that at the practical level, there is a convergence in terms of contract validity, termination and remedies between administrative and civil actions.[64] Therefore, CLUR contracts represent a conjuncture of civil and administrative contracts.

This author believes the CLUR contracts are civil contracts that include certain public law elements, as singled out in Article 348 of the CC. The transfer contract ensures equal rights and obligations for both parties. The main rights of the grantor include collecting land transfer fees, and its primary obligation is to provide land use rights to the other party within a specified period.[65] The main rights of the land user include obtaining land use rights within a certain term, while the primary obligation is to pay the transfer fee and develop the land according to legal and contractual requirements.[66] Regardless of whether it is through

[63] 中日青年交流中心秦皇岛办事处、秦皇岛市自然资源和规划局 [*Sino-Japanese Youth Exchange Center Qinhuangdao Office v. Qinhuangdao Municipal Bureau of Natural Resources and Planning*] (2020) 最高法行申13827号 [(2020) SPC Xing Shen No. 13827].

[64] Peng'Ao Chang [常鹏翱], *China's Real Estate Law in Practice* [《实践中的中国房地产法》] (Peking University Press 2023), pp. 238–40.

[65] Article 16 UREAL.

[66] Article 15 UREAL.

bidding, auction or negotiated agreement, in the contractual agreement for the transfer of the right to use construction land, both the transferor and transferee may choose to participate or not participate in the contract, and their agreement is considered voluntary.[67] Both parties can terminate the contract and claim compensation against a breach.

The model CLUR contract jointly formulated by the former Ministry of Land and Resources and the State Administration for Industry and Commerce includes a provision allowing disputes arising from the contract to be submitted to arbitration for dispute settlement.[68] Suppose the CLUR contracts can be submitted for arbitration to settle disputes. In that case, signing such contracts would be considered a civil act. Under the Arbitration Law, administrative contracts are excluded from arbitration,[69] and disputes cannot be resolved through arbitration designed for disputes between equal civil entities.

7.2.3 Registration

CLUR is established following a mandatory registration system.[70] The establishment of CLUR, with legal effects against third parties, occurs only upon completion of the registration process. The effectiveness of a contract for transferring CLUR does not directly lead to establishing property rights. Instead, it creates contractual obligations, where the transferor has the right to request the transferee to pay the land transfer fee, and the transferee has the right to request the transferor to deliver the land and complete the registration of CLURs. The effectiveness of the CLUR contract is not contingent upon completion of registration. Even before registration, the contract has legal consequences between the parties.

Completion of registration ensures that the CLURs are effective against third parties, providing clarity in property rights. This system

[67] Maohui Qu [屈茂辉], 'Revisiting the Civil Nature of the Land Use Rights Grant Contract for Construction Purposes' [《再论建设用地使用权出让合同的民事属性》] (2023) 6 *China Legal Science* [《中国法学》] 201.

[68] 国土资源部、国家工商行政管理总局发布的《国有建设用地使用权出让合同》示范文本（国土资发）[2008] 第86号 [The Notice from the Ministry of Land and Resources and the State Administration for Industry and Commerce on the Release of the Model Text for State-owned Land Use Rights Transfer Contracts, Circular on Land and Resources [2008] No. 86].

[69] Article 3 Arbitration Law.

[70] Article 349 CC.

reflects the importance of registration in securing and formalising property rights, aligning with broader principles of land management and legal protection in China.

7.2.4 Contract Validity v. Non-compliance with Laws and Departmental Rules

The CLUR contract, while essentially a civil contract, involves administrative governance. Consequently, there are many administrative restrictions placed on the CLUR contract. Therefore, there are many instances where there is a defect in complying with the relevant laws and departmental rules set by the national legislature or relevant ministries of the State Council. The question arises whether the contract is still valid or tainted by non-compliance with administrative formalities. The raw land transfer is discussed to illustrate how Chinese courts resolve this vexing issue.

7.2.4.1 Raw Land Transfer

A departmental rule stipulates that land must meet certain requirements before the local governments engage land supply.[71] These requirements include clear land rights, proper resettlement and compensation without legal or economic disputes, planning conditions such as location, land use and plot ratio, and other basic conditions necessary for development.[72] The land can be granted or transferred if all these requirements are fulfilled. This type of land is often called clean land. On the other hand, raw land is a term used in contrast to clean land. It indicates land for which the government has not yet completed the process of reclaiming land use rights and compensating for the demolition of buildings.

In practice, constrained by the local financial setbacks, many local governments engage in the grant of raw land despite the departmental rule. This is because the local government can shift the burden of paying compensation to the expropriated parties to the grantees, often commercial developers. How would Chinese courts rule if there was a dispute over contract validity due to non-compliance with a department rule?

[71] The Regulations on the Disposal of Idle Land, (2007) Order No. 53 of the Ministry of Land and Resources.

[72] *Ibid.*

One option is to declare the contract invalid because of the defects in administrative formalities, namely non-compliance with a departmental rule. However, there are two perceived drawbacks to this approach. First, the grantee has already incurred substantial expenses to pay compensation and executive the construction work for the land development project. If the contract is invalid, the legal consequence would be that property acquired by the grantee is returned, and if the return is impossible or unnecessary, damages are estimated and paid.[73] However, this remedy is insufficient to compensate for the loss suffered by the grantee, as the project's market value may have increased since it started.

Second, the grantor, the local government, is responsible for ensuring that the land to be granted complies with the administrative rules. If regulations require the local government or the competent government agency to do compliance, that is its responsibility under the law, not the grantee's. In addition, if the competent government agency fails to fulfil any internal requirements, the government agency should be responsible for the consequences.[74] In other words, the faulting party should not benefit from non-compliance.

Therefore, the SPC has taken a clear stance in this scenario that the departmental rule was an internal normative document, not a mandatory regulation in laws or administrative regulations issued by the State Council.[75] As a result, non-compliance was regarded as a mere defect in administrative formalities, and such a defect would not defeat the contract's validity.

7.2.4.2 Twenty-five Per cent of Total Investment Requirement

The raw land transfer violates a departmental rule. How do Chinese courts deal with violating a statutory provision in legislation? Article 39 of the UREAL outlines the conditions for land entering a secondary land market.

[73] Article 157 CC.

[74] 万宁市人民政府与万宁兴隆桃源旅业有限公司 [*Wanning Municipal People's Government v. Wanning Xinglong Taoyuan Tourism Co., Ltd.*] (2018) 琼行终905号 [(2018) Qiong Xing Zhong No. 905].

[75] 乌海市锦邦房地产开发有限责任公司、乌海市自然资源局海勃湾分局[*Wuhai Jinbang Real Estate Development Co., Ltd. v. Wuhai Municipal Bureau of Natural Resources*] (2019) 最高法民终2013号 [(2019) SPC Min Zhong No. 2013].

> When transferring real estate obtained through the transfer of land use rights, the following conditions should be met:
>
> (1) The full payment of the land use right transfer fee has been made per the agreement in the transfer contract, and the land use right certificate has been obtained.
> (2) Investment and development have been carried out as stipulated in the transfer contract. More than 25 per cent of the development investment must be completed for housing construction projects. It should meet industrial or other construction use conditions for land developed.
>
> When transferring real estate with completed buildings, ownership certificates for the buildings should also be held.

The second condition in the preceding provision is that the expenditure should reach at least 25 per cent of the total development investment. In the past, the judiciary was firm that violating this statutory condition renders the CLUR contract void. For example, in a Judicial Reply specifically focused on this provision in 2003 (the "2003 Reply|"), the SPC explicitly stated that "if the transfer lacks both of the above conditions simultaneously, the transfer contract is invalid."[76] The rationale was to cool down overheated land speculation.

Nonetheless, in 2004, the SPC held that the completion of 25 per cent of the total investment requirement is a restrictive condition set for the subject matter of the CLUR contract at the time of property right change.[77] If it does not meet the 25 per cent investment threshold, it constitutes a defect in the subject matter of the contract, namely land, but it does not directly affect the validity of the CLUR contract.[78] The aforementioned provision is not a mandatory rule for determining the validity of the land use right transfer contract. Therefore, if the parties claim that the contract is invalid due to not meeting the 25 per cent investment and development condition, the court should not support it.

[76] 法函[2003]24号 最高人民法院关于土地转让方未按规定完成土地的开发投资即签订土地使用权转让合同的效力问题的答复 [The Reply Regarding the Validity of the Land Use Right Transfer Contract When the Land Transferor Fails to Complete the Development Investment as Required before Signing the Contract Fa Han [2003] No. 24, issued on 9 June 2003].

[77] The SPC gazetted case: 柳州市全威电器有限责任公司、柳州超凡房地产开发有限责任公司与被上诉人南宁桂馨源房地产有限公司案 [*Liuzhou Quanwei Electric Co., Ltd., and Liuzhou Chaofan Real Estate Development Co., Ltd. v. Nanning GuixinYuan Real Estate Co., Ltd*] (2004) 民一终字第46号 [(2004) SPC Min Yi Zhong No. 46].

[78] *Ibid.*

The SPC has infused policy considerations. First, the rigid enforcement of the 25 per cent of total investment conditions cannot achieve a sustainable land development and utilisation market, leading to further land idling. In reality, there are many instances where the transferor is financially unable to carry out the planned real estate development. However, the transferee is financially able and willing to take over.

Nevertheless, this situation is a genuine market practice, not a land speculation. Therefore, a rigid and undifferentiated approach to invalidate the CLUR contracts due to non-compliance with this condition is neither fair nor necessary. Second, where the party transferring the CLUR received the land transfer payment from the transferee, thus receiving the consideration and benefits provided by the contract, it cannot rely on non-compliance of its fault to argue for the contract's invalidity.[79] In other words, it used its own breach of contract as a cause of action, claiming the contract's invalidity due to the land not meeting the transfer conditions. This violates the principle of good faith and fair dealing.

Consequently, in 2013, the SPC repealed the 2003 Reply because it contradicts the principle of separation on the property transfer in the Property Law 2007.[80] One month after the repeal, the SPC, in another case, confirmed that non-compliance with the 25 per cent of total investment condition does not defeat the validity of the CLUR contract.[81]

However, it is important to note that even if the SPC regards the transfer of the CLUR as valid where there is non-compliance with the 25 per cent total investment completion requirement, the land registration office may not be willing to complete the transfer registration given Article 39 of the UREAL. Therefore, despite obtaining a judgment on the contract's validity during litigation, there may be difficulties in the execution process due to the land registration office's reluctance to complete the registration.

[79] 上海枫丹丽舍房地产开发有限公司与上海华夏文化旅游区开发有限公司案 [*Shanghai Fengdan Lido Real Estate Development Co., Ltd. v. Shanghai Huaxia Cultural Tourism Zone Development Co., Ltd*] (2006) 民一终字第57号 [(2006) SPC Min Yi Zhong No. 57].

[80] The Decision of the SPC on Abolishing Some Judicial Interpretations and Documents with Judicial Interpretation Nature Issued from 1 July 1997, to 31 December 2011 (Batch X) – Judicial Interpretation No. 7 of 2013, issued on 26 February 2013.

[81] The SPC gazetted case: 四川省聚丰房地产开发有限责任公司与达州广播电视大学案 [*Sichuan Province Jufeng Real Estate Development Co., Ltd. v. Dazhou Radio and Television University*] (2013) 民一终字第18号 [(2013) SPC Min Yi Zhong No. 18].

To address the dilemma, some local governments issued local rules clarifying that a real estate project with incomplete development investment totalling 25 per cent can undergo real estate transfer pre-registration.[82] The registration procedures can be completed when the investment and development meet the transfer conditions.[83] This provides a new approach to resolving the above dilemma, ensuring investors' rights and facilitating utilising existing land resources.

7.2.5 Duration

The limited term of CLUR refers to a usufructuary right established on the land, allowing individuals or entities to construct buildings on the land with a specified term. People acquire the right to use the land for a limited period while maintaining ownership rights without time restrictions over the buildings and structures constructed on the land. When the term of the land use right expires, it raises questions about how to renew the CLURs and the ownership status of the buildings on the land.

Before the enactment of the CC, the Property Law provided that the right to use residential construction land shall be automatically renewed upon the expiration of the term – the renewal of the right to use non-residential construction land after the term's expiration shall be handled. The ownership of houses and other real properties on the land shall be handled per the agreement if there is one; if there is no agreement or the agreement is unclear, it shall be handled following the provisions of laws and administrative regulations.[84] There is a different way to address residential CLUR and non-residential CLUR. However, further procedures and processes have not been detailed in both situations.

The CC emphasises the automatic renewal principle for residential land use rights.[85] Specifically, the CC provides that upon expiration of the term of CLUR, it shall be automatically renewed. The payment or reduction of

[82] For example, Article 20 of the Guangdong Province State-owned CLUR Transaction Market Management Regulations, Yu Fu Ling No. 304 issued on 13 November 2023 and effective on 1 January 2024; Item 1 of the Implementation Opinions of the General Office of the People's Government of Shaanxi Province on Improving the Secondary Market for the Transfer, Lease, and Mortgage of CLURs, Shan Zheng Ban Fa [2020] No. 17, issued on 10 September 2020.

[83] *Ibid.*

[84] Article 149 Property Law.

[85] Article 359 CC.

renewal fees shall be handled following laws and administrative regulations. The renewal of the right to use non-residential construction land after the expiration of the term shall be handled according to the laws. For example, suppose the term for non-residential CLUR expires, the land user has not applied for renewal or the renewal application has not been approved. In that case, the competent authority of the people's government reports to the people's government that originally approved the land or to the people's government with the approval authority; it may reclaim the CLUR without paying compensation.[86] The ownership of buildings and other immovables on such land shall be as agreed; in the absence of an agreement or if the agreement is unclear, it shall be handled under laws and administrative regulations.

Certain regions in China faced urgent handling of the expiration of the CLUR term by introducing relevant policies for fee reduction. There are practical shortcomings in the existing legislation regarding CLURs. The issues include uncertainties about how to handle the renewal of land use rights and the ownership of buildings when the land use rights expire. Due to the significant practical controversies and lack of a consensus on how to handle the automatic renewal of the CLUR after the expiration of the term, detailed regulations have not been made in the formulation of the CC. In fact, in November 2016, the *Opinion of the CPC Central Committee and the State Council on Improving the System for Protecting Property Rights and Strengthening the Protection of Property Rights through the Rule of Law* proposed to study legal arrangements for the renewal of the right to use land after the expiration of residential construction land and other land use rights and promote the formation of a good and stable expectation of long-term protection of citizens' property throughout society. However, this work still hasn't been completed by relevant departments of the State Council.

Automatic renewal does not mean that residents can use it free of charge. While residential CLURs are specified to be able to renew automatically, it may require payment or a reduction of renewal fees. In 2016 Wenzhou, some apartments faced the expiration of the twenty-year residential land use rights. Without precedence and clear guidance from the national legislation and regulations, the Wenzhou local government required the apartment owners to pay several hundred thousand yuan for renewal, amounting to nearly one-third of the

[86] Article 58 (2) Land Administration Law.

apartment's market value.[87] The high renewal fees brought public attention to the renewal policy and the effect it might have on the wealth of homeowners nationwide. Most urban residents' land use rights on their property certificates are typically set at seventy years. The case of twenty-year land use rights for residential properties in Wenzhou is unique. It stems from flexible measures introduced by the government at that time, driven by the local government's urgency to expedite land transactions.

Nonetheless, in 2001, there was a controversy in Shenzhen regarding the expiration of twenty-year land use rights for a commercial mall building. In response, the Shenzhen government in 2004 introduced the "Shenzhen Regulations on the Renewal of Expired Real Estate," allowing the renewal by paying 35 per cent of the benchmark land price, namely the initial auction price on the land set by the local government.[88] The affected building successfully extended its land use rights under this regulation. Notably, Shenzhen applied a discount of 35 per cent to the benchmark land price, resulting in significant savings for property owners. Subsequently, the Changcheng Building in Shenzhen encountered the renewal of land use rights. Shenzhen government allowed the land use period extension from the original fifty years to seventy years by submitting a renewal application to the government. The homeowner paid a renewal fee of roughly 0.5 per cent of the current market price. If the extended period changed from twenty to seventy years, the renewal fee would be about 2.2 per cent of the total property price.[89]

There is a contrast between the Wenzhou and Shenzhen approaches. Shenzhen's approach is more market driven and protective of private property right. Charging exorbitant fees would be financially destructive and undermine social stability. As a result, after the Wenzhou government issued a high renewal fee plan, the Ministry of National Resources intervened by providing transitional measures for handling the expiration of residential CLURs, which state that no renewal application is

[87] Rong Chen, '温州一批20年产权住在土地使用权到期，须按房价1/3续期' ['In Wenzhou, a batch of residential properties with 20-year land use rights is set to be renewed at one-third of the property price upon expiration'] (*Huanqiu.com*, 15 April 2016) <https://m.huanqiu.com/article/9CaKrnJUYf1> accessed on 10 September 2023.

[88] Article 3 of '《深圳市到期房地产续期若干规定》的通知（2004年4月23日）深府〔2004〕73号'.

[89] Lin Wang [王林], '土地使用权到期怎么办?' ['What should be done when the land use right expires?'] (*victory.itslaw.cn*, 20 April 2016) <http://victory.itslaw.cn/victory/api/v1/articles/article/54baab61-7357-4646-9b89-a3c467ea58f2> accessed on 2 October 2023.

required.[90] This is only a transitional measure before the new law is enacted. It does not necessarily mean that future legislation will be handled according to this provision.

The legal framework for CLURs faces challenges in practical implementation. The existing legislation might not provide clear guidance on procedures and rights concerning renewing CLURs. As a result, there is a need for further clarification or amendments to address these operational deficiencies and ensure a smoother process for handling the expiration and renewal of CLURs.

However, as time passes, the issue of handling the expiration of land use rights becomes more prominent in contemporary society. Consequently, the resulting property disputes will also increase. Therefore, it is necessary to formulate comprehensive regulations on the duration of CLURs as soon as possible, aiming to achieve the effect of resolving disputes and providing clarity.

7.3 Transferability

CLUR can be transferred, leased, exchanged, donated, mortgaged or used as investment equity under certain conditions.[91] Compared with the other four types of usufructuary rights, namely LCMR, homestead rights, servitude and habitation rights, CLUR is the least restrictive and most market-driven land use right under Chinese law. Despite this, the CLUR transfer is subject to certain government approvals and restrictions. The government aims to control and manage land use effectively. The government exercises strict control over land use through land use planning and zoning regulations. These regulations outline the types of development allowed in specific areas, and compliance is crucial for obtaining and maintaining land use rights.

As with its creation, where the CLUR is subject to transfer, exchange, investment, donation or mortgage, the parties should conclude a contract in writing.[92] Parties may stipulate the length of use, provided that such period does not exceed the remaining term of the CLUR.[93]

[90] The Reply on Properly Handling the Issue of Expiring Residential CLURs – Letter from the Office of the Ministry of Land and Resources (Document No. [2016] 1712 from the Ministry of Land and Resources.

[91] Article 353 CC.

[92] Article 354 CC.

[93] Article 43 UREAL.

An application for registration of the change shall be filed at the registration office.[94]

Even if there are defects in the administrative formalities in obtaining approval for the transfer, such administrative formalities will not defeat the validity of the transfer contract or the transfer of the land use rights. This view is consistent with Article 8 of the SPC Interpretation on the State-owned land contracts, which states that after the transferor enters into a land use right transfer contract with the transferee, if one party requests to confirm that the contract is invalid because registration formalities for change of land use right have not been completed between the two parties, it shall not be supported.[95] Therefore, the non-completion of registration of changes is not fatal to the contract's validity. The contract is valid once the transferor and transferee meet the requirements for entering into a CLUR contract.

7.3.1 An Issue of One CLUR Subject to Multiple Transfer Contracts

When the CLUR holder, the transferor, enters into multiple transfer contracts for the same CLUR, all transfer contracts are valid with market value considerations. However, if none of them has been registered to gain publicity, how to determine which transferee has priority over others to acquire the CLUR? The SPC's position is that the first to occupy and develop the land legally acquires priority in obtaining the land.

The starting point is that if one of the transferees has completed the registration and requests the transferor to fulfil obligations to surrender the possession of the land, Chinese courts entertain such a request by the registered transferee.[96] Where none of the transferees has completed registration, the transferee who has lawful occupation of the land and has developed an investment project requests the transferor to fulfil obligations to complete registration; such request should be supported.[97]

94 Article 355 CC.

95 Article 8 of the SPC Interpretation on the Application of Law in the Trial of State-owned Land Use Right Contract Disputes.

96 长沙金霞开发建设有限公司与长沙市交通运输局 [*Changsha Jinxia Development and Construction Co., Ltd. Changsha Municipal Transportation Bureau*] (2015) 民一终字第163号 [(2015) SPC Min Yi Zhong No. 163].

97 Article 9 of the SPC Interpretation on the Application of Law in the Trial of State-owned Land Use Right Contract Disputes.

In *Dongguan Licheng Electronic Industry Co., Ltd.*,[98] Li Bing took control of Changxin Company and lawfully occupied and developed the Lianhu Villa project after signing the land transfer contract. The SPC held that according to the legislative purpose of the possession system in the Property Law, where the possessor has the right to possess to maintain the existing factual and legal order of the property, transferring the land to others is practically impossible. Although Licheng Company and Baoyuan Company also paid the transfer fees to Changxin Company, Li Bing has lawfully taken possession of the involved land, paid part of the transfer price for the land use rights and carried out development and construction. Therefore, Licheng Company and Baoyuan Company's claim for Changxin Company to continue performance cannot be supported.[99]

Where none of the transferees has completed registration, and none of the transferees was in occupation of the land, the transferee who has paid the land transfer fees first will gain priority to request the transferor to perform the contractual obligations.[100] The courts prioritise protecting the performance interests of the party that made prior payments.[101] In the case of *Hebei Jifeng Real Estate Development Co., Ltd.*, the claimant asserts that its submitted notarised documents, invoices, handover lists and receipts are sufficient to prove that it has occupied the relevant land.[102] However, the SPC held that the above evidence can only prove that the claimant has stored some machinery, equipment and materials in the defendant's warehouse.[103] This is insufficient to prove its occupation of the land in question. As a result, the claimant, who was not the first to pay the land transfer fees, is not entitled to seek specific

98 东莞市利成电子实业有限公司等与东莞市大岭山镇房地产开发公司等案 [*Dongguan Licheng Electronic Industry Co., Ltd. v. Dongguan Dalingshan Town Real Estate Development Company and others*] (2012) 民提字第 122 号民事判决书[(2012) SPC Min Ti No. 122.].

99 *Ibid.*

100 Article 9 of the SPC Interpretation on the Application of Law in the Trial of State-owned Land Use Right Contract Disputes.

101 广东富宏房地产开发有限公司与洪妙莲纠纷 [*Guangdong Fuhong Real Estate Development Co., Ltd. v. Hong Miaolian*] (2014) 粤高法民一申字第123号 [(2014) Yue High Court Civil Application No. 123].

102 河北冀丰房地产开发有限公司诉石家庄市金之源化工有限公司 [*Hebei Jifeng Real Estate Development Co., Ltd. v. Jinzhiyuan Chemical Co., Ltd. in Shijiazhuang City*] (2016) 最高法民申1325号 [(2016) SPC Civil Application No. 1325].

103 *Ibid.*

performance against the transferor.[104] This SPC decision clarified that merely storing machinery and equipment on another's land does not amount to the lawful occupation and developing the investment project for Article 9 of the SPC Interpretation on the State-owned land contracts. As a result, the transferee who paid first took priority.

Finally, where none of the transferees has paid the land transfer fees, the transferee who concluded the CLUR contract earliest will take priority over the others.[105] While this situation is rare because the transferee is usually required to pay a deposit upon concluding the contract, it is still necessary for the SPC to provide clarification.

7.3.2 The Transferability of Allocated CLUR

In principle, the allocated CLUR cannot be transferred, mortgaged or leased.[106] However, under certain stipulated conditions, the allocated CLUR can be transferred. Specifically, the right to transfer, lease or mortgage the allocated CLUR and ownership of buildings and other structures on the land can be approved by the competent government agency of the people's government if the following conditions are met: (1) the land user is a company, enterprise, other economic organisation or individual; (2) there is a state-owned land use certificate; (3) there is proof of ownership of buildings and other structures on the land; (4) signing a written land use right transfer contract and making good a payment of the land use right transfer fee to the local people's government or offsetting the fee with the proceeds from the transfer, lease or mortgage of the land use right.[107] In brief, it is essential to obtain approval from the competent government agency to transfer the allocated CLUR[108]; otherwise, the transfer contract is considered invalid unless ratified by the people's government before commencing the legal proceedings.[109]

With the government's approval, the allocated CLUR can be arranged in the following ways. First, the CLUR holder goes through the

104 *Ibid.*
105 Article 9 SPC Interpretation on the Application of Law in the Trial of State-owned Land Use Right Contract Disputes.
106 Article 44 Interim Regulation of Transfer of State-owned Land.
107 Article 45 Interim Regulation of Transfer of State-owned Land.
108 Article 11 SPC Interpretation on the Application of Law in the Trial of State-owned Land Use Right Contract Disputes.
109 *Ibid.*

procedures with the competent government agency to transform allocated land into paid-use land. Subsequently, the CLUR holder transfers the land, now a paid-use CLUR.

Second, the transferee may go through the procedures for transferring the allocated land with the competent government agency. Then, the transferee will pay the land transfer fees to the government agency. In such circumstances, the contract between the transferor and the transferee is regarded as compensatory,[110] as if the land use right was initially obtained by paid use. The rationale is that the transferor loses its right to use the land. In this case, the government reclaims the land and re-grants the land use right.

Third, suppose the transferee qualifies for being allocated land use rights. In that case, the competent government agency may reclaim the allocated land use rights from the transferor and then allocate them to the transferee. In this scenario, it is essentially a re-allocation of land use rights by the government, and the contract between the land use right holder and the transferee is treated as a compensatory contract.[111]

It is permissible for the allocated land use right to be transferred together with the buildings and structures on the land.[112] Transfer of buildings and allocated land use rights must be approved by the people's government with approval authority according to the State Council regulations.[113]

A question arises: If the government has not approved the transfer of real estate built on allocated land, is the transfer contract still valid? A SPC decision reveals how the judiciary tackles this issue. In the case of *Inner Mongolia Puli Real Estate Development Co., Ltd.*, the Hohhot IPC ruled that the contract was invalid because the government had not approved the transfer before the lawsuit.[114] However, in the second instance, the Inner Mongolia Higher People's Court overturned the

[110] Article 12 SPC Interpretation on the Application of Law in the Trial of State-owned Land Use Right Contract Disputes.

[111] Article 13 SPC Interpretation on the Application of Law in the Trial of State-owned Land Use Right Contract Disputes.

[112] Article 40 UREAL.

[113] *Ibid.*

[114] 内蒙古普利房地产开发有限责任公司与北京瑞德康住房开发股份有限公司 (2010) 呼民初字第281号民事判决 [*Inner Mongolia Puli Real Estate Development Co., Ltd. (Puli) v. Beijing Reed Kang Housing Development Co., Ltd.* (2010) Hu Min Chu Zi No. 281].

ruling by upholding the contract's validity, which the SPC affirmed in its retrial decision.[115]

The key facts were that Puli Commercial Center, a project approved by the Hohhot municipal people's government with preferential policies during urban redevelopment, had the legal conditions for conducting real estate transactions; the approval allowed for the development of commercial and residential buildings on the allocated land. The sale of Puli Commercial Center was based on a clear and genuine expression of intent by both parties. The contract explicitly provided that (1) the land at issue was allocated land, (2) the sale price included the land transfer fee and (3) the claimant applied to government authorities for the land transfer procedures. The defendant had already paid the full contract price, and the Hohhot Municipal Housing Management Department had issued the defendant the property ownership certificate, indicating the department's recognition of the transaction. The SPC held that while the approval was expressly given, the project did not violate the Hohhot municipal government's preferential policy or the objectives of national land administration.[116] In the retrial, the Hohhot municipal government legal affairs office responded that the land transfer procedures could be handled if the defendant paid the land transfer fee and was approved after verification. The transaction did not cause a loss over the state-owned allocated land use rights or harm national interests. Hence, the contract is valid.[117]

In summary, where the real estate development project is complete, and government departments recognise the sale of apartments or high-rise buildings and issue the property certificates, the transfer of allocated land without separate approval may not cause the contract to be invalid. Where the competent government agency knew the transaction and issued the property certificates, the failure of the transferor to complete the approval procedures for the allocated land use right does not constitute grounds for the contract's invalidity. The transfer contract remains valid, and neither the transferor nor the transferee can claim its invalidity based on this reason.

[115] 内蒙古普利房地产开发有限责任公司与北京瑞德康住房开发股份有限公司 (2014) 民抗字第41号 [*Inner Mongolia Puli Real Estate Development Co., Ltd. (Puli) v. Beijing Reed Kang Housing Development Co., Ltd.* (2014) Min Kang Zi No. 41].

[116] *Ibid.*

[117] *Ibid.*

7.4 Revocation and Extinguishment

7.4.1 Revocation

The government retains the right to revoke or modify CLURs for public interest, such as urban regeneration[118] or non-compliance with land use regulations.[119] When it is necessary to implement urban planning to regenerate old urban areas and other public interests that require land use, the people's government that originally approved the CLUR or the people's government with the approval authority may revoke the CLUR.[120] In such circumstances, appropriate compensation shall be provided to the holder of the CLUR.[121] Appropriate compensation should be fair and reasonable, considering various factors such as the nature, use, location, assessment methods and reasons for idling of the land being expropriated. Compensation should be determined by referencing market prices.

Where the CLUR originally allocated is no longer used due to reasons such as the dissolution or relocation of the grantee entity, the competent government agency may decide to revoke the CLUR.[122] In addition, in cases of approved abandonment of roads, railways, airports and mines by the competent government agency, the CLUR may be revoked.[123] In these two instances, the government does not need to provide any compensation when the land is abandoned or not used anymore.[124] The revocation of CLURs may also be associated with changes in urban planning and zoning regulations. The government may repurpose the land based on evolving city planning goals and priorities.

The local governments may also revoke the CLUR when the land ought to be in use but the holder remains idle for a certain period after obtaining the CLUR. Chinese law is very restrictive on the commencement date of development when the holder acquires the CLUR for real estate development. For example, where the paid-use CLUR is obtained, it is mandatory to develop the land under the agreed land use and the commencement date of the development specified in the CLUR

[118] Article 358 CC.
[119] Article 26 UREAL.
[120] Para. 1 Item 1 of Article 58 Land Administration Law.
[121] Para. 2 of Article 58 Land Administration Law.
[122] Para. 1, Item 3 of Article 58 Land Administration Law.
[123] Para 1, Item 4 of Article 58 Land Administration Law.
[124] Para. 2 of Article 58 Land Administration Law.

contract.[125] Suppose the developer procrastinates and the granted land remains undeveloped for more than one year since the agreed date. In that case, a land idle fee, equivalent to up to 20 per cent of the land transfer fees, can be levied, but the government agency cannot take back the CLUR.[126] If the development has not been started for more than two years since the agreed date, the land use right can be reclaimed without compensation.[127] However, this does not apply in cases of *force majeure*, actions of governments or related government agencies or delays in commencing development due to necessary pre-development preparatory activities.[128]

Situations in which the land in question requires expropriation, and the expropriation causes a delay in handing over the land to the holder of the CLUR fall within the scope of the government's actions. In the case of *Dengzhou Jinchuan Urban and Rural Construction Co., Ltd. v. Dengzhou Natural Resources and Planning Bureau*, the appellant entered into the CLUR transfer contract with the respondent.[129] The transferred CLUR was intended for commercial and residential purposes. The CLUR contract stipulated that the respondent agreed to deliver the land to the appellant on or before 20 November 2010, and the land should meet the statutory conditions for development. Due to difficulties in reaching an agreement on the amount of expropriation compensation, the land was handed over to the appellant in October 2011. The court held that the respondent is under statutory and contractual obligations to hand over the land at the agreed date.[130] The appellant is not responsible for expropriation matters, but the respondent is. Therefore, the respondent's failure to hand over the land on time constitutes a breach of contract.[131]

Where the government fails to fulfil obligations concerning land requisition, resettlement, pre-development and timely land delivery, leading to delays in handing over the land to the transferee, the government should be responsible for proactively solving the issue. One way to solve this is to enter a supplementary agreement with the transferee to

125 Article 26 UREAL.

126 *Ibid.*

127 *Ibid.*

128 *Ibid.*

129 邓州市金川城乡建设有限公司诉邓州市自然资源和规划局 [*Dengzhou Jinchuan Urban and Rural Construction Co., Ltd. v. Dengzhou Natural Resources and Planning Bureau*] (2018) 豫13行终179号 [(2018) Yu 13 Xing Zhong 179].

130 *Ibid.*

131 *Ibid.*

redefine the deadlines for delivering the land. If the conditions for handing over the land are still not met within the revised time frame, the government may consider withdrawal with compensation through mutual agreement. The two key phrases in this process are "mutual agreement" and "appropriate compensation." The competent government agency should negotiate with the parties involved. The compensation amount should not be lower than the transferee's land acquisition cost, considering reasonable direct losses and referencing market prices. This amount should be mutually agreed upon through negotiations. Once a consensus is reached through negotiation, the competent government agency will draft a plan for the disposal of idle land, seek approval from the local government and execute the compensated withdrawal agreement.

Where the delay in development for more than two years after the agreed date is attributable to the transferee, the CLUR will be reclaimed. According to the *Opinions on Determining the Administrative Nature of Decisions to Revoke Land Use Rights* issued by the National Land Administration (the "1997 Opinion"), revoking land use rights is a significant administrative action undertaken by the people's government and was characterised as an administrative penalty where the land remains undeveloped for more than two years without a good cause.[132] Some judicial decisions have confirmed this characterisation.[133] Therefore, the following steps are generally involved under the Administrative Penalty Law to exercise the administrative penalty power. First, the entity exercising the power of revocation must have statutory authority. The designated entity is the natural resources management department. However, approval from the original land use approving authority is required before making the revocation decision. Second, revocation must follow the due process procedures under the Administrative Penalty Law.[134] For example, the designated agency should notify the transferee, investigate and confirm land idle situations, and issue a revocation decision. The revocation decision notifies the transferee of the intention to reclaim land use rights without compensation, providing details about the facts, reasons and legal basis. The

[132] Article 5 of the 1997 Opinion ([1997] Guotu [Fa] Zi No. 153) (currently in effect).

[133] For example, 海南省人民政府诉海口农村商业银行股份有限公司 [*Hainan Provincial People's Government v. Haikou Rural Commercial Bank Co., Ltd.*] (2020) 最高法行申4439号 [(2020) SPC Xing Shen No. 4439].

[134] Articles 36–41 Administrative Penalty Law.

government agency should inform the mortgagee if there is a legally established mortgage on the idle land. The agency should inform the affected transferees of their right to a hearing and communicate that they will have the opportunity to present statements and defences regarding the decision to reclaim land use rights. If the hearing is conducted, the revoking authority should provide details about the procedure, including the format, venue and any specific rules or guidelines governing the hearing process. When a revocation decision is made, the designated agency should inform the affected parties of their right to apply for administrative reconsideration or file an administrative lawsuit.

In summary, to prevent the waste of land resources due to idleness, Chinese law has given local governments the power to revoke the CLUR in certain circumstances. In a way, the revocation power by local governments is a relief against breach of statutory conditions or contractual terms by the transferee. The most controversial part of the matter is reclaiming the land without compensation if the land remains undeveloped for two years. When the designated government agency decides to revoke for this reason, it should exercise the power to fulfil the statutory due process requirements and to protect other stakeholder's interests, such as the mortgagees.

7.4.2 Grounds for Extinguishment

Apart from the revocation discussed in the preceding sections, three grounds exist for CLUR extinguishment. First, when the agreed term of use in paid-use CLUR contracts expires and the transferee has not applied for an extension, or the application for an extension is not approved, the CLUR is extinguished. As the end of the CLUR term approaches, there may be provisions for renewal or extension. Local authorities may review the situation and decide whether to extend the rights, typically after negotiations with the transferee. The land reverts to the state if the CLURs are not renewed or extended. The government may then decide how to allocate or reuse the land for other purposes, such as redevelopment or new construction projects.

Second, in legal terms, natural disasters or other extraordinary events may be considered *force majeure*. The impact of *force majeure* events on CLURs can depend on the specific terms outlined in the CLUR contract and relevant regulations. *Force majeure* events may trigger compensation provisions, land use rights extension or extinguishment. However, suppose the *force majeure* events are devastating enough to cause partial or total destruction of the land to which the CLUR is attached. In that case, the government may play a role in determining whether the CLUR is extinguished.[135] Local authorities might be involved in decisions related to compensation, land use planning and any potential reclamation or redevelopment of the affected area. If no agreement is achieved through negotiations, disputes arising from the destruction of land and the extinguishment of land use rights may lead to legal proceedings.

Third, the CLUR is extinguished by express or implied release. The express release is usually made for valuable consideration, and an application should be made to cancel relevant entries in the land registration office. Abandonment of the exercise of the right indicates the clear intention to release the CLUR willingly. Under Chinese law, when the abandonment of real property rights occurs, any party – but usually the competent government agency – can unilaterally apply for the cancellation of registration.[136]

Where a property becomes extinct, or the owner willingly relinquishes their rights to it, leading to an application to remove the property from the official records or registry, the grantor shall cancel the registration promptly. The registration office shall take back the title certificate.[137]

[135] Wang, *Property Law* (2015), p. 282.
[136] Article 14 Interim Real Estate Registration Regulations.
[137] Article 360 CC.

8

Servitude and Habitation Right

8.1 Servitude

8.1.1 Concept

The Chinese CC provides the content and contour of a servitude right by stating that the servitude right holder has the right, as agreed in the servitude contract, to use other's immovable property to benefit his/her own immovable property.[1] It defines servitude as a burden on the immovable property, the servient land, to the use and benefit of another immovable property, the dominant land. Therefore, servitude involves the right to use or enjoy the benefits of land owned by someone else. It is defined as a type of usufructuary right under the CC. A servitude entitles the dominant landowner to use the servient land in a particular way or to prevent the servient landowner from using his land in a particular way.[2] A typical example is the right of way.

Servitude is distinguished from purely personal rights. By personal it means rights that have no inherent relationship with land. The servitude binds successive owners and not just the two contracting parties of the bilateral servitude contract. When created by A in favour of B, servitudes certainly bind A and B as a matter of a contract. More than that, servitudes bind the successors of A and B. That is a defining feature of being a property right instead of a personal right. When properly formed, servitudes can have powerful effects on the ownership and use of land against third parties.[3] At its core, servitudes provide a mechanism for tying rights and obligations to land to pass to successive owners and occupiers. Nonetheless, the running-with-the-land feature is curtailed under Chinese servitude law because servitude can only be created through a servitude contract with a specified duration. This will be

[1] Article 372 CC.
[2] Liming Wang, *Property Law* (2015), p. 309.
[3] Articles 382 and 383 CC.

further elaborated upon in the section on the creation of servitude later herre.

The Property Law 2007 established the legal framework for servitude in the PRC for the first time with fourteen articles.[4] The CC merely restates or tweaks existing law contained in the Property Law, with the number of articles remaining at fourteen. For example, the CC introduces several minor changes to the servitude provisions.

First, the CC replaces LCMR with land management right to illustrate the land use rights subject to the creation of a mortgage.[5] This change echoes modifications in the RLCL and highlights that the land management right is mortgageable.[6]

Second, the CC introduces the term "other usufructuary rights" to address the perceived drawbacks of the closed nature of Article 162 of the Property Law.[7] Under the Property Law provision, only the LCMR and homestead rights were provided in an exhaustive list. This unnecessarily narrows the scope of usufructuary rights created over the land burdened with servitude.

Third, a significant and practical change is found in Article 375 of the CC, where the phrase "allowing the servitude holder to use the land" in Article 159 of the Property Law is modified to "allowing the servitude holder to use the immovable property."[8] This modification responds to academic debates regarding whether servitude applies only to land or extends to real estate, explicitly expanding the scope of servitude rights to include real estate.[9] The legislator intends that servitude can benefit or burden not only the land but also the buildings or other constructions upon it.

8.1.2 Defining Characteristics of Servitude

In order to establish servitude, first, there should be two immovable properties or usufructuary rights. One serves as a servient land and the

[4] Article 156 Property Law.
[5] Article 381 CC.
[6] Article 47 RLCL.
[7] Article 378 CC.
[8] Article 375 CC.
[9] Peng'ao Chang [常鹏翱], 'Returning to Tradition: The Path to Improving the Regulation of Servitudes in China' [《回归传统：我国地役权规范的完善之道》] (2018) 5 *Tsinghua Law Journal* [《清华法学》] 142. Of course, the legislator adopted a relatively moderate approach in the amendments, refraining from following the scholars' suggestion of changing "地役权" (servitude) to "不动产役权" (real estate servitude).

other as a dominant land. The CC now clearly states that constructions or buildings can independently acquire the status of a servient or dominant land. As there is no private land ownership in China, servitudes can be created over construction or building or a type of usufructuary right such as LCMR, CLUR or homestead rights. The dominant land (the land benefitting from the servitude) and the servient land (the land burdened by the servitude) do not necessarily need to be adjacent or contiguous.[10] Servitudes are property rights that allow someone to use another's land for a specific purpose, and the lands involved can be situated separately. The key is establishing a legal relationship between the two pieces of land, allowing for the specified use.

The immovable properties must belong to different owners. A servitude is a right over someone else's land or property right. As a result, the same person cannot own and occupy the dominant and servient lands. In principle, a person cannot meaningfully have a right against himself. Nonetheless, Chinese law is unclear whether a servitude can arise where the owner of one immovable property right is also one of the co-owners of the neighbouring immovable right. Nor does Chinese law answer whether a servitude can be created if the same owner owns two different types of usufructuary rights over two pieces of land. For example, the same owner, A, held a CLUR over land X and a land management right over land Y. However, A granted the CLUR to B. Under such circumstances, is it possible to create a servitude, as A has no common occupation over the two pieces of land? Although there is common ownership of dominant and servient land, there is no common occupation. If the very purpose of creating a servitude is to promote the efficient utilisation of land resources, it is feasible for B to be granted a servitude over land Y. However, this academic view needs to be confirmed by a future judicial ruling.

Unlike many other legal systems, servitude rights in China have a specified duration subject to the parties' agreement in the servitude contract. This is because all the usufructuary or land use rights subject to servitude have a limited duration. Where a usufructuary right such as a LCMR, a CLUR or a homestead right has already been created on the land, the landowner shall not create a real servitude without the consent of the usufructuary right holder.[11] The limited duration can be an issue, especially if the intended use or benefit extends beyond the granted

[10] Liming Wang, *Property Law* (2015), p. 296.
[11] Article 379 CC.

period. Parties may stipulate the duration of the servitude, provided that such duration does not exceed the remaining term of the LCMR, the right to use construction land and other property rights.[12] Nonetheless, the law does make it clear whether a servitude is still effective if the LCMR is transferred to a third party after it is renewed upon expiry.

A servitude cannot be transferred separately.[13] Where a right to use construction land or LCMR is transferred, the servitude is transferred together, except as otherwise stipulated in the contract.[14] The successor-in-title of the dominant land is automatically entitled to servitude.[15] Similarly, the burden on the servient land is transferred automatically to the new holder when the land is transferred.[16] It is, therefore, a burden on the property right and enforceable against the servient landholder and all the successors-in-title. A servitude cannot be mortgaged separately. Where there is a mortgage over a usufructuary right, such as a land management right or a CLUR, the servitude held by the mortgagor is transferred simultaneously when realising the mortgage.[17]

8.1.3 Creation of Servitude

Unlike other legal systems where a servitude can be created in various ways, it is striking that Chinese law only recognises a single way to create a servitude, namely express creation by a written contract. To create a servitude, the parties should conclude a servitude contract in writing.[18] Oral grants are not permissible under Chinese law. A servitude contract normally contains the following: (1) names or business names and addresses of the parties; (2) the location of the servient land and the dominant land; (3) purposes and ways of benefits; (4) the duration of servitude; (5) fees and payment methods; and (6) methods of dispute resolution.[19]

In light of the above, a servitude under Chinese law must be created through the conclusion of a servitude contract in writing. The content of servitudes is subject to the parties' agreement as long as it does not violate

[12] Article 377 CC.
[13] Article 380 CC.
[14] *Ibid.*
[15] Article 382 CC.
[16] Article 383 CC.
[17] Article 381 CC.
[18] Para. 1 of Article 373 CC.
[19] Para. 2 of Article 373 CC.

mandatory legal provisions and principles of public order and good customs. While servitude is a general term, it encompasses various specific rights. It can be subject to different conditions and limitations based on the particulars of individual cases, and the agreements reached between parties are flexible enough to accommodate these needs. The right holder of the servitude can take the necessary steps for its use and preservation, and the only caveat is that the dominant landowner should make every effort to minimise restrictions on the property rights of the servient landowner.[20]

It is imperative to explicitly reference the location of the dominant land benefitting from the servitude and the servient land over which it is exercised. In order to be capable of granting, the servitudes must demonstrate a certain quality of clarity as to the purpose of ways of granting the benefits. It is also necessary to specify the servitude duration to conform with certain statutorily defined duration requirements for land use rights subject to servitudes. In most instances, the dominant landholder must pay the servient landholder fees to enjoy the benefits. However, the parties can agree on a gratuitous grant of servitude.

A servitude is created when the servitude contract becomes effective, and a party may apply to the registration office for registration.[21] While registration is not strictly required for a servitude to be effective, it cannot be enforced against a bona fide third party unless it is registered.[22]

One may wonder why there is such a strict formality requirement to conclude a servitude contract in writing. This question is particularly relevant when the servitude contract is required to be registered to complete the creation. Will the servitude contract be invalid due to non-compliance with the written formality? In practice, local Chinese courts have issued divergent rulings on this. In some instances, courts adopt a rigid view by holding the servitude contract, which falls short of written formality, invalid.[23] In other instances, however, courts seem to take a relaxed approach by focusing on the parties' common intentions

20 Article 376 CC.

21 Article 374 CC.

22 *Ibid.*

23 李建新与李亚昔 [*Li Jianxin v. Li Yaxi*] ⑵020⑵ 粤 08 民终 4135 号 [(2020) Yue 08 Min Zhong No. 4135]; 陈科与陈惠芳 [*Chen Ke v. Chen Huifang Civil*] ⑵019⑵ 湘01民终1865号 [(2019) Xiang 01 Min Zhong No. 1865]; 朱瑞彬与李德忠 [*Zhu Ruibin v. Li Dezhong*] ⑵017⑵ 苏06民终3415号 [(2017) Su 06 Min Zhong No. 3415].

through their conduct. As a result, such a servitude contract may be upheld as valid.[24]

To tackle judicial inconsistency, it is suggested that the service contract must be registered for servitude to be effective. First, the registration office will check the existence and formality of servitude contracts when dealing with registration. If there are any defects in formalities, they cannot be duly registered. According to Article 61 of the *Implementation Rules for the Interim Regulations on Real Estate Registration*, the relevant details must be recorded in the registration books, such as the manner of use, purpose of use, scope of use and the term of the servitude.[25] Second, the multiplicity of entitlements and rights over the same land may generate conflicts if not publicised. Publicity through registration may fend off the potential disputes when a bona fide third party is involved. Third, with the wide use of digital technology in a uniform land registration system in China, the benefits of mandatory registration of servitude outweigh the associated costs.

Notably, Chinese law recognises only one type of servitude a written contract creates. As found in other jurisdictions, there is no prescribed statutory servitude, servitude by necessity or servitude through prescription (long use).

Statutory servitude refers to a servitude created and governed by law rather than by agreement between private parties. In various legal systems, including common law jurisdictions, statutory easements can arise through legislation that grants certain rights over land for specific purposes. These purposes often serve the public interest or are deemed essential for the functioning of society. Statutory servitudes can cover a range of rights, such as rights of way, rights to access or rights to use land for utilities like pipelines or power lines.

Servitude by necessity refers to a type of servitude recognised and enforced by law due to the essential need for access to a property. This type of servitude typically arises when a parcel of land is landlocked, meaning it lacks direct access to a public road or right of way. In such cases, the law may imply a servitude by necessity to ensure that the

[24] 吴泽龙诉冯大明 [*Wu Zelong v. Feng Daming*] (2019) 鄂民申 4539 号裁定书 [(2019)] E Min Shen No. 4539]; 张志良、杨月琴与幸安华及海南省乐东黎族自治县千家镇只文村民委员会 [*Zhang Zhiliang, Yang Yueqin, Xing Anhua v. the Village Committee of Zhiwen, Qianjia Zhen, Le Dong Li Zu Zi Zhi Xian, Hainan Province*] (2017) 琼97民终35号 [Qiong 97 Min Zhong No. 35]; 孙文学与张水元、王石柱 [*Sun Wenxue v. Zhang Shuiyuan, Wang Shizhu*] (2018) 晋08民终297号 [(2018) Jin 08 Min Zhong No. 297].

[25] Article 61 Implementation Rules for the Interim Regulations on Real Estate Registration.

landlocked property owner has a reasonable means of ingress and egress, even without an express agreement between the parties. Servitude by prescription refers to acquiring a servitude over another person's land through the passage of time and continuous, open and uninterrupted use. This legal concept is similar to adverse possession or prescriptive acquisition but pertains specifically to acquiring rights to use another's land rather than ownership.

It is noteworthy that Chinese law does not recognise adverse possession or prescriptive acquisition. This explains why servitude by prescription is not provided. However, Chinese legislators believed there was no need to provide statutory servitude, as many administrative regulations control the functional equivalent of statutory servitudes, particularly related to public utilities, environmental protection and other public welfare matters. These mechanisms often impose restrictions on property rights under "temporary land use" provisions, achieving effects similar to those of statutory servitudes. For instance, Article 29 of the *Regulations on the Protection of Oil and Gas Pipelines* states:

> Anyone who, in violation of these regulations, takes soil, digs ponds, builds ditches, constructs aquaculture ponds, discharges corrosive substances, piles up bulk materials, mines stones, constructs houses, builds greenhouses, constructs livestock pens, or builds other structures within a 5-meter range on either side of the centerline of a pipeline shall be ordered to rectify by the department designated by the local people's government at or above the county level. Individuals may be fined up to 2,000 yuan, and entities may be fined up to 50,000 yuan.[26]

Similarly, Article 15 of the *Regulations on the Protection of Power Facilities* states that any unit or individual within the protection zone of overhead power lines must comply with the following regulations: (1) not stacking grains, forage, garbage, slag, inflammables, explosives and other items that affect the safe power supply; (2) not firing kilns or burning fields; (3) not constructing buildings or structures; and (4) not planting plants that may endanger the safety of power facilities.[27] Furthermore, Article 26 of the *Regulations on Nature Reserves* prohibits activities such as logging, grazing, hunting, fishing, harvesting medicinal herbs, reclaiming land, burning fields, mining, stone extraction and sand

[26] Article 29 of the Regulation on Protection of Oil and Gas Pipelines by the State Council, issued on 2 August 2001.

[27] Article 15 of the Regulation on the Protection of Power Facilities by the State Council, first amended on 7 January 1998, second amendment on 8 January 2011.

excavation within nature reserves except where laws and administrative regulations provide otherwise.[28]

The Chinese Academy of Social Sciences drafting team submitted a CC draft, which included provisions on statutory or public interest servitudes. The purpose was to grant entities engaged in public services, such as power grids and telecommunications enterprises, the right to use others' immovable property for laying power lines, cables and pipelines. However, the final version of the CC did not adopt this legislative proposal. Furthermore, the CC did not provide servitude by necessity because Chinese legislators, supported by some Chinese legal scholars, maintain that Chinese law has a natural right to neighbour relations,[29] and it would be redundant to introduce servitude by necessity. The essence of neighbour relations is the extension of the rights of the party exercising the right and the restriction of rights on adjacent immovable property. This extension or restriction is limited to what is necessary and falls under the expansion or limitation due to the lawful exercise of rights. Generally, "necessary" is understood in its usual sense, encompassing natural and objective necessities, such as landlocked property, as well as economic and daily life necessities. Therefore, a natural right of neighbour relation entails a servitude by necessity, including exercising neighbour relation rights for access, water use, drainage and laying pipes and wires.[30]

Accordingly, special attention should be given to distinguishing between servitudes and neighbour relations. The CC has many similarities between neighbour relations and servitude rights, mainly regarding the coordinated use of immovables, involving aspects such as drainage, passage, ventilation and light.

Nonetheless, some key differences between the two exist. First, the rules of neighbour relations do not create an independent property right; they are natural rights that come into being automatically and are not a subject of any servitude contract. Instead, they are an extension or limitation of the content of ownership. Examples are the natural right

[28] The Regulation of the People's Republic of China on Nature Reserves by the State Council, issued on 9 October 1994, effective on 1 December 1994, amended on 7 October 2017.

[29] See Chapter 6 for a more detailed discussion.

[30] Zhuo Geng [耿卓], 'Ascertainment of Servitude—Commentary on a Case Concerning the Right of Way over the Adjacent Roads' [《地役权的认定—相邻道路通行权纠纷案评析》], in Chengxin Peng [彭诚信] (ed), *One Hundred Landmark Cases in Chinese Civil Law* [《民法案例百选》] (2nd edn, Higher Education Press 2021), p. 197.

to support the land and the enjoyment of water flowing naturally. On the other hand, servitude rights are independent property rights, representing a type of usufructuary right within the category of real rights. Second, neighbour relations are inherent to real property rights and arise naturally. Servitude rights, however, arise through the parties' contract and represent a property right. Third, for the rules of neighbour relations to apply, they require the immovables to be adjacent, while servitude rights do not require the servient and dominant lands to be adjacent. Fourth, neighbour relations are restricted to the minimum or absolutely necessary coordination and use of adjacent immovables based on ownership content. The imposition of severe restrictions amounts to an undesirable burden. Therefore, exercising neighbour relations rights usually does not cause harm to neighbours and is typically free of charge. Servitude rights, however, involve an agreement between the parties, which can go beyond the minimum necessary coordination in neighbour relations. It governs the higher-level land utilisation for both parties and is usually obtained by payment.

Given the differences between the two, servitude can relate only to a benefit not already enjoyed as a natural incident of the dominant land. Therefore, it is expected that Chinese legislators must revisit the rule design in servitudes by paying sufficient attention to the nuanced differences between servitudes and neighbour relations. For example, implied servitude may be introduced to address a situation where there is no absolute necessity to imply a right of way but with a highly inconvenient means of access to public roads. However, legislatures and courts did little toward accomplishing systematic and comprehensive reform when the CC was deliberated. In short, the current rules on servitudes are sketchy and short on detail. For example, the extent of use exercisable by the dominant landholder is left unaddressed in the CC. This demands a strategic overhaul of the existing legal regime.

8.1.4 Extinguishment of Servitude

The establishment of servitude is rooted in servitude contracts. Therefore, the creation and extinguishment of servitudes are subject to the Property Book provisions and the relevant provisions of the Contract Book in the CC. Grounds for extinguishing servitudes can be classified into contractually stipulated and statutory. While the servitude does not require registration to be effective, once registered, if there is any alteration, transfer or extinguishment of servitude, a change of registration should be done promptly.[31]

As for contractually stipulated grounds, servitudes may be extinguished by the express release by the dominant landowner. In addition, servitudes can be terminated when the contract term expires. Only the servient landholder can terminate the contract to extinguish a servitude on statutory grounds. This can be done only if a holder of the dominant land does any of the following: (1) abuses the servitude in violation of provisions of law or contractual stipulations; or, (2) in the case of a non-gratuitous contract of real servitude, fails to pay the fees despite their being demanded twice within the reasonable period of time after the expiry of the agreed due date.[32]

The dominant landholder must pay the fees for value within the stipulated period in servitude contracts. If, after two notifications from the servient landowner within a reasonable period, the easement holder still fails to pay the fees, the servient landowner has the right to terminate the contract. A "reasonable period" is determined based on the period required for a reasonable person's interest. If the period expires and the servitude holder fails to make payment, the servient landholder has the right to terminate the easement contract. In cases where the easement contract does not specify a payment deadline, the servient landowner must provide the easement holder with a necessary preparation period.[33]

A servitude can also be extinguished where there is a unity of possession or title between the dominant and servient land. If dominant and servient lands are united into the hands of the same owner due to a sale or gift, the servitude ends. However, if the immovables were to belong to different owners at a later date, a new servitude may arise.

Servitudes may be extinguished by abandonment. This is to say, the dominant landholder has a right to abandon the servitude. The onus of proof rests on the person alleging abandonment. As a servitude is a valuable right, abandonment is not lightly found. If the servitude is obtained for value, the dominant landholder can only abandon its right after paying. On the other hand, if the servient landholder alleges abandonment, the dominant landholder is not presumed to intend to give up a servitude even when they do not enjoy the present use. Therefore, the

[31] Article 385 CC.
[32] Article 384 CC.
[33] Article 511, Item 4 CC.

key test is to ascertain the intention of the dominant landholder. However, legal provisions related to servitudes in the CC lack clarity or specificity, leading to interpretation issues. Ambiguities in the law can result in disputes between the parties involved.

8.2 Habitation Right

8.2.1 Concept

The habitation right (*Habitatio*) refers to the right of possession and use of someone else's housing for residence.[34] It is a personal servitude in the CC as a usufructuary right, meaning it is a right granted to individuals rather than a particular piece of land. This concept was distinct from predial servitudes, rights attached to a particular piece of land (dominant land) to benefit another piece of land (servient land). Providing housing for residents can be considered a crucial political, economic and social issue in contemporary society. Addressing it is beneficial for maintaining social stability and meeting the basic living needs of citizens, but it also contributes to safeguarding fundamental human rights. Habitation rights play a significant catalytic role in effectively resolving this issue.

When the Property Law was drafted, there was significant controversy over whether to stipulate the habitation right. Legislative authorities then believed that rights such as residential leases could meet the need for habitation, and therefore, the habitation right was not provided. Soon after implementing the Property Law, with rapid demographic changes arising from the one-child policy and urbanisation, there has been a growing call for recognising the habitation right as a property right. In response to this societal demand, the CC incorporated the habitation right as a usufructuary right. However, given the scant six articles in total,[35] there are still differing opinions on how to define the characteristics and function of the right of habitation, whether it can be established for value and how to determine the priority against the other property rights, such as a right of mortgage.

The concept of the habitation right was not unfamiliar in judicial practice in China even before the Property Law was enacted in 2007. The SPC issued a judicial interpretation concerning the application of Marriage Law by stipulating that,

[34] Article 366 CC.
[35] Articles 366–371 CC.

> [a]fter divorce, if one party does not have a residence, it constitutes a life difficulty. At the time of divorce, one party may assist the person facing life difficulties in the form of the habitation right or ownership of residential property from their assets.[36]

In practice, this provision has been analogously applied to scenarios such as elderly care.[37] Therefore, it is common to establish the habitation right for a spouse without a residence after divorce.[38] However, while the SPC Interpretation addressed the habitation right, it was not formalised as a property right until it was clearly defined in the CC. In other words, while it employed the same notion of habitation right before the CC, in light of the *numerus clausus* principle, the pre-CC habitation right was only an obligatory right.[39] As a result, both parties have the right to terminate the agreed-upon residential rights at any time.[40]

Establishing the habitation right is mainly for life needs such as support and care. It is a manifestation of the house owner exercising their property rights and an essential way to realise the economic utility of the property. According to the civil law tradition of continental legal systems, the habitation right accrues to the right holder in her personal capacity to utilise someone else's property for residence. It must limit the owner's entitlements, her successor-in-title, and third parties. The habitation right holder not only possesses and uses someone else's

[36] Article 27, para. 3 of the SPCSPC Interpretation on Several Issues Concerning the Application of the Marriage Law (I), Judicial Interpretation No. 30 of 2001.

[37] 蒋琳诉廖联会 [*Jiang Lin v. Liao Lianhui*] (2009) 綦法民初字第3768号民事判决书 [(2009) Qi Fa Min Chu Zi No. 3769 Civil Judgment]; Xiwei Gu [谷昔伟]、and Lu Cao [曹璐], 'The Right of Residence Can Confront the Exclusionary Interference Claims of Property Owners' [《居住权可对抗房屋所有权人排除妨害请求权》] (2015) 18 *People's Judiciary Cases* [《人民司法·案例》] 65.

[38] For example, in the case of 仲林诉熊红波离婚后财产分割纠纷案 [*Zhong Lin v. Xiong Hongbo*] (2011)宿中民终字第1190号 [(2011) Su Zhong Min Zhong Zi No. 1190], although the house was determined to be the personal property of the defendant, the plaintiff, Zhong, had no residence after the divorce, no stable source of income and poor health, falling under the living difficulties stipulated by the Marriage Law. The court ruled that she could continue to reside in the defendant's house.

[39] 曾 诉 陈，上海市闵行区人民法院 (2021) 沪0112民初7461号 [*Zeng v. Chen*, Shanghai Minhang District People's Court (2021) Hu 0112 Min Chu No. 7461]. The Court in this case held that a habitation right is a newly established property right in the CC, and they are not of the same nature as the previously defined residential rights (habitation right, the same notion in Chinese) in laws and regulations or those agreed upon by both parties. According to the legal principle, the types and content of proprietary rights must be clearly defined by law. The divorce occurred in 2009 when there were no provisions for residential rights in the Property Law or related laws.

[40] 李 诉 宿 (2021) 吉0104民初10715号 [*Li v. Su* (2021) Ji 0104 Min Chu No. 10715].

residence but can also exclude others from unlawfully interfering with the residence.

Personal servitudes were typically extinguished upon the death of the individual to whom the right was granted or upon the expiration of a specified period. Unlike predial servitudes, which were tied to the land and passed on to subsequent owners, personal servitudes were generally not inheritable. As it benefits the right holder in his personal capacity, the habitation right is neither inheritable nor transferable.[41] It belongs solely to the rights holder. Therefore, there is no dominant land. The default position in the CC is that the residence on which a habitation right exists cannot be let to another person except as otherwise agreed by the parties.[42] Although it benefits the habitation right holder in her personal capacity and is not inheritable, it is not a personal right but a limited property right. This is because the habitation right is necessarily established on someone else's property. In other words, the habitation right separates ownership from a burden on ownership, benefitting a non-owner. Since the habitation right is a property right when it is infringed, the rights holder can exercise property rights claims to protect their rights.

The CC manifests the characteristics of habitation rights in several aspects. First, only a specific rights holder can enjoy the habitation right. Second, the habitation right is time-limited, either by a specified period in a habitation right contract or the lifetime of the rights holder.[43] Similar to other usufructuary property rights, the habitation right has a duration, usually determined by agreement between the parties or by testament. Essentially, the habitation right is a long-term and stable right. Third, habitation rights are mainly, but not exclusively, established with gratuity for individuals with specific personal relationships, typically characterised by values of generosity and charity.[44]

In summary, under the Chinese CC, a habitation right is a usufructuary right, characterised as a personal servitude. It revolves around the property of others, specifically their residences, to satisfy the residential needs of a specific right holder. The habitation right exhibits a high degree of personal attachment, facing restrictions on market transferability and inheritability, distinguishing it from other usufructuary property rights.

[41] Article 369 CC.
[42] *Ibid.*
[43] Articles 367 and 370.
[44] Article 368 CC.

8.2.2 Creation and Registration

While the rights holder of the habitation right is a natural person, the initiator may not necessarily be a natural person; it could also include legal entities. Therefore, the design of the right of residence in the draft of the CC's Property Rights section must break through traditional limitations on personal servitudes, facilitating a system reconstruction.

There are two ways to create a habitation right: by a contract and by testamentary method.[45] First, as with the servitude right, the parties enjoy ample contract freedom to create a habitation right. The parties conclude the habitation right contract in writing, and the contract normally contains (1) names or business names and addresses of the parties; (2) location of the residence; (3) conditions and requirements of living; (4) duration of the right of habitation; and (5) methods of dispute resolution.[46]

It is important to note that key terms of a habitation rights contract in the CC share many similarities with the ones in a servitude contract. The difference is that there are no fee payments and payment methods in the habitation right contract. It implies that a habitation right contract is a gratuitous arrangement as a default position. It has been forcefully argued that it is inappropriate to strictly limit the creation of the habitation right to gratuitous arrangements.[47] When the habitation right is created through concluding a contract, it implies that it may not be entirely gratuitous. To meet an individual's basic living needs, parties may establish the right of residence with or without compensation as long as it satisfies the resident's housing requirements, which should be legally permissible. Granting parties the autonomy to create the habitation right for consideration is essential to achieving the legislative purpose.[48]

It is worth highlighting that to protect the right holders, the habitation right applies a mandatory registration model, endowing the right of residence with publicity, thereby conferring its effectiveness against third parties. Specifically, the parties must apply to the registration office to register the habitation right to be effective.[49] The Chinese court will not

[45] Articles 367 and 371 CC.
[46] Article 367 CC.
[47] Liming Wang [王利明], 'Discussion on the Several Issues Regarding the Right of Residence in the CC's Property Law Section' [《论民法典物权编中居住权的若干问题》(2019) 51 *Academic Monthly* [《学术月刊》] 91.
[48] *Ibid.*
[49] Article 368 CC.

recognise its existence if the parties do not register the habitation right after concluding a habitation contract.[50] This is different from the servitude right, which does not require registration to be created.

The testamentary method for establishing the habitation right is broadly defined, encompassing both wills and bequests.[51] The question arises whether the habitation right created by will or bequest must be registered to be effective. The Chinese courts held that it does not require registration to create a habitation right by will or bequest.[52] This is because Article 230 of the CC provides that where a property right is acquired by inheritance, the acquisition becomes effective when the inheritance commences.[53] When portioning the estate of the deceased, the holder of a habitation right, as stipulated in the will, has the right to assist the estate administrator in requesting the registration of the habitation right.[54] If the partition of the estate in inheritance is carried out through a court judgment, then the habitation right is established from the effective date of the legal document. After the will becomes effective and before the registration, the holder of the habitation right, without impeding the estate administrator's settlement of inheritance debts, has the right under the will to possess, use and enjoy the property and apply for pre-registration.

8.2.3 Priorities between Habitation Rights and Other Competing Interests

If two or more interests are granted in the same house, how is the priority between them decided? If the interests at issue are granted to clarify the intended priority, there is no conflict between them. However, the habitation right is a newly established usufructuary property right under

[50] 金诉朱（2021）京0106民初34102号 [*Jin v. Zhu* (2021) Jing 0106 Min Chu No. 34102].

[51] Article 371, read with Article 1133 CC.

[52] The Chief Editor of the Leading Group for Implementing the CC of the SPC: 'Understanding and Application of the Property Rights Compilation CC of the People's Republic of China (Volume II),' (People's Court Press 2022), p. 897. Also see 邱某光与董某军居住元执行案子 [*Qiu v. Dong*], The 1st Batch of Typical Cases Illustrating the Implementation CC by the SPC <https://dara.gd.gov.cn/yasf/content/post_3929701.html> accessed on 30 January 2024.

[53] Article 230 CC. Shaokun Fang [房绍坤], 'Discussion on the Right of Residence in the CC' [《论民法典中的居住权》] (2020) 4 *Modern Law Science* [《现代法学》] 85.

[54] Yang Wang [汪洋], 'Regulatory Structure for Establishing the Right of Residence through Testamentary Means' [《遗嘱方式设立居住权的规范构造》] (2023) 5 *Contemporary Law Review*《当代法学》42.

the CC. Currently, the *Interim Real Estate Registration Regulations* and their implementation rules do not have detailed provisions governing registration standards for habitation rights. Only some local regulations (such as the *Several Provisions on Real Estate in Shanghai* and the *Technical Regulations on Real Estate Registration in Shanghai*) have made relevant provisions for the registration of habitation rights.[55] Therefore, it is necessary to ascertain the priority between the competing interests, such as a bona fide house purchaser or a mortgagee.

8.2.3.1 Bona Fide Purchaser

Before introducing the habitation right under the CC, when both parties concluded a real estate purchase agreement, the purchaser only needed to inquire about restrictions such as mortgages, court seizure orders and government expropriation decisions that clog the property. However, with the implementation of the CC, prospective purchasers also need to verify whether the property has a right of residence set up in real estate transactions. For property purchasers, discovering a habitation right will, to some extent, affect the property's value. If the habitation rights contract does not specify a time limit, the habitation rights will extend until their death.[56] Therefore, to safeguard the interests of the parties involved, registration authorities should include whether a habitation right exists in the query when providing information queries and restriction information.

The starting point is that a registered habitation right is a property right. If a habitation right has been established on a certain property, the habitation right holder retains the right regardless of subsequent transfers of ownership. When the property owner granted a habitation right to A and subsequently transferred the property to B without registration of the habitation right, how to determine the priority between the habitation right holder and the bona fide purchaser?

It has been suggested that for a habitation right gratuitously created between individuals with specific relationships, and the right holder having no other residence besides the designated property, it should be handled following the principle that a sale does not break a lease, thus giving priority to the habitation right holder over the bona fide

[55] Article 11 Technical Regulations on Real Estate Registration in Shanghai.
[56] Article 370 CC.

purchaser.[57] If a habitation right was created through a contract for value, it cannot prevail against the bona fide purchaser if it is not registered.[58] However, there is no clear answer for a situation where the habitation right is gratuitously created but the right holder has more than one residence, or where the habitation right was created under a will or bequest.

Nonetheless, it is explicit that the habitation right is created upon registration, and this registration requirement applies to all habitation rights created through a contract, whether gratuitously or for value. Therefore, it appears far-fetched to differentiate a gratuitous contract from a contract for value to determine the priority. In the case of establishing the habitation right through a will, as discussed earlier, the habitation right exists when the will becomes effective. Still, it cannot defeat a bona fide purchaser without notice.

To conclude, where the habitation right has not been registered, only an obligatory relationship exists between the parties. Before the property is registered to change ownership, the habitation rights holder can request the property owner (or the vendor) to register the habitation right. However, if the property has already changed ownership registration, the habitation rights holder can only request the vendor to bear the consequences of the breach of the habitation rights contract. The property was transferred to the transferee free of the habitation right. Hence, the holder of habitation rights is expected to register the habitation rights as soon as possible to avoid potential disputes.

8.2.3.2 Mortgagee

Can a habitation right be established on a mortgaged property? The starting point is that the law does not prohibit the establishment of a habitation right on a property that already has an existing mortgage. This is because the mortgagor, the property owner, does not lose the full disposal rights over the mortgaged property after establishing the mortgage unless the contract specifies otherwise. If the mortgage contract stipulates that the mortgagor cannot create a habitation right during the mortgage term, the mortgagor would be liable for breach if it still creates a habitation right.

[57] Qiang Ma [马强], ‘A Study on Practical Issues Related to the Provisions CC on the Right of Residence’ [《民法典居住权规定所涉实务问题之研究》] (2022) 5 *Journal of Law Application* [《法律适用》] 114, p. 117.

[58] *Ibid.*

Nonetheless, even without a restriction in the contract, creating a habitation right on a mortgaged property may decrease the value of the collateral. Under such a circumstance, the mortgagee may request the mortgagor to cease creating the habitation right or provide other forms of security.[59] To safeguard the interests of the parties involved, obtaining consent from the mortgagee before the mortgagor creates a habitation right is advisable.[60]

Can a property subject to a habitation right create a mortgage on it? Creating a mortgage does not affect the holder exercising the habitation right. Whether the mortgage is created or even realised when defaulted, the holder of the habitation right can still possess and use the property. Article 399 of the CC specifies types of property that cannot be mortgaged and does not include property with a habitation right.[61] Therefore, unless the habitation right contract stipulates otherwise, a property with a habitation right should, in principle, be able to have a mortgage created on it.

It is possible that a mortgage right as a security interest and a habitation right as a usufructuary interest coexist over the same property. A properly registered habitation right is extinguished when the term of the right expires or if the right holder dies.[62] When the mortgaged property is realised if the mortgagor defaults by judicial sale, will the habitation right survive the judicial sale? In other words, will the new owner acquire the property free of the existing habitation right through the judicial sale? How would conflicts between the habitation right and the mortgage right be resolved?

The CC is silent on these questions. According to Article 28(2) of the *SPC Provisions on Auction and Sale of Property in Civil Enforcement 2020 Revision* (the "SPC Provision"), existing lease rights and other usufructuary rights on the auctioned property are not extinguished upon judicial sale or auction.[63] However, suppose the existing rights continue on the

[59] Article 408 CC.

[60] As of now, only Shanghai has imposed restrictions on creating a habitation right on a property with an existing mortgage. According to Article 11.1.4 of the *Technical Regulations on Real Estate Registration in Shanghai*, for real estate that had an established mortgage before 1 January 2021, during the mortgage term, applicants seeking to register a habitation right need to submit written materials with the consent of the mortgagee.

[61] Article 399 CC.

[62] Article 370 CC.

[63] Article 28 (2) of the SPC Provisions on Auction and Sale of Property in Civil Enforcement (2020 Amendment) [《最高人民法院关于人民法院民事执行中拍卖、变卖财产的规定》], adopted on 26 October 2004 and subsequently revised on 29 December 2020.

auctioned property and affect the realisation of earlier created security interests or other priority claims. In that case, the SPC Provision grants the courts the power to remove these rights before proceeding with the auction.[64] This provision establishes the basic principle for resolving conflicts between usufructuary rights and mortgage rights in enforcement procedures by adopting the first-in-time principle. If the habitation right is established first, it remains effective even after the auction of the mortgaged property against the new purchaser. Suppose the mortgage right is established prior to the habitation right. The courts enjoy an inherent jurisdiction to remove the habitation right if satisfied that its continued existence would affect the realisation of the mortgage right. Specifically, when valuing the property subject to a habitation right, if the property value burdened with a habitation right is insufficient to satisfy the creditor's claims fully, the habitation right on the property should be cleared before re-valuing. This process is undertaken to safeguard the interests of the mortgagee. After removing the rights, the prior habitation right on the property is considered extinguished.

The SPC Provision fills the legislative gap by providing certainty. However, it may conflict with Article 367 of the CC, which stipulates that the habitation right can only be extinguished when the term expires or the right holder dies. The CC does not address how the court removes the habitation right before the judicial auction. It is important to note that the binding force of national legislation is higher than any other statutory document, including SPC instruments.[65] Therefore, it is still awaiting further clear changes in the CC.

8.3. Summary

Under Chinese law, a servitude right is a form of predial servitude, and a habitation right is a personal servitude. Both servitude and habitation rights are limited real rights which grant the holder certain entitlements to someone else's property. It is a burden on the property, which is enforceable against the current owner and all successors-in-title and third parties.

[64] *Ibid.*

[65] Article 99 of the Legislation Law stipulates that the force of laws is higher than that of administrative regulations and of local regulations and rules. The force of administrative regulations is higher than that of local regulations and rules. Still awaiting further clear regulations or judicial interpretations (adopted on 15 March 2000 and subsequently amended on 15 March 2015 and 13 March 2023, respectively).

A distinction should be drawn between a servitude and a habitation right. A servitude can only be granted regarding immovable property and always involves two pieces of land, a dominant and a servient land. A servitude is established when a servitude contract is made. While it is not required to be registered to be effective, it is suggested to register the servitude to gain publicity and avoid potential disputes. A habitation right is established by registration in the land register, which burdens the land. However, it accrues to the right holder in his personal capacity. Therefore, it is only concerned about one piece of land being burdened and does not involve two pieces of land.

It is remarkable under Chinese law that the only means of creating a servitude is through signing a servitude contract. All other categories of servitude, such as implied servitude, statutory servitude or servitude by prescription, are not found in the Chinese CC. The habitation rights can be created through signing a contract or leaving a will. The CC is short on details when it comes to the rights and obligations under the servitude and the habitation right.[66] They are expected to be spelt out in the contract between the parties. Suppose we were to speculate on the reasons for the legislators' ultimate choice. In that case, it might be influenced by the cautious and incremental approach and adhering to the traditional legislative method of providing a broad framework rather than detailed specifics. This approach introduces a new system and leaves the specific details for the "judicial practice to handle" in the future. However, servitude and habitation rights must be exercised within reasonable bounds by the right holder. The Chinese courts are expected to develop the criterion of reasonableness using a case-by-case approach.

[66] Lu Xiaoming and Shen Weixing have both put forward their respective draft proposals, each of which includes detailed arrangements for "rights of the right holder," "obligations of the right holder" and "obligations of the property owner" concerning real property obligations. But these proposals were not taken up by the legislature. See details in Lu Xiaoming [鲁晓明], 'The Positioning and Rule Design of the Right of Residence' [《"居住权"之定位与规则设计》] (2019) 3 *Chinese Legal Science*[《中国法学》] 223; Weixing Shen [申卫星], 'From "Having a Residence" to "Residing with Habitat" – Legislative Ideas for the Creation of the Right of Residence System in China's CC' [《从"居住有其屋"到"住有所居"—我国民法典分则创设居住权制度的立法构想》 (2018) 2 *Modern Law Science* [《现代法学》] 105, pp. 113–115.

9

Real Security: Mortgage

9.1 Introduction: Real Security

A security interest is a contingent property right in an asset designed to secure debt repayment.[1] It grants the holder the security to settle the outstanding debt by selling the secured property and establishes a priority for payment over unsecured or lower-priority secured creditors. In essence, security rights encumber a borrower's property to secure a lender's claim, ensuring repayment in the event of borrower default or insolvency. The introduction of the CC in 2020 brought substantial modifications to the realm of property law, particularly in the domain of security interests.

Significant rule changes are often signalled for various reasons. Firstly, codification organises and consolidates existing rules, especially when they have been controversial or sparked public concern. Secondly, security interests, whether in real or personal property, are crucial in promoting credit in economic activities and facilitating homeownership. In China, mortgage transactions have emerged as a primary method of financing homeownership since the introduction of private housing in the mid-1990s. The ideological significance of homeownership often carries political dimensions that influence the formulation of laws and regulations governing mortgage transactions. Thirdly, real security, particularly mortgages, exerts a profound sociological influence on how Chinese people live. It contributes to determining family size and patterns, shaping lifetime savings and the lifestyle of pensioners, and influencing the intergenerational transfer of wealth.[2] Fourthly, globally, there is a growing trend where the traditional model of a mortgage as a

[1] Article 386 CC.

[2] Karl Renner, *The Institutions of Private Law and Their Social Functions* (Routledge and Kegan Paul Ltd. 1949); Kevin Gray and Susan Gray, *Elements of Land Law* (5th edn, Oxford University Press 2009), p. 695.

contract between two private parties securing a loan on the property is evolving towards the social function of mortgage law, emphasising access to homeownership and treating borrowers as consumers.[3] China aligns with this trend and has developed sophisticated sets of security interest rules reflecting these shifts in functions and values.[4]

In the Chinese context, under the GPCL enacted in 1986, only four security interests were recognised and regulated, albeit sketchily: personal guarantee, mortgage, deposit and lien.[5] China enacted the Guarantee Law in 1995,[6] governing real security interests and personal guarantees, before the Property Law in 2007. The Guarantee Law provides a fundamental legal framework governing personal guarantees and real security to deal with real estate financing problems and facilitate the housing privatisation policy. Due to the rapid developments in the real property market practice following the legislation and a still primitive understanding of property law, several apparent defects can be found in the Guarantee Law. For example, it has been stipulated that the mortgage contract over immovable property is invalid if it is not registered.[7] There is no distinction between the effectiveness of the mortgage contract and the effectiveness of the real security right of the mortgage.[8] Hence, the Guarantee Law fell significantly behind the rapidly evolving economic and social landscape.

Nevertheless, the Guarantee Law continued to apply even though it did not address some practical concerns. It is for this reason that in December 2000, the SPC issued the *Interpretation on Several Issues Concerning the Application of the Guarantee Law* (the "Judicial Interpretation of the Guarantee Law"), with a total of 134 articles.[9] The Judicial Interpretation of the Guarantee Law purported to provide nuanced rules where there were some perceived gaps.

[3] Lisa Whitehouse, 'The First Legal Mortgagor: A Consumer without Adequate Protection?' (2015) 38 *Journal Consumer Policy* 161, 163; Irina Domurath, *Consumer Vulnerability and Welfare in Mortgage Contracts* (Hart Publishing 2017), p. 11.

[4] Directive (EU) 2021/2167 of the European Parliament and of the Council of 24 November 2021 on credit servicers and credit purchasers and amending Directives 2008/48/EC and 2014/17/EU (text with EEA relevance).

[5] All the four types of security interests were regulated in one article, i.e. Article 89 of the GPCL 1986.

[6] Enacted on 30 June 1995, became effective on 1 October 1995.

[7] Article 41 Guarantee Law.

[8] Guixiang Liu, 'Several Key Issues in Security Interest under the CC' (2021) 1 *Journal of Law Application* 9.

[9] Issued by the SPC, became effective on 13 December 2000.

When the Property Law was enacted in 2007, it introduced a chapter on real security, encompassing mortgage, pledges and liens laws.[10] Before the Property Law, various departmental rules and administrative regulations had been issued to address emerging issues related to security interests.[11] It is essential to highlight that, in the event of any inconsistency between the Guarantee Law and the Property Law, the provisions of the Property Law take precedence.[12] While many legal provisions from the Guarantee Law were retained or underwent only minor changes, some new rules were introduced, altering the previous legal landscape.[13] Notably, in judicial practice, landmark cases, including guiding cases, have served as a legal foundation for judicial decision-making since the enactment of the Property Law.

Some post-2007 Property Law judicial opinions have shaped the content and contour of the security interests provisions in the CC. Under the CC, a singular term of security system has straddled the laws of contract (e.g. guarantee contract, financial leasing contract, factoring contract) and property (mortgage, pledge and lien). The CC has consolidated many rules and substantiated some new ones. For instance, the rules for transferring moveable property mortgages have been rewritten.[14] The right of mortgage cannot be alleged against the purchaser of such movable property who has paid a reasonable price in the ordinary course of business.[15] The rules concerning assignment security, retention of ownership, financial leases and factoring contracts have been mapped out.[16] It is worth noting that, given the buoyant market practice, the CC balances legal certainty under the *numerus clausus* principle and party autonomy through the principle of freedom of contract.

10 Lei Chen, '100 Years of Chinese Property Law: Looking Back and Thinking Forward', in Lei Chen and C. H. van Rhee (eds), *Towards a Chinese CC* (Brill Nijhoff 2012).

11 For example, the SPC Interpretation of the Guarantee Law, the Circular of the State Administration of Foreign Exchange on Transmitting and Executing the Interpretation of the SPC Application of Judicial Interpretations to Guarantee Dispute Cases and the Determination of Guarantee Liability Forms, as well as the Land Registration Measures and the Real Estate Property Registration Measures, both enacted in 2008.

12 Article 178 Chinese Property Law 2007.

13 Such as the rules on priority order in realising real security and personal security, and right of recourse against other security providers; see Lei Chen, 'Private Property with Chinese Characteristics: A Critical Analysis of the Chinese Law on Property of 2007' (2010) 18 *European Review of Private Law* 983; for more details, see Sections 9.3.1 and 9.3.2.

14 Article 416 CC.

15 Article 404 CC.

16 Articles 388, 642, 735, and 761 CC.

Besides the mortgage, pledge and lien specifically addressed by the property book of the CC, the CC also allows the parties to contractually derogate from the statutory list to create a collateral contract. Article 388 of the CC states, "A collateral contract refers to a contract of charge, a pledge contract, or other kinds of contracts with security functions."[17] It has become clear that the CC adopts an open-ended conception of collateral contracts rather than a closed catalogue as incentivised by the notion of freedom of contract and free market practices. This practice affirms that "fancies are for contract, not for property, to meet the market expectations."[18] This approach facilitates the availability of security over property, promoting secured credit. The growth of individual businesses is supported, and transaction costs for international commerce are reduced. It is expected that the legislative agenda will include the development of a sophisticated secured credit law.

Given the sheer volume of legal disputes concerning the security interest, it is imperative to understand how the security interest rules have evolved in China. In tandem with the security interests provisions in the CC, the SPC Interpretation on the Security System was issued by the SPC to provide further guidance.[19] The SPC Interpretation on the Security System establishes comprehensive regulations for personal guarantees, mortgages, liens, pledges, factoring, finance leasing and retention of title. It is an essential component of the Chinese legal framework concerning security interests, offering practical guidance and promoting consistent application by Chinese courts.

This chapter focuses on mortgage as a real security only. However, it will examine its relationship with the guarantee, which is regulated in the contract law book of the CC. Several questions will be explored. Firstly, were there any needs for changes? Secondly, what are the recent changes? Thirdly, have these changes achieved their purpose? I will reflect critically on the law regarding clarity, simplicity, convenience and fairness. The explanation covers the relevant background and statutory framework of security interests and delves into its theoretical structure and various practical issues. For instance, in the absence of any agreement, where

[17] Article 388 CC.

[18] Bernard Rudden, 'Economic Theory v Property Law: The Numerus Clausus Problem', in John Eekelaar and John Bell (eds), *Oxford Essays in Jurisprudence* (Oxford University Press 1987), p. 243.

[19] The SPC Interpretation on the application CC concerning the Security System, effective on 1 January 2021.

both a personal guarantee and a mortgage secure a loan, will the creditor have the freedom to choose which one to enforce first? Another question is, when more than two different kinds of securities have secured a loan on a joint and several liability basis, can a security provider seek indemnification from the others after fulfilling its security obligation in case of the debtor's insolvency without an agreement?

This chapter centres on mortgages as real security in the context of the CC. It addresses questions such as the accessoriness principle and the necessity for certain departures, priority order in the realisation of mortgage, transfer of mortgaged property and floating charge. The critical reflection considers clarity, simplicity, convenience and fairness. The analysis covers the background, statutory framework, theoretical structure and practical issues of security interests. For example, in the absence of an agreement, if both a personal guarantee and a mortgage secure a loan, does the creditor have the freedom to choose which one to enforce first? Another query pertains to scenarios where more than two securities (including personal guarantees and mortgages) secure a loan on a joint and several liability basis. Without an agreement, can a security provider seek indemnification from others after fulfilling its security obligation in case of the debtor's insolvency?

9.2 Accessoriness and Its Relaxation

9.2.1 Principle of Accessoriness

The Guarantee Law adheres to the accessoriness principle, a concept with roots in Roman law. This principle has become a steadfast rule in China's real security framework.[20] As a result, under Chinese law, a security interest is characterised as (1) an accessory right contingent on having a principal obligation, (2) an indivisible right and (3) a preferential right.

First, a security interest is an accessory, meaning it does not stand independently and is contingent on the secured principal obligation.[21] The CC explicitly provides the fundamental principle that there must be an obligation the security interest secures.[22] The accessory principle indicates that a security right is linked to or dependent on a principal

[20] Lei Chen, 'A Structural Analysis of Chinese Mortgage Law', in Hanri Mostert and Marius J De Waal (eds), *Essays in Honour of CG van der Merwe* (Lexis Nexis 2011), p. 395.

[21] Cornelius G Van der Merwe, 'Security in Immovables', in *International Encyclopaedia of Comparative Law: Property and Trust. Instalment 42* (Mohr Siebeck 2014), pp. 27–29.

[22] Articles 388, 682 CC.

obligation.[23] Since a security interest is an accessory, it cannot exist independently of a valid principal obligation.[24] Under Chinese law, if the creditor's right in the main contract is reassigned, the assignee will inherit the pre-existing secured rights. Additionally, the security interest automatically terminates upon the discharge of the secured debt or principal obligation.[25] While the principal obligation in China is typically monetary, it is conceivable for a non-monetary obligation to be secured. For instance, a non-contractual obligation, such as a tort or unjust enrichment claim, may also be secured, provided it can be quantified as a definite amount of money.[26]

Secondly, a security interest is indivisible. Even if a portion of the underlying principal obligation is discharged, the security remains on the mortgaged property, but only for the outstanding debt. If the creditor permits the debtor, fully or partially, to assign debts to another party, the third-party security provider will no longer be obligated for the corresponding security liability unless there is written consent.[27] The SPC Interpretation of the Guarantee Law stipulates that the mortgagee can execute the security for the entire mortgaged property before fully paying the principal obligation.[28] Article 389 of the CC provides that the scope of secured debts covered by a security interest includes the principal debt and its interest, (agreed) damages, and expenses for keeping collateral in good custody and enforcing the security interest, unless agreed otherwise by the parties.[29]

Thirdly, a claim arising from a security interest holds a preferential position compared to unsecured lenders for debt repayment.

[23] Article 50 Guarantee Law.

[24] Article 2 SPC Interpretation on the Security System provides: "[i]f the parties agree in the guarantee contract that the effectiveness of the guarantee contract is independent of the main contract, or agree that the guarantor shall bear the guarantee responsibility for the legal consequences of the invalidity of the main contract, the agreement on the independence of the guarantee shall be invalid. If the main contract is valid, the invalidity of the agreement on the independence of the guarantee does not affect the validity of the guarantee contract; if the main contract is invalid, the people's court shall determine that the guarantee contract is invalid, unless otherwise provided by law."

[25] Article 393 CC.

[26] Jianyuan Cui [崔建远], *Real Property Law* [《物权法》] (China Renmin University Press 2009), pp. 467–68; see comparative survey of Andrew Steven, 'The Effect of Security Rights *inter partes*', in Ulrich Drobnig, Henk J. Snijders and Erik-Jan Zippro, *Divergences of Property Law, an Obstacle to the Internal Market?* (Sellier 2006), p. 50.

[27] Article 391 CC.

[28] Article 71 SPC Interpretation of Guarantee Law.

[29] Articles 389 and 684 CC.

In situations where the preferential claim secured by the mortgage takes precedence over the proceeds from the sale of the mortgaged property, unsecured lenders may receive minimal or no payment.[30] Arising from this rule, the CC further provides that where the subject matter of a security interest is destroyed, lost or expropriated during the period of security, the security interest holder is entitled to have the priority of debt repayment to the extent of the acquired insurance money, damages or compensation.[31] If the secured debt is not yet due, the rights holder can put the insurance money, damages or compensation in escrow.[32]

9.2.2 Relaxation of Accessoriness

However, exceptions are outlined in the CC despite the accessoriness principle. One exception is that the extent of guarantee liability remains unaffected if the principal contract is modified to increase the principal obligation.[33] Without written consent from the guarantor, if the creditor and the debtor agree to alter the content of the principal obligation contract, the guarantor still bears guarantee liability for the modified obligation even if the principal obligation is reduced.[34] The guarantor does not bear guarantee liability for the increased portion where the principal obligation is increased.[35] Without written consent from the guarantor, if the creditor and the debtor change the time for performance under the principal obligation contract, the guarantee period remains unaffected by such variation.

Second, the accessory principle dictates that a mortgage right cannot be separated from the secured claim and transferred separately. While the CC upholds the accessory principle, it allows for some flexibility in party autonomy. Article 407 of the CC stipulates that

> the mortgage cannot be transferred separately from the main debt or be used to secure another debt. Where the main debt is assigned to another person, the mortgage securing such debt is also transferred, except if otherwise provided by law or agreed by the parties.[36]

[30] Article 394 CC.
[31] Article 390 CC.
[32] *Ibid.*
[33] Article 695 CC.
[34] *Ibid.*
[35] *Ibid.*
[36] Article 407 CC.

The second paragraph of this article indicates that the transfer of the mortgage rights and debt clause is not obligatory, and parties can reach a different agreement. Furthermore, they can mutually exclude its application through an agreement. If the parties decide that the mortgage rights will not be transferred along with the principal debt, the court will not deem the agreement invalid for contravening the provisions on the principle of accessoriness.

The CC does not specifically cover situations where the parties agree to replace the original debt with an entirely new debt. In such cases, whether the novated claim retains its priority ranking with the original mortgage is unclear. The SPC Interpretation on the Security System addresses this gap by stipulating that, under such circumstances, the security provider for the old debt is not responsible for security.[37] This provision helps to clarify the application of the principle of accessoriness in cases involving the assignment of secured debt. Borrowing a new loan to repay the old debt results in extinguishing the old loan and the security provided for it due to debt repayment. In cases where the security provider for the new loan is different from the old loan, or if the old loan is unsecured and the new loan is secured, the court may not support the creditor's claim that the security provider of the new loan assumes liability. This reflects the legal principle that the security interest is tied to the specific debt it was created to secure, and changes in the underlying debt may affect the security provider's obligations.

The rule stipulating that the security provider for the old debt is not responsible for security in cases of replacing the original debt with an entirely new debt aligns with the accessoriness principle. However, it is important to note that if the security provider for the new loan is the same as the old one, the court may hold that the security provider assumes liability for the new loan.[38] Additionally, if the creditor can prove that the security provider knew or should have known that the new loan is intended to repay the old loan, the court may support the creditor's claim.[39] This approach allows for flexibility while considering the circumstances and intentions of the parties involved.

If the security provider of the old loan agrees to continue providing security for the new loan, and the security registration has not been

[37] Para. 1 of Article 16 SPC Interpretation on the Security System.

[38] *Ibid.*

[39] *Ibid.*

cancelled,[40] the same mortgaged property that was established in favour of other creditors before signing the new loan may not allow those other creditors to claim priority in their mortgage rights over the new loan creditors under Chinese law.[41] The court will uphold the surviving security on the new loan as if it were to secure the old loan. This rule eases the rigidity of accessoriness by allowing party autonomy. When borrowing the new loan to repay the old one, the old loan security provider is not liable for the security for the new loan, as the old loan has been extinguished, except that it continues to guarantee the new loan. When the new loan has not been executed, and the old loan has not been paid off, the security interest for the old loan has not been wiped out. If the parties subsequently sign a new loan contract, it is equivalent to extending the old loan. Therefore, the creditor of the new loan still has the right to stand in priority over other creditors when realising the security.

Third, an exception to the accessoriness principle is the concept of a maximum amount mortgage (MAM), designed to secure future debts. In this case, the mortgage contract must specify the maximum amount secured by the mortgage, which should be duly recorded in the land registry.[42] If this amount is less than the total value of the mortgaged property, subsequent mortgages can bring their total amount up to its full value.[43] The MAM allows for flexibility in securing obligations that may arise in the future, providing a predetermined cap on the secured amount that is recognised and registered. Consequently, the maximum mortgage amount is not transferred with a secure claim. Where the creditor assigns some of the debts secured by the MAM to another person before the definition of all the debts,[44] the MAM shall not be transferred simultaneously, except if otherwise agreed by the parties.[45] In other words, a MAM is not an accessory to its principal obligation unless the parties agree otherwise.

Fourth, the holder of a secured interest can relinquish the security right or modify its ranking order. According to paragraph 1 of Article 409 of the CC, a mortgage creditor can abandon the charge or alter the

[40] Para. 2 of Article 16 SPC Interpretation on the Security System.
[41] *Ibid.*
[42] Article 47 SPC Interpretation on the Security System.
[43] Article 420 CC.
[44] Article 423 CC.
[45] Article 421 CC.

priority sequence associated with the mortgage.[46] This provision allows for flexibility in managing the secured interest, granting the creditor the ability to voluntarily release or adjust the security right or its position in the hierarchy of priorities. The parties may modify the priority ranking, the amount of the secured debt and other relevant aspects through mutual agreement. Nevertheless, any such alteration must not disadvantage another mortgage creditor without obtaining its written consent. The accessory features should not be tied exclusively to the original mortgage creditor's rights. Essentially, these accessory principles serve as default rules established by law, but parties can deviate from them through contractual agreements based on their autonomy.

9.3 Real Security versus Personal Security

When an obligation is secured by both personal and real security, such as a guarantee and a mortgage, a crucial question arises regarding the default rule for the order of realisation among the security providers. Furthermore, can the parties agree on the priority order of the security interests to fulfil the creditor's rights? Specifically, is it mandatory to enforce real security before turning to the assets of the personal guarantor? Are there distinct rules when the contract debtor or a third party provides the real security? Should the third party seek recourse against the guarantor after assuming security liabilities when the creditor successfully claims the third party's security interest?

Before enacting the CC, the prevalent stance was the "realising real security first" approach. This principle mandated that in the event of a default by the contract debtor, the creditor must first liquidate the real security before turning to the assets of the personal guarantor.[47] This rule was designed to safeguard the interests of the personal guarantor. The rationale was to make the guarantee obligation less likely to be invoked, as the creditor was required to exhaust the real security before pursuing the assets of the personal guarantor. The drawback of this approach was twofold. Firstly, it deprived the creditor of the flexibility to determine the preference order, as the law mandated a specific sequence. Secondly, the efficacy of the personal guarantee was diminished when real security was

[46] Article 409 CC.

[47] Para. 1 of Article 28 of the Guarantee Law 1995 states that if the same creditor's rights have both guarantee and real security, the guarantor assumes guarantee responsibilities over the creditor's right other than guaranteed by real security.

available for the same contract. The guarantee liability could only be invoked in the absence of real security or if the real security proved inadequate to cover the debt. Thirdly, in light of the above, individuals or companies might readily offer a personal guarantee, especially when aware that the main contract was backed by real security. To address these issues, the SPC Interpretation of the Guarantee Law altered the stance by allowing the creditor to choose between the guarantor and the real security provider for liability when there is a combination of personal guarantee and real security for the same contract.[48] Nonetheless, similar to the Guarantee Law, the SPC Interpretation of Guarantee Law did not address situations where the parties had agreed on the order of realisation of security interests. This created a gap in the legal framework concerning the enforceability of agreements between the parties that deviated from the statutory provision.

When the Property Law was enacted, this loophole seemed to be closed by a refined rule. Article 176 states that where a contract is provided with real security and personal security, the creditor shall realise the security specified in the parties' contractual stipulations if the debtor fails to perform the due debt.[49] Where such stipulation does not exist or is equivocal, the creditor shall enforce the real security first if the debtor provided real security. The creditor has a selection between real security and personal security to enforce if a third party provides real security. After bearing security liabilities, the third party has the right to recover from the debtor.[50]

First, Article 176 of the Property Law respects the party's freedom of contract by upholding the contractual stipulations made by the parties. Second, it distinguishes the contract debtor's real security from a third party's real security. Concerning the former, the debtor's real security must be realised before enforcing against the third party's guarantor.[51] As to the latter, the personal guarantee and a third party's real security are put on equal ranking at the creditor's choice when there is a breach. In other words, the personal guarantee provided by a third party cannot

[48] Article 38(1) SPC Interpretation of the Guarantee Law.

[49] Article 176 Property Law.

[50] *Ibid.*

[51] Hailin Zou [邹海林], 'Interpretation of the "Mixed Guarantee Rules" in the Chinese CC' [《我国〈民法典〉上的"混合担保规则"解释论》] [2020] *Journal of Comparative Law* 91, 95.

be invoked where the contract creditor did not enforce the real security provided by another party first.

The CC adopts the equal ranking approach by retaining Article 176 of the Property Law in Article 392.[52] This is a balanced approach which promotes certainty while preserving contractual freedom. As a result, the Chinese courts uphold that the creditor shall realise the security according to the parties' contractual stipulations.[53] Where there is a contractual stipulation, or the stipulation is unclear, the creditor has a free choice on the sequence when both personal guarantee and real security are provided.[54]

Nonetheless, when there is a contractual stipulation that the creditor can "directly demand the guarantor to assume the security responsibility in the event of default," whether such stipulation causes the guarantor – that is, the personal security – to be enforced ahead of real security? The SPC has been inconsistent in this. In *China Great Wall Asset Management Company Guiyang Office v. Guizhou Liuzhi Special Economic Zone Jiashun Coking Co., Ltd*,[55] it was held by the SPC that such stipulation cannot be regarded as an agreement on the order in realising the security rights because the agreement is unclear. As such, the guarantor must bear only supplementary joint and several liabilities. However, in *China Great Wall Asset Management Corporation Guangzhou Office v. Guangzhou Yunshan Hotel Co., Ltd.*, the SPC held that this type of expression is a clear agreement, and the guarantor is ordered to bear concurrent joint and several liabilities.[56] Despite the judicial inconsistency, the current position regards such an expression to infer the parties' clear intention to realise the security right.

[52] Article 392 CC repeats the wording of Article 176 Property Law almost verbatim.

[53] 钟湘、广州越秀小额贷款有限公司 [*Zhong Xiang v. Guangzhou Yuexiu Small Loan Co., Ltd*] (2017) 粤01民终17661号 [(2017) Yue 01 Min Zhong No. 17661].

[54] 中国民生银行股份有限公司太原分行与山西怀仁中能芦子沟煤业有限责任公司、山西怀仁南窑晋通砂石煤业有限公司 [*China Minsheng Bank Co., Ltd. Taiyuan Branch v. Shanxi Huairen Zhongneng Luzigou Coal Industry Co., Ltd., Shanxi Huairen Nanyao Jintong Sand and Stone Coal Industry Co., Ltd.*] (2017) 京04民初6号 [(2017) Jing 04 Min Chu No. 6].

[55] 中国长城资产管理公司贵阳办事处、六枝特区佳顺焦化有限公司判决书 [*China Great Wall Asset Management Company Guiyang Office v. Guizhou Liuzhi Special Economic Zone Jiashun Coking Co., Ltd*] (2015) 民二终字第280号 [(2015) SPC Final Civil Judgment No. 280].

[56] 中国长城资产管理公司广州办事处与广州云山大酒店有限公司 [*China Great Wall Asset Management Corporation Guangzhou Office v. Guangzhou Yunshan Hotel Co., Ltd,*] (2016) 最高法民终554号 [(2016) SPC Final Civil Judgment No. 554].

Article 393 of the CC provides that the third party has the right to recover from the debtor after bearing security liabilities. It does not address whether the third-party real security provider has a right of recourse against the personal guarantor. If so, under what conditions? This is a pressing question about ascertaining the extent of the co-security providers. In the old legal regime under the Guarantee Law 1995, if a creditor waives the real security, which was supposed to be enforced first, the guarantor will be exempt from the guarantor's rights over the rights that the creditor gave up.[57] Under the CC, where any selected co-security provider bears liability for the whole debt, can the selected co-security provider have a right of recourse against other security providers without any agreement?

9.4 Creation and Registration

A mortgage is usually created through a mortgage contract, and a mortgage contract shall be concluded in writing.[58] Such a mortgage contract normally contains the following: (1) type and amount of the secured debt; (2) time for the debtor to perform the debt; (3) name, quantity and other situations of the subject matter; and (4) scope of the secured debt.[59]

However, it does not require transferring the mortgaged property's possession or title from the mortgagor to the mortgagee. When creating a mortgage on buildings and other fixtures on land, the right to use the land for construction and the right to use sea areas, buildings, vessels and aircraft under construction,[60] the concluded mortgage contract needs subsequent registration at the land register to create a valid mortgage.[61] A mortgage contract can render it legally effective when creating a mortgage over a movable property. Such right of charge is valid between the mortgagor and the mortgagee, but it cannot be alleged against a bona fide third party without prior registration.[62]

A question may arise regarding whether and how the creditor can enforce the mortgage when a concluded mortgage contract has not been

57 Para. 2 of Article 28 Guarantee Law.
58 Article 388 CC.
59 Article 400 CC.
60 Article 395 CC.
61 Article 402 CC.
62 Article 403 CC.

subsequently registered. Initially, it is essential to note that the registration of the mortgage contract is necessary to establish a valid mortgage over an immovable property. If a mortgage contract is concluded but not registered, the mortgage has not been validly established. As a result, a Chinese court will dismiss the creditor's claim to enforce the mortgage in the event of default.

Second, failing to register the property right will not affect the contract's validity.[63] Once the mortgage contract is validly formed, it is binding on the parties. Although the mortgage registration has not been completed, the mortgage contract is valid, so the creditor can request the mortgagor to continue to perform the contract by registering the mortgage.[64] When the mortgage contract cannot be registered, the mortgagor is liable for breach of contract. The determination of the extent of liability depends on the specifics of each particular situation.

Suppose the would-be-mortgaged property is damaged or lost because of *force majeure* or other reasons not attributable to the security provider. In that case, the security provider is not at fault, and the court will not hold the security provider liable for the mortgage liability.[65] However, if the security provider receives compensation from the insurer or the government where the property is destroyed, lost or expropriated, the creditor has the right to request the security provider to bear the compensation liability within the scope of the obtained amount.[66] The security provider is at fault if it fails to register the mortgage. In that case, the creditor may request the security provider to be liable for the debt payment within the agreed extent of secured liability.[67] Such liability for secured debt is a supplementary liability. According to the SPC, if the parties have not agreed on the mortgagor bearing joint and several liabilities, the Chinese courts will not hold the mortgagor to bear joint and several liabilities.[68]

[63] Article 215 CC.

[64] Article 46 (1) SPC Interpretation on the Security System.

[65] Article 46 (2) SPC Interpretation on the Security System.

[66] *Ibid*. It is notable that such a compensation liability is a contractual liability rather than a security liability.

[67] Article 46 (3) of the SPC Interpretation on the Security System; Article 60 of the Notice by the SPC of Issuing the Minutes of the National Courts' Civil and Commercial Trial Work Conference [九民纪要] in 2019 (The 2019 "SPC Trial Minutes").

[68] 最高人民法院民二庭第7次法官会议纪要,第14条【会议日期】2017年12月2日 [Article 14 of the Minutes of the 7th Judges' Meeting of the Second Civil Division of the SPC, Meeting Date: 2 December 2017].

If the mortgage contract is properly registered, Chinese law addresses the situation where the registered terms on the land registry differ from those in the mortgage contract. In the case of *Anyue County Xintong Construction Investment Co., Ltd. v. Chongqing Import and Export Credit Guarantee Co., Ltd.*, the creditor's rights recorded in the land registry were RMB 2 million, while the amount stated in the mortgage contract was RMB 170 million.[69] There is a grave disparity between the two. The issue is: When the mortgage is enforced, which amount should prevail? Usually, the amount recorded in the land registry should match the one in the mortgage contract. In such an exceptional situation, the SPC held that where the content recorded in the land registry is inconsistent with the content agreed in the mortgage contract, the content recorded in the registration prevails.[70]

In extraordinary circumstances, a mortgage may be established by operation of law without a formal contract, commonly referred to as a judicial mortgage. For instance, when a building is designated as the subject of a mortgage, it becomes imperative to encumber the land use rights pertaining to the parcel of land on which the building is situated. Similarly, if the land use rights are subjected to a mortgage, the building on the same land must also be included in the mortgage arrangement. Failure by the mortgagor to concurrently mortgage both the building and the land may result in the unencumbered property being deemed automatically subjected to the mortgage.[71] This appears to clarify the judicial position on this matter. However, four years later, in a judgment delivered by an IPC, the amount agreed in the mortgage contract was held to prevail over the amount recorded in the land registry.[72] It seems to be an unsettled issue which necessitates an SPC interpretation.

Finally, it is essential to recognise that according to Chinese law, not all property rights are mortgageable due to a stringent regulatory framework. Specifically, the CLUR held by a town or village enterprise (TVE) cannot independently serve as the subject matter of a mortgage. Nevertheless, it is permissible to incorporate it within a mortgage

69 安岳县欣通建设投资有限公司等与重庆进出口信用担保有限公司等案(2016)最高法民终268号 [*AnYue County XinTong Construction Investment Co., Ltd. v. Chongqing Import and Export Credit Guarantee Co., Ltd.* (2016) SPC Civil Final Judgment No. 268].

70 *Ibid.*

71 Article 397 CC.

72 中国农业银行股份有限公司怀化分行、张忠民（2020）湘12民终612号 [*China Agricultural Bank Co., Ltd. Huaihua Branch v. Zhang Zhongmin* (2020) Xiang 12 Min Final Judgment No. 612].

arrangement established over assets such as a factory, plant or warehouse owned by the TVE.[73] The Chinese CC has provided two lists, permissible and negative, to indicate what property rights can be mortgageable. The permissible list includes (1) buildings and other fixtures on land; (2) the right to use land for construction; (3) the right to use sea areas; (4) manufacturing devices, raw materials, semi-finished products and products; (5) buildings, vessels and aircraft under construction; (6) transport vehicles; and (7) other assets not prohibited by any law or administrative regulation as the subject matter of a mortgage.[74] Additionally, certain special property rights can be mortgaged, such as mining and exploration rights.[75]

The properties which are not mortgageable on the negative list include (1) land ownership[76]; (2) right to use collective-owned lands, such as homestead land, private plots and hilly land allotted for private use; (3) educational, medical and health, and other public welfare facilities of schools, kindergartens, medical institutions and other non-profit legal persons incorporated for public welfare purposes; (4) the ownership or use right over a property which is equivocal or under dispute; (5) properties that are seized, detained or under public investigation under law; and (6) other properties prohibited by any law or administrative regulation to be the subject matter of a mortgage.

It is worth noting that a mortgage over a movable property does not require registration to be created.[77] Where a movable property mortgage is not registered, the mortgagor subsequently creates another mortgage over the same movable property in favour of another creditor. In such a situation, if the subsequent mortgage is registered, regardless of whether

[73] Article 398 CC. Under Chinese law, the CLUR of a TVE which is located on rural land should not be mortgaged because collectively owned rural land cannot be transferred.

[74] Article 395 CC.

[75] On 24 June 2017, the SPC issued the Interpretation on Several Issues Concerning the Application of Law in the Trial of Mining Rights Disputes (hereinafter the "Judicial Interpretation on Mining Rights Disputes"). Article 15 of this judicial interpretation stipulates: "If the parties request confirmation that the mortgage right of mining rights is established in accordance with the law when registered, the People's Court should support it. The filing procedures for the mortgage of mining rights conducted by the land and resources competent department that issues mineral resources exploration permits or mining permits in accordance with relevant regulations shall be deemed as the registration stipulated in the preceding paragraph."

[76] There is no private land ownership in China. All land is owned by either the state in urban areas or collectively in rural areas. So it is no surprise that land ownership cannot be an object of security in China.

[77] Article 403 CC.

the subsequent mortgagee is in good faith, the prior unregistered movable property mortgagee cannot prevail against the registered one. Article 414 of the CC stipulates that the registered mortgage takes precedence over the unregistered one.[78] This indicates that the proprietary effect of movable property mortgages is limited. Without registration, movable property mortgages lack the publicity to be enforced against third parties, meaning they cannot take precedence over subsequently registered mortgagees or transferees.

9.5 Protection for the Mortgagor

9.5.1 Accessories Exist after the Mortgage Creation

Where the principal thing is mortgaged, are the accessories subject to mortgage in favour of the mortgagee? Suppose the accessories existed before the mortgage's creation. In that case, the mortgagee can claim that they are subject to the mortgage because the owner of the principal thing, the mortgagor, is considered the owner of the accessory unless there is a different agreement between the parties.[79]

The controversy arises when the accessories exist after the mortgage is created. In such a situation, the SPC provides clear guidance that the accessories and auxiliaries are not subject to the mortgage. As a result, the mortgagor has an exclusive say over them. However, if the mortgage is realised later, the accessories can be dealt with along with the principal thing due to their lack of individuality.[80] If divisible, the sale proceeds of the accessories and auxiliaries are not satisfied to the unpaid debt.

9.5.2 Assignment of the Mortgaged Property

Chinese law has not consistently dealt with a lender assigning a mortgaged property. First, a judicial opinion on implementing the General Principles of Civil Law of 1988 stipulated that during the mortgage period, the mortgagor was not allowed to transfer a mortgaged property to others without the mortgagee's consent. Without the mortgagee's consent, a transfer is void.[81] The mortgagor obtains the mortgagee's

[78] Article 414 CC.
[79] Para. 1 of Article 40 SPC Interpretation on the Security System.
[80] Para. 2 of Article 40 SPC Interpretation on the Security System.
[81] *Opinions of the SPC on Several Issues Concerning the Implementation of the General Principles of the Civil Law of the People's Republic of China of 1988*, Article 115(1).

consent before the borrower can dispose of, transfer or assign a mortgaged property. This is called a "no transfer without prior consent" system. However, the Guarantee Law retreated from this rigid approach and required the borrower to notify the lender before transferring a mortgaged property.[82] Simply a notification is sufficient, since it is irrelevant whether or not there is consent. However, in 2000, the Judicial Interpretation of the Guarantee Law stipulated that during the term of a mortgage, if the borrower transfers a mortgaged property without notifying the lender or the party to whom the property is being transferred, the lender can still exercise the mortgage right provided the mortgage has been registered.[83] In addition, the party to whom the property has been transferred can elect to pay all the debts to extinguish the original mortgage and then be entitled to obtain these costs from the original borrower. The Property Law took a stance of prohibiting the mortgagor from transferring the mortgaged property. Specifically, during the mortgage period, the mortgagor cannot transfer the mortgaged property without the mortgagee's consent. Only with the mortgagee's consent can the mortgagor transfer the mortgaged property. Suppose the mortgagor needs to transfer the mortgaged property without obtaining the mortgagee's consent. In that case, the transferee of the mortgaged property can only clear the debt on behalf of the mortgagor to extinguish the mortgage.[84] This is known as a "due-on-transfer" mechanism.[85]

The Property Law prohibits the transfer of mortgaged property without the mortgagee's consent. This restriction is grounded in the understanding that the mortgage right burdens the property's exchange value. Once a mortgage right is established, the property's exchange value control shifts to the mortgagee, limiting the mortgagor's full enjoyment of this value. The mortgagor retains only possession and use rights, obtaining the use value. Allowing unrestricted transfer during the mortgage period could pose a risk of "double sale." Additionally, this prohibition serves as a precautionary measure to protect the interests of the mortgagee, ensuring the mortgage remains an effective remedy throughout its duration.

[82] Article 49 Guarantee Law.
[83] Article 67 SPC Interpretation of the Guarantee Law.
[84] Article 191 Property law.
[85] Dale A. Whitman, 'Chinese Mortgage Law: An American Perspective' (2001) 15 *Columbia Journal Asian Law* 35, pp. 38–41.

To summarise, prior to enacting the CC, the mortgagor must obtain consent from the mortgagee before transferring the mortgaged property. The mortgagee holds the discretion to permit or deny the transfer. If a third party, such as the purchaser of the mortgaged property, wishes to settle the debts on behalf of the borrower, the lender has no control over this action. Similarly, the lender has no discretion if the original borrower repays the loan and the transferee chooses to secure new financing instead of assuming the existing loan.

However, the CC has introduced a new rule. Specifically, the mortgagor can now transfer the mortgaged property during the mortgage term unless otherwise agreed upon by the parties. The mortgage remains unaffected by the transfer of the mortgaged property.[86] In the event of a transfer, the mortgagor must promptly notify the mortgagee.[87] In such a scenario, if the mortgagee can provide evidence that the transfer may pose a risk to the mortgage, the mortgagee has the right to request the mortgagor to use the proceeds from the transfer to repay the debts before they are due or to place the proceeds in escrow.[88] This provision allows the mortgagor to transfer the mortgaged property without requiring explicit consent from the mortgagee, but notifying the mortgagee is mandatory. If the mortgagee can substantiate that the transfer may harm its interests, it is responsible for proving such harm. Otherwise, the mortgagee retains the right to enforce the mortgage against the new transferee.

The reasoning behind this approach is rooted in the mortgage right, which is designed to secure debt repayment by granting the creditor a direct and exclusive right to specific property owned by the debtor or a third party. The fundamental essence of the mortgage right is the right to the thing (*in rem*) rather than the person (*in personam*). Consequently, upon the legal establishment of the mortgage right, the creditor gains an exclusive and priority claim to repayment linked to the mortgaged property. Unless the mortgagee explicitly waives the mortgage right, any alterations to the mortgaged property, whether from voluntary transfer by the mortgagor or judicial enforcement actions, do not impede the mortgagee's capacity to assert their claim to the mortgaged property under the valid mortgage right.

86 Para. 1 of Article 406 CC.

87 Para. 2 of Article 406 CC.

88 *Ibid.*

It is crucial to emphasise that the above legal stance is a default framework. The mortgagor and mortgagee retain the authority to mutually agree to restrict the transfer of the mortgaged property through a mortgage contract.[89] This provision underscores the importance of party autonomy during the contractual formation. The mortgage agreement has the flexibility to incorporate a clause stipulating that if the mortgagor breaches the agreement by transferring the mortgaged property, the mortgagee possesses the right to demand the mortgagor to bear the responsibility for the breach. In the contract, they have the flexibility to explicitly outline liquidated damages or compensation for damages in case of a breach of the prohibition on transferring the mortgaged property. Additionally, if the mortgagor and mortgagee choose to document this restriction on property transfer in the property register, it can exert binding effects on the registration authority responsible for processing the transfer registration of the mortgaged property and the party acquiring the mortgaged property.

The CC's approach ensures the protection of the transferee's interests. Mandatory registration in real estate mortgages promotes transparency, enabling prospective buyers to examine encumbrances, including mortgage rights, through the real estate register. This empowers the transferee to make an informed decision about acquiring a property with such encumbrances. If the transferee chooses to proceed with the purchase despite the existing mortgage, they can negotiate with the mortgagor to establish a fair acquisition price for the mortgaged property.

Conversely, if the transferee prefers not to acquire a property with encumbrances, they can eliminate the mortgage by settling the debt, thereby obtaining a property without any encumbrances. This mechanism fosters transparency in property transactions and offers flexibility for both parties transferring a mortgaged property. The acquirer can make informed decisions by leveraging the information accessible in the real estate register.

9.6 Protection for the Mortgagee

Under Chinese law, the mortgagee, or the holder of the mortgage right, is afforded legal protections to safeguard their interests. In case of the mortgagor's default, the mortgagee is granted a priority position.

[89] Para. 1 of Article 406 CC.

During the foreclosure on the mortgaged property, the mortgagee holds a preferential claim over other creditors. The mortgage right is typically established through registration with relevant authorities, providing a public mortgage record.[90] This registration serves as a notice to third parties and helps to protect the mortgagee's priority.

Should the mortgagor engage in activities leading to a decrease in the property's value, the mortgagee possesses the right to demand that the mortgagor cease such actions.[91] In the event of a decrease in the value of the mortgaged property, the mortgagee has a right to demand the restoration of the property's value or require the provision of additional collateral equivalent to the lost value.[92] If the mortgagor fails to restore the property's value or provide additional security, the mortgagee has the right to demand early repayment from the debtor. Chinese law outlines legal procedures for the enforcement of mortgages.[93] If the mortgagor defaults, the mortgagee can initiate procedures, including foreclosure and property sale, to realise their security. In cases where the mortgaged property is seized by the court due to non-performance by the debtor or other circumstances agreed upon for enforcing the mortgage, the mortgagee is entitled, from the moment of seizure, to collect the natural or civil fruits of the seized property. This entitlement holds unless the mortgagee fails to request the person owing the duty to pay civil fruits.[94] The sale of the mortgaged property entitles the mortgagee to receive proceeds from the sale, which are then utilised to settle the outstanding debt. Subsequently, three specific topics will be examined in detail: the lease of the mortgaged property, the right of recourse among joint security providers without an agreement, and mortgages over illegal structures or allocated CLUR.

9.6.1 Lease of the Mortgaged Property

When a mortgaged property is leased, a potential conflict may arise between the two property interests in the event of a default by the mortgagor. This conflict involves the lessee's right to continue occupying

[90] Article 402 CC. However, the movable property mortgage does not require registration; see Article 403.

[91] Article 408 CC.

[92] *Ibid.*

[93] *Ibid.*

[94] Article 412 CC.

the property despite its sale and transfer and the lender's right to recover the owed money. For example, if A has agreed to grant B a two-year tenancy of his property, what must B do to ensure that her right as lessee has priority over the mortgagee in the sale? Under Chinese law, if a property is leased before the conclusion of a mortgage contract, the existing lease remains unaffected by the subsequent mortgage.[95] The "mortgage does not break the lease" principle applies in this scenario, preserving the lessee's rights even after the property is mortgaged. If a lender needs to enforce a mortgage in a pre-existing lease, they are not entitled to sell the property free of the existing lease.[96] The lessee's rights under the lease agreement are preserved, and the lender must respect the lease terms during the enforcement process. On the other hand, if the borrower leases the mortgaged property after the mortgage has been established, the lease is terminated if and when the lender enforces the sale of the property. In such a scenario, the lender has the right to dispose of the property, overriding the lease agreement.[97]

It is important to highlight that for the "mortgage does not break the lease" principle to apply, the leased property must already be in the lessee's possession. If the lessee does not have possession of the property despite having a valid lease contract concluded before the creation of the mortgage, the lease will be subject to the mortgage. In other words, leasing a property with a pre-existing mortgage, whether it involves immovable or movable property mortgage registration, is legally effective against third parties. As a result, the lessee cannot claim priority over the mortgagee's rights.

9.6.2 Right of Recourse among Joint Security Providers in the Absence of Agreement

Managing the mutual rights and obligations of internal recourse when multiple third parties provide security for the same claim, especially when only some, not all, have been enforced to realise the security, poses a challenge. Despite the Guarantee Law being in effect since 1995, there has been limited guidance on this issue over the past two decades. Only

[95] Article 405 CC.

[96] Article 31 Provisions of the SPC about Auctioning or Selling off Property by the People's Courts in Civil Execution of 2004.

[97] Article 190 Property Law.

Article 19 of the SPC Interpretation of the Guarantee Law has offered a somewhat insufficient provision, mentioning joint and several joint guarantees.[98] In the CC and the SPC Interpretation on the Security System, certain provisions touch upon situations where "the same debt has more than two security providers" and "both real and personal security secures the secured creditor's rights."[99] However, beyond the terms "security provided by two or more third parties" and "agreement to undertake joint and several joint security," the CC does not offer a more detailed definition of joint security.[100]

Joint security is categorised into two primary types based on whether the multiple collaterals are of the same nature: joint security of the same kind and mixed joint security. Joint security of the same kind encompasses joint guarantees, joint mortgages and joint pledges. Conversely, mixed joint security involves combinations of personal guarantees and real security over the same claim. Within joint security, there is a further distinction between joint and several security and joint security with defined shares, depending on whether the creditor can claim the share of security liability from the respective security provider.

Where there are more than two security providers, and a specific security provider is selected to undertake the security liability, the ability of the selected security provider to seek recourse against the other joint security providers for indemnity if the debtor fails to repay can depend on the legal framework and rules in place. The question of recourse among joint security providers has evolved with changes in legislative and judicial rules. The Guarantee Law 1995 marked an important legal development, but subsequent amendments and judicial interpretations may have introduced changes.

Between 1995 and 2007, the legal landscape, including the Guarantee Law and the SPC Interpretation of the Guarantee Law, essentially permitted the right of recourse among joint security providers under specific circumstances. In cases involving joint and several guarantees,[101] mixed

[98] Article 19 of the SPC Interpretation of the Guarantee Law states that "where two or more guarantors secure the same debt simultaneously or respectively, but guarantors and creditor have not agreed on guarantee shares, such guarantee shall be deemed as joint guarantee. Where the joint guarantors defend against creditor with their internal agreement of guarantee shares, such defense shall not be supported by the people's court."

[99] Article 392 CC; Article 13 SPC Interpretation on the Security System.

[100] *Ibid.*

[101] Article 12 Guarantee Law 1995.

joint security[102] and joint mortgages,[103] the security provider who had assumed the guarantee responsibility had the right to demand that other security providers contribute to their respective shares. Where there was no agreement specifying the distribution of shares in the joint security, the joint security providers were generally required to share the responsibility equally.

The Property Law presented ambiguity, as it did not explicitly address the issue of whether a security provider could seek compensation from others in joint mortgages. Unlike the Guarantee Law, the Property Law did not specify whether a security provider in a joint mortgage arrangement could recover compensation from other security providers. In the context of mixed joint guarantees, The Property Law only provides that the third party providing security has the right to recover from the debtor after assuming the responsibility, without clarifying the ability to recover from other security providers.[104] Although the Guarantee Law remained in effect when the Property Law was enacted, according to the Property Law, if there were inconsistencies between the two pieces of legislation, the Property Law would prevail.[105] This led to varying judicial outcomes. To address this, the SPC issued a Trial Minute in 2019, explicitly denying the joint security provider's right of recourse in the case of mixed security.[106]

Since 2021, similar to the Property Law, the CC does not explicitly address the right of recourse among joint security providers. However, Article 13 of the SPC Interpretation on the Security System in 2021 permits the security provider who has assumed liability to exercise the right of recourse against other third-party security providers under specified conditions[107]:

i. where there is an agreement among the guarantors on the proportional liability and the right of recourse;
ii. where there is an agreement among the security providers on the joint and several liabilities or the right of mutual recourse, but it does not specify the proportions;
iii. there is no agreement on the right of recourse, but all security providers signed the same contract with signatures or company seals.

[102] Article 20 (2) SPC Interpretation of the Guarantee Law 2000.
[103] Article 75 (3) SPC Interpretation of the Guarantee Law 2000.
[104] Article 176 Property Law.
[105] Article 178 Property Law.
[106] Article 56 SPC Trial Minutes 2019.
[107] Article 13 SPC Interpretation on the Security System of 2021.

As indicated earlier, neither Article 176 of the Property Law nor Article 392 of the CC explicitly establishes the right of recourse. Nevertheless, Chinese courts appear to acknowledge the existence of such a right for internal recourse. The SPC asserted in the case of *Gu Zhengkang v. Shiyan Ronghua Dongfeng Automobile Franchise Co. Ltd.* that,

> where there is no provision in the Property Law but an explicit provision in the SPC Interpretation of the Guarantee Law, both the first instance court and the appellate Court applied the Interpretation of the Guarantee Law. They found that having the right of recourse against the guarantor was not inappropriate after assuming the guarantee responsibility. The guarantor avers that the mortgagor has no right of recourse, and this Court does not support it.[108]

In addition to the reasoning on the legislative application in support of the right of recourse by the SPC, the Tianjin HPC furnished a cogent analysis in *Tianjin Huaqing Trading Co., Ltd. v. Tianjin Hengjing Recycled Alloy Materials Co., Ltd., Zhejiang Zhihu Investment Management Co., Ltd.* from the perspective of the principle of fairness.[109] It was held that,

> if the guarantor and the real security provider do not agree on how to share the guarantee responsibility, the ex-post balance of their rights and obligations should be realised by applying the principle of fairness. After the guarantor assumes responsibility, it steps into the secured creditor's position. Other security providers are exempted from their responsibility, and they, in a way, have obtained actual legal benefits. If the sharing of security liability is not supported, that causes unfairness. Finally, suppose mutual recovery between security providers is prohibited. In that case, it will encourage creditors to collude with a certain guarantor and maliciously choose other guarantors to assume responsibility, thereby exempting them from the abusive selection.[110]

However, the criteria applied by the SPC do not hinge on whether it is joint and several security or joint security with defined shares. Instead, the underlying rationale appears grounded in the common intention test.

108 顾正康、十堰荣华东风汽车专营有限公司案 [*Gu Zhengkang v. Shiyan Ronghua Dongfeng Automobile Franchise Co., Ltd.*] (2017) 最高法民再137号 [(2017) SPC Fa Min Zai No. 137].

109 天津市化轻贸易有限公司与天津恒景再生合金材料有限公司、浙江致虎投资管理有限公司 [*Tianjin Huaqing Trading Co., Ltd. v. Tianjin Hengjing Recycled Alloy Materials Co., Ltd., Zhejiang Zhihu Investment Management Co., Ltd.*] (2017) 津民初121号 [(2017) Jin Min Chu No. 121].

110 *Ibid.*

In essence, it revolves around whether the parties have explicitly demonstrated a common intention to distribute the security liability in proportion or whether such an intention can be inferred from signing the same contract.[111] No right of recourse exists without a discernible common intention, expressed or implied. The commendable aspect of this common intention test lies in its commitment to upholding party autonomy.

However, there are two unresolved issues with this approach. First, when all security providers sign the same contract, but their security liabilities do not cover the entire debt, recognising the right of recourse against each other becomes problematic. For instance, if A and B commit to securing 40 per cent of the debt each, with C covering the remaining 20 per cent, allowing a right of recourse in such a scenario would be artificial and potentially counterproductive. The prerequisite for recourse should be that a security provider assumes more than its allocated share of liability. If A fulfils his 40 per cent liability commitment, a right of recourse would not arise even if all security providers signed the same document. If A assumes a 50 per cent liability, can A seek recourse against B and C to reclaim the excess 10 percent liability? The answer is negative because the respective shares of security liability have been clearly defined as agreed. Therefore, relying solely on the joint signature on the same contract may be insufficient for invoking a right of recourse. An additional element is required, specifically that all security providers undertake joint and several security liabilities.[112]

Second, if the rationale is to infer a common intention from the parties signing the same contract, is there any other conduct that could serve as evidence of such a common intention? For instance, if the security providers entered into multiple guarantee contracts separately but simultaneously, or if they executed the contracts at different times, they were aware of each other's identity when concluding the guarantee contracts. It is advisable to keep the list of conditions in Article 13 open-ended.[113]

Despite the identified gaps, the SPC prioritises party autonomy by prohibiting the right of mutual recourse among mixed joint security providers unless explicitly agreed upon among themselves. Besides

[111] Lei Chen, 'The Security Interests in Chinese Law: Some Nuances', in Hao Jiang and Pietro Sirena (eds), *The Making of the Chinese CC: Promises and Persistent Problems* (Cambridge University Press 2023).

[112] *Ibid.*

[113] *Ibid.*

explicitly agreeing to mutual recourse rights or entering into joint and several joint guarantees, signing the same contract can indicate mutual recovery intent among the parties.

9.6.3 *Mortgage over New Built Structures, Illegal Structures or Allocated CLUR*

Once a mortgage is established over the CLUR, any new construction erected on the same land is not considered part of the mortgaged subject matter.[114] When enforcing this mortgage, the disposal of the new building will occur concurrently with the CLUR. It is important to note that the mortgagee does not have priority for debt repayment from the sale proceeds of the new building.[115] The rationale behind not granting the mortgagee priority over the sale proceeds of the new building when enforcing the mortgage is to safeguard the rights of third parties, including subsequent purchasers or creditors, who may have vested interests in the new construction. This approach ensures that other legitimate interests are duly considered and protected. By preventing the mortgagee from having disproportionate control over the proceeds, the legal framework promotes fair distribution among various competing interests. This aspect of the legal design may be intended to foster an environment conducive for real estate development by balancing the rights and priorities of different stakeholders in property transactions. Indeed, if the mortgagee were automatically granted priority over the proceeds of a new building, it could create disincentives for property owners to develop or improve their land. Such a scenario might discourage property owners from investing in construction or upgrades, as the automatic priority could limit their control over the resulting value.

Illegal structures or unauthorised construction are not eligible for a mortgage under Article 399 of the CC.[116] This restriction exists because illegal structures are considered assets with unclear or disputed ownership and usage rights. As a result, these types of properties are excluded from being used as collateral in mortgage arrangements. However, practical legal scenarios are often complex, particularly when illegal structures coexist with a legally established CLUR subject to a mortgage. For instance, if a mortgagor initiates a mortgage on a CLUR

[114] Article 417 CC.
[115] *Ibid.*
[116] Item 4 of Article 399 CC.

but argues that the mortgage contract is void due to illegal buildings on the land, what would be the response from Chinese courts? Another situation arises when a mortgage is established on buildings constructed on allocated construction land, and a party contends that the CLUR cannot be mortgaged or that requisite approval procedures are incomplete. In this case, predicting Chinese courts' position is challenging due to the intricate legal considerations involved.

In both scenarios, Chinese courts will reject the claim put forth by the mortgagor.[117] However, in the latter situation, the courts will determine that upon the realisation of the mortgage right, the funds generated from the auction or sale of the buildings will be prioritised for settling the outstanding fees associated with the transfer of the CLUR.[118] The court will dismiss the claim if a mortgage is established solely over the allocated CLUR and the party argues that the mortgage contract is invalid due to the failure to complete the approval procedures. When mortgage registration has been finalised, the court will uphold the mortgagee's request to exercise the mortgage right.[119]

Chinese law strives to balance the rights and interests of various parties participating in property transactions, including mortgage contracts. Illegal structures on a property do not automatically invalidate a mortgage contract. This is primarily due to the following key reasons. First, Chinese law makes clear distinctions between different legal issues, considering illegal structures as matters falling under the jurisdiction of urban planning or construction authorities. However, such issues do not necessarily impact the legal validity of a mortgage contract, and resolutions for illegal structures may follow a distinct legal process. Second, mortgage contracts function as legal instruments establishing a security interest in the property for the mortgagee (lender) benefit. While illegal structures might breach another regulatory framework, they do not automatically void the property rights created through a mortgage. Third, Chinese law generally aims to enforce contracts and adhere to the principle of *pacta sunt servanda* (agreements must be kept). Nullifying a mortgage contract based solely on the presence of illegal structures could jeopardise the stability and predictability of contractual relationships. Fourth, this legal stance serves to protect the interests of mortgagees. Automatically invalidating mortgage contracts due to the

[117] Articles 49 and 50 SPC Interpretation on the Security System.
[118] Para. 1 of Article 50 SPC Interpretation on the Security System.
[119] Para. 2 of Article 50 SPC Interpretation on the Security System.

illegality of structures could result in unfair consequences for lenders unaware of the property's violations. Fifth, if illegal structures hamper the marketability or utilisation of the property, it adversely affects the mortgagee, as the value of the secured property diminishes. In such a scenario, deeming the mortgage contract invalid seems disproportionate.

9.7 Realisation of the Mortgage

Mortgage contracts typically outline procedures for enforcing the mortgage, with enforcement typically initiated when the debtor fails to repay the loan. One notable feature of a mortgage is that it empowers the creditor to seek payment from the proceeds of a property's sale in the event of borrower default. This mechanism provides the creditor with a means to recover the outstanding debt by realising the value tied to the mortgaged property. There are two approaches for a mortgagee to recover the loan. Firstly, the involved parties can negotiate and formulate a supplementary agreement outlining the mortgage's enforcement process. This agreement converts the value of the mortgaged property into cash when the borrower cannot meet the loan repayment obligations.[120] The agreed price must be based on the market value of the mortgaged property.[121] Since this method does not necessitate court intervention, the private agreement offers a swift and cost-effective solution.

Furthermore, prior to the crystallisation of all debts secured by the MAM, the mortgagee and mortgagor have the flexibility to mutually modify the crystallisation period, the range of debts and the maximum amount through an agreement. It is crucial, however, that such an agreement does not disadvantage other mortgagees with claims over the same mortgaged property. This allows the parties involved to adapt the terms within certain limits through mutual consent.[122] The secured creditor has the right to independently auction or sell the secured property to satisfy the debts out of the proceeds where the parties have agreed to allow the secured creditor to do so.[123] Where the secured creditor cannot auction or sell the secured property for reasons attributable to the mortgagor, the secured creditor has the right to demand that

[120] Para. 1 of Article 410 CC.
[121] Para. 3 of Article 410 CC.
[122] Article 422 CC.
[123] Article 45 SPC Interpretation on the Security System.

the mortgagor assume the additional costs incurred.[124] This provision recognises an out-of-court method of security realisation by parties' agreement. It ensures the mortgagor bears responsibility for any hindrances to realising the secured property under the agreement.

Secondly, if the parties cannot reach an agreement, the lender can pursue a judicial sale by applying to the court, requesting the court to conduct an auction or sell the property.[125] The debtor remains liable for any shortfall between the sale proceeds and the amount due under the loan.[126] Any excess money is returned to the borrower.[127] This legal recourse provides a formal and judicially supervised process for selling the mortgaged property to recover the outstanding debt. Two essential conditions must be satisfied to enforce a mortgage: the mortgage payment is overdue, and the lender has not received repayment. However, in the event of borrower default, the creditor cannot directly take possession and obtain the title of the mortgaged property, even if there was an agreement allowing for such a transfer.[128] Any such agreement is considered void (*pactum commissorium*). Instead, the mortgaged property must be sold, and the lender is entitled only to the outstanding amount owed to them. While this approach ensures transparency and fairness by preventing a potentially collusive sale by the lender, court auctions often result in delays and increased costs.

The mortgagee must exercise the mortgage right within the statute of limitations for the main claim.[129] If the mortgagee misses this statutory time limit, the court will not provide legal protection for their interests.[130] The mortgagee must initiate legal proceedings within the specified statutory period, following the prescribed legal procedures to auction or dispose of the mortgaged property to enforce their rights. This provision is designed to incentivise the timely utilisation of mortgage rights, thereby upholding the legitimacy and effectiveness of legal procedures. If, prior to the expiration of the statute of limitations for the main claim, the creditor solely files a lawsuit against the debtor and subsequently, after a judgment or mediation by the Court, fails to apply for compulsory enforcement against the debtor within the stipulated

[124] *Ibid.*
[125] Para. 2 of Article 410 CC.
[126] Article 413 CC.
[127] *Ibid.*
[128] Article 401 CC.
[129] Article 419 CC.
[130] *Ibid.*

period for enforcement application, any assertion of the exercise of the mortgage right against the mortgagor will not be supported by Chinese courts.[131] By imposing these requirements, the legal system seeks to maintain the integrity of legal procedures, uphold the rights of all parties involved and ensure that judgments and mediations are effectively and promptly enforced.

After the mortgage of rural LCMR, any changes to the ownership and usage characteristics of the land are prohibited following the execution of the mortgage unless the specified legal procedures are followed.[132] The rule aims to protect the collective nature of rural land ownership, preventing unauthorised alterations to land ownership relationships through the realisation of mortgages. The rule may be designed to prevent the abuse of mortgage rights, ensuring the rational use of land and societal development. Prohibiting changes to land use without legal procedures may be aimed at maintaining the stability of land use, ensuring that land remains within planned parameters.

Where a discrepancy between the agreed-upon mortgage scope in the mortgage contract and the registered amount of debt in the land register exists, the prevailing practice within the Chinese legal system is to prioritise the information recorded in the registration over the contractual agreement. The content officially registered should take precedence unless there is compelling evidence demonstrating errors in the register.[133] While the agreed-upon scope of security is the outcome of negotiations between the parties, when realising the mortgage, the law prioritises the registration content due to its external effectiveness and legal impact on third parties.[134] Nonetheless, in some other cases, Chinese courts prioritised the contractual stipulations in the mortgage contract over the registration contents.[135] This main reason reflects that some land registers are incomplete or inaccurate in many regions of

[131] Article 44 SPC Interpretation on the Security System.

[132] Article 418 CC.

[133] Article 217 CC states that the title certificate to immovable property is proof of the right holder's entitlement to such property. The items recorded in the title certificate to immovable property shall be consistent with those recorded in the register of immovable property; where there is any inconsistency, the items recorded in the register of immovable property shall prevail unless there is evidence to prove errors in the register of immovable property.

[134] 安岳县欣通建设投资有限公司等与重庆进出口信用担保有限公司 (2016)最高法民终268号 [*Anyue Xintong Construction Investment Co., Ltd. v. Chongqing Import and Export Credit Guarantee Co., Ltd.* (2016) SPC Min Final No. 268].

[135] *Ibid.*

China. The SPC confirmed this approach in its 2019 Judicial Minutes. Specifically, the SPC reasoned that,

> in China, the current real security registration systems implemented vary across different regions. When the courts handle cases, they should pay full attention to the differences in system design and make judgments that align with the actual situation. In most provinces, the registration systems do not have a specific column for the 'scope of security' but only mention the 'amount of the secured principal claim or maximum principal claim amount' and often allow only fixed numbers to be entered. Contract parties often specify that the scope of the real security rights includes the principal claim and its ancillary claims, such as interest and liquidated damages, leading to inconsistencies between the mortgage contract and the registration content. This inconsistency is a common phenomenon caused by the registration system design in that region. Therefore, the Court's choice to recognise the scope of the secured property rights in the mortgage contracts is a practical and appropriate decision. Consistency between the registered scope of real security and mortgage contracts is common in some provinces and regions where the real estate registration systems are relatively standardised, and the registration rules align with mortgage contracts. In such cases, the Court should consider the registered scope valid when handling cases.[136]

9.8 Priority of Mortgages

When multiple mortgages are registered on the same property, their priority is determined by their respective registration dates. Registered mortgages hold precedence over unregistered ones.[137] In the event of realisation, the proceeds from the property will be allocated among the creditors in proportion to their claims. This prioritisation mechanism ensures a systematic and fair property value distribution following the established mortgage registrations.[138] In the context of mortgages on immovable property in China, priority is determined by the time of registration rather than the execution of the mortgage contract. However, a challenge arises when there is a refusal to register. Some unscrupulous borrowers may promise lenders that a mortgage will be established to secure a loan. Subsequently, once the funds have been disbursed, these borrowers may intentionally delay or refuse to register

[136] Article 58 SPC Trial Minutes 2019.
[137] Article 414 CC. This priority rule is also applied to other registrable security interests.
[138] *Ibid.*

the mortgage, leading to potential issues with the enforcement and prioritisation of the security interest. According to the law, the absence of formal registration means no recognised mortgage exists, even if a valid mortgage contract exists. If the failure to register is attributed to the mortgagor, a potential solution is to seek a court order for specific performance to address this issue. This court order would compel the mortgagor to complete the registration process, ensuring that the mortgage is officially recorded and recognised. This approach aims to enforce the legal requirement for registration and protect the mortgagee's interests in cases where the mortgagor is responsible for the registration delay or refusal.

Furthermore, Chinese courts entertain the creditor's request for the mortgagor to bear responsibility within the agreed-upon security scope, treating it as if the mortgage had been officially registered.[139] This approach would allow the creditor to seek redress and hold the mortgagor accountable for the obligations specified in the security agreement, even without formal registration. It allows creditors to enforce the security interests within the agreed-upon parameters, safeguarding their rights despite registration challenges.

Where multiple creditors are to be compensated, a clear rule of priority prevails: *prior tempore, potior iure* (first in time, strongest in law). This principle signifies that the creditor with the earliest-established claim holds a superior legal position and is entitled to receive payment before subsequent creditors. This rule of priority aims to provide a systematic and equitable method for distributing funds among competing creditors based on the timing of their respective claims.[140] In other words, the lender whose mortgage was created first prioritises satisfying his claim from the sale proceeds. This means the lenders whose mortgages were created later are at risk of suffering loss if the total amount of the secured debts exceeds the sale proceeds. Suppose the same property is held by more than one lender simultaneously. In that case, the money from the auction or sale of the property is paid in the following order: (1) if all the mortgages have been registered, the payments are in the sequence of the registration (if the mortgage contracts were registered on the same day, the debts are distributed *pro rata* according to the percentage of each creditor's

[139] Para. 3 of Article 46 SPC Interpretation on the Security System.

[140] Ph. J. Thomas, C. G. Van der Merwe and B. C. Stoop, *Historical Foundations of South African Private Law* (Butterworths 2000).

claims); (2) a mortgaged security that is registered takes priority over one that is not registered; and (3) if no mortgage has been registered, payments are made in proportion to the mortgagees' claims.

Where both a mortgage and a pledge encumber the same property, the sequence of repayment from auction or sale proceeds will be established based on the earlier of the two events: registration or delivery time.[141] The consideration of the time of registration or delivery as a criterion for determining priority is viewed as a convenient and objective method. This principle ensures a clear and orderly process for determining the priority of claims when multiple security interests exist on the same property. It is rooted in establishing a predictable and efficient system for creditors, where the chronological order of registration or delivery determines the priority of interests. The rationale behind this approach is to ensure that creditors with earlier registered or delivered security interests hold a superior claim to proceeds from the sale of the property. The priority system is designed to safeguard the legitimate expectations of creditors and enhance transparency in enforcing security rights.

9.9 Floating Charge

Chinese law recognises the floating charge.[142] An enterprise, industrial and commercial household, or agricultural manufacturer or trader may create a charge over existing and future manufacturing equipment, raw materials, semi-finished products and products so that the creditor is entitled to have the debt repaid with priority to the extent of the value of the movables mentioned above at the moment of crystallisation, in cases of the debtor's non-performance of the due debt or other circumstances of enforcing the charge as agreed by the parties.[143]

The primary advantage of a floating mortgage lies in the fact that, even after establishing the mortgage right, the mortgagor maintains control over the mortgaged property. The mortgagor can operate the property freely and engage in business activities until the floating mortgage is determined. This arrangement allows the mortgagor to utilise the mortgaged property without significant restrictions during the period preceding the final determination of the floating mortgage.

[141] Article 415 CC.
[142] Previously Article 181 Property Law; now Article 396 CC.
[143] Article 396 CC.

Nevertheless, a significant drawback of a floating mortgage stems from the inherent uncertainty linked to the fluctuations of the mortgaged property. The property under a floating mortgage undergoes continuous changes throughout the mortgage period, with the mortgagor possessing the authority to operate, generate income and dispose of the property during this period. The mortgagor's property only becomes the precisely defined mortgaged property when the floating mortgage is crystallised. The efficacy of the floating mortgage applies to the mortgagor's property at the moment of the floating mortgage determination. Before this determination, the property under a floating mortgage remains flexible and subject to movement. Once determined, it loses its flexibility and is referred to as the defined mortgaged property.

Article 181 of the Property Law stipulated that "the creditor shall be paid first from the movable property when the mortgage right is realised." A specific crystallisation time exists between establishing the floating mortgage and the mortgagee's realisation of the mortgage right. This crystallisation time is crucial for accurately determining the scope of the mortgaged property. Therefore, there is a loophole in Article 181 of Property Law, as it did not specify the crystallisation time before the floating charge is realised. The CC rectifies the legislative defect by specifying that the creditor shall be paid first from the movable property when the mortgaged property is crystallised. The determined time for a floating charge property is agreed upon through negotiation between the creditor and the mortgagor. Without such an agreement, Article 411 of the CC provides a default rule on crystallising mortgaged property.[144]

Given that the subject of a floating charge pertains to movable properties,[145] its establishment occurs upon the effectiveness of the floating charge contract.[146] Unlike other security interests, registration is not obligatory for a floating charge. However, it is essential to note that the right of charge associated with a floating charge cannot be asserted against a bona fide third party without prior registration. Registration serves as a crucial step to establish and assert the priority of the floating

[144] Article 411 CC states that where a mortgage is created under Article 396 of this Code, the subject matter of the mortgage is determined under any of the following circumstances: (1) the personal right is not yet realised when the debt becomes due; (2) the mortgagor is declared insolvent or dissolved; (3) in other circumstances of enforcing the mortgage as agreed by the parties; or (4) in other circumstances which severely affect the realisation of the personal right.

[145] Article 396 CC.

[146] Article 403 CC.

charge in cases involving third parties who may not be aware of the security interest.[147]

In a floating charge, after the mortgage right is established, as long as the mortgaged property has not been crystallised, it can be increased or decreased without requiring additional procedures, and the mortgagee has no right to intervene. For movable property already subject to a floating mortgage, specific movable property that "flows in" becomes part of the mortgaged property. In contrast, property that "flows out" is removed from the mortgaged property, no longer serving as part of the mortgaged property. Suppose the movable property flowing into the mortgaged property already has a mortgage right. In that case, it automatically carries the burden of the floating charge, resulting in the coexistence of two mortgage rights on the same property and thus raising priority issues in realisation. The CC introduced the super-priority rule, or the security right over the purchase price, to address this issue. First, the primary claim secured by the movable property flowing into the mortgage collateral is the purchase price of the collateral.[148] In other words, if a specific movable property already has a mortgage right established, it serves as security for the primary claim of the purchase price of that specific movable property, and the amount secured is the purchase price of the specific movable property flowing into the floating mortgaged property.

Second, if the specific moveable property undergoes registration within ten days of flowing into the floating mortgage, the mortgage right acquires super-priority status.[149] Even if its establishment occurs later than the pre-existing floating charge, it enjoys the prioritised position against the pre-existing floating mortgage.[150] Although the mortgaged property with the super-priority right also bears the burden of the floating mortgage right, the holder of the super-priority right takes precedence over other secured rights of the buyer, including the floating mortgage right. As a result, they have the first claim to the proceeds of the property.[151] If multiple super-priority rights exist over the same property, the courts should determine the repayment order based on the registration time.[152]

[147] *Ibid.*
[148] Article 416 CC.
[149] *Ibid.*
[150] Para. 1 of Article 57 SPC Interpretation on the Security System.
[151] Para. 2 of Article 57 SPC Interpretation on the Security System.
[152] Para. 3 of Article 57 SPC Interpretation on the Security System.

Third, except for a possessory lien, the buyer or the floating charger does not include possessory liens in their other secured rights. A possessory lien is an obligatory security interest, not a contractual one. Therefore, the priority effect of the super-priority mortgage right cannot override a possessory lien.[153]

9.10 Validity of a Company's Assumption of a Security Interest

Recently, Chinese courts and arbitration tribunals have grappled with a challenging issue regarding determining a company's security liability in unauthorised contracts. Specifically, there is uncertainty regarding whether Chinese courts will consistently deem such unauthorised agreements void and unenforceable. This uncertainty arises when a company's managing director or legal representative enters into a security undertaking agreement with a third party without adhering to the corporate resolution mandated by Article 16 of the PRC Company Law.

This legal inquiry encompasses contract, property and company laws. Chinese courts face a dilemma without explicit statutory guidance, leading to varied considerations in assessing cases. Numerous factors come into play, including the relationship between the security agreement and the primary contract, the listed status of the security provider, the debtor's role as a shareholder or controller of the guarantor, the creditor's affiliation with the guarantor, and the good faith exhibited by the parties involved in executing the security agreement. Furthermore, the perplexing question arises whether the lack of a corporate resolution can be deemed apparent authority in Chinese contract law. Consequently, the judicial rulings exhibit inconsistency, with a tendency toward favouring the secured party, often to the detriment of the security provider companies. A recent empirical study revealed that out of 226 decisions involving unauthorised security agreements handed down by the provisional HPC level, 79.3 per cent of the decisions were ruled in favour of being enforceable, and even among the remaining 20.7 per cent of cases where the security agreement was held unenforceable, more than a quarter of the decisions held the security provider company partially liable.[154] This

[153] Article 416 CC.

[154] Charles Zhen Qu, 'Corporate Law Issue, Civil Law Solutions: Resolving Disputes Arising from Unauthorized Corporate Security Contracts in People's Republic of China High Courts' (2020) 1 *Corporate and Business Law Journal* 12.

situation could create opportunities for legal arbitrage, as it may incentivise the managing director or the company's legal representative to engage in such misconduct.

The CC and the SPC Interpretation on the Security System have clarified the conditions requiring a company to undergo corporate resolutions when offering a security guarantee. In instances involving an unauthorised security agreement, the validity and enforceability are contingent on the good faith of the counterparty. If the counterparty acted in good faith, the security agreement is recognised as valid and enforceable. Conversely, the agreement is deemed unenforceable if the counterparty acted in bad faith. The legal standard presumes good faith unless proven otherwise.

> If the counterparty does not know and should not have known that the legal representative exceeds the authority when concluding the guarantee contract. The counterparty has evidence that a reasonable review of the company's resolution has been conducted. The People's Court shall determine that it constitutes good faith unless the company has evidence that the counterparty knew or should have known that the resolution was forged or altered.[155]

The legal implications are evident. Firstly, the burden of proof lies with the counterparty to demonstrate that it has undertaken a thorough review to meet the good faith requirement. Secondly, the counterparty must proactively engage in a diligent examination of the corporate resolutions. Although the SPC Interpretation does not explicitly define the parameters of a "reasonable review," it is anticipated that the standard for such a review is higher than the mere formality check outlined in the initial trial guidance document issued by the SPC.[156]

Moreover, the SPC outlines a relatively narrow set of exceptions where a corporate resolution may not be required to authorise a guarantee or security provision. As a standard practice, corporate resolutions are deemed necessary unless one of the following exceptions applies:

> 1, issuance of a letter of credit by financial institutions or granting of a guarantee and security by licensed guarantee companies (担保公司);
>
> 2, granting of a guarantee or security by a non-listed company for the operation of wholly owned subsidiaries; and

[155] Article 7 SPC Interpretation on the Security System.

[156] Notice by the SPC of Issuing the Minutes of the National Courts' Civil and Commercial Trial Work Conference [九民纪要] in 2019 (the 2019 "SPC Trial Minutes").

3, consent by signing the guarantee or security document by the shareholders of a non-listed company, constituting not less than two-thirds of shareholder voting rights.[157]

Ultimately, where a listed company or a publicly disclosed subsidiary of a listed company extends security by entering into an agreement, it is mandated that the listed company publicly announces the approval of corporate resolutions for providing the guarantee or security. This practice is praiseworthy because it significantly limits the legal representative's capacity to sign unauthorised security agreements. Additionally, certain department rules for listed companies necessitate transparency through disclosure.[158] The expectation is that a listed company publicly discloses any security undertakings, and it is logical to anticipate that the counterparty would be required to furnish evidence to establish the liability of a listed company in this regard.

The SPC has taken a nuanced approach to fill the gap identified above. However, it is important to note that the security provider remains liable for an invalid security contract even if the main contract is valid. A security contract is invalid for several reasons, such as where the intended property interest to be secured is legally prohibited from being mortgaged,[159] the property to be mortgaged is entangled in a title dispute[160] or when the board of a company has not approved it to act as the security provider.

In the event of an invalid security contract, it does not necessarily absolve the security provider from all liabilities. Chinese law employs a refined typology based on the fault test. In other words, the extent of the security provider's liability will be determined by assessing whether and to what degree they were at fault in creating the invalid security contract. To be specific, Article 17 of the SPC Interpretation on the Security System specifies that when the main contract is valid but the guarantee contract provided by a third party is invalid, the courts shall ascertain the security liability based on different situations:

(1) where both the creditor and the security provider are found to be at fault, the liability of the security provider for compensation shall be limited to one-half of the outstanding amount owed by the debtor.

[157] Article 8 SPC Interpretation on the Security System.
[158] Article 6 Listed Company Information Disclosure Regulatory Measures.
[159] Article 399 CC.
[160] *Ibid.*

(2) should the security provider be deemed at fault while the creditor is not, the security provider shall bear responsibility for the portion of the debt remaining unpaid by the debtor.
(3) if the creditor is found at fault and the security provider is not, the security provider shall be exempt from any obligation for compensation.[161]

It can be seen from the above that the SPC Interpretation of the Security System does not explicitly outline a fault test, and it appears that a common-sense approach is employed to allocate liability in such scenarios. What stands out in Chinese law is that if the principal contract is invalid, the security contract provided by a third party should also be deemed invalid, adhering to the accessory principle. Under this principle, the security provider will not be liable for compensation if it is not at fault. However, if the security provider is found to be at fault, the liability for compensation will be limited to one-third of the portion that the debtor cannot pay. This delineation reflects a nuanced and context-specific approach to determining liability in invalid security contracts.[162]

9.11 Termination of Security Interest

As explained earlier, Chinese law follows the accessory principle, albeit with some deviations. Consequently, the mortgage interest is terminated upon the discharge of the secured claim through payment or other means. Furthermore, a security interest can be extinguished through the waiver or release of the mortgage. The CC presents a somewhat concise list of situations in which the security interest can be terminated, including cases where:

1) the main debt is extinguished;
2) the security interest is realised;
3) the creditor waives the security interest or
4) any other circumstances of the termination of security interest provided by law.[163]

The discharge of a secured obligation (main debt) does not automatically result in the cancellation of the mortgage; it necessitates registration in

[161] Article 17 (1) SPC Interpretation on the Security System.
[162] Article 17 (2) SPC Interpretation on the Security System.
[163] Article 393 CC.

the land registration office.[164] When a mortgage on a building is established, registration is a mandatory step, and the mortgage comes into effect upon registration.[165] However, it is notable that the CC lacks provisions governing the registration of mortgage cancellations. This absence of explicit guidelines could lead to disputes concerning the timing of the termination of the security interest. The need for clarity in the registration process for mortgage cancellations becomes apparent in ensuring a smooth and unambiguous resolution of such matters.

The termination of a mortgage is brought about by the waiver or release of the mortgage.[166] However, the terminology used in the CC is "abandon." The provision does not explicitly clarify whether a bilateral agreement is necessary for abandonment, whether the secured creditor can unilaterally waive the mortgage, or if both unilateral and bilateral actions are permissible. Additionally, the question arises as to whether abandonment can be exercised implicitly or only explicitly. For instance, if a mortgage creditor agrees to transfer the mortgaged property free from the mortgage, does this constitute abandonment? Furthermore, it is unclear whether abandonment necessitates a change in the land registration. The CC remains silent on these issues, leaving room for interpretation and potential disputes surrounding the mechanisms and requirements for mortgage abandonment.

The list above does not encompass scenarios where the mortgaged property is destroyed, the title of the mortgage debtor is expropriated beyond their control or where the mortgage creditor becomes the owner of the mortgaged property. The SPC fills this gap by providing detailed rules to address these situations. When the mortgaged property is damaged, lost or expropriated, and the mortgagee requests that insurance compensation, expropriation compensation or damages be prioritised and paid according to the order of the original mortgage, the court is expected to support such a request. This underscores the importance of preserving the priority rights of the mortgagee in cases of unforeseen events affecting the mortgaged property.[167] Where compensation is paid to the mortgagor, and the mortgagee requests the party liable for compensation to pay directly to the mortgagee, the court

[164] Lei Chen, 'Land Registration, Property Rights and Institutional Performance in China: Progress Achieved and Challenges Ahead' (2014) 44 *Hong Kong Law Journal* 841.

[165] Article 402 CC.

[166] Article 409 CC.

[167] Article 42 (1) SPC Interpretation on the Security System.

is typically not inclined to support such a request. An exception is only made when the party responsible for compensation continues to pay the mortgagor even after the mortgagee has served a payment request. This signifies that, under Chinese law, the creation of a mortgage is not automatically terminated upon expropriation or destruction, and the mortgagee's rights remain contingent on specific conditions and legal proceedings.

When the mortgaged property is lost or expropriated before registration, and it is not attributable to the mortgagor, but the mortgagor receives compensation when the creditor requests the mortgagor to assume mortgage liability, the court is expected to support this request.[168] This principle, often referred to as the "surviving mortgage rule," is based on the condition that the loss or expropriation is not the fault of the mortgagor. The continued existence of the mortgage is tied to the continuation of the mortgage debtor's interest in the building, offering protection to the mortgage creditor.

However, the SPC Interpretation on the Security System does not explicitly address whether the mortgage is terminated when expropriation is uncompensated. In cases of under-compensation or delayed compensation, it remains uncertain how this might affect the scope of security liability agreed upon in the original mortgage. This aspect may be clarified through future case law developments.

While property law in China may not specifically address the situation where the mortgage creditor becomes the owner of the mortgaged property, according to the principle in Chinese contract law, this scenario can be viewed as a form of merger, leading to the termination of the contract.[169] However, an important question arises, even if the mortgage is considered extinguished based on contract rules: whether the mortgage creditor, now the owner of the mortgaged property, retains the right to enforce the mortgage against subsequent creditors. This issue is not explicitly clarified and may depend on the specific circumstances and legal interpretations that may arise through court decisions or further legislative developments. The interplay between contract law, property law and the rights of subsequent creditors in this context may require additional clarification from the legal system.

[168] Article 46 (2) SPC Interpretation on the Security System.
[169] Article 557 CC.

9.12 Conclusion

The CC has brought about notable enhancements in security interests by clarifying and refining existing laws. The SPC has introduced intricate legal tests through the SPC Interpretation on the Security System, aiming to strike a nuanced balance among the interests of the debtor, creditor and security provider. Furthermore, the recent regulations appear to modify the long-standing accessory principle in Chinese law.

Strict adherence to the accessory principle seems to be losing significance, leading to somewhat of a departure from this principle in the CC. Evident in this shift is the growing prominence of instruments such as MAM[170] and floating charges in China.[171] Furthermore, the existing legal framework governing security interests is inclined toward private initiatives. Parties are granted the freedom to establish non-standard security arrangements through contracts, enhancing the effectiveness of security measures. However, these approaches are still in early stages of development and necessitate additional legal clarifications from the judiciary.

Nonetheless, certain provisions remain unclear, requiring further elaboration, particularly in conflicts between publicly registered standard security and privately contracted non-standard security lacking public disclosure. Additional clarification is needed for internal recourse rules among security providers and the termination of security interests. It is anticipated that the courts will need to establish detailed legal tests and rules through judicial decisions to address these intricacies.

170 Article 420 CC.
171 Article 396 CC.

10

Pledge and Lien

10.1 Introduction

Besides mortgages, Chinese law acknowledges two additional forms of real security, specifically pledge (质权) and lien (留置权). A pledge involves the delivery of movable assets or a property right certificate to the creditor or registration, whereas a right certificate exists as collateral for fulfilling an obligation.[1] When the debtor fails to meet the outstanding debt or under agreed-upon circumstances for enforcing the pledge, the creditor holds the right to prioritise repayment up to the value of the pledged subject matter.[2] In this context, the party receiving the collateral, usually the creditor, is called the pledgee while the party providing the collateral is the pledgor. The property provided as collateral is called the pledged property (including the incorporeal rights). In Chinese law, a pledge is divided into two categories: a chattel pledge and a pledge over rights. A pledge over rights involves the pledge of certain property rights or entitlements, often intangible property rights rather than physical assets. Real property cannot be subject to a pledge. A lien (留置权) is a security interest that allows a person (the "lienholder") to retain possession of another person's property until a debt or obligation is satisfied.[3]

From the Property Law to the CC, the main provisions regarding pledges have not undergone any significant changes, making it the most conservative part of the real security system. Although China's legal system provides non-possessory security for movables, such as pledges over movables, it is still unpopular because its rule design is not business friendly. The floating mortgage system suffers from an expanded scope of mortgagors and deficiencies in enforcement rules, leading to its

[1] Article 425 CC.
[2] *Ibid.*
[3] Article 447 CC.

unpopularity.[4] On the other hand, chattel mortgages are essentially a barely used security system. The designated registration authorities have hardly processed any registrations for chattel mortgages.[5] Likewise, the traditional pledge over movables involving the transfer of actual possession of movable properties is not commonly used in commercial transactions. The most notable one is the dynamic inventory pledge. It refers to a pledging arrangement in which, within a pledge contract, the debtor uses its inventory as collateral, and these inventories may change during the contract period. Inventory typically includes a company's stock, raw materials, work-in-progress and finished goods.

By contrast, a pledge over the rights in commercial practice gained ground due to its flexibility. Among others, the accounts receivable pledge is a focal point of the rights pledge in Chinese commerce. This is largely due to its involvement in rules related to the transfer of claims and its status as one of the most prevalent forms of security in commercial practices. Therefore, in this chapter, the creation, exercising and realisation of pledges will be discussed by reference to statutory provisions and landmark cases. The accounts receivable pledge will be examined more pertinently to evaluate the current legal framework. Finally, the lien as a separate security right will be investigated to reveal its function and characteristics.

10.2 Pledge

10.2.1 Creation of Pledge

A pledge is typically established through a written agreement between the pledgor and the pledgee. Both parties must consent to the arrangement, and a pledge contract normally contains the following information: (1) type and amount of the secured debt; (2) time for the debtor to perform the debt; (3) name, quantity and other situations of the subject matter; (4) scope of the secured debt; and (5) time and methods of delivering the subject matter of the pledge.[6]

[4] Peng Sun and Dajiang Deng [孙鹏、邓达江], 'The Logic of Creation and Legislative Expression of Dynamic Movable Property Pledge – Centred on the Legislation of Movable Property Security in the Property Law CC' [《动产动态质押的生成逻辑与立法表达——以民法典物权编动产担保立法为中心》] (2019) 5 *Social Science Research* [《社会科学研究》] 92.

[5] Jinqiang Ye [叶金强], 'Critique of the Current Movable Property Security Model' [《现行动产担保模式之批判》] (2022) 6 *Law Science Magazine* [《法学杂志》] 39.

[6] Article 427 CC.

After the pledge contract takes effect, the creditor has the right to request the pledgor to deliver the pledged property. Upon delivery of the pledged property, the pledge right becomes effective, and the creditor begins to enjoy the pledge right. This is to say, the effectiveness of a pledge over movables is contingent on the delivery of the pledged property. This legally mandatory requirement overrides any contrary agreements between the parties.[7]

Not all the movables are capable of creating a pledge.[8] One example is property for which the right of use is uncertain or subject to dispute. It may involve disputes over ownership rights, unclear identification of right holders or conflicts among multiple claimants. The objects of pledge over rights primarily include negotiable securities, mutual fund units and company shares, intellectual property rights and receivables. Specifically, the rights that can be pledged may include but are not limited to (1) bills of exchange, promissory notes and checks; (2) bonds and certificates of deposit; (3) warehouse receipts and bills of lading; (4) transferable mutual fund units and company shares; (5) transferable patrimonial rights in intellectual property such as the right to exclusive use of a registered trademark, patent right and copyright; (6) current and after-acquired receivables; and (7) other patrimonial rights allowed by any law or administrative regulation to be the subject matter of a pledge.[9]

The pledge is effective upon registration or delivery of negotiable securities, such as a bill of exchange, promissory note, check, bond, certificate of deposit, warehouse receipt or bill of lading. The right of pledge is created when the right certificate is delivered to the pledgee. Where no such right certificate exists, the right of pledge is created when the pledge is registered.[10] When using a promissory note for a pledge, if the parties endorse the promissory note with the word "pledge" and sign it, and the promissory note has been delivered to the pledgee, the pledge is established from the time when the promissory note is delivered to the pledgee.[11] Likewise, if the holder of the inventory or warehouse receipt endorses the warehouse receipt with the word "pledge" and obtains the custodian's signature, and the warehouse receipt has been delivered to the pledgee, the pledge is established when the warehouse receipt is

[7] Article 429 CC.
[8] Article 426 CC.
[9] Article 440 CC.
[10] Article 411 CC.
[11] Article 58 SPC Interpretation on the Security System.

delivered to the pledgee.[12] If any other specific legislative provision addresses the creation of a pledge over negotiable securities, such provision shall prevail. This shows that the CC only provides a principle-based framework, leaving other special laws to flesh out the details.

Nonetheless, its creation is effective upon registration when a pledge is over mutual fund units, company shares, accounts receivable or intellectual property rights, such as exclusive use of a registered trademark, patent or copyright. A pledge over accounts receivable occurs when a company uses its accounts receivable as collateral for a loan or other financial arrangement.

However, no uniform registration authority and procedures exist for creating a pledge. For example, where a pledge is over company shares in a limited liability company or a company limited by shares, the Administration for Market Regulation is the responsible registration authority.[13] However, a pledge over a listed company shares can be registered at the securities depository and clearing institution.[14] While a pledge over a patent or a registered trademark is registered at the National Intellectual Property Administration, a pledge over a copyright is with the National Copyright Administration.[15] It is important to note that under the Unified Registration Measures for Chattel and Property Rights Security issued by the People's Bank of China (PBOC) on 1 February 2022, pledges over production equipment, raw materials, semi-finished products and finished products, pledges over accounts receivable and pledges over deposit certificates, warehouse receipts and bills of lading are registered with the PBOC Credit Reference Center.[16]

In practice, it is common to encounter situations where a pledge contract over company shares has been signed but the pledge registration was not processed after that. In this case, does the pledgor still bear legal responsibility? If so, what kind?

[12] Para. 1 of Article 59 SPC Interpretation on the Security System.

[13] The Administrative Measures for the Pledge Registration of Equity, issued on 1 September 2008 and revised on 29 April 2016 and most recently revised on 31 December 2020.

[14] See the Securities Registration and Settlement Management Measures. This institution plays a crucial role in the securities market by facilitating the registration, transfer and settlement of securities transactions.

[15] Article 2 of the Copyright Pledge Registration Measures, effective 1 January 2011; Article 2 of the Patent Pledge Registration Measures, effective 15 November 2021; Article 1 of the Registered Trade Work Pledge Registration Measures, effective 1 May 2020.

[16] Article 2 Unified Registration Measures for Chattel and Property Rights Security.

Pledge registration is a mandatory step to record the pledge over company shares with the competent registration authority, ensuring that the creditor can effectively exercise their rights in case of any transfer of the pledged shares or default events. The pledge is not legally effective without proper pledge registration, and the creditor may face difficulties in enforcing their pledge rights based on the pledge. However, the failure to register the pledge of shares does not affect the validity of the pledge contract. In other words, the pledge contract remains effective. If the pledgor fails to register the pledge over company shares as agreed, it bears the liability for breach of contract unless the pledgor can prove that they have valid grounds for exemption from such liability. The extent of liability the pledgor should bear is based on the contract terms, extent of fault, contractual expectations and other relevant circumstances specified in the pledge contract.

In *Guizhou Shangchu Shengji Warehouse Logistics Co., Ltd v. Liu*, the respondent undertook a pledge in the appellant's favour to secure a debtor loan.[17] The pledged asset is a holding of a 10 per cent stake in a company valued at 10 million RMB when the pledge agreement was signed. The respondent did not proceed with the pledge registration or notify the appellant to handle the pledge registration on his behalf. Due to the debtor's failure to repay the debt on time, the appellant filed a lawsuit claiming that the respondent took responsibility for the undertaken security.

The SPC held that the pledge was not established due to failing to complete the pledge registration.[18] The pledgee does not enjoy a priority right to be repaid from the pledged shares. Although the pledge was not created, the agreement between both parties is a genuine expression of their mutual intent and, therefore, valid. Consequently, there is a pledge contractual relationship between the parties.[19] According to contractual stipulations, the respondent is responsible for applying to register to create the pledge. The failure of registration has resulted in the appellant being unable to enjoy priority repayment rights under the pledge. This constitutes a breach of contract, and the respondent should bear liability for the breach.

[17] 贵州商储胜记仓物流有限公司诉刘某 [*Guizhou Shangchu Shengji Warehouse Logistic Co., Ltd vs. Liu*] (2019) 最高法民再202号 [(2019) SPC Min Zai No. 202].

[18] *Ibid.*

[19] *Ibid.*

Further, while the respondent did not complete the pledge registration as agreed, the appellant also failed to provide evidence demonstrating it had sent any notice to the respondent urging the completion of the pledge registration throughout. The appellant remained idle in exercising its right. Considering the various breaches and the degree of fault from all parties involved, the SPC decides that the respondent bears 50 per cent of the liability for the value of the pledged asset for his breach of contract.[20]

While it is generally agreed that a pledgor failing to register the pledge of shares should bear breach-of-contract liability, the extent of such liability differs on a case-by-case basis. In *Li v. Wang*, the parties signed a pledge agreement, but the pledgor failed to complete the registration to create a pledge at law.[21] The Sichuan HPC held that Wang failed to complete the pledge registration, thus improperly evading the pledged collateral responsibility.[22] This caused the loss of Li's pledge rights and frustration with the real security right to safeguard the loan repayment. Therefore, the court did not consider the fault of the pledgee and ruled that the pledgor violated the registration obligation and should bear the entire civil liability.[23] This entire liability approach starkly contrasts with the proportional liability approach taken by the SPC, which considered various breaches and the degree of fault of both parties.

As a matter of practicality, the responsibility for pledge registration is generally assigned to the pledgor, as they are responsible for submitting the application and providing relevant materials. The pledgees often cannot access these materials, as the pledgor owned the pledged property. Therefore, even the SPC has taken a holistic assessment by taking into account both parties' degree of fault in performing the pledge contract. Where the contract explicitly states that the pledgor has the responsibility to handle the pledge registration, imposing the duty of notice on the pledgee and determining a 50 per cent liability seem unfair. The proportion of fault distribution in the SPC case is worth reconsidering. Likewise, the Sichuan HPC approach is worth revisiting because such an entire liability approach was reasoned as if the registration had been completed. In other words, with or without registration, the pledgor faces the same legal consequences: the full pledge liability as agreed in the pledge

20 *Ibid.*

21 李某诉王某 [*Li v. Wang*] (2018) 川民再790号 [(2018) Chuan Min Zai No. 790].

22 *Ibid.*

23 *Ibid.*

contract. Such an entire liability approach may further incentivise the parties not to complete the registration.

Another thorny issue concerning the pledge over company shares is that the share price fluctuates over time. There is a good chance of a significant difference in value between when the pledge agreement was signed and when the dispute arose. While the SPC adopted a 50 per cent portion of liability, it determines the price as fixed when the pledge contract has been signed. This makes sense to secure a loan with an ascertained amount absent any agreement to the contrary between the parties. This is because the parties intended to provide the security to ensure the loan repayment. If the loan amount is fixed, the parties' common intention can be inferred to cover the loan amount. However, where the loan amount is not fixed, it is suggested that the parties make a provision in the contract to specify the details.

Several solutions are proposed. First, it is recommended that the pledge contract over company shares explicitly stipulates the consequences for the pledgor's failure to complete the pledge registration as a breach of contract. This will encourage the parties to complete the required registration formality and stipulate the agreed remedies if this contractual obligation is breached. If the pledge agreement is silent on this, the risk of uncertain judicial outcomes rises. Second, the pledgees are recommended to promptly notify the pledgor to complete the pledge registration under the contract. This would alleviate or exempt its liability when a dispute arises later when realising the pledge right. Third, the pledgees and pledgors are recommended to agree in the pledge agreement on the calculation basis for the pledged share value as of a specified reference date. If there are no specified details in the agreement, the courts can conduct the calculation without any contractual basis but instead follow the trade usage and common market practice in the same industry. The determined price value may be leaning against the pledgee in favour of the pledgor because the pledgee can protect itself by incorporating such a provision in the pledge contract to secure a loan in its favour. If the pledgee did not take active steps to provide such a provision to protect its own interests, neither should the courts.

A pledgor and a pledgee may agree to create a maximum amount pledge (MAP).[24] The MAP is intended to secure future, continuous and unspecified claims. Before the MAP is determined, the pledgee and the

[24] Para. 1 of Article 439 CC.

pledgor can negotiate to change the period for confirming the claims, the scope of the claims and the maximum amount of the claims. However, it should not adversely affect other rights holders. Determining the claims secured by the MAP refers to Article 423 of the CC. After determining the claims, the MAP is consistent with an ordinary pledge.[25] Claims arising after that are no longer included in the scope of the security provided by the MAP.

10.2.2 Exercising the Pledge

Once a pledge is created, the pledgee can directly or indirectly possess the pledged property. If possession is lost due to no fault of the pledgee, the pledgee can request the possessor to cease infringement, restore the original state and return the property. In addition, the pledgee is entitled to collect the fruits of the pledged property unless the pledge contract stipulates otherwise.[26] The collected fruits are used to offset the costs of collecting the fruits first[27] and then be used to satisfy the pledge, with any remainder returned to the pledgor.

During the pledge period, if the pledged property is likely to be damaged or destroyed or its value may be significantly reduced for reasons not attributable to the pledgee, and such damage is determined to be sufficient to infringe the pledgee's right, the pledgee can claim against the pledgor to provide additional security. If the pledgor fails to provide such, the pledgee may dispose of the pledged property by auction or sale and agree with the pledgor to have the debt repaid in advance by the proceeds of the auction or sale or to escrow the proceeds.[28]

During the period of the pledge, if the pledgee uses or disposes of the pledged property[29] or transfers the pledge[30] without the consent of the pledgor, causing damage to the pledgor, the pledgee is liable for compensation. A dispute arises over the re-pledging of the same property to a third party, the second pledgee. The pledgor cannot set up another security on the same movable without the pledgee's consent. If the pledgor violates this provision and re-pledges the same property, the

[25] Para. 2 of Article 439 CC.
[26] Para. 1 of Article 430 CC.
[27] Para. 2 of Article 430 CC.
[28] Article 433 CC.
[29] Article 431 CC.
[30] Article 434 CC.

subsequent pledge is invalid, and the original pledgee retains the priority right to repayment. However, what is the legal consequence if the pledgee consents to re-pledge? In practice, when a pledgee allows the pledgor to use the pledged property for external financing to satisfy the creditor's claim, a situation arises where both parties claim rights over the proceeds from the auction or sale of the pledged property. Which one's claim prevails over the other? The CC does not address this, so it is necessary to examine the judicial practice.

In *Xiong Weijie v. Peng Xin*,[31] on 12 December 2013, Panxing Company signed a loan agreement with Peng Xin, the defendant, borrowing 30 million yuan. On the same day, Hongchang Company, the pledgor, provided a pledge for the involved pledged property and signed a pledge contract with the defendant.[32] Four months later, the pledgor signed a loan agreement with Xiong Weijie, the claimant, borrowing 20 million yuan. Hongchang Company signed a pledge agreement with the claimant on the same day. Therefore, the claimant is the second pledgee and the defendant is the first pledgee. Subsequently, the first pledgee, Peng Xi, applied to the Chengdu Railway Intermediate Court to enforce the pledged property by an effective court judgment.[33] The Chengdu Railway Intermediate Court lawfully sealed the pledged property and issued a seizure order.[34] Later, the pledged property stored at the pledgor was transferred to a new premise, Warehouse No. 1. Both the claimant and defendant individually locked the door of Warehouse No. 1 and arranged for security guards. On 15 April 2015, the claimant objected to judgment enforcement, arguing that the seized goods were pledged to him by Hongchang Company. The Chengdu Railway Intermediate Court dismissed the claim.[35] The claimant appealed to the Sichuan HPC.

The Sichuan HPC held that the claimant, the second pledgee, holds a pledge over the pledged goods.[36] The claimant and Hongchang Company

[31] 熊伟杰诉彭鑫 [*Xiong Weijie v. Peng Xin*] (2016) 川71民初12号民事判决 [(2016) Chuan 71 Min Chu No. 12].

[32] *Ibid.*

[33] 彭鑫诉熊伟杰 [*Peng Xin v. Xiong* Weijie] (2014) 成铁执字第244号《执行通知书》 [(2014) Cheng Tie Zhi Zi No. 244 Enforcement Notice].

[34] *Ibid.*

[35] 熊伟杰诉彭鑫 [*Xiong Weijie v. Peng Xin*] (2016) 川71民初12号民事判决 [(2016) Chuan 71 Min Chu No. 12 Civil Judgment].

[36] 熊伟杰诉彭鑫 [*Xiong Weijie v. Peng Xin*] (2018) 川民终572号 [(2018) Chuan Min Zhong No. 527].

signed a pledge agreement, delivered the goods, and controlled and possessed the pledged property in Warehouse 1 with a padlock. Therefore, the claimant's pledge has been legally established. Further, the claimant can realise the pledge he holds. The transfer of possession of chattels is a prerequisite to exercising a pledge right.[37] Only when the pledgee possesses the pledged property can the risks associated with the pledge as collateral be minimised and the function of the pledge as security be fulfilled. If the pledgee returns the pledged property to the pledgor, there is a risk that the mortgage rights may be difficult to exercise due to the mortgagee's loss of control over the pledged property. This risk arises from the pledgee's abandonment of control over the pledged property and should be borne by the pledgee. After the defendant, the first pledgee, returned the pledged property to the pledgor Hongchang Company, his pledge lost publicity.[38] As a third party, the claimant cannot identify that the defendant had established an earlier pledge on the involved goods. In this case, in the absence of evidence proving any fault or negligence on the part of the second pledgee, he is considered a bona fide third party. Hence, the first pledgee's assertion of pledge rights over the involved goods cannot prevail against the bona fide third party, specifically the second pledgee's security right. Therefore, the claimant can realise the pledge he holds.[39]

It can be seen from the above case that the current Chinese law position is that if the first pledgee consented to create a second pledge by transferring the possession of the same pledged property, the second pledgee's claim would prevail over the first pledgee's as it was taken as a bona fide third party. There will be no publicity of the first pledge when the possession of the pledged movable property is transferred.

The pledgee must keep the pledged property in good custody; otherwise, the pledgee is liable for compensation for the damaged or destroyed pledged property.[40] Where the pledgee's conduct is likely to damage or destroy the pledged property, the pledgor has the right to claim against the pledgee to escrow it or to return it by repaying the debt in advance.[41] From the pledgee's perspective, the law imposes burdens and compensation liability on the pledgee regarding safeguarding and upkeeping the

[37] *Ibid.*
[38] *Ibid.*
[39] *Ibid.*
[40] Para. 1 of Article 432 CC.
[41] Para. 2 of Article 432 CC.

movables in commercial transactions. If the pledgee's improper custody damages the pledged property, the pledgee is liable for compensation. If the pledge is extinguished, the pledgee's debt becomes an unsecured ordinary debt. The same obligation applies to the transferee of the pledge. Also, the pledgee cannot freely use the pledged property without consent from the pledgor. In other words, the efficient use of the pledged property is severely restricted.

On the other hand, establishing a pledge over movables requires delivery of the pledged property to the pledgee. As such, the pledgor loses its possession and use during the pledge. Given this rule design, the pledge over moveables has gradually lost its popularity in practice.

In cases of pledges involving bills, bonds, deposit certificates, warehouse receipts or bills of lading, if the maturity or delivery date precedes the expiration of the main creditor's right, the pledgee is entitled to honour or claim for delivery and enter into an agreement with the pledgor to have the debt repaid by the proceeds of honour or delivery or to escrow such proceeds.[42] The right of the pledgor to dispose of the pledged right is restricted to protect the interests of the pledgee. A complete prohibition could increase the transaction cost and limit the use of the pledged property. Hence, the CC reasonably limits this. The pledgor cannot transfer the rights without the pledgee's consent for pledges involving fund shares, equity, intellectual property rights and accounts receivable.[43] However, the pledgee and pledgor may agree to transfer the pledged right, but the proceeds must be used to settle the debt in advance or be escrowed.[44]

10.2.3 *Realising the Pledge*

Where the debtor performs the obligation or the pledgor pays the secured debt to the pledgee in advance, the pledgee returns the pledged property.[45] As with the mortgage rules, the pledgee cannot directly acquire the title of the pledged property when exercising the right to realise the pledge. Where an agreement exists that the pledged property shall be owned by the creditor when the debtor fails to perform the due

[42] Article 442 CC.

[43] Articles 443, 444 and 445 CC.

[44] Baoyu Liu [刘保玉], 'Suggestions for Improving the Pledge System in China' [《完善我国质权制度的建议》] (2017) 6 *Modern Law Science* [《现代法学》] 56.

[45] Para. 1 of Article 436 CC.

debt, the pledgee can have the debt repaid with priority only to the extent of the value of the pledged property.[46] In cases of the debtor's non-performance of the due debt or other circumstances of enforcing the pledge as agreed, the pledgee may agree with the pledgor to have the debt repaid by converting the pledged property into money or by the proceeds of an auction or sale.[47] If the amount of money obtained through trade-in, auction or sale of the pledged property is higher than the amount of the secured debt, the excess belongs to the pledgor.[48] If there is an outstanding debt after the repayment, the debtor shall pay the debt to the pledgee.[49]

Where the parties fail to agree to realise the pledge, does the pledgee notify the pledgor before auctioning or selling the pledged property? Neither the CC nor the SPC Interpretation on Security System answers this. The pledgee already possesses the pledged property and holds a favourable position in realising the pledge. To better balance the interests between the pledgor and the pledgee, it is recommended to provide the pledgor with an opportunity to substitute the debtor's performance of the obligation or terminate the pledge through other means. Guided by the principle of good faith, the pledgee should notify the pledgor before auctioning or selling the pledged property. However, this notification requirement may be waived if the pledgee cannot provide such notice.

In the case of an auction or sale of the pledged property, it is carried out by reference to the market price.[50] The market price of the pledged property, whether movables or intangible rights, fluctuates over time. Suppose the pledged property is devalued or the proceeds from auctioning or selling the pledged property are lower than the agreed value set when the pledge was established. In that case, the prevailing market value of the pledged property at the time of realisation will settle. The debtor should cover the shortfall. In the absence of an agreement between the parties, the proceeds from the devaluation or auctioning/selling of the pledged property are settled in the following order: (1) expenses incurred in realising the pledge; (2) interest on the principal debt; (3) the principal debt.

[46] Article 428 CC.
[47] Para. 2 of Article 436 CC.
[48] Article 438 CC.
[49] *Ibid.*
[50] Para. 3 of Article 436 CC.

Generally, the realisation of the pledge is a right of the pledgee rather than an obligation. However, since the pledged property is under the control of the pledgee, its value may fluctuate in the market. The pledged property is, therefore, subject to the risk of a decrease in value or unexpected loss. The failure of the pledgee to timely exercise its rights may lead to a decrease in the value of the pledged property or other damaging events, such as destruction or loss, rendering the pledged property unable to realise its original appraised value. For example, if the pledged property was expected to have a surplus after clearing the debt, the surplus might be lost. If the appraised value was originally sufficient to cover the debt, it may no longer be adequate. If the pledged property was initially capable of covering a significant portion of the debt, it might now only be enough to cover a small fraction. In such cases, while the delayed exercise of rights by the pledgee may result in a diminished ability to recover the debt, it also causes financial losses for the pledgor. The law encourages pledgees to exercise their rights to mitigate these risks or harms timely. Specifically, Article 437 of the CC stipulates the legal responsibility for the pledgee's failure to exercise the pledge right timely[51]:

> The pledgor may request the pledgee to exercise the right of pledge promptly after the debt becomes due. If the pledgee fails to exercise this, the pledgor may ask the People's Court for a People's Court-ordered auction or sale of the pledged property. Where the pledgee has received notice from the pledgor to exercise the right promptly but neglects to exercise the right, causing damage to the pledgor, the pledgee shall be liable for compensation.

When the debt is not fully repaid upon the expiration of the performance period, the pledgee has the discretion to either continue retaining the pledged property to compel the debtor to fulfil the obligation, negotiate with the pledgor for a discounted settlement involving the pledged property or auction/sell the pledged property to prioritise repayment with its proceeds. It is the creditor's right to choose the appropriate course of action, and the pledgee is not obliged to exercise the pledge right in any specific manner initially. However, if, upon the expiration of the debt performance period, the pledgor requests the creditor to exercise the right timely, and the creditor's failure to do so results in a decrease in the value of the pledged property, the creditor should be held liable for

[51] Article 437 CC.

the resulting loss and may be required to compensate the pledgor for the damages incurred due to the delayed exercise of rights.

The pledgor must first initiate a request for the pledgee to exercise the pledge right promptly. The expiration date of the debt performance period is crucial because the pledgor can only request a timely exercise of right upon or after the expiration date of the performance period.[52] Subsequently, evidence should demonstrate that the harm incurred resulted from the pledgee's delay in exercising the pledge right. The facts of the damage should have a causal relationship with the pledgee's failure to exercise the pledge right.

This underscores the importance of the pledgor actively communicating and urging the pledgee to take timely action. The subsequent evidence should establish a clear link between the pledgee's inaction and the resulting harm suffered by the pledgor. The right to resort to legal recourse granted to the pledgor by requesting the court to auction or sell the pledged property achieves the equilibrium of interests of both the pledgor and the pledgee in the realisation process.

The pledgee has the right to waive the pledge.[53] The pledgee can explicitly waive the pledge right. However, if the pledgee returns the pledged property to the pledgor, does it automatically extinguish the pledge? As shown in *Xiong Weijie v. Peng Xin*, the Chinese judicial approach is that if the pledgee returns the pledged property to the pledgor, the pledgee cannot allege against bona fide third parties based on the pledge. However, it does not explicitly state whether the pledge right is completely extinguished. Since one of the prerequisites for establishing a pledge is delivery of possession to the pledgee, returning the pledged property means losing possession by the pledgee. Thus, returning or abandoning the pledged property should be considered the pledgee waiving the pledge right.

If the debtor pledges its own property and the pledgee waives this pledge right, other guarantors are released from the guarantee liability within the scope of the pledgee's loss of priority for repayment.[54] However, this exemption from guarantee liability does not apply to other guarantors who have explicitly committed to continuing to provide guarantees.[55]

[52] Para. 1 of Article 437 CC.
[53] Article 435 CC.
[54] *Ibid.*
[55] *Ibid.*

10.2.4 Priority of Claims

Where both a pledge over warehouse receipts and a pledge over the stored goods of the warehouse exist against the same pledgor, there is an issue of priority. Priority is determined by the order of publicity (registration or delivery). If it is difficult to determine, the order is based on the proportion of the debt.[56] Suppose the custodian issues multiple warehouse receipts for the same goods, and the pledgor establishes multiple pledge rights on different warehouse receipts. In that case, the repayment order shall be determined according to the order of publicity. If it is difficult to determine the order, repayment shall be made in proportion to the amount of the debt.[57] Therefore, assessing the priority of the pledge concerning other existing security interests or creditors depends on the timing of registration and delivery. Where the creditor provides evidence to prove that their losses are caused by the joint actions of the pledgor and the custodian, the pledgor and the custodian assume joint and several liability.[58]

10.2.5 Pledge over Accounts Receivable

The pledge over accounts receivable is a focal point for Chinese property law scholars, mainly because it involves the connection with rules related to the transfer of claims. It is the most widespread form of guarantee in commercial practice. Unlike a pledge over movables, a pledge over accounts receivable is a popular financing security method due to its simple registration process and relatively light financing burden. The CC, for the first time at the legislative level, stipulates that accounts receivable include both existing and future such accounts.[59] However, the CC does not legally define accounts receivable. Its definition is provided in a departmental rule issued by the People's Bank of China. The Measures for Unified Registration for Movables and Rights Security states:

> Accounts receivable refers to the right of an accounts receivable creditor to demand payment from the accounts receivable debtor due to the provision of certain goods, services, or facilities. This includes the right

[56] Para. 2 of Article 59 SPC Interpretation on the Security System.
[57] Para. 3 of Article 59 SPC Interpretation on the Security System.
[58] Para. 4 of Article 59 SPC Interpretation on the Security System.
[59] Item 6 of Article 440 CC.

> to receive existing and future monetary claims but excludes payment claims arising from bills or other negotiable securities and payment claims prohibited from transfer according to laws or administrative regulations.[60]

Specifically, this departmental rule provides a list of account receivables including (1) claims arising from sales or leases, including the sale of goods, provision of water, electricity, gas, heating, licensing of intellectual property rights and leasing of chattels or real estate; (2) claims arising from the provision of services or labour in areas such as healthcare, education and tourism; (3) rights to income from infrastructure and public utility projects in areas such as energy, transportation, water conservancy, environmental protection and municipal engineering; (4) claims arising from the provision of loans or other credit activities; and (5) other contract-based monetary claims.

Existing accounts receivable mainly refer to monetary claims that can be determined or specific amounts of accounts receivable from the debtor when creating a pledge. According to the SPC Interpretation on the Security System, future accounts receivable mainly include income rights from infrastructure and public utility projects, claims arising from providing services or labour, and other future accounts receivable.[61] Before the implementation of the CC, relevant cases had already recognised income rights from sewage treatment projects,[62] electricity revenue rights[63] and gas project revenue rights[64] as objects of accounts receivable pledges. The SPC further explains that future accounts receivable refer to monetary claims from the debtor or the pledged subject that are not yet determined or specific at the time of pledging. This includes real estate charging rights, other chargeable rights that can be pledged according to law, and other

[60] Para. 1 of Article 3 Measures for Unified Registration for Movables and Rights Security.

[61] Para. 4 of Article 61 SPC Interpretation on the Security System.

[62] 最高人民法院指导案例 53 号: 福建海峡银行股份有限公司福州五一支行诉长乐亚新污水处理有限公司、福州市政工程有限公司 [SPC Guiding Case No. 53: *Fujian Haixia Bank Co., Ltd., Fuzhou Wuyi Branch, Changle Yaxin Sewage Treatment Co., Ltd v. Fuzhou Municipal Engineering Co.*].

[63] 青海西宁农村商业银行股份有限公司与白恩青、青海永丰化工建材有限责任公司 [*Qinghai Xining Rural Commercial Bank v. Bai Enqing & Qinghai Yongfeng Chemical Construction Materials Ltd., Co.*] ⑵016⑹ 最高法民终341号 [(2016) SPC Min Zhong No. 341].

[64] 中国工商银行股份有限公司桑植支行与桑植裕轮远航燃气工程有限公司、重庆市中宝投资（集团）股份有限公司等 [*ICBC Limited, Sangzhi Branch and Sangzhi Yulun Long-distance Voyage Gas Engineering Co., Ltd v. Chongqing Zhongbao Investment (Cooperation) Co., Ltd etc.*] ⑵016⑹ 湘民终324号 [(2016) Xiang Min Zhong No. 324].

future accounts receivable for pledging.[65] Under the principle of *numerus clausus*, recognising the accounts receivables pledge in the CC aligns with past judicial practices. It invigorates the accounts receivable pledging business, expanding the financing space for enterprises.

To create an accounts receivable pledge, three requirements need to be met. First, there must be specificity of the accounts receivable. Second, following the publicity principle of property rights, it is necessary to obtain the public and credible effect of property rights against third parties. Third, the collateral must be transferable. This involves meeting the accounts receivable's retention requirements and control as collateral. Only when the claim is transferable can the pledgee step in the pledgor's shoes in collecting the accounts receivable from the underlying debtor. Claims that are non-assignable by nature, prohibited from assignment by specific agreement or subject to the prohibition of attachment cannot be pledged. Regarding transferability, the *Measures of Unified Registration for Movables and Rights Security* includes the catch-all provision under "other transferable claims," which inherently encompasses the transferability requirement for accounts receivable.

Accounts receivable, as a subject of security interest, are related to a specific right. In the legal relationship of an accounts receivable pledge, three parties are involved: the pledgee, the pledgor/accounts receivable creditor and the accounts receivable debtor. Although the accounts receivable debtor is a party in realising the pledge, it is not a party to the contract, and establishing an accounts receivable pledge is not contingent on notifying the debtor.[66] This has proven to be problematic. However, when considering accounts receivable as the subject of a security interest, inherent challenges may arise from defences raised by the debtor. Very often, the debtor may challenge that the accounts receivable does not exist or assert defences against the pledgor's rights claimed by the pledgee.

[65] Wenxue Lin, Yongqing Yang, Jinliang Ma and Guangrong Wu [林文学、杨永清、麻锦亮、吴光荣], 'Understanding and Application of the Interpretation on the Application of Relevant Guarantee Systems in the CC' [《<关于适用民法典有关担保制度的解释>的理解和适用》] (2021) 4 *Legal Application* [《法律适用》] 30.

[66] 梅劲松与金元顺安基金管理有限公司、上海光大证券资产管理有限公司 [*Mei Jinsong, Jinyuan Shunan Fund Management Co., Ltd. v. Shanghai Guangda Securities Asset Management Co., Ltd.*] (2018)苏民终638号 [(2018) Su Min Zhong No. 638]; 神雾科技集团股份有限公司等与南京银行股份有限公司北京分行 [*Shenwu Environmental Technology Co., Ltd etc v. Bank of Nanjing Co., Ltd Beijing Branch*] (2019) 京民终86号 [(2019) Beijing Min Zhong No. 86].

Under the current legal regime, verification is required to ensure that the pledgee can exercise its rights without being challenged by the debtor.[67] It needs to be confirmed that the pledgor of the accounts receivable has fulfilled its obligations under the underlying contracts with its debtor, such as delivering goods or providing services. When the underlying debtor has not fulfilled its payment obligations, the pledgor has the right to claim the agreed payments from the debtor. Future accounts receivable require a commitment from the underlying debtor. Even though the accounts receivable have not yet arisen when establishing the pledge, the right is expected to arise in the future, and the underlying debtor commits not to exercise defences against the pledgor in the future.

The accounts receivable pledge is established when the parties sign a valid written accounts receivable pledge contract and register the pledge. The pledge right is established once the accounts receivable pledge registration is completed.[68] The *Measure for Unified Registration for Movables and Rights Security* specifies that "the Credit Reference Center of the People's Bank of China is the registration authority for chattel and property rights security, responsible for specific service-oriented registration work, without conducting prior approval registration, and not conducting the substantive examination of the registration content."[69] This provision explicitly states that the Credit Reference Center of the People's Bank of China is only responsible for service-oriented registration work and does not conduct substantive examination of the registration content, thereby assigning the responsibility of reasonably identifying the truthfulness and speciality of the account receivables to the parties.[70] Therefore, selecting genuine and enforceable accounts receivable and registering them effectively is crucial for the pledgee.

A question arises whether a notification is sufficient to defeat the potential defence the accounts receivable debtor raises, given that the pledgee is responsible for conducting a substantive review to verify. In *Mizuho Bank (China) Co. Ltd. v. Shanghai Baihong Trading Co. Ltd.*, Mizuho Bank entered into a revolving credit agreement with

[67] Article 61 SPC Interpretation on the Security System.
[68] Article 445 CC.
[69] Article 4 Measure for Unified Registration for Movables and Rights Security.
[70] Article 53 SPC Interpretation on the Security System.

Shanghai Baihong.[71] On 20 March 2019, the parties signed a pledge agreement, providing pledge security for the receivables from transactions between Shanghai Baihong and its trading partners for a certain period. The future accounts receivables involved were properly registered. After registration, the plaintiff sent the receivables pledge notices to each receivable debtor. Later, Shanghai Baihong failed to repay the principal and interest as agreed. When Shanghai Baihong entered bankruptcy liquidation proceedings, Mizuho Bank filed a lawsuit seeking the priority right on the pledge to be paid from the receivables. Shanghai Baihong has no disputes regarding the facts and claims of the plaintiff. However, the accounts receivable debtors raised the defence that they did not receive the receivables pledge notices, and each company has terminated cooperation with Shanghai Baihong. In addition, two debtors counter that they have agreed to settle the relevant claims and debts with Shanghai Baihong. Another two debtors acknowledge the existence of outstanding amounts to be settled but claim offsetting mutual debts. The Shanghai Putong Court held that the pledges had been properly registered and lawfully established against the various debtors.[72] Once established, while the legislation does not require notification to the accounts receivable debtors, the pledge will not be effective against the debtors without proper notification.[73] The court reasoned that when a notification has been sent to the accounts receivable debtors, the pledgee needs to request a reply to confirm from the debtors, as happened in this case. However, if the accounts receivable debtors did not send a reply as requested and subsequently the pledgee did not follow up to communicate with the debtors, the pledge cannot gain priority over the subsequent set-off dealings between the pledgor and the debtors.[74] This is in line with Article 61 of the SPC Interpretation on Security System, which requires a confirmation from the accounts receivable debtors.

While the CC is silent on the notification requirement to the debtor in the accounts receivable pledges, the judiciary maintains that notification to the debtor is required. In other words, establishing an accounts

[71] 瑞穗银行（中国）有限公司与上海百红商业贸易有限公司案 [*Mizuho Bank (China) Co., Ltd. v. Shanghai Baihong Trading Co., Ltd.*]（2020）沪0115民初40268号 [Shanghai Pudong New District People's Court (2020) HU 0115 Min Chu No. 40268].

[72] *Ibid.*

[73] *Ibid.*

[74] *Ibid.*

receivable pledge should require notification to the accounts receivable debtor; otherwise, it would not be legally effective.[75]

The CC does not specify how to realise accounts receivable pledge rights. However, as the accounts receivable pledge falls under the category of rights pledge, the relevant rules of pledge over movables apply to the pledge over rights.[76] These methods include the pledgee and the pledgor agreeing to use the pledged property as a set-off or prioritising the proceeds obtained from auctioning or selling the pledged property.[77] Further, neither the CC nor Article 61 of the SPC Interpretation on the Security System specifies whether the pledgee has the right to demand the debtor to fulfil the obligation directly without going through auction or judicial sale. However, considering the nature of accounts receivable as a monetary debt, the prevailing opinion is inclined to suggest that, after notifying the debtor about the establishment of the accounts receivable pledge and obtaining confirmation from the debtor regarding the truthfulness of the accounts receivable, when the conditions for realising the accounts receivable pledge are met, the pledgee has the right to demand the debtor directly pay the accounts receivable to them and enjoy the priority right to be satisfied from the accounts receivable.[78] This judicial approach has been confirmed in an SPC guiding case – *Fujian Haixia Bank Co., Ltd., Fuzhou Wuyi Branch*

[75] 程晓春与重庆文化产业融资担保有限责任公司 [*Cheng Xiaochun v. Chongqing Stated Culture Assets Administration Co., Ltd.*] (2019) 渝民终325号 [Chongqing HPC (2019) Yu Min Zhong No. 325]; 深圳融易商业保理有限公司、深圳市英维克科技股份有限公司与深圳市中兴康讯电子有限公司 [*Shenzhen Yirong Commercial Factoring Co., Ltd., Shenzhen Envicool Technology Co., Ltd. v. Shenzhen Zhongxing Kangxun Telecommunication Co., Ltd.*] (2016) 粤03民终19804号 [Shenzhen City, Guangdong Province Intermediate People's Court (2016) Yue 03 Min Final No. 19804].

[76] Article 446 CC.

[77] Para. 2 of Article 436 CC.

[78] 最高人民法院指导案例 53 号: 福建海峡银行股份有限公司福州五一支行诉长乐亚新污水处理有限公司、福州市政工程有限公司案 [SPC Guiding Case No. 53: *Fujian Haixia Bank Co., Ltd., Fuzhou Wuyi Branch v. Changle Yaxin Sewage Treatment Co., Ltd and Fuzhou Municipal Engineering Co., Ltd.*] The Court held that revenue rights from sewage treatment projects fall under future monetary debts. In such cases, the pledgee may request the court to order the direct collection of money from the debtor of the pledgor and exercise the priority right to be satisfied from that money. Therefore, there is no need to resort to discounting or sale by auction. Additionally, revenue rights are typically associated with certain obligations, and the operating entity has a specific nature. Therefore, considering the nature of these rights, auctioning or selling is not appropriate. As a result, the pledgee has the right, based on the agreement, to directly collect sewage treatment fees from the transferor of the concessionaire and exercise the priority right to be satisfied from the collected sewage treatment service fees.

v. Changle Yaxin Sewage Treatment Co., Ltd., and Fuzhou Municipal Engineering Co., Ltd.[79] In this ruling, the SPC held that the revenue rights of the sewage treatment project constitute future monetary claims, and the pledgee may request the court to collect money directly from the debtor of the pledgor and exercise priority repayment rights over such money.[80] Therefore, there is no need to adopt a discount or auction/sale method.

Moreover, revenue rights are inherently encumbered, and their operational entity possesses specificity; hence, their nature is unsuitable for auction or sale.[81] This approach can avoid the cumbersome procedures of discounting, auctioning and selling when realising the accounts receivable pledge, reducing the exercise cost for the pledgee and expediting the resolution of disputes between the parties.[82] However, absent explicit means of realising the ledge in the CC, the direct assertion of payment by the pledgee from the debtor is a discretionary remedy exercised by the courts.

According to the SPC Interpretation of Security System, depending on whether the parties set up a specific account for accounts receivable, there are two ways to realise the pledge involving future accounts receivable.[83] When the parties set up a specific account for accounts receivable, the pledgee has the right to request priority satisfaction from the funds in that specific account directly when a statutory or agreed cause for realising the pledge arises. When the funds in the specific account are not sufficient to satisfy the debt or no specific account is set up, the pledgee has the right to request a discount or auction, sale or other means for the future accounts receivable, and the funds obtained shall have priority satisfaction of claims.[84]

Finally, it is recommended that the pledge contract clearly defines events of default and specifies the procedures for realisation. This includes determining whether the pledgee has the right to collect receivables directly from account debtors upon default. Second, it is suggested to establish mechanisms for notifying and monitoring the accounts

[79] *Ibid.*
[80] *Ibid.*
[81] *Ibid.*
[82] Weiheng Zhong [仲伟珩], 'The Practical Difficulties, Systematic Interpretation, and Practical Approaches to Accounts Receivable Pledge Rights' [《应收账款质权的现实困境、体系解释与实务进路》] (2022) 28 *People's Judicature*《人民司法》38.
[83] Para. 4 of Article 61 SPC Interpretation on the Security System.
[84] *Ibid.*

receivable, including regular reporting to the pledgee. The communications between the pledge and the accounts receivable debtors help to ensure that the pledged assets maintain their value and that the pledgee can take prompt action in case of default.

10.3 Lien

10.3.1 Concept and Nature

A lien is a right of retention exercisable by a creditor on the debtor's property, granting the creditor the ability to retain possession until a debt is satisfied.[85] Where the debtor fails to perform the due debt, the creditor is entitled to retain possession of the debtor's movable property, which has already lawfully been in the creditor's possession, and to have the debt repaid with priority to the extent of the value of such movable property.[86] The creditor realises the lien in receiving the proceeds from selling, auctioning or disposing of the property at a discounted price.[87] Therefore, the lien exhibits a dual nature: compelling the debtor to fulfil the obligation and realising the secured debt. Meeting the conditions specified by the law, the lien holder can initially refuse to return the possessed movables. Subsequently, following the legal procedures, they can obtain priority from the proceeds of selling or disposing of the retained property. Since the promulgation of the General Principles of the Civil Law in 1986, the lien has consistently been treated by Chinese law as a real security right by operation of law. The ultimate purpose for a creditor to exercise the lien is to satisfy the debt through the proceeds obtained from the disposition of the retained movable property.

Unlike mortgages and pledges, where the parties must agree to their creation, the lien is a real security right by operation of law. The lien arises based on legal provisions and does not require the parties to agree. However, the parties can agree to exclude the application of the right of retention. Therefore, its scope is strictly defined by law. The lien can only secure existing claims and cannot provide security for claims that may arise in the future.

[85] While under Chinese law a lien may apply to all kinds of contractual relationship, it is notable that a lien cannot be created in the course of an employment contract. See details at 长三角商品交易所有限公司与卢海云 [*YRD Commodity Exchange Co., Ltd. v. Lu Haiyun*] (《最高人民法院公报》2017年第1期 (2014) 锡民终字第1724号) [Notice by the SPC 2017 Issue 1, (2014) Xi Min Zhong Zi No. 1724].

[86] Article 447 CC.

[87] Article 453 CC.

The CC stipulates certain types of liens in some nominate contracts: for example, a lien exercisable by the contractor against the non-payment of remuneration and material costs by an ordering party in a work contract[88]; a lien exercisable by a carrier against a consignor or a consignee's non-payment of carriage and storage fees in a contract for carriage of goods[89]; and a lien exercisable by the depository against a depositor's non-payment of safekeeping fees in a safekeeping contract.[90] These specific lien rights are concrete examples of liens, and their creation, legal consequences and rules for exercising the rights are governed by the provisions under Articles 447–457.

Nonetheless, there are some distinctive liens provided in some specific legislation. For example, the Trust Law provides that after the termination of a trust, the trustee, when exercising the right to claim remuneration or obtain compensation from the trust property according to this law, may retain the trust property.[91] In addition, the Maritime Law includes provisions related to maritime liens. For example, Article 25 (2) stipulates that shipbuilders or repairers can retain the vessels they possess if the other party fails to fulfil the contract, ensuring the right to receive payment for shipbuilding or repair costs.[92] Article 87 outlines the carrier's retention rights in maritime freight contracts, Article 141 specifies the lessor's retention rights, and Article 161 addresses the tugboat operator's retention rights.[93] These provisions constitute special retention rights under commercial laws, not discussed in this chapter.

10.3.2 Creation

A lien is a security right by operation of law and does not require a concluded contract to be created. However, a lien needs to meet the following conditions to be established. First, the creditor must have

88 Article 783 CC: Where the ordering party fails to pay the contractor its remuneration or expenses in relation to the materials, et cetera, unless otherwise agreed by the parties, the contractor is entitled to a lien over, or to refuse to deliver, the work.

89 Article 836 CC: Where the consignor or the consignee fails to pay the carriage, storage or other fees, the carrier is entitled to a lien over the corresponding goods, unless otherwise agreed by the parties.

90 Article 903 CC: Where the depositor fails to pay safekeeping fees or other fees in accordance with the contract, the depository is entitled to have a lien over the deposited item, unless otherwise agreed by the parties.

91 Article 57 Trust Law.

92 Article 25(2) Maritime Law.

93 Articles 87, 141 and 161 Maritime Law.

already legally possessed the debtor's movable property, and retaining such property should not violate mandatory legal provisions or public order and good morals.[94] The lien arises only if the lien holder is in possession of the movable property to which its claim relates and for as long as it retains possession. It is not valid if possession is acquired through unlawful means or infringement. Possession A lien is generally specific to a particular property or assets the creditor possesses and does not extend to the debtor's other assets.

Second, the debt must have reached its maturity for repayment and the debtor has not fulfilled the obligations on time. A lien enables its holder to demand payments owed to it regarding the movable property to which its lien relates when the debt is due to be repaid. Generally, a lien is a defence mechanism and does not give a cause of action.

Third, the retained movable property is not prohibited by law or excluded by the parties' agreement to be the subject matter of a lien.[95] Note that a lien cannot be established on all movable property. If the parties agree not to retain certain specified movable property, and such agreement does not affect public interests or the interests of third parties, the law respects the parties' intention. Some legislation disallows certain movable properties to be subject to a lien. For example, according to Article 37(1) of the Customs Law, customs-supervised goods may not be retained.[96] Also, Article 15(3) of the Resident Identity Card Law stipulates that no organisation or individual may withhold a resident's identity card.[97] Retaining an identity card has the same effect as withholding, and an identity card should be considered as movable property that cannot be retained according to legal provisions. If retaining movable property violates public order or good morals, the creditor is not allowed to retain it. For example, retaining fire trucks would impact public safety. In cases where a carrier transports disaster relief materials for the sake of public interest, the carrier is not allowed to retain the materials.

Fourth, the movable property possessed by the creditor and the debt must be in the same legal relationship. Usually, the possessed movable property must be the debtor's property. If it is the personal property of a

[94] Article 447 and Article 153 CC.

[95] Article 449 CC.

[96] Article 37(1) of the Customs Law provides that customs-supervised goods shall not be unpacked, removed, delivered, shipped, exchanged, modified, pledged, hypothecated, retained, transferred, re-marked, diverted for other uses or otherwise disposed of without the permission of the customs.

[97] Article 15(3) Resident Identity Card Law.

third party, it must be based on the same legal relationship. Retaining a movable property not related to the debt violates the principles of good faith and fairness. Therefore, the same legal relationship limitation is intended to avoid unfettered expansion of the scope of retained property.

Whether a lien can be established on property not owned by the debtor is a contentious issue. In *Shenzhen Kingkey Real Estate Co., Ltd. Kingkey 100 Phase 1 Parking Management Ltd v. Beijing China Auto Renting Inc. Shenzhen Branch*,[98] a vehicle registered under the name of the defendant, Beijing China Auto Renting Inc. Shenzhen Brach, was leased to Huang from 3 May 2012 to 30 December 2012. After the lease term, Huang failed to return the vehicle. On 17 December 2012, the vehicle was parked in the parking lot operated by the plaintiff. The person who parked the car did not pay the parking fee, and the vehicle's tyres were locked. On 5 June 2018, someone from the defendant company drove the vehicle through the exit gate of the plaintiff's parking lot. Subsequently, based on the lien over the involved vehicle, plaintiff filed a lawsuit requesting the court to order defendant and other related subsidiaries to pay parking fees and interest jointly. Defendant argued that there was no contractual relationship with plaintiff. Therefore, the plaintiff has no lien right over the vehicle.

The focal issue in this case is whether the plaintiff has a lien over the vehicle. The first-instance judgment decided that the plaintiff did not possess a right of retention over the property of the defendant and dismissed the plaintiff's lawsuit. The reasoning was that the vehicle was parked during Huang's lease in the parking lot. The party parking the vehicle should be considered the debtor. The plaintiff failed to prove that the defendant is the debtor; therefore, it does not have the lien over the vehicle. The plaintiff filed an appeal, claiming that the defendant violated its right of lien. The second-instance judgment issued by the Shenzhen IPC determined that the plaintiff does have a lien over the vehicle. As a result, the second-instance judgment was in favour of the plaintiff.

The Shenzhen IPC held that the plaintiff's possession of the vehicle in question is based on lawful possession under a contract. In this case, the party with whom the plaintiff formed a contractual relationship is responsible for parking. Even though the specific identity of this person

[98] 深圳市京基房地产股份有限公司京基一百大厦一期停车场、北京神州汽车租赁有限公司深圳分公司 [*Shenzhen Kingkey Real Estate Co., Ltd. Kingkey 100 Phase 1 Parking Management Ltd v. Beijing China Auto Renting Inc. Shenzhen Branch*] (2019) 粤03 民终28944 号民事判决 [Shenzhen IPC (2019) Yue 03 Min Zhong No. 28944].

cannot be ascertained, it does not affect the existence of the contractual relationship. Secondly, the plaintiff has the right to retain the vehicle in question, which the person responsible for parking lawfully possessed. The court reasoned,

> In real life, situations where creditors possess property not owned by the debtor often occur, especially in small-amount contracts, such as storage contracts, which facilitate everyday life. In entering such contracts, requiring creditors to scrutinise whether the property belongs to the debtor would incur significant transaction costs. Furthermore, insisting that creditors can only establish a lien over property owned by the debtor would not be conducive to ensuring transaction security. Therefore, without a clear legislative provision specifying that creditors can only retain property owned by the debtor, the Court held that the parking lot retains the vehicle lawfully possessed by the person responsible for parking. The lien is lawfully established when parking fees have not been paid.

From this landmark case, it appears to be permissible for a lien to be created over a property not owned by a debtor. The SPC has confirmed this approach in its Interpretation on the Security System.[99] The plaintiff needs to satisfy the following requirements to create a lien over a third party's property: (1) the person responsible for parking possesses the vehicle through a leasing arrangement; (2) the plaintiff lawfully possesses the vehicle based on a storage contract; (3) the plaintiff's retention of the vehicle is related to the same contractual relationship as the debt; (4) the plaintiff was unaware of the person responsible for parking lacking the right to dispose of the vehicle at the time of possession.

10.3.3 *Rights and Obligations of the Lien Holder*

The lien holder has the right to retain the movable property, establishing a lawful possession right that can be asserted against the debtor and third parties. The lien holder has the right to collect the fruits of the subject matter of the lien, such as interest.[100] The collected fruits can be used to offset the costs of collecting them first,[101] followed by the settlement of the principal debt's interest and then the principal debt itself.

The lien holder is obligated to safeguard the lien property but has the right to request the debtor to pay necessary custodial expenses to compel

[99] Article 62 SPC Interpretation on the Security System.

[100] Para. 1 of Article 452 CC.

[101] Para. 2 of Article 452 CC.

the debtor's performance.[102] As the lien serves as security, the lien holder can agree with the debtor to discount the lien property if the debtor defaults. Alternatively, the lien holder can auction or sell the lien property to prioritise repayment, taking into account market prices.[103]

Regarding the lien holder's obligations, where the lien property is divisible, the lien holder can only retain items of value equivalent to the secured debt.[104] The lien holder can exercise rights over the entire lien property if indivisible. In addition, the lien holder is prohibited from disposing of or re-pledging the lien property. After the debtor satisfies the debt, the lien is extinguished, and the lien holder must return the lien property. In addition, the lien holder must keep the subject matter of the lien in good custody. Otherwise, the lien holder shall be liable for compensation for the damaged or destroyed subject matter.[105] The standard for good custody is that the holder of the lien should manage the property with care and in a prudent manner. There are different views on how to interpret "a prudent manner." According to the Legislative Affairs Commission of the National People's Congress, as long as the holder of the right of retention does not cause significant intentional damage or loss of the property, it cannot be deemed improper custody.[106] The SPC held that the standard for custody should be based on the concept prevalent in general transactions, using the standard of care possessed by a knowledgeable and experienced person of integrity.[107] This SPC approach is preferred because whether the holder of the right of retention has fulfilled the duty of good custody

[102] Article 83 Guarantee Law. While the Guarantee Law was repealed when the CC came into effect on 1 January 2021, the rule allowing the lien holder to claim the necessary custodial expenses against the debtor remains as a received wisdom. See Weiheng Zhong [仲伟珩], 'Research on Difficult Issues Regarding the Establishment Requirements of Right of Lien' [《留置权成立要件疑难问题研究》] in *Compilation of the First Division of Civil Adjudication of the SPC: Civil Judgment Guidelines and References* [最高人民法院民事审判第一庭编：《民事审判指导与参考》] (Law Press China 2010), pp. 83–84.

[103] Article 453 CC.

[104] Article 450 CC.

[105] Article 451 CC.

[106] Wei Huang [黄薇], *Interpretation of the Property Rights Section CC of the People's Republic of China* [《中华人民共和国民法典物权编解读》] (China Legal Publishing House 2020), p. 816.

[107] Chief Editor of the Leading Group for the Implementation CC by the SPC [最高人民法院民法典贯彻实施工作领导小组主编], *Understanding and Application of the Property Rights Section CC of the People's Republic of China* [《中华人民共和国民法典物权编理解与适用》] (People's Court Press 2020), p. 1296.

should be based on an objective third-party standard rather than a subjective one.[108]

10.3.4 *Realising the Lien*

Upon retaining the property when the debt is due, the creditor should promptly establish the grace period for performance. The commencement of the grace period is calculated from when the debtor receives notice from the creditor. Without proper notification, the creditor is not allowed to exercise the right of retention. If the debtor fails to fulfil the obligation within this period, the creditor can proceed to realise the lien by selling the retained property for priority repayment. Both parties agree upon the grace period; without an agreement, the creditor can unilaterally set a period, but it must not be less than sixty days except where the subject matter of the lien is difficult to keep in good custody, such as the perishables.[109]

If in disagreement on a discount, the creditor can apply for auction or sale without requiring debtor consent or court approval. After prioritised repayment, any surplus should be returned to the debtor.[110] If there is an outstanding debt after the repayment, the outstanding debt shall be paid by the debtor. If complete restitution is impossible, the surplus should be placed in escrow, and fees are deducted from the remaining amount. If the surplus is insufficient to cover all expenses, the creditor retains the right to seek further payment from the debtor.[111]

According to the CC, when multiple security interests coexist on the same moveable property, the priority order for satisfaction is as follows: the lien > registered mortgage or pledge (in the order of public notice time) > unregistered mortgage.[112] There are two explanations for why a lien gains priority against a mortgage or pledge. First, a lien is a security by operation of law, whilst the mortgage or pledge is a security arising from a parties' agreement. The legislative policy is that security rights by operation of law take precedence over security rights derived from an

[108] Liyan Hao [郝丽燕], 'The Commentary on CC Articles 447–452: The Constituent Elements and Effectiveness of a General Lien' [《民法典》第447—452条 （一般留置权的成立要件与效力）评注] (2023) 2 *Nanjing University Law Review* [《南京大学法律评论》] 128.

[109] Article 453 CC.

[110] Article 455 CC.

[111] *Ibid.*

[112] Article 456 CC.

agreement. Second, a lien generally arises because the lien holder has provided goods or services related to the subject matter. Granting a lien a priority will reduce enforcement costs in directly realising the security. The lien holder's actual possession of the subject matter provides the convenience of prioritising the realisation of rights.

A lien is extinguished when the lien holder loses possession of the subject matter of the lien or accepts another security provided by the debtor.[113] It is important to note that a lien will be relinquished if the lien holder voluntarily abandons the possession. If the possession of the movable property is taken away involuntarily – say, being stolen by requisitioned by the government agency – the lien will not be extinguished. In addition, if the lien holder willingly accepts another form of security provided by the debtor in place of the original subject matter, the lien on the initial property may be extinguished. This could happen if the debtor offers a substitute asset or provides an alternative form of collateral. What happens if the lien holder does not accept the new adequate collateral the debtor provides? Given that the lien is a type of real security to secure the repayment of the debt, more likely than not, Chinese courts will uphold the extinguishment of the lien over the initial property, provided the new collateral is adequate to secure the outstanding debt.

113 Article 457 CC.

11

Possession and Expropriation

11.1 Possession

The concept of possession is important in defining and determining property rights.[1] Possessing an object gives the impression to others that the person has a title to the object. It is the starting point in any disputes about the title. Despite a crucial notion, possession has long lacked concise judicial explication in China. Defining possession is difficult, as the concept expands in meaning to adapt to changing social circumstances.[2] It is also not helped by the fact that the CC has omitted defining the term, even though the concept is one of the five major parts of the legislation.

The main legislation governing possession is in Part V of the Property Law Book in the Chinese CC, titled "Possession." Articles 458 to 462 comprise this entire last part of the Property Law Book. It deals mainly with the protection of possession: Article 458 states that possession arising out of a contractual relationship shall be governed by its stipulation or otherwise by the law. Article 459 spells out the compensations that can be sought against a malicious possessor. Article 460 sets out the remedies available to a property holder from a bona fide possessor. Article 461 determines the consequences when the property being maliciously or innocently possessed is destroyed or damaged. Lastly, Article 462 provides the legal rights of a possessor. Remarkably, prescriptive acquisition or adverse possession is not found in Chinese law.

The chapter will begin with a brief discussion of the significance of possession in the property system. This will be followed by examining the fundamental issues in possession: the nature of possession. Next,

[1] Gray Kevin and Gray Susan, *Elements of Land Law* (5th edn, Oxford University Press 2009), pp. 152–154.

[2] Thomas W. Merrill, 'Ownership and possession' In Chang Yun-chien, ed. *Law and Economics of Possession* (Cambridge University Press 2015) pp. 1–4.

different categories of possession will be dealt with in detail concerning its practical use. Lastly, protection of possession will be addressed.

11.1.1 The Significance of Possession

Possession serves as a cornerstone of any property law system. While the term is becoming more abstract in its modern interpretation, possession, as it refers to a factual condition, can offer instant and temporary relief to any title disputes. Without any other indications of legal title, possession can be the first and determinative indicator of where that title should lie.[3] Possession thus takes on a presumptive role as a starting point for determining the rightful owner in any title disputes.

Moreover, possession is a sign to a purchaser that the person possessing the object has a right to sell such object. While for some types of property, a registration system can easily replace the need to rely on possession to ensure the right to the title, a registration system is impracticable for movable objects, such as cell phones and cameras. Thus, purchasers need to rely on possession alone to secure sellers' title to those objects. Because possession is a state of fact, it often takes an auxiliary role in determining property issues.[4] These issues include finder's rights, rights to abandoned objects, and as a determinative factor of title to property with no owners. The property concerned can be a movable or an immovable object,[5] where protective rights of a possessor are available to both movable and immovable objects' possessors.

Last by not least, possession is one way of protecting property. By recognising possession, the law can give owners or other rightful holders adequate means to protect their properties by possession. This protection is a form of self-remedy, allowing the processors to take necessary steps to protect others from infringing their property rights.

[3] Carol M. Rose, 'The Law Is Nine-Tenths of Possession: An Adage Turned on Its Head', in Chang Yun-chien (ed), *Law and Economics of Possession* (Cambridge University Press 2015).

[4] Peng'ao Chang [常鹏翱], 'Normative Analysis of Possessory Act' [《占有行为的规范分析》] (2014) *Science of Law: Journal of Northwest University of Political Science and Law* [《法律科学（西北政法大学学报）》] 106.

[5] As illustrated through Part V of the Property Law Book CC, where both movable and immovable properties are included.

11.1.2 *The Nature of Possession: A Fact or a Right?*

The archaic and limited way to determine the nature of possessory rights is physical control. It was doubtlessly straightforward in determining questions of possession, but it was not without problems. Applied strictly, it would give away a person's rights as a possessor should that person solicit the help of others to hold the objects temporarily. In such a situation, the principal would lose possessory protection of the object when it was in the hands of agents or others in actual possession, since, by handling the object, the person would be considered to have lost possession of it. In this sense, possession was merely occupancy. Hence, physical possession of the object does not necessarily translate to having legal possession of it.

Possession was more than physical control and mere occupancy. To possess something involves having control, physical or not, of the property to the exclusion of others. This meaning changes with circumstances and functions it performs; for example, possession in exchange for property takes a more abstract form, while possession in innocent misappropriation strongly depends on actual possession. The concept is relative.

Being heavily influenced by the civil law tradition, the consensus among the Chinese legal community is that possession is a fact instead of a right.[6] It is a fact that leads to legal rights pertaining to possession. Although the laws protect possessors, wrongful possessors must return the benefits deriving from the property to the property holders.

Possession can have different meanings. First, possession can be understood as a fact of physical control of an object, although it may not attract legal recognition of such control as possession. Second, possession can be understood as a factual circumstance with certain legal consequences.[7] It is widely supported that possession in the Chinese CC mostly takes the second form – possession as a fact with legal consequences,[8] which determines a particular relationship between a person and a thing.[9]

[6] Yun-chien Chang, 'The Economy of Concept and Possession', in Chang Yun-chien (ed), *Law and Economics of Possession* (Cambridge University Press 2015).

[7] Chengxin Peng [彭诚信], 'Re-determination of Possession and Its Practical Application' [《占有的重新定性及其实践应用》] (2009) 27 *Science of Law: Journal of Northwest University of Political Science and Law* [《法律科学（西北政法大学学报）》] 92.

[8] Although the law lays down certain requirements before a person is regarded as a possessor to realise the legal consequences, as shown in Articles 459–462 CC.

[9] Shaokun Fang [房绍坤] and Lan Ma [马兰], 'On Several Issues of Possession' [《论占有的几个问题》] (1999) *Legal System and Social Development* [《法制与社会发展》] 33.

11.1.2.1 Factual Possession (Objective Element)

Under general circumstances, possession takes its natural meaning to stand for the state of being of having physical control or custody of something. The protective function of possession derives mainly from factual possession, as it is hardly available for an indirect possessor or constructive possessor to offer immediate protection of the property without soliciting the factual possessor's help.

To say that factual possession refers to a fact of control exercised on the property must mean that there is factual and effective control of the property. The interpretation of what is considered "factual and effective control" is determined by societal understanding of it, referring to what is constituted in the market. There is no one-size-fits-all approach to determine whether there is "factual and effective control" on a certain property. The interpretation of that term is best understood based on the circumstance. For example, leaving a car in a parking lot will not mean losing possession. Leaving a phone unattended on a table at a local library will mostly be considered a "lost" item. It is affected not only by the proximity between the object and the person but also by the period it is in control of and the nature of the object.

Control of the property must have existed for a certain and continuous period of time. A transient amount of time must not be enough to constitute "control" on the property. It has a quality of consistency. Control must be exclusive. This, however, does not necessarily have to be physical exclusion. It also includes exclusion that arises out of moral and legal standards. Hence, a person does not have to lock up everything to be considered legally in possession of all his assets. The requirement is fulfilled when it is clear to others that the item is in someone's possession. It is enough to show or infer from the circumstances that the item is not abandoned or without a holder. Possessory activities need to be transparent. Although it is not required that a third person know exactly who the factual possessor of a property is, a third person should, by the circumstances, be able to tell that the property belongs to a certain someone and is not just abandoned.

Finally, this factual control does not relate to how the possession comes about. The possessor may be in possession by wrongful means, such as stealing, but that alone does not affect the fact that he becomes a factual possessor if the other elements are satisfied. It must be stressed that although possession may be based on one's legal rights to the property, those property rights and rights as possessors are not directly related. In other words, the rights of possessors, once in legal possession, are available to the property's owner and the thieves in possession.

11.1.2.2 Intention to Possess (Mental Element)

The CC does not specify the constituting element of intention to possess. There used to be a lack of consensus on whether possession requires a mental element.[10] Historically, there were three views. The first view is that there must be an accompanying intention to possess.[11] A different view was that a separate element was unnecessary and that it was enough that such intention could be inferred from actions.[12] The third view held that there was no need for a mental element at all.[13] It is generally taken that the mainstream view is the second view. That is, the action taken to exercise control over an item must be capable of representing an intention to possess to a third person. In other words, intention is implicit in possession. Relevant evidence of animus (intention) is normally left to be inferred from conduct.

It is now commonly viewed that an intention is indeed needed.[14] However, the intention needed to show here is not necessarily that of the legal definition of the term. It emphasises whether there is an intention to possess the item. In other words, whether the person has the legal capacity to act will not restrict the finding of the person having an intention to possess. However, it must be realised that such intention is inferred from the facts and thus would more likely be determined by an objective standard. On the same note, the intention must be understood or taken by a third party, knowing the circumstance.

11.1.3 Categories of Possession

The commonly recognised categories of possession among academics are factual versus constructive possession and rightful versus wrongful

[10] Qinguo Meng [孟勤国], 'Historical Development of the Concept of Possession and the System of Possession in China' [《占有概念的历史发展与我国占有制度》] (1993) *Chinese Social Sciences* [《中国民法》] 75.

[11] Jia'an Liu [刘家安], 'Ambiguities in "Possession": Analysis of the Concept of "Possession" in the Draft Property Law' [《含糊不清的"占有"–〈物权法〉草案"占有"概念之分析》] (2006) *Perking University Law Journal* [《中外法学》] 116.

[12] Shuanggen Zhang [张双根], 'Fundamental Issues of Possession: A Review of Chapter Twenty of the Draft Property Law' [《占有的基本问题 评〈物权法草案〉第二十章》] (2006) 18 *Perking University Law Journal* [《中外法学》] 118.

[13] Fang and Ma (n. 9).

[14] Liming Wang [王利明], *Property Law* [《物权法》]，457.

possession.[15] Determining factual and constructive possession is based on whether control is through physical (actual possession) or other means, such as an agent (constructive possession). The differentiation between rightful and wrongful possession is through their legal basis – that is, whether one has a legal right to possess the item, for example as the owner's right. It must be noted, however, that legislation does not explicitly differentiate between actual and constructive possession.[16]

Although factual possession stresses the person's ability to control the object, the capacity to possess is granted beyond just natural persons. Natural persons have the capacity to possess property. This can be reasonably inferred after considering that possession is defined as a fact. Thus, natural persons are legally capable of being a possessor. Legal persons are also capable of becoming possessors. Properties may come under their possession if the representative of the legal person possesses the property through the prescribed means with authorisation. This also applies to other non-legal persons such as partnerships and unincorporated associations where their status as persons is not legally recognised but may deal with property for the benefit of a group.

11.1.3.1 Rightful Possession v. Wrongful Possession

Rightful possession can be obtained on a legal basis. The legal basis refers to contractual stipulations or statutory provisions.[17] Rightful possessors can legitimately exclude legal owners, as in the case of landlord–tenant relationships. On the other hand, wrongful possession is a general term that refers to possession that lacks legal basis. A finding of wrongful possession is usually made due to a claim filed by the property holder. The rights and liabilities of a wrongful possessor are determined by whether the possessor does so with malicious intent.[18] A wrongful possessor cannot reject a rightful owner's request to exercise the right to

[15] Xihe Li [李锡鹤], 'On Good Faith Possession as Possession with Right' [《论善意占有为有权占有》] (2012) *Law Science* [《法学》] 39.

[16] Yun-chien Chang, 'The Economy of Concept and Possession', in Chang Yun-chien (ed), *Law and Economics of Possession* (Cambridge University Press 2015), pp. 103–125.

[17] Article 458 CC states that as for possession based on contractual relationships, issues of the use, profit, liability for breach and so forth in relation to immovables or movables are governed by contractual stipulations. Where a contractual stipulation does not exist or is equivocal, provisions of law shall apply.

[18] Pingji Shan [单平基], 'Proof of the Right to Compensation for Unauthorized Possession Expenses – A Review of Article 243 of the Property Law of the People's Republic of China' [《无权占有费用求偿权之证成——〈中华人民共和国物权法〉第243条检讨》] (2014) 31 *Legal and Business Studies* [《法商研究》] 63.

demand possession. At the same time, simply because the possession is wrongful does not deprive it of the protection given to persons in possession by law. Persons in wrongful possession can still be protected against others with no rights to the property. The difference in legal protection between the rightful possessor and the wrongful possessor is a matter of degree.

In general, the time limit to pursue claims against malicious possessors is longer than against innocent possessors, and malicious possessors are asked to compensate for the losses caused to the rightful claimant for loss of possession. In contrast, innocent possessors are only responsible for returning the property and profits obtained during the wrongful possession.

11.1.3.2 Bona Fide Possession and Mala Fide Possession

How to differentiate between bona fide possession and malicious possession often attracts fierce discussions. Regarding claims against wrongful possession, the emphasis seems to be placed on the knowledge of the possessor, that is, whether the possessor knows that he is in wrongful possession of others' property.[19] Wrongful possession is presumed to be bona fide unless proven otherwise.[20] For example, malicious possession can be found when it is proved that the wrongful possessor was made aware of his defective right to the property because the rightful owner demanded to return the property.

The significance of differentiating the two lies in the following aspects. First, only a bona fide possessor can invoke the bona fide acquisition rule in Article 311 of the CC to defeat a claim of the original owner. The mala fide possessor cannot. Second, when the possessed property is requested to return to the true owner, the bona fide possessor has no duty to make restitution to the extent that the enriched is no longer enriched.[21] Nonetheless, the malicious possessor must make restitution for the value of the subject matter not diminished. If the returned property diminishes the value, the malicious possessor is liable for compensation to recover the loss of value.[22] Third, where the true owner claims against the possessor and asks for the return of the property and its fruits, the true owner pays the bona fide possessor the expenses necessarily incurred for maintaining the property. However, the malicious possessor cannot

[19] *Ibid.*
[20] Li (n. 15).
[21] Article 986 CC.
[22] Article 987 CC.

claim against the necessary maintenance expenses.[23] Fourth, a mala fide possessor is liable for compensation if she causes damage to the property when she possesses and uses the property.[24] A possessor is responsible for returning "the insurance money, damages or indemnities obtained from the said destruction of loss to the holder" when the property has been damaged or is lost.[25] However, the CC only requires a malicious possessor to be "liable for additional compensations where the damage suffered by the right holder is not adequately compensated."[26] Thus, it can be inferred that the CC purposely excuses bona fide possessors from needing additional compensation.

11.1.3.3 The Assistant in Possession: Occupation

In many situations, a person comes in possession of an item not because of one's rights to the property but for the assistance provided to a person with rights to the property, such as in an employment relationship. In these cases, the assistant uses the property for the sole benefit of the persons with rights to the property and is obliged to handle the property based on the directions of the person with rights to the property. The person in actual control of the property can be said to be the person directing the assistant rather than the assistant himself. An assistant does not earn a status as a possessor. The assistant is better understood as occupying the property instead of possessing it.[27] This is because the assistant does not have any ties with the property: as the assistant does not profit from possession of the item, such profits belong solely to the persons the assistant is acting for. Therefore, the law does not offer separate protection for assistants. An assistant is different from an agent, where an agent is given certain freedom in dealing with the property. Because the assistant is taken as an occupier of the property, it is inappropriate for others to claim against the assistant for possession-related matters. At the same time, the person directing the assistant can resort to legal remedies if the assistant refuses to return the property.

Of particular importance is the relationship between the assistant and the principal. The key factor is the assistant's purpose in handling the

[23] Article 460 CC.
[24] Article 459 CC.
[25] Article 461 CC.
[26] *Ibid.*
[27] Hongliang Wang [王洪亮], 'Reconstruction of the Legal System of Possession' [《占有法律制度重构》] (2017) 25 *Journal of National Prosecutors College* [《国家检察官学院学报》] 27.

property: Is it for the sole benefit of the principal and under the sole direction of the principal? Since factual possession requires that a third person can reasonably infer that the person is in factual possession, it must be obvious to a third party that the assistant in the occupation of the property has such a relationship with the principal. It is not a requirement that the assistant must be in a financially inferior position. For example, a business owner in financial difficulties may be in debt to his employees, but this does deprive the owner of her status as the rightful possessor.

11.1.4 Recovery of Possession

A property holder has a right to recovery of possession of the property. This is a right belonging to the holder against both bona fide and malicious possessors. The law only grants the right to seek compensation to the owner of real or personal property against a possessor with malicious intent.[28] However, a possessor acting in good faith and causing damage to the possessed property through its use is not obligated to bear liability for damages.[29] In *Maonan Yin Hai Leather Co., Ltd. v.and Wu Longhan in Maoming City*, the appellant, when entering into the land lease agreement with the third party in the original trial, relied on the original forestry right certificate provided by the third party to determine the ownership of the disputed land.[30] By signing the land lease agreement, the appellant had already fulfilled the duty of reasonable and prudent attention.

Moreover, after signing the lease agreement, the appellant duly paid the corresponding consideration under the contract. The appellant's occupation of the disputed land under this lease agreement is characterised as bona fide and rightful possession. Although leasing the disputed land resulted in a loss to the respondent's interests, the appellant is not at fault and should not be liable for compensation.

In general, when a person gains profits belonging to others by illegal means, that person must return the profits to the rightful owner. Article 985 of the CC requires a return of the profits to the right holder "if profits

[28] Article 459 CC.

[29] 茂名市茂南银海皮业有限公司诉吴隆汉二审民事判决 [*Maonan Yin Hai Leather Co., Ltd. v. Wu Longhan in Maoming City*] (2018) 粤09民终331号 [Maoming IPC (2018) Yue 09 Min Zhong 331].

[30] *Ibid.*

are acquired improperly and without a lawful basis."[31] The basis for claims against bona fide possessors is in Article 460, which states: "In case a possessor possesses a real property or movable property, the holder may request the return of original object and its fruits."[32] Fruits refer to natural produce, such as crops, and legal produce, such as interests, rents and other benefits arising from legal relationships.

Nonetheless, a bona fide possessor has a right to expenses used for property maintenance, as it requires the holder of the property to "pay the necessary expenses to the bona fide possessor for maintaining this real property or movable property."[33] From the wording of the legislation, this payment of expenses does not require the bona fide possessor to make a claim. However, it automatically arises when the holder demands possession of the property. Thus, a bona fide possessor has a right to make necessary deductions from the profits or even the property to treat as payment of the expenses used for maintaining the property. Can the malicious possessor claim the necessary expenses? In *Wan Daxuan v. Wan Dalian*,[34] the Chongqing court held that the registered owner of the property involved in the case had the right to request the return of the house from the unauthorised possessor. As the malicious possessor of the house in question, the possessor lacks legal basis to claim repair expenses for the house without the right holder's consent, and the court does not support such a claim.[35]

11.1.5 Remedies

11.1.5.1 Self-Remedy

The laws do not explicitly govern situations where a possessor resorts to owning means when its property is trespassed. The absence of a self-help remedy for possessors in possession protection signifies a legislative omission.[36] These self-remedies can be categorised into protective means and recovery means. Protective means refer to actions the possessor takes to protect his possession when others interfere with the property. This is appropriate when the property is still within the possession of the rightful

[31] Article 985 CC.
[32] Article 460 CC.
[33] *Ibid.*
[34] 万大轩与万大民事判决书 [*Wan Daxuan v. Wan Dalian*] (2020) 渝02民终740号 [Chongqing Second IPC (2020) Yu 02 Min Zhong 740].
[35] *Ibid.*
[36] Zhang (n. 12).

possessor. On the other hand, when the possessor has lost possession of the property, the actions he relies on are referred to as recovery means.

To resort to self-protection, there must be immediate and actual interference with the property. If the possessor has already lost possession of the property, the possessor must resort to other means. Self-protection methods are understandably only available to those in factual possession of the property, since they require action to stop or prevent immediate encroachment of the property from others. This is also available to occupiers. Unrelated third parties may also act against a person by interfering with the properties of others. Thus, the person protecting the property is not required to be an authorised person of the possessor or related to the possessor.

The methods taken to protect the property must not exceed what is necessary for effective protection. It is to be considered given due regard to the circumstances including an assessment of all the available methods available to the protector at the time. The first requirement to employ self-recovery actions is that possession has been completely lost. Otherwise, the actions taken are considered self-protection means. Possessors are only available for self-recovery when the person taking away the property has not established possession of his own. This is a matter of time. Thus, possessors having lost possession can only resort to self-recovery immediately after losing possession. Whether the action is taken as "immediate" depends on the circumstance.

Like other self-remedies, self-recovery must be done with reasonable care and not exceed necessary. It is to be encouraged that, when it is available, the person should do what he can to protect his property, but it is not a bar to a claim if the person chooses to do nothing personally and later resorts to seeking the court's help.

11.1.5.2 Spoliation Order

When possession has been wrongly deprived by others who refuse to return the property upon demand, the possessor has a claim to demand the return of the property. The first sentence of Article 462 of the CC provides that "in case a real property or movable property under possession is encroached on, the possessor shall be entitled to demand the return of the original object (property)."[37] A spoliation order offers a speedy trial for the rightful possessor to recover the property from

[37] Para. 1 of Article 462 CC.

wrongful possessors. To apply for a spoliation order, the person must establish that at the time, right before infringement, she was in possession of the property. It is, however, not required for the claimant to prove that she had the right to possession at that time, but only that she was in possession of the property.

It is necessary that the property still exists at the time the claim is made. If the property has been destroyed, the only remedy available is to seek compensation.[38] It is stated in the above-mentioned provision that "The claim of a possessor for returning the original object shall be exercised within one year as of the date of encroachment. Otherwise, such claim shall perish."[39] This clearly shows that the time limit for making the claim is a year from the time of the infringement.

11.1.5.3. Prohibitory Interdicts

The same section that gives the right to apply for a spoliation order states that "for any act that may impair the possession, the possessor shall be entitled to require the elimination of impairment or danger."[40] This can be understood as a prohibitory interdict claim. A person may resort to this when possessing the property is being wrongly interfered with without taking possession away from the person.

The situation that calls for this must pose an actual threat to the possessor's possession. It is not based on the possessor's understanding of the circumstance but must be objectively inferred from the facts.[41] A common situation is when a development plan reveals that it will encroach on the boundary of neighbouring land.

11.1.5.4 Tort Claim: Damages and Return of Profits

If the infringer has caused damage to the property, he is liable to compensate the possessor.[42] The principle is to restore the property to its original state before the infringement. They share the same requirements, since they rely on the same article as spoliation claims and

[38] Xiangxiang Wu [吴香香], 'On Compensation for Damage Caused by Infringement of Possession' [《论侵害占有的损害赔偿》] (2013) 25 *Peking University Law Journal* [《中外法学》] 598, pp. 598–603.

[39] Para. 2 of Article 462 CC.

[40] Para. 1 of Article 462 CC.

[41] Xianghong Bu [卜祥洪], 'On the Basis and Scope of the Right to Claim Compensation for Possession Damage' [《论占有损害赔偿的请求权基础与范围》] [2011] *Contemporary Law Review* [《当代法学》] 61.

[42] Para. 1 of Article 462 CC.

prohibitory interdicts. This means the person must be in possession immediately before the damage to the property occurred and that the property must still exist when the claim is made. It must be noted that the time limit only applies in recovering possession by a possessor but not in seeking compensation for damage to the property.

While the brief section on possession in the Chinese CC does not explicitly provide a return of profits to possessors as they do for holders of property, the possessor may be, in the limited circumstance, able to rely on the same ground for a return of profits that result in the infringer's possession of the property. Article 985 of the CC in the section of unjust enrichment provides a possessor with a claim to return profits if (1) the infringer is without lawful excuse and has made a profit due to the infringement and (2) the infringement has caused the possessor a loss.[43] However, it should be noted that any wrongful possessor is responsible for returning profits to the property holders.[44]

Aside from restrictions under private laws, there are situations whereby the laws make it possible for the state to intervene with one's use of his or her property. Expropriation and requisition are, among others, the most severe interference a state can cause to one's ownership rights. There are other obligations placed on owners under public laws to refrain from causing harm to the public, such as limiting activities that produce substances harmful to the environment. It is also required for owners to obey the laws in exercising their ownership right, such as staying within the speed limit while driving.

11.2 Expropriation

The extensive use (and abuse) of government power to order forced evictions or expropriation has given the Chinese citizenry and the rest of the world the impression that Chinese property rights are very precarious. The emphasis on economic development or urban regeneration in the past four decades encouraged land expropriation.[45] The increase in the number of cases of land seizures across the country has been fuelled in part by the

[43] Article 985 CC.

[44] Article 460 CC.

[45] Jiang Xu, Anthony Yeh and Fulong Wu, 'Land Commodification: New land Development and Politics in China since the Late 1990s' (2009) 33 *International Journal of Urban and Regional Research* 890.

government's urban regeneration policies.[46] In a way, economic development or urban regeneration is synonymous with and necessary in the wider public interest of the whole country. The danger of this thinking was felt and seen almost everywhere regularly. When the unconstrained capitalist enterprise marries the state's coercive land-taking power, coupled with corruption at the local government level, the media coverage of the appalling life of the evicted farmers sparks public outcries.[47] In addition, the perception of China's attractiveness as a recipient of foreign investment hinges upon China's commitment to the legal protection from expropriation.[48] China has concluded many bilateral investment treaties (BITs) or other international agreements that provide protections for foreign investors, including provisions related to expropriation.[49] In any event, China cannot sustainably accomplish economic development without a properly functioning, comprehensive property law.

11.2.1 Legislative History of Expropriation Law

The concept of expropriation, in the Chinese legal language, "zheng shou" (征收), is relatively new in the Chinese legal system. From 1949 until 2003, Chinese law did not employ the notion of expropriation at any level of the legal system. Instead it employed the concepts of "repatriation, requisition or nationalisation" (征购、征用或者收归国有).[50] To gain a clear understanding of the expropriation concept and rules

[46] Sally Sargeson, 'Violence as Development: Land Expropriation and China's Urbanization' (2013) 40 *The Journal of Peasant Studies* 1063.

[47] Hualing Fu, 'What Does Wukan Offer? Land-Taking, Law, and Dispute Resolution,' in Hualing Fu and John Gillespie (eds), *Resolving Land Disputes in East Asia: Exploring the Limits of Law* (Cambridge University Press 2014).

[48] Article 20 of the Foreign Investment Law states that "the state does not implement expropriation for the investments of foreign investors. Under special circumstances, for the needs of the public interest, the state may, in accordance with the law, implement expropriation or requisition of the investments of foreign investors. Expropriation or requisition shall be conducted in accordance with statutory procedures and timely and provide fair and reasonable compensation." However, it is worth noting that the Foreign Investment Law or its implementation regulation does not specify the "statutory procedures," and therefore it is necessary to refer to the procedures contained in the Land Administration Law and other property law–related statutory instruments.

[49] Leon E. Trakman, Qiao Liu, and Lei Chen, 'Investor-State Arbitration in China: A Comparative Perspective', in Lei Chen and André Janssen (eds), *Dispute Resolution in China, Europe and World* (Springer 2020); Yuwen Li and Cheng Bian, 'China's Stance on Investor-State Dispute Settlement: Evolution, Challenges, and Reform Options' (2020) 67 *Netherlands International Law Review* 503.

[50] For example, in the Land Administration Law 1988 and 1998 versions.

in China, it is apposite to examine the evolutionary development of the relevant legal concepts from 1949 to now.

The 1954 Constitution, the first constitution enacted after the PRC was founded, did not set out the concept of "expropriation" but adopted instead the distinct concepts of "repatriation, requisition or nationalisation."[51] As with the 1954 Constitution, the 1975 Constitution also did not use the term expropriation and stipulated that "the state may, in accordance with the conditions prescribed by law, repatriate, requisite and nationalise urban and rural land and other means of production."[52]

The 1982 Constitution was a product of China's reform and opening-up policy after the Cultural Revolution. This version of the constitution is in force today, albeit with numerous subsequent amendments. From the time the 1982 Constitution was first adopted and until 2004, Article 10 provided that "to meet the needs of the public interest, the land may be requisitioned per the provisions of the law."[53] On 14 May 1982, the State Council announced the Land Requisition Regulation for State Construction, which put forward the concept of rural collective land acquisition systematically for the first time. Again, the concept of expropriation was still not employed. In 1986, the Land Administration Law was promulgated, stipulating that "the state may requisite collectively owned land per the law to meet the needs of public interests."[54]

China amended its Constitution in 1988 to recognise privately owned, transferable urban land use rights for the first time.[55] In other words, before the 1988 Constitutional Amendment, no privately held and commercially transferable land use right existed. It was not until the middle 1990s that China started a "housing reform policy" introducing private housing and apartments. The Chinese legislature incorporated procedural legality as a core requirement for administrative action for the first time in the 1989 Administrative Litigation Law.[56]

The 2004 amendment of the constitution provides a property clause that "citizens' legally obtained private property rights" should not be violated.[57] For the first time, the notion of expropriation was used in

[51] Article 13 of the 1954 Constitution.

[52] Article 6 of the 1975 Constitution.

[53] Article 10 of the 1982 Constitution.

[54] Article 2 Land Administration Law 1986 version.

[55] Article 10 Constitution 1988 version.

[56] Article 54 Administrative Litigation Law 1989 version.

[57] Para. 2 of Article 13 of China's Constitution, amended on 14 March 2004 at the 2nd session of the 10th NPC.

the Chinese Constitution. Furthermore, the amendment requires compensation whenever private property is expropriated or requisitioned.[58] In other words, a limitation of a private property right is permissible but subject to explicit safeguards or conditions. This means that under the Chinese constitutional property clauses, the private property of citizens may be infringed only for public interest and upon compensation.[59] As opposed to expropriation, requisition is a temporary taking of property by the state without obtaining consent from the owner.[60]

During the time of requisition, an owner is deprived of the right to exercise any powers he or she has by virtue of the ownership. Accordingly, when necessitated by an emergency such as a rescue situation or disaster relief, the state may require any movable or immovable property owned by a unit or the state. The same provision also provides that the state must return and compensate for any damage or loss of property suffered due to the state's use of the property.

It must be noted, however, that compensation does not include compensation for loss of usage during the time of requisition. Since such requisition is done within the law, a person has no recourse under torts for any harm suffered due to requisition, as there are no "improper acts."[61]

Property rights cannot exist as a social and economic institution without laws that define their content and structure. Following the 2004 Constitutional Amendment, the Property Law came into effect in 2007. This legislation aims to secure property rights by safeguarding legal protection, thus providing greater economic stability in the marketplace. Article 42 of the Property Law reiterates this position, expanding the scope of expropriation to include any lands owned by collectives or units or houses and other immovable property of individuals.[62]

Land expropriation became a primary source of lucrative revenues and financing for some local governments, as the affected farmers are

[58] Para. 3 of Article 13 of China's Constitution: "The State may, in the public interest and in accordance with law, expropriate or requisition private property for its use and make compensation for the private property expropriated or requisitioned."

[59] Hanri Mostert and Lei Chen, 'The Dynamics of Constitutional Property Clauses in the Developing World: China and South Africa' (2010) 17 *Maastricht Journal of European and Comparative Law* 377.

[60] Article 44 Property Law; Article 245 CC.

[61] Wang Liming [王利明], *Research on Real Property Rights Law* (Vol. 1) [《物权法研究（上卷）》] (3rd edn, China Renmin University Press 2013), p. 416.

[62] Article 42 Property Law (2007).

drastically under-compensated for their expropriated land.[63] Farmers are perceived to be weak and vulnerable to property rights infringement by local governments and property developers. The ruling party and the government have not been oblivious to the continuous accumulation and eruption of contradictions and conflicts in land expropriation and compensation.[64] In fact, under pressure to maintain stability, the central government has taken a series of steps to alleviate the conflicts arising from land expropriation and compensation.[65] One way to tackle this is to ensure that the expropriation is explicitly required to act within the laws' limits and follow the procedures outlined in the relevant regulations, such as the Regulation on Expropriation and Compensation for Houses on State-Owned Land (the "2011 Housing Expropriation Regulations") in 2011.[66]

The 2011 Housing Expropriation Regulations heralded a big leap forward in China's legal framework for state-orientated expropriations. The statutory intent behind it was to regulate the procedure governing expropriation and compensation while upholding the public interest and protecting the legal interests of property owners.[67] First, the different types of public interest that justify and legitimise expropriation were demarcated for the first time.[68] Second, concerning compensation, payment levels would have to consider the property's location and market value based on independent third-party assessments.[69] Third, it introduces some detailed procedural safeguards, including public hearings, ensuring the participation of the property owners affected, the selection of a property value appraiser and dispute settlement during an

[63] Qun, Wu, Li Yongle and Yan Siqi, 'The Incentives of China's Urban Land Finance' (2015) 42 *Land Use Policy* 432.

[64] Guoyin Dang [党国英], 'A Theory on Social Stability and Its Application in China's Countryside' [《关于社会稳定的一个理论及其在农村分析中的应用》] (1996) *China Rural Survey* [《中国农村观察》] 52.

[65] Chun Peng, 'Rural Land Expropriation Law in the Reform Era: A Story of Continuity', in Chun Peng (ed), *Rural Land Takings Law in Modern China: Origin and Evolution* (Cambridge University Press 2018).

[66] State Council Order No. 590. It replaced the Regulation on Administration of Demolition and Relocation of Urban Premises effective since 1 November 2001, State Council Order No. 78.

[67] Lei Chen, 'Legal and Institutional Analysis of Land Expropriation in China', in Hualing Fu and John Gillespie (eds), *Resolving Land Disputes in East Asia: Exploring the Limits of Law* (Cambridge University Press 2014).

[68] Article 8 Housing Expropriation Regulations (2011).

[69] Article 19 Housing Expropriation Regulations (2011).

expropriation process.[70] Fourth, it gave property owners objecting to expropriation the right to file an administrative lawsuit.[71]

Still up to this day there is no overarching legal framework governing expropriation. Notwithstanding the developments described above, including the constitutional amendments, China still lacks a comprehensive and specific expropriation law. For instance, all the legislation or regulations described up to this point provide no legal definition of expropriation. In addition, the 2011 Housing Expropriation Regulations, technically, is not a piece of national legislation made by the NPC, the Chinese national legislature. It is an administrative regulation issued by the State Council. Furthermore, as the full title suggests, the Housing Expropriation Regulation does not cover the expropriation conducted over rural land or mineral rights.

The most recent amendment to the Land Administration Law was approved on 26 August 2019. The amendment introduced provisions to fill the gap by improving the legal protection of rural land expropriation. First, it clarifies the scope of public interests in land expropriation through enumeration.[72] The list of public interests largely aligns with that of the 2011 Housing Expropriation Regulation. Given the specified scope of public interests, the local governments' power of land expropriation has been effectively constrained, and the traditional model of land supplies originating in rural land expropriation became more costly than ever.

The two strategies adopted by the State Council to address the land supply issue are unsurprising, given the centralized nature of policy-making in China. These strategies include activating the secondary land market for Construction Land Use Rights (CLUR) and allowing rural construction land to enter the market with fewer regulatory restrictions. The top–down nature of these measures reflects the State Council's authority and control over land policy. This approach is consistent with China's governance structure, where centralized decision-making often drives policy reforms. Furthermore, alternative bottom–up strategies are uncommon or largely restricted in China's land management framework, making the reliance on these centralized strategies expected.[73]

[70] Articles 10 and 11 Housing Expropriation Regulations (2011).

[71] Articles 13 and 14 Housing Expropriation Regulations (2011).

[72] Article 45 Land Administration Law.

[73] The General Office of the State Council issued the "Guiding Opinions on Improving the Secondary Market for Transfer, Lease, and Mortgage of CLURs" on 6 July 2019 (State

Despite the needed clarifications, Article 45 of the Land Administration Law does not define the term "planned development of a block of land" in item 5 of the list of specified public interests. This statutory lacuna may cause the risk of local governments expanding the scope of land expropriation because the governments at all levels have the right to formulate overall land use plans and designate planned development. To prevent the local governments from abusing "planned development" for land expropriation, it is suggested that the State Council or the Natural Resources Administration Department formulate clear standards to define planned development.

Second, three situations that require approval from the State Council for land expropriation are stipulated, namely (1) permanently designated primary farmland; (2) non-primary farmland exceeding thirty-five hectares; and (3) other land exceeding seventy hectares.[74] For the expropriation of land not falling within the categories that require approval from the State Council, the people's government of the province, autonomous region or municipality directly under the central government is the approving authority.[75] While it is unnecessary to report to the State Council for the record,[76] the state, including approving authorities at all levels, provides special protection for arable land, strictly restricts the conversion of agricultural land into construction land and controls the total amount of construction land.[77]

Third, it states that the compensation and resettlement funds must be fully in place, and agreements must be signed with the owners and users of the land to be expropriated regarding compensation and

Council Document [2019] No. 34). This opinion is the first top-level design in China specifically regulating the secondary market for CLURs, establishing a series of fundamental and systematic institutional arrangements. With the gradual standardisation and institutionalisation of the secondary market for CLURs, the secondary land market will become more active, and construction entities can obtain construction land through this market.

74 Para. 1 of Article 46 Land Administration Law.

75 Para. 2 of Article 46 Land Administration Law.

76 Minister of the Ministry of Natural Resources, Lu Hao, stated during the first submission of the "Amendment to the Land Management Law (Draft)" to the 7th session of the 13th National People's Congress Standing Committee that the role and purpose of filing with the State Council after the provincial government approves land expropriation are unclear. After the removal of the filing requirement, according to the principle of whoever has the power and makes the decision takes the responsibility, the provincial government that makes the land expropriation decision will be responsible, and eliminating the filing requirement is more conducive to strengthening local accountability.

77 Article 244 CC.

resettlement.[78] Although these obligations were already practices that the government should fulfil in expropriating the state-owned land, incorporating them into the national legislation undoubtedly demonstrates the state's commitment to protecting farmers' rights.

Fourth, it specifies that the extant living standards of the farmers losing the land are not reduced and their long-term livelihoods are guaranteed. It replaces the previous method of determining land compensation and resettlement subsidies based on the multiple annual output values with a comprehensive regional land price. Instead, it introduces compensation for rural villagers' residences and social security for the affected farmers, aiming to construct a more comprehensive safeguard mechanism for the affected farmers.[79] The law emphasises the importance of not reducing the original living standards of the land-deprived farmers and ensuring their long-term livelihoods.

The most recent legislation concerning land expropriation is in the CC. However, the provisions in the CC largely retain the wording of Article 42 of the Property Law. Still, Article 243 of the CC introduced one notable technical change. It requires compensation to be paid promptly when expropriating collectively owned land.[80] In practice, there is often a long delay in paying compensation for the expropriation of collectively owned land, leading to the failure to protect farmers' legitimate rights and interests. The CC clarifies that compensation for the rural residential houses should be paid promptly and in full in addition to compensations for land taking, resettlement allowances and attached structures and crops.[81] Specifying compensation fees for rural residents' houses is intended to protect the interests of farmers and ensure their living conditions. Likewise, Article 245 of the CC largely follows Article 44 of the Property Law by providing that organisations' and individuals' immovable or movable property may be requisitioned in emergency rescue, disaster relief or epidemic prevention and control.[82] The requisitioned property shall be returned to the owner after use, and compensation shall be provided to the owners if the requisitioned property is damaged or lost due to the requisition.[83]

[78] Para. 4 of Article 47 Land Administration Law.
[79] Article 48 Land Administration Law.
[80] Para. 2 of Article 243 CC.
[81] *Ibid.*
[82] Article 245 CC.
[83] *Ibid.*

11.2.2 Procedures and Due Process

There are three pillars in the expropriation law: public interest requirement, just compensation and procedural safeguards. An expropriation must be in the public interest.[84] This requirement prevents the expropriation of private property for unlawful purposes and restricts the exercising of the power to expropriate. In the preceding analysis, the 2011 Housing Expropriation Regulation and the 2019 Land Administration Law specify the circumstances where the public interest requirement is met. Likewise, the compensation amount cannot be lower than the market value of similar housing on the day of the announcement of the expropriation decision. This sets up a market value–based mechanism to calculate compensation.

It has been revealed in an empirical study that Chinese courts focus on expropriation procedures while rarely supporting claims on the grounds of public interest requirements or just compensation.[85] There are two main reasons to explain this phenomenon. First, technically, procedural rules are determinate and, therefore, easier to enforce than substantial public interest standards and just compensation. Second, strategically, it is a natural choice for Chinese courts to focus on procedures to confine their power of judicial review for self-preservation in an authoritarian state that empowers the courts to monitor local governments but does not want their power unfettered.[86]

Therefore, it is necessary to determine what procedural steps must be taken to conduct the expropriation. Compared with the Land Administration Law 2004 amendment, the new Land Administration Law 2019 amendment and its revised implementation regulation introduce the procedure of pre-approval public announcement.[87]

[84] Para. 1 of Article 243 CC.

[85] Wenzheng Mao and Shitong Qiao, 'Legal Doctrine and Judicial Review of Eminent Domain in China' (2021) 46 *Law & Social Inquiry* 826.

[86] Shitong Qiao and Marc Chien, 'A Rural-Urban Crossroads in Chinese Law: Qiao Shitong on the Development and Future of Chinese Eminent Domain: Bulletin' (2022) *Columbia Journal of Transnational Law*, 3 March, <www.jtl.columbia.edu/bulletin-blog/a-rural-urban-crossroads-in-chinese-law-qiao-shitong-on-the-development-and-future-of-chinese-eminent-domain> accessed 16 February 2024.

[87] Para. 2 of Article 47 of the Land Administration Law states that local governments at or above the county level intending to apply for land expropriation should conduct a current status survey and social stability risk assessment for the land they plan to expropriate. They are required to publicly announce, with at least a thirty-day notice, the expropriation scope, current status of the land, purpose of expropriation, compensation standards, resettlement methods, social security, etc., within the scope of the township (town)

Additionally, the law establishes a hearing procedure, stating that if the majority of the members of the collective economic organisation of the rural area to be expropriated believe that the compensation and resettlement plan does not comply with legal provisions, the local government at or above the county level shall organise a hearing and modify the plan based on legal provisions and the hearing's results.[88] This provides the farmer's rights of participation and supervision, thus ensuring their voice is heard and responded to in the process.

There are nine steps under the Implementation Regulation of the Land Administration Law.[89] The first step is to make a pre-announcement of land expropriation, which includes information such as the scope of expropriation, the purpose of expropriation and the arrangements for conducting a land status survey.[90] The pre-announcement of land expropriation should be conducive to public awareness by being published within the township (town) and village and the villagers' group where the intended expropriation is located. The pre-announcement period should be no less than ten working days.[91] From the date of the pre-announcement of land acquisition, no individual or entity is allowed to plant or construct within the proposed acquisition area. Violators who engage in unauthorised planting or construction are not entitled to compensation for the affected portions.[92]

Second, a survey of the land to be expropriated is conducted, including information about the location, ownership, land type and area, as well as the ownership, type and quantity of rural villagers' residences, other surface attachments and crops.[93] Third, a social stability risk assessment is carried out to comprehensively assess the social stability risks of the

and village where the land to be expropriated is located, including village and villagers' group levels. The authorities should also solicit opinions from the collective economic organisations and their members, village committees and other stakeholders affected by the expropriation.

88 Para. 3 of Article 47 Land Administration Law.

89 Articles 26–32 of the Implementation Regulations of Land Administration Law, initially issued on 27 December 1998, through the State Council Order No. 256. The regulations have undergone three revisions: the first revision was based on the State Council's decision to abolish and amend certain administrative regulations on 8 January 2011, the second revision was based on the decision to modify certain administrative regulations on 29 July 2014, and the third revision was made on 2 July 2021, according to the State Council Order No. 743.

90 Para. 2 of Article 26 Implementation Regulations of Land Administration Law.

91 *Ibid.*

92 *Ibid.*

93 Para. 3 of Article 26 Implementation Regulations of Land Administration Law.

expropriated land, identify risk points, propose risk prevention measures and prepare contingency plans.[94] The assessment should involve the affected rural collective economic organisations, their members, village committees and other stakeholders, with the results being a crucial basis for the land expropriation application.[95]

Fourth, based on the social stability risk assessment results and the land status survey, the local government at or above the county level should organise various relevant government departments to draft a land compensation and resettlement plan (LCRP).[96] The plan should cover the expropriation scope, land status, purpose of expropriation, compensation methods and standards, resettlement targets, resettlement means, social security and other relevant aspects.[97]

Fifth, after formulating the LCRP, the local government at or above the county level should announce it within the township (town), the village and the villagers' group where the intended expropriation is located. The announcement period should be no less than thirty days.[98] The announcement should also specify the registration process, deadlines and objection feedback channels.[99] In the case of expropriating the urban housing, the municipal and county-level people's governments shall organise relevant departments to demonstrate and publicise the expropriation and compensation plan, soliciting public opinions, and the period for soliciting opinions shall not be less than thirty days.[100]

Sixth, if most of the affected rural collective economic organisations' members believe that the proposed LCRP does not comply with legal regulations, the local government at or above the county level should organise a public hearing.[101] The plan should be modified based on legal regulations and the hearing outcomes if necessary. Seventh, after determining the LCRP according to legal regulations and the hearing outcomes, the local government at or above the county level should organise relevant departments to sign land compensation and resettlement

94 Para. 4 of Article 26 Implementation Regulations of Land Administration Law.
95 *Ibid.*
96 Para. 1 of Article 27 Implementation Regulations of Land Administration Law.
97 *Ibid.*
98 Para. 1 of Article 28 Implementation Regulations of Land Administration Law.
99 Para. 2 of Article 28 Implementation Regulations of Land Administration Law.
100 Article 10 Urban Land Expropriation Regulation.
101 Para. 3 of Article 28 Implementation Regulations of Land Administration Law.

agreements with land use rights holders.[102] Suppose it is genuinely difficult to reach an agreement for individual cases. In that case, the local government at or above the county level should truthfully explain the situation when applying for land expropriation.[103]

Eighth, after completing the required pre-expropriation work, the local government can apply for land expropriation at or above the county level, seeking approval from the higher-level government.[104] The approving authority reviews the necessity, reasonableness, compliance with the requirements of Article 45 of the Land Administration Law and adherence to legal procedures for land expropriation.[105]

Ninth, once the application for land expropriation is legally approved, the local government at or above the county level should, within fifteen working days of receiving the approval, issue an announcement of land expropriation within the township (town) and village, and the villagers' group where the intended expropriation is located.[106] The announcement should detail the expropriation scope, timing and other specific work arrangements. For cases where individual land compensation and resettlement agreements have not been reached, the local government should issue a decision on land compensation and resettlement and lawfully execute the decision.[107]

It is worth highlighting that the local people's governments at the county level or above applying for land acquisition promptly implement the compensation fees for land, resettlement subsidies, compensation for rural villagers' residences, other compensation fees for surface attachments and crops, as well as social security fees, ensuring that the funds are fully and exclusively allocated. The land acquisition cannot be approved if the relevant funds are not fully in place.[108]

From the above it is clear that the local government at or above the county level can only apply to land expropriation once the required pre-expropriation work is completed. In practice, it is common for some farmers not to agree to the LCRP within the announced time frame due to dissatisfaction with compensation standards, among other reasons.

[102] Para. 1 of Article 29 Implementation Regulations of Land Administration Law. The provincial governments formulate model texts for these agreements.
[103] Para. 2 of Article 29 Implementation Regulations of Land Administration Law.
[104] Para. 1 of Article 30 Implementation Regulations of Land Administration Law.
[105] Para. 2 of Article 28 Implementation Regulations of Land Administration Law.
[106] Article 31 Implementation Regulations of Land Administration Law.
[107] *Ibid.*
[108] Article 32 Implementation Regulation of the Land Administration Law.

It is suggested that the competent government agency conduct on-site notarisation of the registration status. More to the point, the threshold for the percentage of signed compensation and resettlement agreements before applying is not explicitly specified in the law. The wording in the legislation uses the phrase "individuals who are genuinely difficult to reach an agreement with." The determination of a specific percentage for "individual cases" is left to the discretion of local authorities. For example, in Shandong Province, the proportion of signed agreements generally should not be less than 95 per cent of the total number of individuals affected by the expropriation.[109] This indicates that the legislative intent of the Land Administration Law was to establish a very high percentage threshold.

While the Implementation Regulation of the Land Administration Law requires the local governments to announce land expropriation after the approval is obtained, it does not explicitly specify the procedure for making compensation and resettlement decisions. Before making compensation and resettlement decisions, it is necessary to go through pre-decision negotiations with the expropriated parties. For example, before the compensation and resettlement decisions are made, a notice is made to the affected parties with a request for their response within the specified period. Suppose the response from the affected party violates mandatory legal provisions and cannot be entertained with a good cause. In that case, the local government can promptly issue a written decision on compensation and resettlement.

Furthermore, the relevant government departments sign agreements with the expropriated persons regarding compensation and resettlement matters. This procedural step is the beginning of the approval process. This implies that there might be a time gap between the signing of the agreement and the issuance of the expropriation decision. Additionally, provincial and municipal governments may adjust the LCRP during approval.

In practice, many disputes arise from fluctuations in land and house prices and changes in the compensation and resettlement plan during this time gap. Therefore, the issue is whether the expropriated person can request a change to the signed agreement. The agreement reached by both parties voluntarily should be respected as long as they do not violate the laws. Without a contractual stipulation, the person affected by

[109] Article 2 Item 6 of the Opinion on Regulating the Management of Land Acquisition by the People's Government of Shandong Province (Lu Zheng Ban Zi (2022) No. 13).

expropriation can only request a change based on the principle of fairness if significant changes were unforeseeable at the time of contract formation and not attributable to *force majeure*. Usually, the rise and fall of land and house prices fall within the scope of business risks and are considered foreseeable. Therefore, the courts generally do not support purely using the fluctuation of land and house prices as a reason to request a contract change. However, adjustments to the LCRP by the higher-level government during the approval process might go beyond what the expropriated person could foresee. In such cases, if the approved compensation and resettlement standards are higher than those agreed upon in the signed agreement, the expropriated person can request a change to the compensation clauses based on the doctrine of change of circumstances.[110]

11.2.3 Malpractices by the Local Governments

The forced eviction without going through the due process and prior approval is not uncommon in China. This is particularly the case when there is a disagreement on the LCRP and the parties fail to reach compensation and resettlement agreements. In such a circumstance, the expropriation was considered procrastinated because the land is desperately needed for an urban regeneration project, such as a science park complex. Some local government officials boldly believed that a "bulldoze first and pay compensation later" approach might show their creativity in getting things done in their assessment of key performance indicators. As a result, if the building has been torn down, what has been done cannot be undone. If this happened, what approach did the Chinese courts take in remedying the expropriated farmers?

In *Li Xuenong v. Zouping County Government*, the LCRP was announced in the village. However, the appellant disagreed with the compensation standard and did not sign an expropriation agreement, but the competent administrative authority expropriated the land without approval.[111] While confirming the illegality of the expropriation

[110] Yan Wei [阎巍], 'The Impact of China's Rural Land Reform on Compensation and Distribution in Collective Land Expropriation' [《国农村土地改革对集体土地征收补偿分配的影响》] (2022) *Legal Application* [《法律适用》] 89.

[111] 李学农诉被申请人邹平县政府、邹平县孙镇党里村村委会行政赔偿案 [*Li Xuenong v. Zouping County Government*] (2019) 最高法行赔申51号 [SPC (2019) SPC Administrative Compensation Application No. 51].

conduct in violation of the statutory procedures, the SPC chose not to revoke the administrative action because revocation would cause significant harm to national or public interests.[112] As a result, the SPC ordered the administrative authority to complete the land expropriation procedures and simultaneously fulfil compensation and resettlement obligations.[113]

In this case, the Zouping County government has constructed the supporting project of Phase I of the South-to-North Water Diversion Project over the expropriated land. This was done to address industrial water needs in Zouping County and ensure drinking water safety for residents. A significant amount of construction funds has already been invested, and the project has been completed. There is no practical way to restore the expropriated land to its original state. Therefore, the SPC ruled that revoking the administrative action under litigation would cause significant harm to the public interest. The SPC adopted a proportionality test on economic efficiency in balancing protecting individual property rights and the greater and wider public interest.

However balanced this judicial approach may be, the downside of the judicial outcome is that wherever there is a grand project or wider public interest at stake, the due process procedures may not be strictly followed. The bold and illegal government conducts can be rectified later, and no official is held accountable for violating the statutory procedures. This may encourage the local governments to take a dim view of the due process procedures.

To better protect the rights of the individuals affected by expropriation, relevant government agencies should promptly inform these individuals in writing of the specific basis and compensation amounts. If they refuse to accept the compensation, the relevant procedures for depositing the compensation should be carried out. Additionally, once the administrative authorities obtain expropriation approval and issue a decision on land compensation and resettlement to the appellant, the appellant is entitled to lodge an administrative review or file an administrative lawsuit.[114]

Public interest is an abstract legal concept that often manifests different purposes and forms in individual cases of expropriation. Usually, administrative authorities have undertaken specific expropriation work

[112] Article 74 (1) Administrative Litigation Law.

[113] *Ibid.*

[114] Article 14 Housing Expropriation Regulations (2011).

and often cite reasons related to advancing the progress of expropriation, serving the overall local development and having a broad scope of involvement as justifications for public interest requirements. However, the courts should not simplify such grounds as fulfilling the public interest requirement.

In another SPC ruling, *Wang Xianwu v. the Xixiu District Government, Anshun City, Guizhou Province*,[115] the Xixiu district government claimed that public interests were seriously damaged, primarily in terms of constraining the development of urban transportation, ineffective recovery of upfront project construction investment and the existence of significant public safety hazards. The SPC held that although there is an objective need to improve urban transportation, enhance living environments and develop new urbanisation, it is not sufficient to establish the legitimacy and urgency of collective land expropriation without the statutory approval of the provincial-level people's government.[116] Additionally, the contested expropriation decision involves a relatively small number of signed compensation agreements and actual demolished houses, minimising the impact of revoking the expropriation decision. Furthermore, whether the expropriation decision is revoked is not directly related to whether public safety hazards are in the houses subject to expropriation. Therefore, the existing evidence from the Xixiu district government is insufficient to prove that revoking the expropriation decision will cause significant damage to national and social public interests.[117]

To summarise, when most affected parties have reached compensation agreements, the SPC may confirm the illegality of the expropriation decision without revoking it. SPC believes this approach helps to avoid introducing new conflicts into stable legal relationships.[118] It is conducive to protecting the legitimate rights of the parties involved, striking a balance between conflicting interests. Conversely, revocation may be considered when the expropriation decision has not been specifically implemented or even if it has been initiated but is stalled for various reasons, such as when only a few compensation agreements are concluded relative to the total number of the affected parties.

115 王贤武诉贵州省安顺市西秀区人民政府 [SPC ruling *Wang Xianwu v. the Xixiu District Government, Anshun City, Guizhou Province*] 最高人民法院（2020）最高法行再276号 [(2020) SPC administrative retrial No. 276].

116 *Ibid.*

117 *Ibid.*

118 *Ibid.*

The danger of the SPC approach is that whenever a legitimate public interest is involved in expropriation, the "bulldoze first and pay compensation as determined later" local government policy will be justified. Consequently, those who do not reach an agreement with the government agency may be bypassed or ignored despite a well-designed due process in the legislation.

A dispute may arise when the competent government agency discovers an error in an issued land use right certificate and decides to rectify the mistake by issuing a revocation decision. Where the registration occurred more than a few years ago, the relevant government agency must specify the legal and factual basis stipulated in laws and follow due process under PRC law to revoke the alleged wrongful registration. Otherwise, it may amount to expropriation. In the past, there were two main ways to rectify a mistake in the land register: by registering for cancellation[119] or by revoking the administrative act of registration.[120] However, the Interim Regulation of Real Estate Registration, which is currently in effect, does not provide any provision addressing cancellation of registration. Therefore, the land registration office cannot register for cancellation. There appears to be only one way to correct if the relevant authority decides to revoke the earlier issued land use right certificate, namely revoking the administrative act of registration.

Nonetheless, when the relevant government authority – usually the county people's government or higher – issues a revocation decision, it should meet the specified statutory conditions[121] and follow the due process procedures.[122] It is essential to accurately identify the reasons for erroneous administrative actions and distinguish the responsibilities of the administrative authority and the affected individuals. The trust in an administrative act lies in its certainty and stability. An administrative act cannot be credible if an administrative authority can revoke it without legitimate grounds and without following procedural due process.[123]

[119] Article 50 Land Registration Measures (repealed in 2017).

[120] Article 62 Administrative Litigation Law; Article 69 Administrative Licensing Law.

[121] The Minutes of the 6th Judges' Meeting of the First Circuit Court of the SPC in 2018: Administrative agencies should have sufficient factual and legal basis for self-correction.

[122] Administrative Adjudication Tribunal of the SPC, 'Compliance with the principles of due process and protection of legitimate expectations in administrative rectification actions', in *Minutes of the Judges' Meetings of the Administrative Adjudication Tribunal of the SPC* (Vol. 1) (People's Court Press 2022), pp. 120–133; Article 8 Administrative Licensing Law.

[123] *Ibid.*

In the case of *Zhengzhou Zhongyuan District Yuxing Spices Factory v. Zhengzhou Municipal People's Government of Henan Province*, the SPC held that when deciding to revoke a land use right certificate issued by mistake many years ago, the following due process requirements apply.[124] Specifically, the SPC stresses that,

> *according to the basic requirements of due process, before making an administrative decision unfavourable to the administrative counterparty or interested party,* ***the administrative authority shall inform it and allow it to make representations and contend****. . . . The Government of Zhengzhou Municipality neither informed Yuxing Seasoning Factory in advance nor allowed it to make representations and contend, which* ***is obviously an improper process****. In such a case, prior to the Revocation Decision, the Factory was not informed enough to make representations and contend in a targeted way, which obviously cannot meet the requirement of due process. Therefore, the Government of Zhengzhou Municipality made the revocation decision under the inappropriate procedure, and the accused administrative act constituted a violation of the law.*[125]

Similarly, in *Tan Chengri v. People's Government of Hengyang*, the SPC held that while the current laws do not explicitly mandate a hearing in the provisions regarding administrative cancellations, the administrative body must adhere to the principles of due process.[126] This ensures the complete protection of the administrative counterpart's right to be informed and to defend themselves. Consequently, despite notifying Tan Chengri of the hearing and deciding to conduct one, the Hengyang Municipal Bureau of Land and Resources proceeded to revoke Tan Chengri's state-owned land use certificate without conducting the scheduled hearing, resulting in a lack of proper procedural fairness.[127]

11.2.4 Summary

Chinese law is still nascent in terms of developing its expropriation laws and jurisprudence. While the CC sets out the principle-based provisions

[124] 郑州市中原区豫星调味品厂诉郑州市人民政府行政处理决定案 [*Zhengzhou Zhongyuan District Yuxing Spices Factory v. Zhengzhou Municipal People's Government of Henan Province*] (2014) 行提字第21号 [(2014) Xing Ti Zi No. 21].

[125] *Ibid* (emphasis added).

[126] 谭成日与衡阳市人民政府、湖南省人民政府其他一案 [*Tan Chengri, Hengyang Municipal People's Government and People's Government of Hunan Providence etc.*] (2018) 最高法行再97号 [(2018) SPC Xing Zai No. 97].

[127] *Ibid.*

on expropriation, the detailed rules and procedural requirements are found mainly in the Implementation Regulation of the Land Administration Law and other administrative statutes. Nonetheless, the Chinese judiciary has advanced expropriation jurisprudence by emphasising the fulfilment of stipulated legal reasons and due process procedures.

There is no such notion of indirect expropriation as found in other jurisdictions. Indirect expropriation refers to situations where a government or regulatory authority takes actions or implements measures that, while not directly taking ownership of private property, result in a de facto deprivation of the value or use of that property. Indirect expropriation can take various forms, including changes in zoning laws, environmental regulations or other governmental actions that significantly reduce the value or use of private property. It is a concept often discussed in international investment law, where foreign investors may seek compensation for measures that effectively expropriate their investments without formally taking ownership.

How far should the government go in its efforts to avoid frustrating the owners' expectations about what they can do with their property? There appears to be a trend toward property rights taking root in China.[128] As shown in Section 11.2.1, the Chinese legal framework governing expropriation has experienced gradual and incremental developments since the early 1980s. The current laws and regulations narrowly demarcate the scope of public interest requirements for expropriation in urban and rural lands. It outlines procedures, criteria and compensation principles for land expropriation, including public purposes requirements, fair compensation and resettlement arrangements. Compensation standards may be based on market value and replacement costs. It also strengthens the procedural safeguards against the superior bargaining power of local governments in negotiating compensation for expropriations. One may argue that periodic revisions and law amendments demonstrate a commitment to refining the legal provisions.

In order to avoid the abuse of power, it is necessary to make the expropriation process more transparent and to allow the affected parties an easier way to seek redress through judicial channels. Ensuring that

[128] Xueyang Cheng [程雪阳], 'The Identification and Judicial Review of Collective Land Expropriation Decision' [《论集体土地征收决定的识别与司法审查》] (2022) *The Jurist* [《法学家》] 88.

affected parties are adequately informed and have opportunities for participation remains a challenge. There have been instances of local authorities not fully adhering to legal requirements, leading to disputes and concerns over fairness and procedural justice. This is particularly needed when some affected parties disagree with the announced compensation and resettlement plan. At the enforcement level, implementing expropriation laws may vary across regions. Disparities in implementation over expropriation of state-owned and rural collective land could lead to inconsistent outcomes and unequal treatment of affected individuals.

12

Conclusion

China's property law framework is underpinned by a series of fundamental laws and statutory reforms that define the ownership, usage and transfer of both urban and rural property. First, the Constitution establishes the legal foundation for property rights within the country. Significant constitutional amendments over the years have progressively recognised and protected private property rights alongside state and collective ownership. These constitutional guarantees provide the overarching legal ethos from which specific property laws derive. Second, the Civil Code, which came into effect in 2021, consolidates and revises previous separate laws related to personal rights and property laws, including the Property Law of 2007. The CC includes detailed provisions on ownership, co-ownership, usufruct rights (rights to use and profit from property owned by another) and security interests. It represents a modernised and unified legal framework intended to simplify and clarify property rights and duties, making the legal system more accessible to the public and more adaptable to contemporary economic and social conditions. Third, the Land Administration Law is the primary legislation governing land use and regulation in China. It distinguishes between urban land, which is owned by the state, and rural land, which is typically owned collectively by rural communities. The dichotomy between urban and rural lands is a distinguishing feature of Chinese property law. The law regulates the conditions under which land can be leased, transferred and utilised, ensuring that land use aligns with national and local development plans.

These statutes not only reflect the evolution of property law in China but also highlight the country's ongoing efforts to balance state control with private property rights, aiming to foster economic development while ensuring social stability and equity. The dynamic nature of China's property law framework continues to evolve in response to domestic and international economic pressures, requiring continuous analysis and adaptation.

In addition, the SPC issues judicial interpretations to clarify and elucidate the provisions of laws passed by the legislature. These interpretations help to fill any gaps in the legislation and provide guidance on how laws should be applied in practice. The SPC's interpretations guide lower courts on how to apply laws consistently, preventing regional disparities in legal practices that could undermine the real estate market and property rights protection. Judicial interpretations allow the legal system to adapt flexibly to new challenges and changes in society and the economy without the need for immediate legislative reform. In the context of property law, as China's economy evolves and new forms of property and property interests emerge (such as digital property or new forms of real estate investment), the SPC can issue interpretations that address these modern issues effectively. Overall, the SPC's judicial interpretations are integral to the functioning of property law in China, ensuring that the laws are current, coherent and capable of meeting the country's social and economic needs. These interpretations not only dictate the application of the law by courts but also inform public understanding and compliance, shaping the landscape of property rights and transactions in China.

Notwithstanding the ongoing signs of progress, Chinese property law faces several challenges that stem from rapid economic development, urbanisation, ideological inertia and the legal complexities of transitioning to a market-oriented economy. There remains considerable ambiguity over land management rights, particularly in rural areas where land is collectively owned. This can impact long-term investments and improvements on the property, as usufructuaries may be hesitant to invest significantly in assets that they do not own. The pressure of urban expansion often leads to the expropriation of rural lands, sometimes resulting in disputes over compensation and resettlement terms. Ensuring fair compensation and protecting the rights of landowners or users are significant challenges. Rapid increases in property values in urban areas have raised concerns about affordability and speculative bubbles. The government frequently intervenes with cooling measures, but managing these fluctuations without sacrificing the level of protection of private property rights remains a challenge.

Although significant reforms have been implemented, there is a continuous need for updates to accommodate new economic realities, especially concerning rural land reforms and the rights to trade or mortgage rural land use rights. Increasing transparency in real estate transactions and property registration remains a significant challenge, but it is necessary to combat corruption and enhance market confidence.

There is often a lack of clear and detailed legal provisions regarding the rights and obligations of and between usufructuaries (such as servitude holders and habitation rights holders) and property owners. This can lead to disputes over the extent of use, maintenance responsibilities and the rights to profits derived from the property. Ensuring that these rights are enforceable in courts can also be problematic, especially when the judiciary faces inconsistent application of laws across different regions.

Drawing upon property theories to understand the development of Chinese property law involves examining the evolution of legal concepts and frameworks in light of broader economic, social and political changes. This analysis can help to identify the underlying principles that have guided the transformation of property rights in China and anticipate future trends.

The conventional perspective, exemplified by Lord Denning, asserted that individuals had the unrestricted right to demolish their homes or remove their trees, regardless of the consequences for others, such as being deprived of shelter from the wind or shade from the sun.[1] Perhaps a simpler way to term the classic view of the property is "despotic dominion."[2] In essence, the classical liberal view of property entailed that its owner had no obligations toward it or the society. What, specifically, does "social function" demand? By introducing the notion of social obligations tied to property, Duguit aimed to navigate a path acknowledging individual property rights while emphasising the broader societal responsibilities of ownership.[3] This perspective allowed for a nuanced approach that considered both the interests of property owners and the welfare of the community, offering a compromise between the extremes of unbridled individualism and collectivism.

Nevertheless, the idea of property's inherent social function has been deeply rooted in China's long history. For example, ancient Chinese philosopher Mengzi indicated that a person who owned property had a higher level of morality and behaved more disciplined than those who

[1] *Phipps v. Pears* [1965] 1 QB 76, 83 per Lord Denning MR.

[2] Thomas Cooley, *Commentaries on the Law of England (Blackstone's Commentaries)* (Chicago Callaghan and Co 1871), 2.

[3] Lei Chen et al., 'The Norm of Property's Social Function: A Chinese Perspective,' in P. Babie and J. Viven-Wilksch (eds), *Léon Duguit and the Social Obligation Norm of Property* (Springer 2019), pp. 331–354.

did not own property.[4] From this stance, the right to private property promotes a harmonious and ordered society. Property can represent both personal freedom and obligation/restraint simultaneously. From physical to intellectual property, Confucianism bestowed respect for past knowledge and believed it should be shared without restrictions. Authors, for example, were not encouraged to create works primarily for income generation.[5]

The book, drawing insights from Chinese property law and practices, argues that the "social function" of property requires land and its resources to be employed to generate a positive societal influence. The exemplification of this concept is particularly evident in the exercise of property rights within a condominium living arrangement. Specifically, the Chinese CC stipulates that property owners shall abide by the laws, regulations and management rules and act in accordance with the requirements for resource conservation and ecological and environmental protection. Property owners shall co-operate with property service companies or other managers when implementing emergency response management measures.[6]

Certainly, discussions surrounding property inherently carry value judgements. Any discourse on property is intricately tied to the social legitimacy of the respective claims. The qualifications for what constitutes property and the authority over its use or exclusion are essential considerations. If one contends that property law involves value judgements that express cultural norms and mirror the political economy within a community, it becomes reasonable to assert that property law functions as a conveyance for ideology.

It is intriguing that in China, a country undergoing transformative socialist development, the concept of property seems to align well with socialist ideology, particularly in emphasising the social function of property. China's distinctive blend of socialist authoritarianism and a market economy contributes to its unique political and economic system. The nation is undergoing comprehensive economic and political reforms, although some observers contend that legal reforms in China are

[4] English version: "The people . . . will not have constant hearts if they are without constant means. Lacking constant hearts, they will go astray and fall into excesses, stopping at nothing." See D. C. Lau, *Mencius* (Chinese University of Hong Kong Press 2003), p. 23.

[5] William. P. Alford, *To Steal a Book Is an Elegant Offense: Intellectual Property Law in Chinese Civilization* (Stanford University Press 1995), pp. 18–24.

[6] Article 286 CC.

progressing slowly. Critics argue that the current legal system in China may not be entirely compatible with its rapidly expanding economy.[7] They posit that a robust economy necessitates an impartial and efficient legal system. The definition of property rights is becoming a significant legislative focus in China, as the state is actively engaged in transforming the property system. This commitment is reflected in the legislative activities of the Chinese government. Article 206 of the CC states, "The State upholds and improves the basic socialist-economic system, under which public ownership shall be the core, together with other diverse forms of ownership economies."[8] This legal provision underscores the state's dedication to maintaining and enhancing a socialist economic system with public ownership and other forms of ownership at its core. Article 206 continues that, "the State consolidates and develops the public sector of the economy, and encourages, supports and guides the development of the non-public sector of the economy. The State safeguards all market actors' equal legal status and development rights."[9] It is clear from the above provision that China upholds a property rights system where public ownership is at par with collective and private ownership. The equal protection principle, inspired by the Constitutional Amendment of 2004,[10] has been integrated into the CC. However, a need remains to elucidate how the fundamental principle of public ownership as a core concept aligns with the equal protection principle in practical application. Understanding the interplay and reconciliation between these two fundamental principles is essential for clarifying how they coexist and operate within the legal framework and in the day-to-day implementation of laws in China.

How do property rights evolve in a transitional socialist jurisdiction like China? Upon closer scrutiny, private law designs in China – property rights and land reform – are more complex than many legal comparatists suggested.[11] Without a clear understanding of how domestic institutional arrangements cope with transplanted foreign laws, it would not be easy

[7] Larry Diamond, 'Can the whole world become democratic? Democracy, development, and international policies' (2003) UC Irvine: Centre for Study of Democracy, < https://escholarship.org/uc/item/7bv4b2w1> accessed 6 January 2023

[8] Article 206 CC.

[9] *Ibid.*

[10] Article 13 PRC Constitution (amended on 14 March 2004 at the 2nd session of the 10th NPC).

[11] Shitong Qiao and Frank Upham, 'Evolution of Relational Property Rights: A Case of Chinese Rural Land Reform' (2015) 100 *Iowa Law Review* 2479.

to provide an insightful answer on how the legal system evolves.[12] Therefore, a detailed depiction of the existing institutional context in such a transitional society is provided in detail.[13]

While much has been written on the importance of property rights to economic development, relatively little seems to be understood about how changes take place in the complex property system. Law and economics rhetoric applies cost–benefit analysis to predict the evolution of the property system towards efficiency and net social welfare amid competitive conditions.[14] However, this optimistic picture does not match reality in many developing countries like China.[15] Rather, it seems to provide only a general conceptual framework. The extent to which it operates in a particular country depends on the government-driven policies, economic development level, customs and other relevant factors.

In contrast, the pessimistic view sees property transitions through political processes.[16] Powerful interest groups induce changes in the property system to capture a disproportionate share of the benefits associated with the changes[17] without compensating those who lose under the new property regime. The result is less optimistic than evolutionary perspectives, as it encompasses changes favouring well-connected interest groups more likely to influence property policy.

Despite the attractiveness of these theories in providing insights into the diverse factors influencing property systems, it is worthwhile to investigate the impact of law on the evolution of property systems. Many sociological studies have challenged the efficacy of formalising property rights as disregarding cultural and social variations of place.[18] Law itself seems less effective in resolving property-related conflicts than

[12] Donald Clarke, 'China's Stealth Urban Land Revolution' (2014) 62 *The American Journal of Comparative Law* 323. While acknowledging the detriments with a complete absence of a formal legal system, "it would be profoundly misleading to view the real barrier to economic development in such a society as the lack of an effective formal legal system."

[13] Gunther Teubner, 'Legal Irritants: Good Faith in British Law or How Unifying Law Ends Up in New Differences' (1998) 61 *Modern Law Review* 11.

[14] Harold Demsetz, 'Toward a Theory of Property Rights' (1967) 57 *The American Economic Review* 347.

[15] Daniel Fitzpatrick, 'Evolution and Chaos in Property Rights Systems: The Third World Tragedy of Contested Access' (2006) 115 *Yale Law Journal* 996.

[16] Richard A. Epstein, 'The Allocation of the Commons: Parking on Public Roads' (2002) 31 *Journal of Legal Studies* 515.

[17] Stuart Banner, 'Transitions between Property Regimes' (2002) 31 *Journal of Legal Studies* 359.

[18] C. M. Hann, *Property Relations: Renewing the Anthropological Tradition* (Cambridge University Press 1998).

the cultural-ethical legitimacy in which law is embedded.[19] Blackletter or bright-line approaches to property rights distinguish between formal law (state law) and informal law (local norms and practices). This binary approach does not adequately capture the dynamics of the interrelationship between the various factors – cultural or historical, social or moral – both in public and private spheres.[20]

Nevertheless, recognising cultural variations and informal factors does not deter legal formalisation.[21] From the government's viewpoint, sustainable development requires respecting property rights, ensuring policy accountability, and judiciously applying state intervention to uphold good governance.[22] Legislation is a precise and reliable tool for distributing/delegating power to individuals and, thus, an efficient solution to the lack of legal institutions that cannot be left to a good conscience, informal rules or traditional civil customs.[23] More fundamentally, the solution to incomplete property systems is to incorporate existing property systems in the informal sectors to create a "unified property system."[24] The real question, then, is not whether the law needs to reflect and respond to the interaction and compromise among legal and sub-legal/extra-legal factors and state and non-state actors in the underlying property regimes; rather, it revolves around how the state, users and rights holders utilise legislation to facilitate a seamless shift from incongruent social norms to a legal-oriented and efficiently coordinated property system.[25]

This draws upon a comparative examination of the international authority and statutory analysis and evaluates them from both the Chinese and Western scholarship perspectives. It analyses the trends

19 Ryan Bubb, 'The Evolution of Property Rights: State Law or Informal Norms?' (2013) 56 *The Journal of Law & Economics* 555; Daniel Abramson, 'Transitional Property Rights and Local Developmental History in China' (2011) 48 *Urban Studies* 553.

20 Randy Peerenboom, 'The Future of Rule of Law: Challenges and Prospects for the Field' (2009) 1 *Hague Journal on the Rule of Law* 5; John Gillespie, 'Commentary: Theorising Dialogical Property Rights in Socialist East Asia' (2011) 48 *Urban Studies* 595.

21 Lei Chen and Hanri Mostert, 'The Unavoidable Necessity of Formalizing Condominium Ownership in China: A Pilot Study' (2007) 2 *Asian Journal of Comparative Law* 1.

22 Ann Seidman and Robert. B. Seidman, *State and Law in the Development Process* (Palgrave Macmillan Press 1994), pp. 5–22.

23 Ronald C. Keith, *China's Struggle for the Rule of Law* (St. Martin's Press 1994), pp. 137–41; Donald. C. Clarke, 'Economic Development and the Rights Hypothesis: The China Problem' (2003) 51 *The American Journal of Comparative Law* 89.

24 Hernando de Soto, *The Mystery of Capital: Why Capitalism Triumphs in the West and Fails Everywhere Else* (Basic Books 2000), pp. 52–54.

25 Yun-chien Chang, 'Property Law with Chinese Characteristics: An Economic and Comparative Analysis' (2012) 1 *Brigham-Kanner Property Rights Conference Journal* 345.

behind improving the statutory law that governs property rights in the PRC. Epistemic assumptions supporting the socialist approach to land remain. Rather than a linear transition to private ownership, China's institutional reform of rural land markets is more complex than economic theory, law and development theory suggests. In many ways, property rights emerge through political processes in which all the relevant stakeholders intentionally seek to implement changes to property rights arrangements.[26] This book provides up-to-date legislative provisions, analysis of landmark cases and scholarly literature to facilitate conversations and enhance a deep understanding of property law in China.

[26] Meg E. Rithmire, *Land Bargains and Chinese Capitalism: The Politics of Property Rights under Reform* (Cambridge University Press 2015), pp. 171–92.

BIBLIOGRAPHY

Primary Sources

Legislation and Regulations

Property Law of the PRC 2007 (repealed on 1 January 2021 when the Civil Code became effective)

Civil Code of the PRC 2000

Land Administration Law of the PRC 1986 (amended in 1988, 1998, 2004 and 2019)

Constitution of the PRC 1954 (amended in 1988, 1993, 1998, 2004 and 2018)

Land Reform Law of the PRC 1950

Town and Village Enterprise Law of the PRC 1996

Urban Real Estate Management Law of the PRC 1994 (amended in 1997, 2009 and 2019)

Rural Land Contract Management Law of the PRC 2002 (amended in 2018)

Forest Law of the PRC 1984 (amended in 1998, 2009 and 2019)

Mineral Resources Law of the PRC 1986 (amended in 2009)

Maritime Law of the PRC 1992

Civil Aviation Law of the PRC 1995

Law on Desert Prevention and Control of the PRC 2001 (amended in 2018)

Grassland Law of the PRC 1985 (amended in 2002, 2009, 2013 and 2021)

Law on the Mediation and Arbitration of Rural Land Contract Disputes of the PRC 2009

Intangible Cultural Heritage Law of the PRC 2011

Fisheries Law of the PRC 1986 (amended in 2000, 2004, 2009 and 2013)

Water Law of the PRC 1988 (amended in 2002, 2009 and 2016)

Law on the Administration of Sea Areas of the PRC 2001

Wetlands Conservation Law of the PRC 2021

Water and Soil Conservation Law of the PRC 1991 (amended in 2010)

Urban and Rural Planning Law of the PRC 2007 (amended in 2015 and 2019)

Construction Law of the PRC 1997 (amended in 2011 and 2019)

Trust Law of the PRC 2001

Law on the State-Owned Assets of Enterprises of the PRC 2008

Foreign Investment Law of the PRC 2019
Provisions Concerning the Administration of Private Houses Owned by Foreigners (1984)
Interim Regulations on the Assignment and Transfer of Rights to Use State-Owned Land in Urban Areas (1990)
Guiding Rules on the Management Corporation and Its Executive Council (promulgated by the municipal government of Shenzhen City on 17 January 2005)
Regulation on Realty Management (Issued by Order No. 379 of the State Council on 8 June 2003; Amended for the first time on 26 August 2007; Amended for the second time on 6 February 2016; Amended for the third time on 19 March 2018)
Interim Regulation on Real Estate Registration (Issued by Order No. 656 of the State Council of the People's Republic of China on 24 November 2014; Amended according to the Decision of the State Council on Amending Some Administrative Regulations on 24 March 2019)
Regulation on the Expropriation of Buildings on State-owned Land and Compensation (Adopted at the 141st executive meeting of the State Council on 19 January 2011)
Regulations of the People's Republic of China on Nature Reserves (Adopted at the 24th executive meeting of the State Council on 2 September 1994)
Provisions Concerning the Administration of Private Houses Owned by Foreigners (1984)
Interim Regulations on Assignment and Transfer of Rights to Use State-Owned Land in Urban Areas (1990)
Detailed Rules for the Implementation of the Interim Regulations on Real Estate Registration, Ministry of Natural Resources Decree No. 63 (Published on January 1, 2016, Ministry of Natural Resources Decree No. 63; Amended according to the decision of the 2nd Departmental Meeting of the Ministry of Natural Resources on July 16, 2019, regarding the abolition and modification of the first batch of departmental regulations)
State Council Decree No. 313 on 'Regulation on Protection of Oil and Gas Pipelines' by the State Council of the People's Republic of China, issued on 2 August 2001
State Council Decree No. 239 on the 'Regulation on the Protection of Power Facilities' by the State Council, first amended on 7 January 1998, second amendment on 8 January 2011
State Council Decree No. 167 on the 'Regulation of the People's Republic of China on Nature Reserves' by the State Council of the People's Republic of China, published on 9 October 1994, became effective on 1 December 1994 and amended on 7 October 2017
Universal Declaration of Human Rights, GA Res 217A, UM GAOR, 3rd Session, first plenary meeting, UN Doc A/810 (12 December 1948)

Case Law

England and Wales

AA v Persons Unknown & Ors, Re Bitcoin [2019] EWHC 3556 (Comm)
Clydesdale Bank plc v Davidson [1998] SLT 522
Keppell v Bailey [1834] EWHC Ch J77, [1834] 2 My & K 517
Phipps v Pears [1965] 1 QB 76

China

吴某与上海耀志网络科技有限公司、浙江淘宝网络有限公司案 (2019) 浙0192民初1626号 [*Wu v Shanghai Yaozhi Internet Technology Co., Ltd., Zhejiang Taobao Network Co., Ltd.,* (2019) Zhejiang 0192 Min Chu No. 1626]
李某、布兰登·斯密特诉闫某等案 (2019) 沪01民终13689号 [*Li, Brandon Smit v Yan, etc.,* (2019) Hu 01 Min Zhong No. 13689]
辽宁中集哈深冷气体液化设备有限公司、徐沛欣民事判决书 [*Liaoning CIMC Haisheng Cryogenic Gas Liquefaction Equipment Co., Ltd., Xu Peixin*] (2020) 最高法民再328号 [(2020) SPC Min Zai No. 328]
陈某诉张某案 (2020) 苏1183民初3825号 [*Chen v Zhang,* (2020) Su 1183 Min Chu No. 3825]
程红与施玉莲民事判决 (2020) 沪 0113 民初 23704号 [*Cheng Hong and Shi Yulian* (2020) Shanghai 0113 Civil First 23704]
屈保龙诉南昌市林业局二审行政判决书 [*Qu Baolong v Nanchang City Forestry Bureau*] (2015) 洪行终字第 5 号行政判决书 [(2015) Hong Xing Zhong Zi No. 5 Administrative Judgment]
屈保龙诉南昌市林业局一审行政判决书 [*Qu Baolong v Nanchang City Forestry Bureau,* First Instance Administrative Judgment], (2014) 东行初字第 14号行政判决书 [(2014) Dong Xing Chu Zi No. 14]
上海民生投资有限公司与吉林省东力投资集团公司, (2006) 民二终字第145号[*Shanghai Minsheng Investment Co., Ltd. v Jilin Dongji Comprehensive Investment (Group) Co., Ltd.,* SPC (2006) Min Er Zhong Zi No. 145]
昊壮公司诉百桂公司、达胜公司、房铁公司 (2016) 桂0102民初2228号民事判决[*Nanning Haozhuang Real Estate Development Co., Ltd v Nanning Dasheng Real Estate Development Co. Ltd & Hangtie Co Ltd.* (2016) Min Chu No. 0102]
徐振富诉徐文有 (2019)津01民终2401号 [*Xu Zhenfu v Xu Wenyou* (2019) Min Zhong No. 2401]
郑诉蒋 (2015) 二中民终字第01033号 [*Zheng v Jiang* (2015) Min Zhong No. 01033]
山东日发纺织机械有限公司诉华融金融租赁股份有限公司金华分公司 (2016) 浙07民终5303号 [*Shandong Rifa Textiles Machinery Co., Ltd v Huarong Leasing Co., (Subsidiary Company)* (2016) Min Zhong No. 5303]
河南金石联科工程技术有限公司与中国建设银行股份有限公司周口分行案 [*Henan Jinshi Lianke Engineering Project Technology Co Ltd and China*

Construction Bank Co Ltd Zhoukou Branch etc.] (2018) 最高法民申5669 [(2018) SPC Min Shen No. 5669]

交通银行股份有限公司陕西省分行诉王菊梅 (2018) 最高法民申4883号 [*Bank of Communications Co Ltd Shaanxi Branch v. Wang Jumei*, (2018), SPC Min Shen. No. 4883]

胡喜柱邢磊民事判决书 (2018) 冀民终737号 [*Hu Xizhu v. Xing Lei*, (2018) Ji Min Zhong. No. 737]

胡建军、高有林民事判决书 (2019) 赣民终705号[*Hu Jianjun v. Gao Youlin* [2019] Gan Min Zhong. No. 705]

韩高伟、青海怡海房地产开发有限公司 (2020) 青民终83号二审民事判决 [*Han Gaowei v. Qinghai Yihai Real Estate Development Co Ltd* (2020) Qing Min Zhong. No. 83]

孙良与吴焕堂审判监督民事裁定书 (2015) 粤高法民一申字第1187号 [*Sun Liang v. Wu Huantang* [2015] Yue Gao Fa Min Yi Shen No. 1187]

北京京华信托投资公司与王会文 (2019) 京民终145号 [*Beijing Jinghua Trust and Investment Co Ltd v. Wang Huiwen* (2019) Jing Min Zhong No. 145]

北京京华信托投资公司与刘九海, (2016) 京02民初217号 [*Beijing Jinghua Trust and Investment Co Ltd v. Liu Jiuhai* (2016) Jing 02 Min Chu No. 217]

成敏瑜、黄清文与魏彩莲、深圳市金融联融资担保有限公司二审判决书 (2019) 粤03民终21735号 [*Cheng Minyu v. Wei Cailian* (2019) Yue03 Min Zhong. No. 21735]

大冶市保安镇城镇化建设有限责任公司;刘继平二审民事判决书 (2021) 川16民终10号 [*Daye Baoan Urban Development Co Ltd v. Liu Jiping* (2021) Chuan16 Min Zhong No. 10]

李瀚洋、左亮 (2017) 苏01民终1869号民事判决 [*Li Hanyang v. Zuo Liang* (2017) Su 01 Min Zhong No. 1869]

A SPC gazetted case (2014) 12: 杨某某 诉 刘某某 (2014) 三中民终字第09467号 [*Yang v Liu*, (2014) San Zhong Min Zhong Zi No. 09467].《最高人民法院公报》2014年第12期 [*SPC Gazette* (2014) 12]

四川省聚丰房地产开发有限责任公司与达州广播电视大学 (2014) 民申字第56号[*Sichuan Jufeng Real Estate Development Co Ltd v. Dazhou Radio and Television College*, (2014), SPC Min Shen No. 56]

赵国权、赵国良等与李元顺、镇江市住房和城乡建设局[2016] 苏民申5948号民事裁定书 [*Zhao Guoquan et al. v. Li Yuanshun and Zhenjiang Housing and Urban-Rural Development Bureau* [2016] Su Min Shen No. 5498 Civil Ruling]

常援朝、陈霞等与夏邑县住房和城乡规划建设管理局[2016] 豫民申376号民事裁定书 [*Chang Yuanchao et al. v. Xiayi County Housing and Urban-Rural Planning and Development Bureau*, [2016] Yu Min Shen No. 376 Civil Ruling]

中国农业银行股份有限公司黄石东方支行诉梅荷花案 [2017] 鄂02民终1078号 [*Huangshi Dongfang Sub-branch of the Agricultural Bank of China Co Ltd v. Mei Hehua et al.* E 02 Min Zhong No. 1078]

中国农业银行股份有限公司黄石东方支行诉梅荷花等 [2014]鄂黄石中执字第00211–4号 [*Agriculture Bank of China Co., Ltd Huangshi Dongfang branch v Mei Hehua etc.*[2014] E Huangshi Zhong Zhi Zi No. 00211-4]

中国农业银行股份有限公司黄石东方支行与被告梅荷花、任超 (2016) 鄂0202民初1291号 [*Agriculture Bank of China Co., Ltd Huangshi Dongfang branch v Mei Hehua, Ren* Chaoyi, (2016) E 0202 Min Chu No. 1291]

邵仁忠诉威海广信房地产开发有限责任公司案 [2020]最高法民申3576号民事裁定书 [*Shao Renzhong v Weihai Guangxin Real Estate Development Co Ltd* [2020] SPC Min Shen No. 3576 Civil Ruling]

青岛源宏祥纺织有限公司诉港润（聊城）印染有限公司案 [*Qingdao Yuanhongxiang Textile Co Ltd v Gangrun (Liaocheng) Printing and Dyeing Co Ltd,* a SPC gazetted case accessible at <http://gongbao.court.gov.cn/Details/3cd383841a8014afb01979f91ddb35.html> accessed 10 September 2023

最高人民法院公告案例：张一诉郑中伟、中国联合网络通信有限公司武汉分公司案 [SPC gazetted case: *Zhang Yi v Zheng Zhongwei, China Unicom Co., Ltd. Wuhan Branch* <http://gongbao.court.gov.cn/Details/6a9a70d224268146817a72b6a0702d.html?sw=%e5%bb%ba%e7%ad%91%e7%89%a9.> accessed on 1 July 2023

陈秀碧与厦门源昌房地产开发有限公司案 (2014) 厦民终字第1085号[*Chen Xiubi v. Xiamen Yuanchang Real Estate Development Co., Ltd. and Other Owners* (2014) Xia Min Zhong Zi No. 1085]

夏浩鹏等人诉上海市闸北区精文城市家园小区业主委员会案，上海市闸北区人民法院 2010 [Xia Haopeng et al. and Owners Association of Jingwen City Home Community in Zhabei District, Shanghai Zhabei District People's Court 2010]. SPC gazetted case (2011) 10

上海市虹口区久乐大厦小区业主大会诉上海环亚实业总公司案 [*Property Owners' Association of Jiule Building Community in Hongkou District, Shanghai v. Shanghai Huanya Industry Corporation,*] (2011) 沪二中民二（民）终字第1908号 [(2011) Hu Er Zhong Min Er (Min) Zhong Zi No. 1908]

杭州市江干区人民政府、任月英、邹飞等 (2020)浙行终821号 [*Jianggan District People's Government, Hangzhou, Zhejiang v. Ren Yueying and others* (2020) Zhe Xing Zhong No. 821]

梁安平与梁安均等 (2015)宜民终字第485号[*Liang Anping v. Liang Anjun and Another*, (2015) Yi Min Zhong Zi No. 485号]

刘柯妤诉刘茂勇、周忠容 (2015) 渝五中法民再终字第00043号 [*Liu Keyu v. Liu Maoyong and Another* (2015) Yu Wu Zhong Fa Min Zai Zhong Zi No. 00043]

enant川公达信律师事务所、何开发等与四川皇嘉农业集团有限公司 民事判决书 (2019)川0781民初2658号 [*Xunchuan Gongdaxin Law Firm and He Kaifa v. Sichuan Huangjia Agricultural Group Co., Ltd.* (2019) Chuan 0781 Min Chu No. 2658]

绻传颂、高玉珊(2022) [Quan Chuansong and Gao Yushan, (2022)] 豫05民终488号 [Yu 05 Min Zhong No. 488]

上诉人涂婷婷与林添珠等人二审民事判决书 (2020) [*Tu Tingting (the Appellant) v. Lin Tianzhu and Another*, the Second Instance Civil Judgment (2020)] 闽05民终3145号 [Min 05 Min Zhong No. 3145]

新疆维吾尔自治区建筑木材加工总厂与中国民主同盟新疆实业发展总公司案 (2000) 民终字第115号[*Xinjiang Uygur Autonomous Region Construction Timber Processing Plant v. China Democratic League Xinjiang Industrial Development Corporation* (2000) SPC Min Zhong Zi No. 115]

屠福炎诉王义炎案 [*Tu Fuyan v Wang Yiyan*] (2013) 3《最高人民法院公报》[the SPC Gazette] <http://gongbao.court.gov.cn/Details/9e1b67636e6957ad92d13ff880308f.html?sw=%e7%9b%b8%e9%82%bb%e9%80%9a%e8%a1%8c%e6%9d%83> accessed on 5 September 2023

辽宁英巍良种猪专业合作社诉辽宁省高等级公路建设局案 [*Liaoning Yingwei Fine Breed Pig Professional Cooperative v. Liaoning Provincial High-grade Highway Construction Bureau*] (2013)民一终字第83号 [(2013) SPC Min Yi Zhong Zi No. 83]

新华日报社诉南京华厦视野有限公司案 [*Xinhua News Agency v. Nanjing Huaxia Ltd*] (1996) 47《最高人民法院公报》[(the SPC *Gazette*] <http://gongbao.court.gov.cn/Details/74005c35afb4548e624e195230aa6b.html> accessed on 22 January 2024

袁科威诉广州嘉富房地产发展有限公司案 (2015) 穗中法民一终字第5108号 [*Yuan Kewei v. Guangzhou Jiafu Real Estate Development Co., Ltd.* (2015) Sui Zhong Fa Min Yi Zhong Zi No. 5108]

沈海俊与机械工业第一设计研究院民事裁定书 (2016) 皖民申840 [*Shen Haijun v No. 1 Design and Research Institute of Machinery Industry* (2016) Wan Min Shen No. 840]

吴国金与中铁五局（集团）有限公司、中铁五局集团路桥工程有限责任公司、贵州建工监理咨询有限公司、贵州贵安新区管理委员会，(2015) 筑环保民终字第2 [*Wu Guojin v. China Railway No. 5 Bureau (Group) Co., Ltd. and China Railway No. 5 Bureau Group Road and Bridge Engineering Co., Ltd., Guizhou Construction Supervision Consulting Co., Ltd, Guizhou Guian New Area Management Committee*, (2015) Zhu Huan Bao Min Zhong Zi No. 2]

曲忠全诉山东富海实业股份有限公司案 [*Qu Zhongquan v. Shandong Fuhai Industrial Co., Ltd.*] (2014)民申字第1782号 [(2014) SPC Min Shen Zi No. 1782]

袁科威诉广州嘉富房地产发展有限公司案 (2015) 穗中法民一终字第5108号 [*Yuan Kewei v. Guangzhou Jiafu Real Estate Development Co., Ltd.* (2015) Sui Zhong Fa Min Yi Zhong Zi No. 5108]

尚贤菊诉励国定案 (2007)甬民一终字第152号 [*Shang Xianju v. Li Guoding*, (2007) Yong Min Yi Zhong Zi No. 152]

王某诉王某[*Wang v. Wang*]，民 事 判 决 书(2021) 京0119民初5100号 [Civil Judgment (2021) Jing 0119 Min Chu No. 5100]

王某诉王某（2021）云0623民初1614号 [*Wang v Wang* (2021) Yun 0623 Min Chu 1614]

马某诉马某(2021）吉0112民初2518号 [*Ma v Ma* (2021) Ji 0112 Min Chu No. 2518]

蒋元桂、蒋守良 (2021）湘12民终1760号[*Jiang Yuan Gui v. Jia Shoulaing* (2021) Xiang 12 Min Final 1760]

李乾胜与武隆区白马镇鱼光村何家沟村民小组，渝0156民初3035号 [*Li Qiansheng and the Village Committee of Hejiagou, Yuguang Village, Bai Ma Town, Wulong District*. (2021) Yu 0156 Min Chu 3035]

管永恒等诉山西省长治市郊区人民政府，行政裁定书. （2018）最高法行申1731号 [*Guan Yongheng and others v. the People's Government of Changzhi Suburban District, Shanxi Province*, (2018) SPC Administrative Application No. 1731]

韩明利与延津县榆林乡大韩庄村村民委员会 （2015）新中民五终字第401号 [*Han Mingli v. The Village Committee of Dahanzhuang Village, Yulin Township, Yanjin County*, 2015 Xin Zhong Min Wu Zhong Zi No. 401]

黄某诉李某 (2015)延民初字第821号 [*Huang v Li* (2015) Yan Min Chu No. 821]

许德仁诉辽宁省沈阳市人民政府，最高人民法院行政裁定书 （2020）最高法行申14503号[*Xu Deren v. Shenyang People's Government, Liaoning Province*, (2020) SPC Admin Decision No. 14503]

廊坊市荣达通房地产开发有限公司与廊坊市自然资源和规划局广阳区分局案 [*Langfang Rongda Tong Real Estate Development Co., Ltd. v Langfang Natural Resources and Planning Bureau Guangyang Branch*], （2020）最高法民终168号 [(2020) SPC Min Zhong 168]

萍乡市亚鹏房地产开发有限公司诉萍乡市国土资源局，（2014）萍行终字第10号 [*Pingxiang Asia Peng Real Estate Development Co., Ltd. v. Pingxiang Land and Resources Bureau* (2014) Ping Hang Zhong Zi No. 10]

葫芦岛市自然资源局、葫芦岛鸿亿房地产开发有限公司审判监督行政裁定 （2020）最高法行申11749号 [*Huludao City Natural Resources Bureau v. Huludao Hongyi Real Estate Development Co* (2020) SPC Hang Shen No. 11749]

中日青年交流中心秦皇岛办事处、秦皇岛市自然资源和规划局审判监督行政裁定，（2020）最高法行申13827号 [*Sino-Japanese Youth Exchange Center Qinhuangdao Office v. Qinhuangdao Municipal Bureau of Natural Resources and Planning and Qinhuangdao Municipal People's Government* (2020) SPC Hang Shen No. 13827]

万宁市人民政府与万宁兴隆桃源旅业有限公司 （2018）琼行终905号[Wanning Municipal People's Government and Wanning Xinglong Taoyuan Tourism Co., Ltd. [(2018) Qiong Xing Final No. 905]

乌海市锦邦房地产开发有限责任公司、乌海市自然资源局海勃湾分局（2019）最高法民终2013号[Wuhai Jinbang Real Estate Development Co., Ltd. and

Wuhai Municipal Bureau of Natural Resources (2019) Final Civil Judgment no. 2013]

柳州市全威电器有限责任公司、柳州超凡房地产开发有限责任公司与被上诉人南宁桂馨源房地产有限公司案(2004) 民一终字第46号 [*Liuzhou Quanwei Electric Co., Ltd., and Liuzhou Chaofan Real Estate Development Co., Ltd. v. Nanning GuixinYuan Real Estate Co., Ltd* (2004) SPC Min Yi Zhong Zi No. 46]

上海枫丹丽舍房地产开发有限公司与上海华夏文化旅游区开发有限公司案(2006) 民一终字第57号 [*Shanghai Fengdan Lido Real Estate Development Co., Ltd. v. Shanghai Huaxia Cultural Tourism Zone Development Co., Ltd* (2006) SPC Min Yi Zhong Zi No. 57]

四川省聚丰房地产开发有限责任公司与达州广播电视大学案（2013）民一终字第18号[*Sichuan Province Jufeng Real Estate Development Co., Ltd. v. Dazhou Radio and Television University Joint Venture*, (2013) SPC Min Yi Zhong Zi No. 18]

长沙金霞开发建设有限公司与长沙市交通运输局二审民事判决书（2015）民一终字第163号[*Changsha Jinxia Development and Construction Co., Ltd. v. Changsha Municipal Transportation Bureau* (2015) SPC Min Yi Zhong Zi No. 163]

东莞市利成电子实业有限公司等与东莞市大岭山镇房地产开发公司等案(2012) 民提字第 122 号民事判决书 [*Dongguan Licheng Electronic Industry Co., Ltd., Dongguan Dalingshan Town Real Estate Development Company and others v. Maizanxin and Cai Yuehong*,] [(2012) SPC Min Ti Zi No. 122]

广东富宏房地产开发有限公司与洪妙莲 （2014）粤高法民一申字第123号 [*Guangdong Fuhong Real Estate Development Co., Ltd. v. Hong Miaolian* (2014) Yue High Court Civil Application No. 123]

河北冀丰房地产开发有限公司与石家庄市金之源化工有限公司（2016）最高法民申1325号, [*Hebei Jifeng Real Estate Development Co., Ltd. v. Jinzhiyuan Chemical Co., Ltd. In Shijiazhuang City* (2016) Civil Application No. 1325]

内蒙古普利房地产开发有限责任公司与北京瑞德康住房开发股份有限公司 (2010) 呼民初字第281号民事判决 [Inner Mongolia Puli Real Estate Development Co., Ltd. (Puli) and Beijing Reed Kang Housing Development Co., Ltd. (2010) Hu Min Chu Zi No. 281]

内蒙古普利房地产开发有限责任公司与北京瑞德康住房开发股份有限公司（2014）民抗字第41号 [Inner Mongolia Puli Real Estate Development Co., Ltd. (Puli) and Beijing Reed Kang Housing Development Co., Ltd. (2014) Min Kang Zi No. 41]

邓州市金川城乡建设有限公司、邓州市自然资源和规划局 （2018）豫13行终179号[Dengzhou Jinchuan Urban and Rural Construction Co., Ltd. and Dengzhou Natural Resources and Planning Bureau (2018) Yu 13 Xing Zhong 179]

海南省人民政府、海口农村商业银行股份有限公司（2020）最高法行申4439号[*Hainan Provincial People's Government v. Haikou Rural Commercial Bank Co., Ltd.* (2020) SPC Hang Shen No. 4439]

李建新与李亚昔（2020）粤 08 民终 4135 号 [*Li Jianxin v Li Yaxi,* (2020) Yue 08 Min Zhong No. 4135]

陈科与陈惠芳（2019）湘01民终1865号[*Chen Ke v Chen Huifang* (2019) Xiang 01 Min Zhong No. 1865]

朱瑞彬与李德忠,（2017）苏06民终3415号 [*Zhu Ruibin v Li Dezhong*, Civil Second Instant Judgment (2017) Su 06 Min Zhong No. 3415]

吴泽龙、冯大明（2019）鄂民申 4539 号裁定书[Wu Zelong and Feng Daming (2019)] E Min Shen No. 4539]

张志良、杨月琴与幸安华及海南省乐东黎族自治县千家镇只文村民委员会（2017）琼97民终35号 [Zhang Zhiliang, Yang Yueqin, Xing Anhua and the Village Committee of Zhiwen, Qianjia Zhen, Le Dong Li Zu Zi Zhi Xian, Hainan Province (2017) Qiong 97 Min Zhong No. 35]

孙文学与张水元、王石柱二审民事判决书（2018）晋08民终297号 [*Sun Wenxue v Zhang Shuiyuan, Wang Shizhu,* (2018) Jin 08 Min Zhong No. 297]

蒋琳诉廖联会（2009）綦法民初字第3768号民事判决书 [*Jiang Lin v Liao Lianhui* (2009) Qi Fa Min Chu Zi No. 3769]

仲林诉熊红波离婚后财产分割纠纷案 (2011)宿中民终字第1190号 [*Zhong Lin v. Xiong Hongbo* (2011) Su Zhong Min Zhong Zi No. 1190]

曾 诉 陈（2021）沪0112民初7461号 [*Zeng v Chen*, (2021) Hu 0112 Min Chu No. 7461]

李 诉 宿（2021）吉0104民初10715号 [*Li v Su*, (2021) Ji 0104 Min Chu No. 10715]

金诉朱,（2021）京0106民初34102号 [*Jin v Zhu*, (2021) Jing 0106 Min Chu No. 34102]

邱某光与董某军居住元执行案子 [*Qiu v Dong*], see The First Batch of Typical Cases Illustrating the Implementation of the CC by the SPC <.https://dara.gd.gov.cn/yasf/content/post_3929701.html > accessed 30 January 2024

钟湘、广州越秀小额贷款有限公司（2017）粤01民终17661号 [*Zhong Xiang and Guangzhou Yuexiu Small Loan Co., Ltd* (2017) Yue 01 Min Zhong No. 17661]

中国民生银行股份有限公司太原分行与山西怀仁中能芦子沟煤业有限责任公司、山西怀仁南窑晋通砂石煤业有限公司（2017）京04民初6号 [*China Minsheng Bank Co., Ltd. Taiyuan Branch v. Shanxi Huairen Zhongneng Luzigou Coal Industry Co., Ltd., Shanxi Huairen Nanyao Jintong Sand and Stone Coal Industry Co., Ltd.* (2017) Jing 04 Min Chu No. 6]

中国长城资产管理公司贵阳办事处、六枝特区佳顺焦化有限公司（2015）民二终字第280号[*China Great Wall Asset Management Company Guiyang Office and Guizhou Liuzhi Special Economic Zone Jiashun Coking Co., Ltd*，[(2015) SPC Final Civil Judgment No. 280]

中国长城资产管理公司广州办事处与广州云山大酒店有限公司 (2016) 最高法民终554号[*China Great Wall Asset Management Corporation Guangzhou Office and Guangzhou Yunshan Hotel Co., Ltd*, (2016) SPC Final Civil Judgment No. 554]

安岳县欣通建设投资有限公司等与重庆进出口信用担保有限公司等追偿权纠纷上诉案，(2016)最高法民终268号. [*AnYue County XinTong Construction Investment Co., Ltd., et al. v. Chongqing Import and Export Credit Guarantee Co., Ltd., and others*. (2016) SPC Civil Final Judgment No. 268]

中国农业银行股份有限公司怀化分行、张忠民 (2020) 湘12民终612号 [*China Agricultural Bank Co., Ltd. Huaihua Branch and Zhang Zhongmin*, (2020) Xiang 12 Min Final Judgment No. 612]

顾正康、十堰荣华东风汽车专营有限公司再审案 (2017) 最高法民再137号 [*Gu Zhengkang and Shiyan Ronghua Dongfeng Automobile Franchise Co., Ltd.* (2017) SPC Fa Min Zai No. 137]

天津市化轻贸易有限公司与天津恒景再生合金材料有限公司、浙江致虎投资管理有限公司[(2017) 津民初121号*Tianjin Huaqing Trading Co., Ltd. and Tianjin Hengjing Recycled Alloy Materials Co., Ltd., Zhejiang Zhihu Investment Management Co., Ltd.* (2017) Jin Min Chu No. 121]

安岳县欣通建设投资有限公司等与重庆进出口信用担保有限公司案 (2016)最高法民终268号. [Anyue Xintong Construction Investment Co., Ltd. and Chongqing Import and Export Credit Guarantee Co., Ltd. (2016) SPC Min Final No. 268]

贵州商储胜记仓物流有限公司、刘某 (2019) 最高法民再202号 [*Guizhou Shangchu Shengji Warehouse Logistic Co., Ltd v. Liu* (2019) SPC Min Zai No. 202]

李某、王某 (2018) 川民再790号 [*Li v. Wang*, (2018) Chuan Min Zai No. 790]

熊伟杰诉彭鑫 (2016) 川71民初12号民事判决 [*Xiong Weijie v Peng Xin* (2016) Chuan 71 Min Chu No. 12]

彭鑫诉熊伟杰 (2014) 成铁执字第244号《执行通知书》[*Peng Xin v Xiong Weijie* (2014) Cheng Tie Zhi Zi No. 244 *Enforcement Notice*]

熊伟杰诉彭鑫 (2016) 川71民初12号民事判决 [*Xiong Weijie v Peng Xin* (2016) Chuan 71 Min Chu No. 12 Civil Judgment]

熊伟杰、彭鑫案 (2018) 川民终572号 [*Xiong Weijie v. Peng Xin* (2018) Chuan Min Zhong No. 527]

最高人民法院指导案例 53 号: 福建海峡银行股份有限公司福州五一支行诉长乐亚新污水处理有限公司、福州市政工程有限公司金融借款合同纠纷案 [SPC Guiding Case No. 53: A Financial Loan Contract Dispute between Fujian Haixia Bank Co., Ltd., Fuzhou Wuyi Branch, Changle Yaxin Sewage Treatment Co., Ltd and Fuzhou Municipal Engineering Co., Ltd]

青海西宁农村商业银行股份有限公司与白恩青、青海永丰化工建材有限责任公司(2016) 最高法民终341号[Qinghai Xining Rural Commercial Bank and

Bai Enqing & Qinghai Yongfeng Chemical Construction Materials Ltd., Co. (2016) SPC Min Zhong No. 341]

中国工商银行股份有限公司桑植支行与桑植裕轮远航燃气工程有限公司、重庆市中宝投资（集团）股份有限公司等（2016）湘民终324号[*ICBC Sangzhi Branch v. Sangzhi Yulun Long-distance Voyage Gas Engineering Co., Ltd and Chongqing Zhongbao Investment* (Cooperation) Co., Ltd etc (2016) Xiang Min Zhong No. 324]

梅劲松与金元顺安基金管理有限公司、上海光大证券资产管理有限公司(2018)苏民终638号[*Mei Jinsong v. Jinyuan Shunan Fund Management Co., Ltd. and Shanghai Guangda Securities Asset Management Co., Ltd.* (2018) Su Min Zhong No. 638]

神雾科技集团股份有限公司等与南京银行股份有限公司北京分行（2019）京民终86号 [*Shenwu Environmental Technology Co., Ltd etc. v. Bank of Nanjing Co., Ltd Beijing Branch* (2019) Beijing Min Zhong No. 86]

瑞穗银行（中国）有限公司与上海百红商业贸易有限公司（2020）沪0115民初40268号[*Mizuho Bank (China) Co., Ltd v. Shanghai Baihong Trading Co., Ltd.* (2020) HU 0115 Min Chu No. 40268]

程晓春与重庆文化产业融资担保有限责任公司 (2019) 渝民终325号[*Cheng Xiaochun v. Chongqing Stated Culture Assets Administration Co., Ltd.* (2019) Yu Min Zhong No. 325]

深圳融易商业保理有限公司、深圳市英维克科技股份有限公司与深圳市中兴康讯电子有限公司（2016）粤03民终19804号[*Shenzhen Yirong Commercial Factoring Co., Ltd., Shenzhen Envicool Technology Co., Ltd. v. Shenzhen Zhongxing Kangxun Telecommunication Co., Ltd* (2016) Yue 03 Min Final No. 19804]

长三角商品交易所有限公司与卢海云返还原物纠纷 [*YRD Commodity Exchange Co., Ltd. v Lu Haiyun*, Dispute over Return of an Original Object]（《最高人民法院公报》2017年第1期 (2014) 锡民终字第1724号）[Notice by the SPC 2017 Issue 1, (2014) Xi Min Zhong Zi No. 1724]

深圳市京基房地产股份有限公司京基一百大厦一期停车场、北京神州汽车租赁有限公司深圳分公司（2019）粤03 民终28944 号民事判决. [Shenzhen Kingkey Real Estate Co., Ltd. Kingkey 100 Phase 1 Parking Management Ltd and Beijing China Auto Renting Inc. Shenzhen Branch (2019) Yue 03 Min Zhong No. 28944]

茂名市茂南银海皮业有限公司诉吴隆汉（2018）粤09民终331号 [*Maonan Yin Hai Leather Co., Ltd. v. Wu Longhan* (2018) Yue 09 Min Zhong 331]

万大轩与万大连二审民事判决书 （2020）渝02民终740号 [*Wan Daxuan v. Wan Dalian* (2020) Yu 02 Min Zhong 740]

李学农诉被申请人邹平县政府、邹平县孙镇党里村村委会案 （2019）最高法行赔申51号[*Li Xuenong v. Zouping County Government*, and the Sunzhen Village Committee of Zouping County (2019) Xing Pei Shen No. 51]

王贤武诉贵州省安顺市西秀区人民政府（2020）最高法行再276号[*Wang Xianwu v. the Xixiu District Government*, Anshun City, Guizhou Province (2020) SPC administrative retrial No. 276]

郑州市中原区豫星调味品厂诉郑州市人民政府案 (2014) 行提字第21号 [*Zhengzhou Zhongyuan District Yuxing Spices Factory v. Zhengzhou Municipal People's Government of Henan Province* (2014) SPC Xing Ti Zi No. 21]

谭成日与衡阳市人民政府、湖南省人民政府案（2018）最高法行再97号 [*Tan Chengri v. Hengyang Municipal People's Government and People's Government of Hunan Providence* (2018) SPC Xing Zai No. 97]

Secondary Sources

Articles

Abramson D., 'Transitional Property Rights and Local Developmental History in China' (2011) 48 *Urban Studies* 553.

All-China Women's Federation[中华全国妇女联合会], 'Safeguarding Rural Women's Rights and Interests in Land'[《维护农村妇女的土地权益》] (2015) 3 *Chinese Women's Movement* [《中国妇运》] 15.

Arruñada B., 'Property Enforcement as Organized Consent' (2003) 19 *The Journal of Law, Economics, and Organization* 401.

Banner S. 'Transitions between Property Regimes' (2002) 31 *Journal of Legal Studies* 359.

Bell A. and Parchomovsky G., 'A Theory of Property' (2005) 90 *Cornell Law Review* 531.

Benkler Y., 'From Consumers to Users: Shifting the Deeper Structures of Regulation toward Sustainable Commons and User Access' (2000) 52 *Federal Communications Law Journal* 561.

Bramall C., 'Chinese Land Reform in Long-Run Perspective and in the Wider East Asian Context' (2004) 4 *Journal of Agrarian Change* 107.

Brandt L., Debin Ma and Thomas. G. Rawski, 'From Divergence to Convergence: Re-evaluating the History behind China's Economic Boom' (2014) 52 *Journal of Economic Literature* 45.

Bu X. [卜祥洪], 'On the Basis and Scope of the Right to Claim Compensation for Possession Damage' [《论占有损害赔偿的请求权基础与范围》] (2011) *Contemporary Law Review* [《当代法学》] 61.

Bubb R., 'The Evolution of Property Rights: State Law or Informal Norms?' (2013) 56 *The Journal of Law & Economics* 555.

Cai Y., 'China's Moderate Middle Class: The Case of Homeowners' Resistance' (2005) 25 *Asian Survey* 777.

Chang P. [常鹏翱], 'Normative Analysis of Possessory Act' [《占有行为的规范分析》] (2014) *Science of Law: Journal of Northwest University of Political Science and Law* [《法律科学（西北政法大学学报）》] 106.

[常鹏翱], 'Returning to Tradition: The Path to Improving the Regulation of Servitudes in China' [《回归传统：我国地役权规范的完善之道》] (2018) 5 *Tsinghua Law Journal* [《清华法学》] 142.

Chang Y., 'Property Law with Chinese Characteristics: An Economic and Comparative Analysis' (2012) 1 *Brigham-Kanner Property Rights Conference Journal* 345.

Chang Y. and Smith H. E., 'An Economic Analysis of Civil versus Common Law Property' (2012) 88 *Notre Dame Law Review* 1.

'The Numerus Clausus Principle, Property Customs, and the Emergence of New Property Forms' (2015) 100 *Iowa Law Review* 2275.

Chen L., 'The New Chinese Property Code: A Giant Step Forward?' (2007) 11 *Electronic Journal of Comparative Law* 1.

'The Developer's Role in the Surging Chinese Condominium Housing: Through the Comparative Lens of the US System' (2010) 18 *Asia Pacific Law Review* 233.

'The Historical Development of the Civil Law Tradition in China: A Private Law Perspective' (2010) 78 *The Legal History Review* 159.

'Private Property with Chinese Characteristics: A Critical Analysis of the Chinese Law on Property of 2007' (2010) 18 *European Review of Private Law* 983.

'Land Registration, Property Rights and Institutional Performance in China: Progress Achieved and Challenges Ahead' (2014) 44 *Hong Kong Law Journal* 841.

'Continuity and Change: Some Reflections on the Chinese CC' (2021) 29 *Asia Pacific Law Review* 287.

'Self-Governing Organizations and Culture: Addressing Condominium Law Developments in China' (2024) 16 (1) *Journal of Property, Planning and Environmental Law* 20.

Chen L. and Kielsgard M. D., 'Evolving Property Rights in China: Patterns and Dynamics of Condominium Governance' (2014) 2 *The Chinese Journal of Comparative Law* 21.

Chen L., Liu Z. and Tang Y., 'Judicial Transparency as Judicial Centralization: Mass Publicity of Court Decisions in China, Journal of Contemporary China' (2021) 31 *Journal of Contemporary China* 726.

Chen L. and Mostert H., 'The Unavoidable Necessity of Formalizing Condominium Ownership in China: A Pilot Study' (2007) 2 *Asian Journal of Comparative Law* 1.

Chen L. and Van der Merwe C., 'Reflections on the Role of the Managing Agent in South African and Chinese Sectional Title (Condominium) Legislation' (2009) 1 *Journal of South African Law (TSAR)* 22.

Chen S. [陈甦], 'The Mechanism of Inheritance of Land Contract Management Rights and Its Interpretive Debate' [《土地承包经营权继承机制及其阐释辨证》] (2016) 3 *Tsinghua Law Journal* [《清华法学》] 57.

Chen X. [陈小君] and Xiao C.[肖楚钢], 'The Legal Nature of Rural Land Management Rights and the Distinction of Its Object: A Commentary on the Land Operation Rights Rules in the Property Law of the CC' [《农村土地经营权的法律性质及其客体之辨——兼评〈民法典〉物权编的土地经营权规则》] (2020) 12 *Zhongzhou Academic Journal* [《中州学刊》] 48.

Cheng X. [程雪阳], 'The Identification and Judicial Review of Collective Land Expropriation Decision' [《论集体土地征收决定的识别与司法审查》] (2022) *The Jurist* [《法学家》] 88.

Clark W. A. V., Huang Y. and Yi D., 'Can Millennials Access Homeownership in Urban China?' (2021) 36 *Journal of Housing and the Built Environment* 69.

Clarke D. C., 'Economic Development and the Rights Hypothesis: The China Problem' (2003) 51 *The American Journal of Comparative Law* 89.

'China's Stealth Urban Land Revolution' (2014) 62 *The American Journal of Comparative Law* 323.

Coase R. H., 'The Problem of Social Cost' (1960) 3 *The Journal of Law and Economics* 1.

Cui J. [崔建远], 'A Positivist Analysis of the Concept of Juridical Act of Real Rights and Chinese Civil Law' [《从解释论看物权行为与中国民法》] (2004) *Journal of Comparative Law* [《比较法研究》] 60.

Dang G. [党国英], 'A Theory on Social Stability and Its Application in China's Countryside' [《关于社会稳定的一个理论及其在农村分析中的应用》] (1996) *China Rural Survey* [《中国农村观察》] 52.

Deakin S. and Meng G., 'Resolving Douglass C. North's "puzzle" concerning China's household responsibility system.' (2022) 18 *Journal of Institutional Economics* 521.

Demsetz H., 'Toward a Theory of Property Rights' (1967) 57 *American Economic Review* 347.

Diamond, L. *Can the Whole World Become Democratic? Democracy, Development, and International Policies* (2003) UC Irvine Centre for Study of Democracy.

Ding Y. [丁宇翔], 'Constructing the System of Restitution of Things in the CC' [《民法典中返还原物制度的构建》] (2019) *Financial and Economic Law Review* [《财经法学》] 67.

Edgeworth B., 'The Numerus Clausus Principle in Contemporary Australian Property Law' (2006) 32 *Monash University Law Review* 387.

Ellickson R. C., 'The Costs of Complex Land Titles: Two Examples from China' (2011) 1 *Property Rights Conference Journal* 281.

Epstein R. A., 'The Allocation of the Commons: Parking on Public Roads' (2002) 31 *Journal of Legal Studies* 515.

Fang S. [房绍坤], 'On the Method and Effectiveness of the Judgment for the Division of Co-owned Property' [《论共有物裁判分割的方法与效力》] (2015) 11 *Shandong Social Sciences* [《山东社会科学》] 58.

[房绍坤], 'Discussion on the Right of Residence in the CC' [《论民法典中的居住权》] (2020) 4 *Modern Law Science* [《现代法学》] 85.

Fang S. [房绍坤] and Ma L. [马兰], 'On Several Issues of Possession' [《论占有的几个问题》] (1999) *Legal System and Social Development* [《法制与社会发展》] 33.

Fitzpatrick D., 'Evolution and Chaos in Property Rights Systems: The Third World Tragedy of Contested Access' (2006) 115 *Yale Law Journal* 996.

Gao S. [高圣平], 'Allocation of Contracted Land Rights After the Amendment of the Rural Land Contract Law' [《农村土地承包法修改后的承包地法权配置》] (2019) 5 *Chinese Journal of Law* [《法学研究》] 44.

Ge Y. [葛云松], 'Study on the Theory of Real Juridical Act' [《物权行为理论研究》] 16 (2004) *Peking University Law Journal* [《中外法学》] 702.

Gillespie J., 'Commentary: Theorising Dialogical Property Rights in Socialist East Asia' (2011) 48 *Urban Studies* 595.

Gray K., 'Equitable Property' (1994) 47 *Current Legal Problems* 157.

Gu X. [谷昔伟] and Lu C. [曹璐], 'The Right of Residence Can Confront the Exclusionary Interference Claims of Property Owners' [《居住权可对抗房屋所有权人排除妨害请求权》] (2015) 18 *People's Judiciary Cases* [《人民司法·案例》] 65.

Hansmann H. and Kraakman R., 'Property, Contract, and Verification: The Numerus Clausus Problem and the Divisibility of Rights' (2002) 31 *The Journal of Legal Studies* 373.

Hao L. [郝丽燕], 'The Commentary on CC Articles 447–452: The Constituent Elements and Effectiveness of a General Lien' [《民法典》第447—452条（一般留置权的成立要件与效力）评注] (2023) 2 *Nanjing University Law Review* [《南京大学法律评论》] 128.

He X. [贺雪峰], 'On the Scale of Rural Land Management: Taking Anhui Fanchang City as a Subject of Discussion'[《论农地经营的规模——以安徽繁昌调研为基础的讨论》] (2011) 11 *Journal of Nanjing Agricultural University: Social Science Edition* [《南京农业大学学报: 社会科学版》] 6.

Heller M. A., 'The Boundaries of Private Property' (1999) 108 *The Yale Law Journal* 1163.

Ho P., 'Who Owns China's Land? Policies, Property Rights and Deliberate Institutional Ambiguity' (2001) 166 *The China Quarterly* 394.

Huang P. C. C., 'Rural Class Struggle in the Chinese Revolution: Representational and Objective Realities from the Land Reform to the Cultural Revolution' (1995) 21 *Modern China* 105.

Huang Y., Yi D. and Clark W. A. C, 'Multiple Home Ownership in Chinese Cities: An Institutional and Cultural Perspective' (2020) 97 *Cities* 102518.

Jin K. [金可可], 'On the Ownership of Ebony Wood: Also on the Types and Limits of State Ownership' [《论乌木之所有权归属—兼论国家所有权之种类及其限度》] (2015) 3 *Oriental Law* [《东方法学》] 82.

Kelly D., 'Citizen Movements in China's Public Intellectuals in the Hu-Wen Era' (2006) 79 *Pacific Affairs* 183.

Kielsgard M. D. and Chen L., 'The Emergence of Private Property Law in China and Its Impact on Human Rights' (2014) 15 *Asian-Pacific Law & Policy Journal* 94.

Kirby W. C., 'China Unincorporated: Company Law and Business Enterprise in Twentieth-Century China' (1995) 54 *The Journal of Asian Studies* 43.

Kremzner M. T., 'Managing Urban Land in China: The Emerging Legal Framework and Its Role in Development' (1998) 7 *Pacific Rim Law & Policy Association Journal* 611.

Kung J. K. S., 'Equal Entitlement versus Tenure Security under a Regime of Collective Property Rights: Peasants' Preference for Institutions in Post-reform Chinese Agriculture' (1995) 21 *Journal of Comparative Economics* 82.

'Choice of Land Tenure in China: The Case of a County with Quasi-private Property Rights' (2002) 50 *Economic Development and Cultural Change* 793.

Lee J., 'From Welfare Housing to Home Ownership: The Dilemma of China's Housing Reform' (2000) 15 *Housing Studies* 61.

Li X. [李锡鹤], 'On Good Faith Possession as Possession with Right' [《论善意占有为有权占有》] (2012) *Law Science* [《法学》] 39.

Li Y. and Cheng B., 'China's Stance on Investor-State Dispute Settlement: Evolution, Challenges, and Reform Options' (2020) 67 *Netherlands International Law Review* 503.

Liang H. [梁慧星], 'Is Juridical Act of Real Rights Recognised in Chinese Civil Law?' [《我国民法是否承认物权行为》] (1989) 6 *Chinese Journal of Law* [《法学研究》] 56.

Lin G. C. S and Ho S. P. S, 'The State, Land System, and Land Development Processes in Contemporary China' (2005) 95 *Annals of the Association of American Geographers* 411.

Lin W., Yang Y., Ma J. and Wu G. [林文学、杨永清、麻锦亮、吴光荣], 'Understanding and Application of the Interpretation on the Application of Relevant Guarantee Systems in the CC' [《<关于适用民法典有关担保制度的解释>的理解和适用》] (2021) 4 *Legal Application* [《法律适用》] 30.

Lin Y. [林鹰], 'Discussion on Cases Concerning Rural Neighbour Disputes' [《浅谈农村相邻纠纷案件》] (2014) 31 *Legal System and Society* [《法制与社会》] 218.

Liu B. [刘保玉], 'Suggestions for Improving the Pledge System in China' [《完善我国质权制度的建议》] (2017) 6 *Modern Law Science* [《现代法学》] 56.

Liu G., 'Several Key Issues in Security Interest under the CC' (2021) 1 *Journal of Law Application* 9.

Liu J. [刘家安], 'Ambiguities in "Possession": Analysis of the Concept of "Possession" in the Draft Property Law' [《含糊不清的"占有"–〈物权法〉

草案"占有"概念之分析》] (2006) *Perking University Law Journal* [《中外法学》] 116.

Liu Z., Klöhn L. and Spamann H., 'Precedents and Chinese Judges: An Experiment' (2021) 69 *The American Journal of Comparative Law* 93.

Lu X. [鲁晓明], 'The Positioning and Rule Design of the Right of Residence' [《"居住权"之定位与规则设计》] (2019) 3 *Chinese Legal Science* [《中国法学》] 223.

Ma Q. [马强], 'A Study on Practical Issues Related to the Provisions of the CC on the Right of Residence' [《民法典居住权规定所涉实务问题之研究》] (2022) 5 *Journal of Law Application* [《法律适用》] 114.

Mao W. and Qiao S., 'Legal Doctrine and Judicial Review of Eminent Domain in China' (2021) 46 *Law & Social Inquiry* 826.

McDermott J. P., 'Charting Blank Spaces and Disputed Regions: The Problem of Sung Land Tenure' (1984) 44 *The Journal of Asian Studies* 13.

Meng Q. [孟勤国], 'Historical Development of the Concept of Possession and the System of Possession in China' [《占有概念的历史发展与我国占有制度》] (1993) *Chinese Social Sciences* [《中国民法》] 75.

Merrill T. W. and Smith H. E., 'Optimal Standardization in the Law of Property: The Numerus Clausus Principle' (2000) 110 *The Yale Law Journal* 1.

Merill T. W. and Smith H. E., 'Making Coasean Property More Coasean' (2011) 54 *Journal of Law and Economics* 77.

Michelson E., 'Climbing the Dispute Pagoda: Grievances and Appeals to the Official Justice System in Rural China' (2007) 72 *American Sociological Review* 459.

Mostert H. and Chen L., 'The Dynamics of Constitutional Property Clauses in the Developing World: China and South Africa' (2010) 17 *Maastricht Journal of European and Comparative Law* 377.

Niu Z. and Van Dijck G., 'The Impact of Culture on Chinese Judges' Decision-Making in Contractual Damages Cases' (2019) 6 *Asian Journal of Law and Society* 359.

Ostrom E., 'Beyond Markets and States: Polycentric Governance of Complex Economic Systems' (2010) 100 *American Economic Review* 641.

Palmer M. J. E., 'The Surface–Subsoil Form of Divided Ownership in Late Imperial China: Some Examples from the New Territories of Hong Kong' (1987) 21 *Modern Asian Studies* 1.

Peerenboom R., 'The Future of Rule of Law: Challenges and Prospects for the Field' (2009) 1 *Hague Journal on the Rule of Law* 5.

Peng C. [彭诚信], 'Re-determination of Possession and Its Practical Application' [《占有的重新定性及其实践应用》] (2009) 27 *Science of Law: Journal of Northwest University of Political Science and Law* [《法律科学（西北政法大学学报）》] 92.

Pils E., 'Land Disputes, Rights Assertion and Social Unrest: A Case from Sichuan' (2005) 19 *Columbia Journal of Asian Law* 235.

'Land Disputes, Rights Assertion and Social Unrest: A Case from Sichuan' (2006) 19 *Columbia Journal of Asian Law* 365.

Pound R., 'Chinese CC in Action' (1954) 29 *Tulane Law Review* 277.

Prosterman R. L., Hanstad T. and Li P., 'Can China Feed Itself?' (1996) 5 *Scientific American* 90.

Qiao S., 'The Authoritarian Commons: Divergent Paths of Neighborhood Democratization in Three Chinese Megacities' (2023) 71 *The American Journal of Comparative Law* 388.

Qiao S. and Chien M., 'A Rural-Urban Crossroads in Chinese Law: Qiao Shitong on the Development and Future of Chinese Eminent Domain' (2022) *Columbia Journal of Transnational Law*. www.jtl.columbia.edu/bulletin-blog/a-rural-urban-crossroads-in-chinese-law-qiao-shitong-on-the-development-and-future-of-chinese-eminent-domain

Qiao S. and Upham F., 'Evolution of Relational Property Rights: A Case of Chinese Rural Land Reform' (2015) 100 *Iowa Law Review* 2479.

Qu M. [屈茂辉], 'Revisiting the Civil Nature of the Land Use Rights Grant Contract for Construction Purposes' [《再论建设用地使用权出让合同的民事属性》] (2023) 6 *China Legal Science* [《中国法学》] 201.

Quigley J., 'Socialist Law and the Civil Law Tradition' (1989) 37 *American Journal of Comparative Law* 781.

Radin M. J., 'Personhood and Property' (1982) 34 *Stanford Law Review* 957.

Raff M., 'Characteristics of the International Model of Land Title Registration Illuminated by Comparative Study of the German and Torrens Systems' (2012) 1 *European Property Law Journal* 54.

Read B., 'Assessing Variation in Civil Society Organizations: China's Homeowner Associations in Comparative Perspective' (2008) 41 *Comparative Political Studies* 1240.

Rose C., 'The Comedy of the Commons: Custom, Commerce, and Inherently Public Property' (1986) 53 *The University of Chicago Law Review* 711.

Sagaert V., 'Property Law: Beyond Dogmas?' (2017) 6 *European Property Law Journal* 119.

The Background and General Principles of the New Belgian Property Law (2021) 10 *European Property Law Journal* 3.

Sargeson S., 'Full Circle? Rural Land Reforms in Globalizing China (2004) 36 *Critical Asian Studies* 637.

'Violence as Development: Land Expropriation and China's Urbanization' (2013) 40 *The Journal of Peasant Studies* 1063.

Shan P. [单平基], 'Proof of the Right to Compensation for Unauthorized Possession Expenses: A Review of Article 243 of the Property Law of the People's Republic of China' [《无权占有费用求偿权之证成 —〈中华人民

共和国物权法〉第243条检讨》] (2014) 31 *Legal and Business Studies* [《法商研究》] 63.

Shen W. [申卫星], 'From "Having a Residence" to "Residing with Habitat": Legislative Ideas for the Creation of the Right of Residence System in China's CC' [《从"居住有其屋"到"住有所居"—我国民法典分则创设居住权制度的立法构想》] (2018) 2 *Modern Law Science* [《现代法学》] 105.

Singer J. W. and Beermann J. M., 'The Social Origins of Property' (1993) 6 *Canadian Journal of Law & Jurisprudence* 217.

Stroup R. and Baden J., 'Externality, Property Rights, and the Management of Our National Forests' (1973) 16 *The Journal Law and Economics* 303.

Sun P. and Deng D. [孙鹏、邓达江], 'The Logic of Creation and Legislative Expression of Dynamic Movable Property Pledge Centred on the Legislation of Movable Property Security in the Property Law of the CC' [《动产动态质押的生成逻辑与立法表达——以民法典物权编动产担保立法为中心》] (2019) 5 *Social Science Research*[《社会科学研究》] 92.

Sun X. [孙宪忠], 'The Principle of Separation between the Reason and the Result of the Alteration of Property Rights' [《论物权变动的原因及其结果的区分原则》] (1999) 5 *Chinese Journal of Law* [《法学研究》] 28.

Teubner G., 'Legal Irritants: Good Faith in British Law or How Unifying Law Ends Up in New Differences' (1998) 61 *Modern Law Review* 11.

Treffers S. T and Lippert R. K., 'Condominium Self-Governance? Issues, External Interests, and the Limits of Statutory Reform' (2020) 35 *Housing Studies* 1025.

Tu S., 'From Demolition to Expropriation: Problems, Solutions and Difficulties in China' (2010) 3 *Wuhan University Law Review* 49.

Van der Merwe C., 'A Comparative Study of the Distribution of Ownership Rights in Property in an Apartment or Condominium Scheme in Common Law, Civil Law and Mixed Law Systems' (2002) 31 *Georgia Journal of International and Comparative Law* 101.

'Things' (2002) 27 *The Law of South Africa*.

Van Erp S., 'Ownership of Data: The Numerus Clausus of Legal Objects' (2017) 6 *Brigham-Kanner Property Rights Conference Journal* 235.

Vandevelde K. J., 'The New Property of the Nineteenth Century: The Development of the Modern Concept of Property' (1980) 29 *Buffalo Law Review* 325.

Wang H. [王洪亮], 'Reconstruction of the Legal System of Possession' [《占有法律制度重构》] (2017) 25 *Journal of National Prosecutors College* [《国家检察官学院学报》] 27.

Wang J. [王敬波] and Li X. [李晓果], 'A New Exploration of Dispute Resolution in State-Owned Land Use Right Transfer: A Case Study of the Dispute over the Construction Land Use Right Transfer Contract of Jiangsu Ruihao Real Estate Company' [《国有土地使用权出让争议解决新探索——以江苏瑞豪置业公司建设用地使用权出让合同纠纷案为例》] (2017) 4 *Legal Application* [《法律适用》] 7.

Wang L. [王利明], 'On Several Issues Concerning Juridical Act of Real Right' [《物权行为若干问题探讨》] (1997) 3 *Chinese Legal Science* [《中国法学》] 58.

[王利明], 'Discussion on the Several Issues Regarding the Right of Residence in the CC's Property Law Section' [《论民法典物权编中居住权的若干问题》] (2019) 51 *Academic Monthly* [《学术月刊》] 91.

Wang R. [王荣珍], 'Judicial Dilemma and Legislative Reflection on the Compensatory Liability of Real Estate Registration Organizations in Our Country' [《我国不动产登记机构赔偿责任的司法困境与立法反思》] (2019) 37 *Tribune of Political Science and Law* [《政法论坛》] 106.

Wang Y. [汪洋], 'Study on the Succession of Land Contract Management Rights: Explanation of the Legal Construction of the Existing Norms and Consideration of Legal Policies' [《土地承包经营权继承问题研究》] (2014) 4 *Tsinghua Law Journal* [《清华法学》] 129.

[王轶], 'How Does the CC Protect Property Rights' [《民法典如何保护物权》] (2019) *Chinese Law Review* [《中国法律评论》] 71.

[汪洋], 'Regulatory Structure for Establishing the Right of Residence through Testamentary Means' [《遗嘱方式设立居住权的规范构造》] (2023) 5 *Contemporary Law Review*《当代法学》42.

Wen S. [温世扬], 'The Conservation, Progress and Defects of Property Ownership'[《<民法典>物权编的守成、进步与缺憾》] (2021) 2 *Law Science Magazine* [《法学杂志》] 56.

Whitehouse L., 'The First Legal Mortgagor: A Consumer without Adequate Protection?' (2015) 38 *Journal Consumer Policy* 161.

Whitman D. A., 'Chinese Mortgage Law: An American Perspective' (2001) 15 *Columbia Journal Asian Law* 35.

Wily L. A., 'Collective Land Ownership in the 21st Century: Overview of Global Trends' (2018) 7 *Land* 68.

Women's Rights and Interests Department of All-China Women's Federation (全国妇联权益部), 'Land Contract and Women's Rights and Interests: A Survey on Violation of Women's Rights and Interests during the Second Round of Rural Land Contracting'[《土地承包与妇女权益 – 关于农村第二轮土地承包工作中妇女权益被侵害情况的调查》] (2000) 3 *Chinese Women's Movement* [《中国妇运》] 30.

Wu Q., Li Y. and Yan S., 'The Incentives of China's Urban Land Finance' (2015) 42 *Land Use Policy* 432.

Wu X. [吴香香], 'On Compensation for Damage Caused by Infringement of Possession' [《论侵害占有的损害赔偿》] (2013) 25 *Peking University Law Journal* [《中外法学》] 598.

Wu Y. and Yip N., 'The Homeowners' Protest in Beijing and Guangzhou: Rightful Resistance and Beyond' (2010) 5 *The International Journal of Interdisciplinary Social Sciences: Annual Review* 513.

Wu Z. and Chen L., 'Revisiting Property Transfer Theory: English Law and Chinese Law Compared' (2023) 43 *Legal Studies* 259.

Xu D. [徐涤宇], 'A Teleological Explanation of the Abstraction Principle' [《物权行为无因性理论之目的论解释》] (2005) 2 *Chinese Legal Science* [《中国法学》] 84.

Xu J., Yeh, A. and Wu F., 'Land Commodification: New Land Development and Politics in China Since the Late 1990s' (2009) 33 *International Journal of Urban and Regional Research* 890.

Xu T., and Gong W., 'Community-Based Individual Property Rights: Developing the 'Bundle of Rights' Perspective in the Chinese Context' (2020) 28 *Asia Pacific Law Review* 138.

Yan W. [阎巍], 'The Impact of China's Rural Land Reform on Compensation and Distribution in Collective Land Expropriation' [《国农村土地改革对集体土地征收补偿分配的影响》] (2022) *Legal Application* [《法律适用》] 89.

Ye J. [叶金强], 'Critique of the Current Movable Property Security Model' [《现行动产担保模式之批判》] (2022) 6 *Law Science Magazine* [《法学杂志》] 39.

Zhang J., 'China's Slow Motion Land Reform' (2010) 159 *Policy Review* 59.

Zhang S. [张双根], 'Fundamental Issues of Possession: A Review of Chapter Twenty of the Draft Property Law' [《占有的基本问题 评〈物权法草案〉第二十章》] (2006) 18 *Perking University Law Journal* [《中外法学》] 118.

Zhang T., 'Social Hierarchies and the Formation of Customary Property Law in Pre-Industrial China and England' (2014) 62 *The American Journal of Comparative Law* 171.

'Beyond Information Costs: Preference Formation and the Architecture of Property Law' (2020) 12 *Journal of Legal Analysis* 1.

Zhen C. Q., 'Corporate Law Issue, Civil Law Solutions: Resolving Disputes Arising from Unauthorized Corporate Security Contracts in People's Republic of China High Courts' (2020) 1 *Corporate and Business Law Journal* 12.

Zhong W. [仲伟珩], 'The Practical Difficulties, Systematic Interpretation, and Practical Approaches to Accounts Receivable Pledge Rights' [《应收账款质权的现实困境、体系解释与实务进路》] (2022) 28 *People's Judicature [《人民司法》]* 38.

Zhu J. and Wang C., 'Seniors Defending Their Rights – Strategies and Culture in Collective Action: The Homeowners Rights Movement in Lijing Garden, Guangzhou' (2007) 40 *Chinese Sociology & Anthropology* 5.

Zhu Y. and Fu Q., 'Deciphering the Civic Virtue of Communal Space: Neighbourhood Attachment, Social Capital and Neighbourhood Participation in Urban China' (2017) 49 *Environment and Behavior* 161.

Zou H. [邹海林], 'Interpretation of the "Mixed Guarantee Rules" in the Chinese CC' [《我国〈民法典〉上的"混合担保规则"解释论》] (2020) *Journal of Comparative Law* 91.

Books (including chapters in contributed volumes)

Administrative Adjudication Tribunal of the SPC [最高人民法院行政审判庭], 'Compliance with the principles of due process and protection of legitimate expectations in administrative rectification actions' [《行政纠错行为对正当程序和信赖保护原则的遵循》], in *Minutes of the Judges' Meetings of the Administrative Adjudication Tribunal of the SPC (Volume One)* [《最高人民法院行政审判庭法官会议纪要(第一辑)》], (People's Court Press 2022).

Akkermans B., *The Principle of Numerus Clausus in European Property Law* (Intersentia 2008).

Alford W. P., *To Steal a Book Is an Elegant Offense: Intellectual Property Law in Chinese Civilization* (Stanford University Press 1995).

Barzel Y., *Economic Analysis of Property Rights* (Cambridge University Press 1997).

Beekhuis J. H. et al., *International Encyclopaedia of Comparative Law* (vol. VI) (Mohr 2004).

Blackstone W., *Commentaries on the Laws of England (Volume 1)* (J. B. Lippincott Co. 1893).

Blaustein A. P., *Fundamental Legal Documents of Communist China* (Fred B. Rothman & Co 1962).

Bookchin M., *The Ecology of Freedom: The Emergence and Dissolution of Hierarchy* (Cheshire Books 1982).

Butler W. E., *Soviet Law* (2nd edn) (Butterworths 1988).

Chang P. [常鹏翱], *China's Real Estate Law in Practice* [《实践中的中国房地产法》] (Peking University Press 2023).

Chang Y., 'The economy of concept and possession', in Chang Y. (ed), *Law and Economics of Possession* (Cambridge University Press 2015).

Chen A., 'Socialist law, civil law, common law, and the classification of contemporary Chinese law', in Otto J., Polak M., Chen J. and Li Y. (eds), *Law-Making in the People's Republic of China* (Kluwer Law International 2000).

Chen H. [陈华彬], *Study on Modern Condominium Ownership* [《现代建筑物区分所有权研究》 (Law Press 1995).

Chen J., *From Administrative Authorisation to Private Law: A Comparative Perspective of the Developing Civil Law in the People's Republic of China* (Springer 1995).

Chen L., *The Making of Chinese Condominium Law: A Comparative Perspective with American and South African Condominium Laws* (Intersentia 2010).

'A structural analysis of Chinese mortgage law', in Mostert H. and De Waal M. J. (eds), *Essays in Honour of CG van der Merwe* (Lexis Nexis 2011).

'100 years of Chinese property law: Looking back and thinking forward', in Chen L. and Van Rhee C. H. (eds), *Towards a Chinese CC* (Brill Nijhoff 2012).

'Legal and institutional analysis of land expropriation in China', in Fu H. and Gillespie J. (eds), *Resolving Land Disputes in East Asia: Exploring the Limits of Law* (Cambridge University Press 2014).

'The legal and institutional analysis of land expropriation in China', in Gillespie J. and Fu H. (eds), *Resolving Land Disputes in East Asia* (Cambridge University Press 2015).

'The changing landscape of condominium laws and urban governance in China', in Lehavi A. (ed.), *Private Communities and Urban Governance* (Springer 2016).

'Relaxations of contractual privity and the need for third party rights in Chinese contract law', in Chen-Wishart M., Loke A. and Vogenauer S. (eds), *Studies in the Contract Laws of Asia II: Formation and Third Party Beneficiaries* (Oxford University Press 2018).

'The evolution of the property system in China: Between the socialist heritage and liberal market', in Fu H., Gillespie J., Nicolson P. and Partlett W. E. (eds), *Socialist Law in Socialist East Asia* (Cambridge University Press 2018).

'The security interests in Chinese law: Some nuances', in Jiang H. and Sirena P. (eds), *The Making of the Chinese CC: Promises and Persistent Problems* (Cambridge University Press 2023).

Chen, L., Michalek, A. and Wang, J. 'The norm of property's social function: A Chinese perspective', in Babie P. and Viven-Wilksch J. (eds), *Léon Duguit and the Social Obligation Norm of Property* (Springer 2019).

Chen L. et al. (eds), *The CC of the People's Republic of China: English Translation* (Brill 2021).

Chief Editor of the Leading Group for the Implementation of the CC by the SPC [最高人民法院民法典贯彻实施工作领导小组主编], *Understanding and Application of the Property Rights Section of the CC of the People's Republic of China* [《中华人民共和国民法典物权编理解与适用》] (People's Court Press 2020).

Cooley T. M., *Commentaries on the Law of England (Blackstone's Commentaries)* (Chicago Callaghan and Co 1871).

Cui J. [崔建远], *Real Property Law* [《物权法》] (China Renmin University Press 2009).

[崔建远], *Property Law* [《物权法》] (China Renmin University Press 2010).

[崔建远], *Commentaries of the Chinese CC: Book on Property Rights (vol. I.)* [《中国民法典释评：物权编（上下卷）（上)》] (China Renmin University Press 2020).

Dagan H., *Property: Values and Institutions* (Oxford University Press 2011).

A Liberal Theory of Property (Cambridge University Press 2021).

Dannemann G. et al. (eds), *German CC: Bürgerliches Gesetzbuch (BGB): Article-by-article Commentary* (C.H. Beck 2020).

De Soto H., *The Mystery of Capital: Why Capitalism Triumphs in the West and Fails Everywhere Else* (Basic Books 2000).

Deininger K., *Land Policies for Growth and Poverty Reduction* (Vol. 1) (World Bank 2003).

Domurath I., *Consumer Vulnerability and Welfare in Mortgage Contracts* (Hart Publishing 2017).

Enforcement of CC Group of the SPC (ed.), *Understanding and Applying the Book on Contracts of the Chinese CC* (People's Court Press 2020).

Fu H., 'What does Wukan offer? Land-taking, law, and dispute resolution', in Hualing F. H. and Gillespie J. (eds), *Resolving Land Disputes in East Asia: Exploring the Limits of Law.* (Cambridge University Press 2014).

Geng Z. [耿卓], 'Ascertainment of Servitude: Commentary on a Case Concerning the Right of Way over the Adjacent Roads' [《地役权的认定–相邻道路通行权纠纷案评析》], in Peng C. [彭诚信] (ed), *One Hundred Landmark Cases in Chinese Civil Law* [《民法案例百选》] (2nd edn, Higher Education Press 2021).

Gray K. and Gray S., *Elements of Land Law* (5th edn, Oxford University Press 2009).

Guo X. [郭晓鸣], *Coordinating Urban and Rural Development and Rural Land Transfer Reform: An Empirical Study on Chengdu Model* [《统筹城乡发展与农村土地流转制度变革: 基于成都"试验区"的实证研究》] (Science Press China 2012).

Hann C. M., *Property Relations: Renewing the Anthropological Tradition* (Cambridge University Press 1998).

Hase P. H., *Custom, Land, and Livelihood in Rural South China: The Traditional Land Law of Hong Kong's New Territories, 1750–1950* (Hong Kong University Press 2013).

Hazard J. N., *Communists and Their Law: A Search for the Common Core of the Legal System of the Marxian Socialist States* (The University of Chicago Press 1969).

Ho P., *Developmental Dilemmas: Land Reform and Institutional Change in China* (Routledge 2009).

Huang P. C. C., *Civil Justice in China: Representation and Practice in the Qing* (Stanford University Press 1996).

Code, Custom, and Legal Practice in China: The Qing Dynasty and the Republic Compared (Stanford University Press 2002).

Huang W. [黄薇], *Interpretation of the Property Rights Section of the CC of the People's Republic of China* [《中华人民共和国民法典物权编解读》] (China Legal Publishing House 2020).

Jiang P., *Chinese Property Law* (China Intellectual Property Press 2007).

Keith R. C., *China's Struggle for the Rule of Law* (St. Martin's Press 1994).

Kennedy D., 'Laws and developments', in Hatchard J. and Perry-Kessaris A. (eds), *Law and Development: Facing Complexity in the 21st Century: Essays in Honour of Peter Slinn* (Cavendish Publishing 2003).

Kevin G. and Susan G., *Elements of Land Law* (5th edn, Oxford University Press 2009).

Kishimoto M., 'Ming Qing Shidai de Zhaojia Huishu Wenti' ['The issue of 'Zhaojia' and 'Dian' redemption in the Ming and Qing'], in Hiroaki T. (ed), *Empirical Studies on Chinese Legal History* [《中国法制史考证》] (China Social Sciences Press 2003).

'Property rights, land, and law in Imperial China', in Ma D. and van Zanden Jan. L. (eds), *Law and Long-Term Economic Change: A Eurasian Perspective* (Stanford University Press 2011).

Lau D. C. *Mencius* (Chinese University of Hong Kong Press 2003).

Li P. and Prosterman R. L., 'From collective to household tenure: China and elsewhere', in Prosterman R. L., Mitchell R. and Hanstad T. (eds), *One Billion Rising: Law, land and the Alleviation of Global Poverty* (Leiden University Press 2009).

Liang H. [梁慧星], *Research on Civil Law Doctrine, Cases, and Legislation (Part II)* [《民法学理论、案例与立法研究（下）》] (National Administrative College Press 1999).

[梁慧星], *Commentary on Chinese Property Law Draft* [《中国物权法草案建议稿》（合著）] (Social Science Literature Press 2000).

The Draft CC of the People's Republic of China (Brill 2010).

Liang H. and Chen H. [梁慧星、华彬], *Property Law* [《物权法（第六版）》] (6th edn, Law Press China 2016).

Liang H. [梁慧星]and Chen H. [陈华彬], *Property Law* [《物权法（第7版）》] (7th edn, Law Press China 2020).

Lippert R. and Treffers S., 'Turnover or rollover? Property developer legal avoidance and influence on condominium governance in New York City and Toronto', in Lippert R. and Treffers S. (eds), *Condominium Governance and Law in a Global Urban Context* (Routledge 2021).

Lippit V., *The Economic Development of China* (M. E. Sharpe 1987).

Liu J. [刘家安], *Property Law* [《物权法论》] (Chinese University of Political Science and Law Press 2009).

Low K. and Wu Y., 'The characterization of cryptocurrencies in East Asia', in Fox D. and Green S. (eds), *Cryptocurrencies in Public and Private Law* (Oxford University Press 2019).

Macauley M., *Social Power and Legal Culture: Litigation Masters in Late Imperial China* (Stanford University Press 1998).

Marshall M., *Organizations and Growth in Rural China* (Palgrave Macmillan 1985).

McDermott J. P. 'Village institutions in the early and mid-Ming', in *The Making of a New Rural Order in South China* (Cambridge University Press 2013).

Meng Q., *A Study on China's Rural Land Reform* (Law Press China 2009).

Merrill T. W., 'Ownership and possession' In Chang Y. (ed), *Law and Economics of Possession.* (Cambridge University Press 2015).

Merrill T. W. and Smith H. E., *The Oxford Introductions to US Law: Property* (Oxford University Press 2010).

Ostrom E., *Governing the Commons: The Evolution of Institutions for Collective Action* (Cambridge University Press 1990).

Peng C., 'Rural land expropriation law in the reform era: A story of continuity', in Peng C. (ed), *Rural Land Takings Law in Modern China: Origin and Evolution* (Cambridge University Press 2018).

Pils E., 'Peasants' struggles for land in China' in Ghai Y. and Cottrell J. (eds), *Marginalized Communities and Access to Justice* (Routledge-Cavendish 2009).

Pleissis P. D., *Borkowski's Textbook on Roman Law* (6th edn, Oxford University Press 2020)

Randolph P. and Lou J., *Chinese Real Estate Law* (Kluwer Law International 2000).

Rawls J., *Justice as Fairness: A Restatement* (Harvard University Press 2001).

Raz J., *The Morality of Freedom* (Clarendon Press 1986).

Read B., 'Property rights and homeowner activism in new neighbourhoods', in Zhang L. and Ong A. (eds), *Privatizing China: Socialism from Afar* (Cornell University Press 2008).

Renner K., *The Institutions of Private Law and Their Social Functions* (Routledge and Kegan Paul Ltd. 1949).

Rithmire M. E., *Land Bargains and Chinese Capitalism: The Politics of Property Rights under Reform* (Cambridge University Press 2015).

Rose C. M., 'The law is nine-tenths of possession: an adage turned on its head', in Yun-chien C. (ed), *Law and Economics of Possession* (Cambridge University Press 2015).

Rudden B., 'Economic theory v property law: The Numerus Clausus problem', in Eekelaar J. and Bell J. (eds), *Oxford Essays in Jurisprudence* (3rd edn, Clarendon Press 1987).

Sagaert V., 'Consensual versus delivery systems in European private law: Consensus about tradition?', in Faber W. and Lurger B. (eds), *Rules for the Transfer of Movables* (Sellier 2008).

Seidman A. and Seidman R. B., *State and Law in the Development Process* (Palgrave Macmillan Press 1994).

Selden M. and Lu A., 'The reform of landownership and the political economy of contemporary China', in Selden M. (ed), *The Political Economy of Chinese Development* (Armonk & ME Sharpe 1993).

Steven A., 'The effect of security rights *inter partes*' in Drobnig U., Snijders, H. J. and Zippro, E.-J. (eds), *Divergences of Property Law, an Obstacle to the Internal Market?* (Sellier 2006).

Sun X. [孙宪忠], *General Principles of Real Rights Law of China* [《中国物权法总论》] (2nd edn, Law Press China 2009).

Sun X. and Zhu G. [孙宪忠与朱广新], *Commentaries of the CC: Book on Property Rights* (Vol. I) [《民法典评注: 物权编（上卷）》] (China Legal Publishing House 2020).

SPC Property Law Research Group [最高人民法院物权法研究小组], *The Interpretation and Application of the Articles of 'the Property Law of the People's Republic of China'* [《<中华人民共和国物权法>条文理解与适用》] (People's Court Press 2007).

Suzuki R., *Real Estate Law Lecture (Bukkenhō Kōgi)* (5th edn, Sobunsha 2007).

Swadling W., 'Restitution and bona fide purchase', in Swadling W. (ed), *The Limits of Restitutionary Claims: A Comparative Analysis* (UKNCCL 1997).

The Legal Affairs Committee of the Standing Committee of the National People's Congress (ed), *The Interpretation of the Property Law of the People's Republic of China* (Law Press 2007).

Thomas Ph. J, Van der Merwe C. and Stoop B. C., *Historical Foundations of South African Private Law* (Butterworths 2000).

Tian Y. [尹田], *Comments and Thoughts on Property Law Theories* [《物权法理论评析与思考》] (China Renmin University Press 2004).

Trakman L. E., Liu Q. and Chen L., 'Investor-state arbitration in China: A comparative perspective', in Chen L. and Janssen A. (eds), *Dispute Resolution in China, Europe and World* (Springer 2020).

Tsao J. T. H., *China's Development Strategies and Foreign Trade* (Lexington Books 1987).

Van der Merwe C., *The Law of Things* (Butterworths 1987).

Apartment Ownership (Mohr Siebeck 1994).

'Modern application of the Roman institution of fiducia cum creditore contracta', in Vacca L. (ed), *La Garanzia nella prospettiva storico-comparatisca* (G. Giappichelli Editore 2003).

Sectional Titles 14-66 (2007).

'Security in Immovables' in *International Encyclopaedia of Comparative Law: Property and Trust. Instalment 42* (Mohr Siebeck 2014).

European Condominium Law (Cambridge University Press 2015).

Van der Walt A. J., *Property in the Margins* (Bloomsbury Publishing 2009).

Verdery K., 'Fuzzy property: Rights, power, and identity in Transylvania's collectivization', in Burawoy M. and Verdery K. (eds), *Uncertain Transition: Ethnographies of Change in the Post-socialist World* (Rowman and Littlefield Publishers 1999).

Wang L. [王利明], *Annotated Draft of China's Law of Things* [《中国物权法草案建议稿及说明》] (Legal Press 2000).

[王利明], *Research on Contract Law* [《合同法研究》] (2nd edn, China Renmin University Press 2012).

[王利明], *Research on Real Property Rights* [《物权法研究》] (3rd edn, Renmin University of China Press 2013).

[王利明], *Research on Real Property Rights Law* (Vol. 1) [《物权法研究（上卷）》] (3rd edn, China Renmin University Press 2013).

[王利明], *Property Law* [《物权法》] (China Renmin University Press 2015).

Wang W., *The History of Chinese Land Systems* [《中国土地制度史》] (Cheng Chung Book 1988).

Wang Y. [王轶], *On the Transfer of Real Rights* [《物权变动论》] (China Renmin University Press 2001).

Yang Y., *Chinese Contemporary Legal History* [《中国近代法制史》] (Zhonghua Wenhua Shiye Chubanshe 1958).

Zhong W. [仲伟珩], 'Research on difficult issues regarding the establishment requirements of right of lien' [《留置权成立要件疑难问题研究》] in *Compilation of the First Division of Civil Adjudication of the SPC: Civil Judgment Guidelines and References* [最高人民法院民事审判第一庭编：《民事审判指导与参考》] (Law Press China 2010).

Zhou Q., *Property Rights and Institutional Transformation: Empirical Study of China* (Peking University Press 2004).

Zimmermann R., Visser D., and Reid K., 'Co-ownership', in Zimmermann R., Reid K., and Visser D. (eds), *Mixed Legal Systems in Comparative Perspective: Property and Obligations in Scotland and South Africa* (Oxford University Press 2005).

Newsletters & Websites

Gu Zhang [张谷], Can the "Property Rights" of the CC be "reborn"? [《民法典"物权编"能否"浴火重生"？》] (2016) *Speech at the International High-Level Forum on the Rule of Law and Reform* ["法治与改革国际高端论坛"中的演讲] <www.ghls.zju.edu.cn/ghlscn/2016/1112/c13708a1142666/page.htm> accessed 24 January 2024.

Lin Wang [王林], '土地使用权到期怎么办?' ['What should be done when the land use right expires?'] (*victory.itslaw.cn*, 20 April 2016) <http://victory.itslaw.cn/victory/api/v1/articles/article/54baab61-7357-4646-9b89-a3c467ea58f2> accessed 2 October 2023.

'深圳住宅小区业委会成立比例约三成，上海超九成 [About 30% of Shenzhen Residential Communities have set up HOAs, and more than 90% in Shanghai]' (深圳商报 [Shenzhen Business Daily], 24 August 2021) <www.sohu.com/a/485334915_121010226> accessed 6 June 2022.

Rong Chen, '温州一批20年产权住在土地使用权到期，须按房价1/3续期' ['In Wenzhou, a batch of residential properties with 20-year land use rights is set to be renewed at one-third of the property price upon expiration'] (*Huanqiu.com*, 15 April 2016) <https://m.huanqiu.com/article/9CaKrnJUYf1> accessed 10 September 2023.

INDEX

Printed by Integrated Books International,
United States of America